# LEGAL INNOVATION & TECHNOLOGY

## A Practical Skills Guide for the Modern Lawyer

**Dyane O'Leary**
*Suffolk University Law School*

WEST
ACADEMIC
PUBLISHING

© 2023 LEG, Inc. d/b/a West Academic
    444 Cedar Street, Suite 700
    St. Paul, MN 55101
    1-877-888-1330

West, West Academic Publishing, and West Academic are trademarks of West Publishing Corporation, used under license.

Printed in the United States of America

**ISBN:** 978-1-63659-574-0

to my students, for being eager to learn new skills
to my parents, for filling the bookshelves in our home
to my husband, for tolerating me with
my head in a book
to my children, for keeping their heads
in a book just like mom
. . . and inspiring me to write one myself

# ACKNOWLEDGMENTS

---

A common refrain in legal technology circles is "people first, technology second." This book is "people first, writing second." Many people sparked ideas, shared resources, gave time, lent expertise, shared a helpful tweet, asked great questions, chatted at a conference, or encouraged me to put this project together. Thank you to Suffolk University Law School for its support and Dean Andrew Perlman's dedication to preparing lawyers for modern practice. The work of modern-lawyer-to-be research assistant Samantha Ahearn was invaluable.

If readers don't get what they want out of this book, it's on me. If they do enjoy it, it's because I stood on the shoulders of colleagues. Friend and legal innovation and technology leader Gabriel Teninbaum knocked on my office door years ago to invite me to join a call with a technology company. I've been grateful for his inclusiveness, encouragement, and advice ever since. Teachers have a hard enough time keeping up with reading student work and their own writing but a group of excellent teachers took the time to read mine: David Colarusso, Sarah Boonin, Richard Buckingham, Adam Eckart, Lori Johnson, Joseph Regalia, Jennifer Romig, Sarah Schendel, Gabriel Teninbaum, and my legal practice skills mentor Kathleen Elliott Vinson. Their students are lucky to have them and so am I.

I decided early on not to write a book about technology without technology. I'm grateful for the enthusiasm from vendors and industry specialists, many of whom provided quotes or screenshots. Special thanks to Carolyn Hall from CS Disco, Inc. and e-discovery specialist Jessica Tseng Hasen for reviewing the chapter on electronically stored information.

As a first-time book author, I experimented and took risks. As a reader, I hope you'll do the same.

*"To rid yourself of old patterns, focus all your energy not on struggling with the old, but on building the new."*

DAN MILLMAN, WAY OF THE PEACEFUL WARRIOR:
A BOOK THAT CHANGES LIVES (2000).

# TABLE OF CONTENTS

# LEGAL INNOVATION & TECHNOLOGY

## A Practical Skills Guide for the Modern Lawyer

# CHAPTER 1

# INTRODUCTION TO MODERN LEGAL PRACTICE SKILLS

| LIT TIP |
|---|
| "[A]ll lawyers, unless they are retiring today, are tomorrow's lawyers."[1] |
| Richard Susskind |
| Legal Futurist and Author |

Before a soccer tournament in college, my coach shared some advice from Benjamin Franklin: when you fail to plan, you plan to fail. This book is not about failing. It's about planning. I invite you to plan what type of lawyer to be.

By "type" I don't mean what you've heard in law school: the decision between criminal law or torts, for example, or between a public interest or in-house position. I mean the choice between being a forward-thinking, modern lawyer who understands that innovation and technology enhance their skillset—or being content as one who does not. In fact, early congratulations are in order. By opening this book, you've already made your choice.

Let's back up. You entered law school to be a lawyer. You learn how lawyers read, think, speak, and write. But you also learn what lawyers do and how they do it: how does "everyday" lawyering work?

Here's the problem: what lawyers do and how they do it is not as simple today as it was decades ago. The practice of law today is different than in the past and it will continue to change during your career.

Don't believe me? Take a simple challenge: name any profession, service, or aspect of everyday life that has *not* changed from technology. Changed over your lifetime? The past ten years? Five? Even the past six months? Perhaps the way a plumber uses a wrench to fix a leaky kitchen sink is the same as it's always been. Or how an electrician replaces a light bulb. But

1

none of us bought groceries with a click or flash of our cell phone a few years ago. We never got them delivered by an automated delivery robot. We never followed our friends' exact locations with the tap of a screen. Parents never before tracked how fast children were driving in a moving car hundreds of miles away by installing apps on their smartphones. Years ago, artificial intelligence technology (more on this later) didn't help doctors differentiate between patients having a heart attack and those suffering from everyday heartburn. People used to save thick photo albums but today it takes a few seconds to save thousands of photos to a magical place called "the cloud." And I'm not sure about you, but I left my last dentist appointment with a recommendation for a smart toothbrush to measure brushing time, gauge plaque accumulation, and send notifications to my dental patient portal. Based on the cavities I had as a teenager, that technology must be new!

Examples like this could fill an entire book. Back to how technology and innovation have changed lawyering skills. Spoiler alert: a lot. At the risk of boring you with "back in my day" legal practice stories, let's warm up in this introduction with a "then v. now" comparison showing side-by-side some skills of the past next to skills expected today. It's hard to understand where the profession is headed if you don't know where it has been.

### Practice skill: fact and information collection

| then . . . | now . . . |
|---|---|
| ✓ get boxes of hard copy papers from a client or witness or company and thumb through them one at a time<br>✓ use a sticky note to mark important documents for assistant to photocopy | ✓ review facts about a matter by contracting with an e-discovery vendor to collect gigabytes of electronic data from custodians (witnesses, clients, companies)<br>✓ process uploaded files to an artificially intelligent cloud-based software platform |

| | |
|---|---|
| ✓ stick thick white tape strips to cover up privileged information that would need to remain confidential | ✓ use software to identify potentially relevant and "hot" documents and create electronic automatic redactions of privileged content |

### Practice skill: research and writing

| *then . . .* | *now . . .* |
|---|---|
| ✓ read cases or a legal encyclopedia excerpt from office bookshelf or local library<br><br>✓ dictate original content aloud to an associate or secretarial assistant taking notes on a legal pad<br><br>✓ use a pen to sign the document typed on a typewriter or computer and mail or walk for service or filing | ✓ review jurisdiction-specific analytics such as the percentage of times the assigned judge has granted the motion being drafted<br><br>✓ create persuasive documents from an online brief-builder tool by clicking among suggested authorities and pre-filtered arguments<br><br>✓ format electronic filings with optimal design for a digital reader |

## Practice skill: client communication & practice management

| then . . . | now . . . |
|---|---|
| ✓ drive or fly hundreds of miles for in person client intake<br>✓ mail a client engagement letter and create a hard copy file folder for case communication<br>✓ play "phone tag" when client calls and give random case updates by phone<br>✓ mail follow-up communication for billing and open and record each hard copy check payment received | ✓ meet client by virtual web conference after reviewing information from online intake forms<br>✓ set client up with secure 24/7 access to case portal for real-time updates and Q&A<br>✓ populate automatic calendar entries for client and legal team for key dates<br>✓ receive notification of client credit card payments through secure third-party service |

## Practice skill: marketing & business development

| then . . . | now . . . |
|---|---|
| ✓ publicize services with a print advertisement in community phonebook<br>✓ share expertise at local conferences and events<br>✓ draft newspaper editorials on key legal issues | ✓ publicize services online with advice from a search engine optimization consultant<br>✓ share expertise with blog posts and updates to web profile<br>✓ develop LinkedIn page and engage with clients and colleagues daily |

| ✓ stay in touch with network with a printed holiday card in the mail | ✓ stay in touch with network through social media posts, and videos |
|---|---|

The backbone principle of this book is that fundamental lawyering skills are the same but the way a modern lawyer does them is different. You'll still draft documents and do legal research, create and execute transactional documents or court filings, communicate with and manage clients, review information for fact development and investigation, and advertise and network with other professionals and prospective clients. These fundamental skills that lawyers have practiced for centuries are, in fact, still fundamental—but they certainly don't look the same. Our "then v. now" examples scratch the surface; there are many more in the chapters to come. The goal of this book is to introduce you to the many "now" examples of the skills a modern lawyer should have.

Innovation and technology (we'll add the "legal" and call it LIT) can be abstract topics. I hope to make them less so for you. We'll move beyond buzzwords like "artificial intelligence" (OK, that's two words), and put broad ideas into real-world lawyering examples an aspiring lawyer can grasp: more hypotheticals, more examples, more exercises, more practice opportunities, more questions, and more information about technologies and innovations impacting the traditional profession you've chosen to enter—a profession now shedding its reputation as an old-fashioned guild resistant to change. Law school teaches you to avoid risk as a lawyer. All change brings risk. It can also bring great reward. Avoiding change might be the plan for some lawyers, but not for you. So read on.

Before we turn to chapter 2 and some early legal innovation & technology Need to Knows to set the stage, take a sneak peek at what's next. Skim the Table of Contents. The chapters following our Need to Knows represent broad categories where technology and innovation have made, and will continue to make, a real impact on legal practice skills. Each chapter integrates basic explanations of concepts alongside multiple-choice questions, extension exercises, visuals, screenshots, and LIT TIP examples, quotes, and personal perspectives from lawyers and technologists who create, use, and navigate the same tools and topics you'll be learning.

Here's the general framework to expect in each chapter:

---

✓ **Core Concepts**: basic LIT lingo on each topic to expand your vocabulary.

✓ **Knowledge Kickoff**: an initial question to warm up your thinking before you read—plan to revisit the question and the answer explanation after you read.

✓ **LIT TIP**: tips, quotes, definitions, rules, and decisions throughout each chapter that reinforce what you're reading—don't skim past them!

✓ **Review Your Knowledge**: concluding questions to gauge understanding after you read—review the answer explanations whether you answered correctly or not.

✓ **Practice Your Knowledge**: two exercises to dive deeper with hands-on application of ideas.

✓ **Expand Your Knowledge**: optional additional resources to expand your understanding.

---

I wrote this book for hundreds—maybe even thousands—of new lawyers, not just you. Not every aspect we cover will pertain to your career and interests, now or in the future. One size doesn't fit all. A solo real estate lawyer might not have much of a need for legal analytics or remote courtroom technology. A public defender might not have much interest in the ethics of accepting cryptocurrency as payment for legal services. But every lawyer can benefit from seeing new concepts in different professional contexts and becoming aware of how changes impact the other lawyers, clients, and people they'll meet along whatever career path they choose.

This book is for beginners. It offers a broad, working foundation—not comprehensive coverage of everything under the legal tech sun. This book will not teach you how to code software. It will not explain the intricate mysteries of a blockchain network (if you figure that out, let me know) or answer the latest questions about NFTs (non-fungible tokens) in the metaverse. It will not dive deep into particular software features, platforms, online tools, or specific mobile applications, although by no means will we ignore them completely. I mention specific companies and legal technology products and include visual screenshots to help concepts come to life, but I do so knowing these companies and tools will change—they'll go out of business, get acquired, change their user interface, or update their software. Just like you learn legal research using one database but transfer that learning elsewhere, you can apply foundational LIT concepts and skills throughout your career no matter the tool you use. The goal of this book is a solid baseline familiarity with the concepts and available categories of tools—not expertise with any one feature, vendor, or software.

---

**LIT TIP**

"[O]peness to, and affinity for, the newest tools of the legal trade are now fundamental to competent lawyering (and in several jurisdictions, an ethical requirement too). Software is daily growing its capacity to perform legal tasks. Whether you buy these tasks or sell them, it's imperative that you know what's available . . . [t]here's not a single profession—accounting, medicine, communications, education, the list goes on—that doesn't routinely use technology. Law will never again be an exception to the rule."[2]

Jordan Furlong
Principal, Law21
Legal Analyst & Consultant

---

We'll cover a lot in this book. I've separated the topics but the lines are blurry. Electronically stored information (ESI) blends into metadata, which blends into document proficiency, which blends into remote lawyering, which blends into law practice management, which blends into security. I've drawn dividing lines where they make sense, recognizing that no single aspect of law practice fits squarely into any one box. For the lawyering you'll do, half the battle will be recognizing what you don't know but need to know—and knowing who or what to consult for support. The future is impossible to predict. This book helps create the mindset you'll need, because the ins and outs of the concepts we cover will change faster than I'll be able to write a second edition.

If you want to springboard from this book's introduction to become a "legal tech" guru and keep going, go for it. Become an expert, take on a role like Chief Innovation Officer, Legal Data Analyst, or Technology & Knowledge Management Director, build a new product, or design some legal technology software. That's terrific. But for most readers, I suspect the goal is simple: familiarity, awareness, and a willingness to set your intention to be a lawyer open to learning new ways of doing things—not just today, but throughout your career, long after your coursework ends.

At this point, you might be wondering why you should listen to me. Am I a technologist? Software developer? Chief Innovation Officer? Inventor? No. I teach fundamental skills of legal practice:

- ✓ case briefing
- ✓ rule synthesis
- ✓ legal analysis
- ✓ drafting & editing
- ✓ client communication
- ✓ oral advocacy
- ✓ fact investigation
- ✓ research

Why, then, am I writing a book about innovation and technology and not one of those things? In fact, this book is about *all* of those things. Innovation and technology touch every basic lawyering skill. I've spent years learning how LIT has changed the practice of law. LIT concepts and techniques are just as much practice skills for a modern lawyer as many traditional tasks taught in law school like drafting an objective memorandum or presenting an oral argument. I hope this short introduction has convinced you of that.

---

### LIT TIP

Lawyers in many states complete mandatory continuing legal education (CLE) to maintain active status as a member of the bar. Two states (Florida and North Carolina) require CLE relating to technology on an annual or periodic basis. Maine's rule describes competence in technology as a goal of its CLE, Delaware includes a course on Fundamentals of Law Practice Management & Technology for new lawyers, and in 2022 New York implemented mandatory CLE training every two years related to cybersecurity, privacy, and data protection.

---

One final caution. If you mention this book to other students or lawyers (or a stranger on the train who glances over your shoulder and spots the title), be ready for skeptics. Folks challenging my perspective might claim the legal tech "hoopla" is overblown. Sure, it impacts some lawyering but it's a minuscule percentage in the big scheme of things. And won't you figure it out after law school? After all, you're a digital native who grew up with technology. You'll learn as you go with some on-the-job training. Let your employer or clients worry about getting you up to speed. These naysayers might urge you to focus instead on traditional fundamentals as a junior lawyer. Learn to think like a lawyer.

I agree. You should learn to think like a lawyer. But lawyering fundamentals do not exist in a vacuum as an abstract and fixed thing we do. They change. Even the strongest naysayer would agree legal research is not what it was with stacks of library books in 1970 (or 2010, for that matter), and no client would pay for hours of a lawyer's time spent updating case law using hard copy case reporters when an online tool does it in seconds. The many ways we "think like a lawyer" play out by what we do in courtrooms, boardrooms, offices, social media platforms, videoconferences, and everywhere in between with real clients, cases, negotiations, problems, and demands—all of which technology impacts. Don't let anyone convince you otherwise.

---

**LIT TIP**

"Here is the great excitement for tomorrow's lawyers. As never before, there is an opportunity to be involved in shaping the next generation of legal services. You will find most senior lawyers to be of little guidance in this quest. Your elders will tend to be cautious, protective, conservative, if not reactionary. They will resist change and will often want to hang on to their traditional ways of working, even if these are well past their sell-by date . . . I urge you to join a growing movement of people who I say are 'upgrading justice'—exploiting technology in forging new paths for the law, our most important social institution."[3]

Richard Susskind
Legal Futurist and Author

---

Hold your head up high when you express interest in legal innovation and technology or when someone sees you reading this book. Explain to them what modern lawyering skills are. Fundamentals are the same but the game has changed. Broadening your context about how lawyers deliver legal services today (and how they'll deliver them tomorrow) makes your skillset stronger, not weaker. You'll still be:

- ✓ a creative problem solver—only now you'll solve problems with the benefit of analytics based on jurisdiction-specific relevant data or create new tools to help individuals solve legal problems using principles of automation

- ✓ an available advocate who communicates with clients—only now you'll do so through convenient client portals and messaging systems, and at virtual court hearings and videoconferences

- ✓ a terrific researcher and writer—only now you'll do your work with the benefit of efficient document creation, editing, and citation software and advanced search and data visualization tools

- ✓ a careful lawyer who maintains client confidences—only now you'll make reasonable efforts to ensure a secure third-party cloud platform instead of a lock-and-key file cabinet

\* \* \* \*

As you move past this Introduction, remember these final thoughts:

Are robots and machines going to take over all legal jobs? Nope.

Will innovation and technology replace lawyers? Nope.

Will innovation and technology replace and change some of what lawyers used to do and how they do it? You bet—they already have.

Can you be a good lawyer without integrating innovation and technology into your everyday practice skills? Maybe.

Can you become an excellent lawyer if you use innovation and technology to create a more modern skillset? Definitely.

Let's get started.

## Endnotes

¹  RICHARD SUSSKIND, TOMORROW'S LAWYERS: AN INTRODUCTION TO YOUR FUTURE xi (2017).

²  Jordan Furlong, *How to Be a Legal Marvel: 8 Super Skills for the Modern Lawyer*, at 21, LOD (2015), https://www.lodlaw.com/documents/10/How_to_be_a_Legal_Marvel. PDF [https://perma.cc/P2TF-PVXZ].

³  RICHARD SUSSKIND, TOMORROW'S LAWYERS: AN INTRODUCTION TO YOUR FUTURE 195–96 (2017).

CHAPTER 2

# GETTING STARTED: LIT NEED TO KNOWS

*Core Concepts*

| | |
|---|---|
| *technology of law practice* *law of technology* *legal innovation* *ethical duty of technology competence* *legal regulatory reform* | *alternative legal service providers* *non-traditional legal jobs* *access to justice (A2J) gap* *cross-disciplinary lawyer* *artificial intelligence* |

Ever find yourself at a networking event or reception standing with a group of people but not understanding what they're talking about? You nod your head along as if you share their experience and knowledge when really, you feel like a lost, out-of-place imposter. Don't worry, I've been there too. Many times. I don't want you to feel like that while reading the upcoming chapters in this book.

This chapter gets us started with nine big-picture ideas I'll call LIT Need to Knows (aka "You'll be in the know at the cocktail party when folks are chatting about legal innovation and technology."). These Need to Knows are for beginners; no technical expertise or background is necessary. You "need" to know them before moving on in this book to put smaller concepts and examples in context, whether that's one new research tool or a new mobile timekeeping law practice management app.

Before we turn to the substantive chapter-by-chapter topics, I want you to grasp the bigger industry picture first. We'll paint it in this chapter through short introductions to some definitions, rules, trends, and concepts that shape today's legal profession. Think of these puzzle pieces as together forming the backdrop landscape that runs across the rest of this book. I'll refer to these Need to Knows in the chapters that follow. Each Need to Know could be its own chapter—so we'll keep our overview high level.

## Need to Know #1: Technology of Law Practice v. Law of Technology

First, let's get some terminology straight. When I use the phrases "**technology of law practice**" or "legal technology" or "practice skills" in this book, I mean technology lawyers use, should use, or might encounter as part of delivering legal services. This is everything from a desktop computer to a mobile document application to software for e-signatures to complex cloud-based virtual data rooms. The words "innovation" and "technology" in the LIT acronym focus on the act of lawyering, with at times minimal connection to the underlying subject. While some technologies like contract management software are more context-specific than others, technology of law practice applies whether a lawyer is drafting a licensing contract, negotiating a plea agreement, leading an investigation, showing exhibits to a jury, or mediating a custody arrangement. It touches everywhere and everyone. It applies to family law lawyers, criminal prosecutors, transactional deal lawyers, clerks, in-house lawyers, associates and partners at large and small firms, government lawyers, and just about anyone else practicing law. Technology of law practice is what this book is all about.

Don't confuse this with **law of technology**—statutes, regulations, and cases that govern new emerging legal issues brought about by advances in technology. It can take months, years, or decades for laws to catch up to new aspects of society. Examples aren't scarce:

- ✓ Smart cars driving around in your community—who is liable if they crash?

- ✓ Enjoying a smart doorbell camera outside your home—can the police get the video with a warrant?

- ✓ Using your Alexa device to keep a personal shopping list—can Amazon sell your IoT (Internet of Things) information to advertisers?

- ✓ Inventing something new with artificial intelligence technology—can a machine be named as an inventor on a patent application?

✓  Representing a criminal defendant denied bail based on a court's new algorithm that evaluates flight risk—does that violate the defendant's constitutional rights?

✓  Sharing an embarrassing video of a friend's avatar driving in the metaverse digital space—can they sue for infliction of emotional distress?

As technology evolves at a lightning speed, lawmakers, regulators, and judges struggle to keep pace. Substantive legal issues with law of technology today are fascinating and complicated. But they aren't the subject of this book.

---

**LIT TIP**

technology of law practice: technology that lawyers use, should use, or might encounter as part of delivering their legal services, no matter the underlying subject or context

law of technology: primary legal authority that governs (or is needed to govern) new emerging substantive issues of law brought about by advancements in technology

technology of teaching: classroom and teaching techniques that include technology to deliver educational content to students

---

One more clarification: the technology of law practice this book covers has little to do with whether you use technology in school to learn it or how your teacher uses technology to teach it. Those idea fall under the umbrella of technology of teaching, meaning the hybrid or online classes you've taken, or the learning management system such as Canvas or Blackboard your professor might use to post course files. Technology of teaching is growing in popularity as schools experiment with distance education, due to the Covid-19 pandemic or otherwise. Legal innovation and technology concepts covered in this book existed well before the pandemic and can (and should) be taught anytime, anywhere, and using anything—from a 100% online class to an old-fashioned classroom lecture hall and chalkboard (although I admit practicing document creation shortcuts or new legal research approaches on a chalkboard would be interesting,

I hope you'll have fun on your own laptop or device trying out some tips and tools we cover).

## Need to Know #2: What's Innovation?

What do I mean by **legal innovation**, and how does it connect to technology? It's a hot topic buzzword. I'm willing to bet readers have a general sense of what it's all about, but let's put a finer point on it given the different contexts in which we hear it—Chief Innovation Officers at companies and law firms, Legal Innovation Awards each year for the industry's brightest, and even my own title at a law school as a director of the legal innovation and technology concentration. Black's Law Dictionary, a go-to source, does not include the word "innovation" (alone an interesting fact). I've heard it defined as the action or process behind a new idea, method, or product. Here's my simple equation we can take throughout this book:

> *Innovation: new idea + hands-on implementation =*
> *a better way of doing something*

Combining innovation with law just means we put the concepts together within endless different lawyering contexts, from groundbreaking changes to incremental improvements:

- ✓ Updating billing practices to reduce the administrative load at a large government agency? Innovative.

- ✓ Scanning yellow notepads and manila folders into electronic form to create a paperless solo law firm? Innovative.

- ✓ Outsourcing e-discovery file collection to a vendor and saving hours of expensive attorney billing time? Innovative.

- ✓ Replacing manual signatures on hundreds of corporate deal documents sent back and forth across the globe with an e-signature tool? Innovative.

✓  Dividing up drafting of a summary judgment brief on a cloud-based sharing platform instead of 10 lawyers working on 10 different versions? Innovative.

✓  Creating an interactive app to help people unable to afford a lawyer challenge a housing eviction? Innovative.

Innovation and technology often go hand in hand, but they need not. Typing on a keyboard uses technology but it's not innovative (at least not today—it was a different story decades ago). Restructuring a case management workflow in a corporate legal department might be innovative but it need not require technology. Technology might be one path to innovation but it's not the only one. This book gives examples in both contexts. Paired together, though, innovation and technology can create forward-looking improvements whether by creating efficiencies that affect the bottom line or by improving processes that affect lawyer well-being. It's the mindset not to be satisfied with the status quo where greater opportunities lie. I hope to steer you toward welcoming creative and positive change no matter where your professional path leads.

## Need to Know #3: Ethical Duty of Technology Competence

Technology of law practice relates to many ethical rules under the American Bar Association's Model Rules of Professional Conduct[1] for lawyers, adopted in some form in every jurisdiction in the United States (other countries have similar ethical frameworks). We'll weave them throughout the book, including Rule 1.4 (Communications), Rule 1.6 (Confidentiality of Information), and Rule 7.1 (Communications Concerning a Lawyer's Services). Our catch-all, most important starting point is Rule 1.1 (Competence). Understanding technology might be a nice-to-have plus factor but *must* you do so to be a competent lawyer? If you practice in one of 40 United States jurisdictions or Canada, the answer to that question is yes.

Model Rule 1.1 creates a baseline expectation that lawyers be competent. It's no surprise this concept is broad, whether applying to written work, research, supervision of staff, adherence to deadlines, or substantive understanding of legal rules. But in 2013, after an American Bar Association Commission on Ethics report, Comment 8 to Rule 1.1 was amended to add the underlined language here:

---

### LIT TIP

"A lawyer shall provide competent representation to a client. Competent representation requires the legal knowledge, skill, thoroughness and preparation reasonably necessary for the representation."

Comment [8]: "To maintain the requisite knowledge and skill, a lawyer should keep abreast of changes in the law and its practice, <u>including the benefits and risks associated with relevant technology,</u> engage in continuing study and education and comply with all continuing legal education requirements to which the lawyer is subject."[2]

Model Rule 1.1 (emphasis added)

---

As of this book's publication, 40 states have adopted some form of Comment 8 since 2013. Lawyers navigate jurisdiction-specific enforcement guidance and formal and informal bar opinions and notices to determine how to keep "abreast" of "the benefits and risks associated with relevant technology." Does it mean:

✓ updating your practice technology for things such as word-processing or cloud computing? (yes)

✓ obtaining some understanding of your client's technology as relevant to representation? (yes)

✓ becoming a technology expert? (no)

✓ recognizing when to ask for an expert's help? (yes)

✓ learning to code software? (no)

✓ asking questions of a potential third-party service relating to cybersecurity of privileged work product? (yes)

✓ using a computer instead of a typewriter? (yes—yes please!).

There are countless variables and questions about what the **duty of technology competence** means for the modern lawyer. We'll touch on more Comment 8 interpretation in the chapters that follow, but here's one early example from years ago to kick us off. You know what a spreadsheet is. But in 2013, one lawyer didn't. A Delaware court sanctioned a lawyer for not producing an accurate spreadsheet as part of the discovery phase of a case, citing that state's adoption of Model Rule 1.1 Comment 8. Put this next LIT TIP example in the "don't let this be you" category:

---

**LIT TIP**

"When James' counsel put National's counsel on the spot about neXVel's role, National's counsel claimed ignorance . . . during the hearing on the motion for sanctions, National's counsel offered a different explanation: 'I have to confess to this Court, I am not computer literate. I have not found presence in the cybernetic revolution. I need a secretary to help me turn on the computer. This was out of my bailiwick.' Professed technological incompetence is not an excuse for discovery misconduct. Deliberate ignorance of technology is inexcusable . . . if a lawyer cannot master the technology suitable for that lawyer's practice, the lawyer should either hire tech-savvy lawyers tasked with responsibility to keep current, or hire an outside technology consultant who understands the practice of law and associated ethical constraints."[3]

*James v. National Finance LLC*

---

This kickoff summary of the duty of technology competence oversimplifies a topic that's not simple. It's a duty woven throughout this book. Technology competence for tomorrow's modern lawyer is specific to one's practice and resources. Technology is dynamic; what helps a client one day might harm it the next. That's why this book focuses on ideas and concepts more than specific technology tools. The only bright-line rule to heed at the starting line of your career is that Rule 1.1 Competency no longer "just" means you should know what the law is. Competency never "just" meant that. What the benefits and risks with technology are will seesaw throughout your future law practice and will depend on more variables than there are pages in this book.

Don't be intimidated. Be excited. This book gives you a head start with your eyes open and gets you running in the right direction.

## Need to Know #4: Legal Services Without (or Alongside) Lawyers

Wait a minute. How can people get legal services without a lawyer? Isn't this the select, specialized, highly regulated, insulated, lifetime, traditional, exclusive profession you've worked so hard for the privilege to join? Sure, on-demand custom streaming services from Netflix might have put the local video store from the 1990s out of business, and yes, thumbnail-size smartphone cameras signaled doom for photography companies like Kodak and Polaroid—but that can't happen to lawyers, right?

Wrong. There's been a bubble around lawyers for hundreds of years. It hasn't outright popped yet, but it's stretching, weakening, and shrinking.

We'll touch on three pieces to the complicated story of how legal services get delivered without lawyers:

1) state-by-state legal regulatory reform

2) growth in alternative legal service providers

3) new non-traditional lawyer and legal jobs

As to each, innovation and technology don't always play lead roles but they're important supporting actors.

1)   Legal Regulatory Reform

Reform of what? Remember that the only place to seek "official" legal advice in the United States is at a law firm owned and run by lawyers. The Model Rules of Professional Conduct:

✓   ensure that only licensed lawyers practice law

✓   forbid lawyers from joining forces and sharing legal fees with individuals who aren't lawyers

> **LIT TIP**
>
> "A lawyer or law firm shall not share legal fees with a nonlawyer . . . a lawyer shall not form a partnership with a nonlawyer if any of the activities of the partnership consist of the practice of law."[4]
>
> Model Rule 5.4
>
> "A lawyer shall not practice law in a jurisdiction in violation of the regulation of the legal profession in that jurisdiction, or assist another in doing so."[5]
>
> Model Rule 5.5

Pushback about someone or something besides a lawyer delivering services or delivering them in an untraditional way is old. But it's exploding in interest and growth today. Rewind a century: nearly a hundred years ago, radio was a new hot technology. A national radio show featured judges responding to callers' legal questions—before it got shut down. Fast-forward to 1999. You may be familiar with the popular online tool LegalZoom founded as a way for individuals to create legal documents such as a will. We'll discuss LegalZoom in chapter 6 about improved efficiency and legal automation. The regulatory framework around lawyering has always threatened to stifle competition and it's often assumed that lawyers face little of it. After all, where else can the public get legal advice? There are restrictions in every jurisdiction as to who can practice law. Given stringent regulations around unauthorized practice of law and the bar licensing structure in the United States, it's almost always the case that lawyers still get to be the only players in town.

Not anymore, perhaps. We're seeing slow signs of **legal regulatory reform** that may change this landscape, such as by allowing lawyers and non-lawyers to work together or creating new lawyer-*ish* positions. While some states maintain a strict line, other jurisdictions like Utah, Arizona, California, Oregon, North Carolina, Florida, and Washington have experimented in different ways:

> ➤ In 2015, Washington launched a Limited License Legal Technician program to offer more reasonably priced family law services to the public (in 2020 the

state's supreme court voted to sunset its LLLT program).

➢ In 2020, under Utah's Office of Legal Services Innovation, Utah began a seven year "regulatory sandbox" period to experiment with different business models, including licensing for Alternative Business Structures (ABS) that allow for nonlawyer owners of firms that provide legal services (something Model Rule 5.4 otherwise prohibits).

➢ In 2020 and 2021, Arizona and Minnesota pursued development of new licensing options beyond the traditional "JD" bar exam competency such as legal paraprofessionals who provide limited, subject-specific services.

➢ In 2022, Arizona became the first state to approve a temporary license under new law firm ownership rules and allow technology and consulting company Elevate Services, Inc. to combine with an integrated law firm ElevateNext (it also granted an Alternative Business Structure license to Axiom Law).

I don't have a crystal ball but more changes could be on the horizon during your career. You may be familiar with the Big Four accounting firms such as Deloitte and Ernst & Young. Accounting firms aren't law firms and can't compete with lawyers, right? Not in the United States—not yet at least. They have thousands of lawyers competing with traditional law firms in countries around the globe.

2)    Growth in Alternative Legal Service Providers (ALSPs)

**Alternative Legal Service Providers** (ALSPs) aren't all that "alternative" anymore. They are becoming mainstream, coexisting with what we've always thought of as traditional lawyers and firms. Think of an ALSP like you might a nurse practitioner at an urgent care walk-in setting providing you medical services instead of an MD physician at your traditional doctor's office. The behind-the-scenes license and the physical setting is different, but as far as you're concerned at your appointment, the goal is outstanding healthcare. If you're like me, you care more about the provider, convenience, cost, and quality of service—not so much the abbreviation on someone's nametag.

---

### LIT TIP

Alternative Legal Service Providers (ALSPs) are third-party providers that deliver select legal services as an "alternative" to using lawyers for certain tasks related to a legal matter but they are not considered engaged in licensed law practice. These are non-law firm companies that lawyers or clients work with to handle matters efficiently and often with niche expertise lawyers might not have. Examples include accounting firms, auditors, electronic discovery and investigation companies, staffing services, compliance companies, and legal technology companies. The process of "unbundling" some of a legal matter and handing off a task (or more) to a different provider is called Legal Process Outsourcing (LPO).

---

As a modern lawyer, you may not be the only player in town on a matter. If the life cycle of a case involves 20 steps, in the past a lawyer (or the legal team) probably performed all 20. Today, often lawyers might perform only 10 or 15. For example, instead of relying on lawyers at a large firm to handle all company legal matters, an in-house general counsel at a life sciences drug company might "cut out the middle" and reduce costs by outsourcing compliance tasks directly to a third-party ALSP that only focuses on that work (and thus sits at the cutting edge of technology relevant to those processes). Or a large law firm might partner with an e-discovery provider to handle that aspect of a matter on a per-project basis with greater efficiency and expertise. The scenarios are as plentiful as the many categories of ALSPs such as:

✓ legal research

✓ contract lifecycle management (CLM)

✓ e-discovery

✓ intellectual property services

✓ investigation support

✓ practice management

✓ electronic billing and payment

- ✓ security
- ✓ document automation
- ✓ captioning and transcription

The growth of—and demand for—ALSPs shows no signs of slowing down: one study termed ALSPs a "mainstream segment of the legal market" and reported accelerated market growth, finding that 79% of law firms and 71% of corporations now use ALSPs in a nearly $14 billion market.[6]

---

**LIT TIP**

Growth of legal technology companies and ALSPs will fluctuate with market and trends, but overall financial interest and investment in legal technology has exploded in recent years. In 2021 and 2022, legal technology companies in the United States received billions of dollars in investment; legal technology companies that went public include LegalZoom.com Inc. (online legal help), Intapp Inc. (cloud-based software), and CS Disco Inc. (electronic discovery software).

---

3) New Non-Traditional Lawyer and Legal Jobs

Where does this change leave you? Conventional lawyering positions are still there for you. But so are some **non-traditional legal jobs**, as more legal services come from someone and somewhere other than a lawyer (or come from a lawyer in new ways). New positions and new opportunities in the legal industry are out there for individuals who aren't licensed lawyers as well as for lawyers (like you!) willing to embrace a modern, consumer-centric practice of law. Here are a few examples:

- ✓ Hub Innovation Manager
- ✓ Technology Training Attorney
- ✓ Chief Innovation Officer
- ✓ E-Discovery Specialist
- ✓ Legal Analytics Manager
- ✓ Knowledge Management Director
- ✓ Online Dispute Resolution Court Facilitator

- ✓  Legal Operations Director
- ✓  Legal Resource Manager
- ✓  Legal Project Manager

That's your Need to Know about legal services without or alongside lawyers. Your future clients will be watching these industry developments carefully. You should too.

## Need to Know #5: Access to Justice (A2J) Gap

With that introduction to *how* aspects of the legal profession are changing, I'll fill you in on one reason *why* they are—and why they must. It's because people who need legal help in the United States often can't get it. There are other more market-driven reasons such as private business opportunities and financial investment in legal technology. But a critical driving reason is to close what's known as the **access to justice gap**.

As an author, it's difficult to tee up such a complex societal topic with a mere overview. I urge you to dive into this issue if you aren't familiar with it. Access to justice, called A2J, should be on the mind of any and every lawyer, but especially a future lawyer thinking about modern legal practice skills and efficient delivery of legal services. Many industry analysts compare basic legal services to a public utility such as oil or gas or electricity for a home: something to which everyone should have access.

Everyone doesn't have access. Statistics suggest that more than three-quarters of low-income people needing civil legal help in the United States receive either no help or help that is inadequate. Those are people needing, for example, help with a will, custody arrangement, small business loan, or housing eviction. Many scholars, advocates, and lawyers suggest the percentage is even higher; the United States tied for 108th place out of 126 countries in a 2020 Rule of Law Index by the World Justice Project measuring "accessibility" and "affordability of civil justice."[7] 108 out of 126. Not good.

---

**LIT TIP**

"Imagine if lawyers, judges, and decision makers used rigorous evidence to design and run the U.S. justice system. They could enable far more people, especially those who can't afford to hire lawyers, to access civil justice; make the criminal justice system fairer and more efficient; and promote the dignity and respect of individuals and families as they encounter the justice system."[8]

A2J Lab Harvard Law School

---

There's some light at the end of what feels like a doom-and-gloom tunnel. Access to Justice is a Need to Know in a book about legal innovation and technology because those concepts impact how law can become more efficient, affordable, and accessible. The theory is this: better processes, better technology, doing more with less, and serving people more efficiently—in turn create the time, capacity, resources, and capability to serve more.

These principles fuel many efforts at improving delivery of legal services, from the creation of a new limited license lawyer role discussed earlier to help people in court to the development of online legal tools the public can access regardless of socioeconomic status. Lawyers in the traditional sense working alone won't make a dent in the A2J crisis; it will require the ultimate team effort among lawyers, third-party vendors, ALSPs, paralegals, legal services corporations, data scientists, and many others. Closing the gap is not a guarantee; technology and innovation are not an overnight quick fix. They can, however, fuel movement in the right direction.

## Need to Know #6: Law as a Business Product

My neighbor is a culinary expert and nutritionist. Years ago, friends asked for her help with meal planning. She started a small business going to homes to talk about food preferences and map out healthy meal plans. She became bored with going into autopilot mode four evenings a week: her introduction to each client was the same, as was her explanation of the downsides of sugar and optimal times to eat. So she created a universal video for clients to watch beforehand, which freed up time in the meeting for a more personalized discussion. She later built a tool for custom meal planning where clients could choose among her prepackaged "know-how" and recipes and tips. Two years in, she was helping more people and making more money—all the while enjoying more free time!

In law school, we talk about lawyers who "serve" or "represent" or "counsel" individual clients with a unique problem. A one-to-one lawyer-to-client ratio. While that's still true in some ways, in other ways it's not. The individualized practice of law is moving (maybe tiptoeing) toward a more commoditized, "off-the-shelf" business of law. What my nutritionist friend did is what lawyers today might consider for repetitive, often mundane aspects of lawyering:

- ✓ If we work more efficiently, can we serve more people using less time and effort?

- ✓ Can we replicate what we do and package and scale it for others?

- ✓ Does every client need a bespoke and often expensive service tailored precisely to their needs?

- ✓ Can we duplicate and automate legal tasks to free up time for deeper, more personalized client counseling and strategizing?

- ✓ Might we be able to serve more people this way? (Need to Know #5 Access to Justice).

Innovative thinking (often combined with technology) is what helps a lawyer package their legal "know-how" or "how-to" into a bite-sized version scalable for many. This is sometimes called productizing legal work and this brief explanation is just the leading edge. We'll tackle the concept when we turn to efficiency and automation in chapter 6. You might think of this concept as "TurboTax" for legal services. Years ago, accountants created that system by packaging tax knowledge and creating a step-by-step platform for clients to get tax answers. TurboTax changed aspects of accounting work, but the accountants I know are still in business today. TurboTax changed the profession but it didn't ruin it. Same will go for lawyers.

Chatter about automated legal work either scares you or excites you. Some lawyers view it as a personal affront to the "old" way of doing things. The principles in this book should get you energized by the thought of automating aspects of practice and freeing up time for "higher level" legal analysis and creative counseling. Or freeing up much-needed time to focus on rest and well-being in our demanding profession.

## Need to Know #7: There May Be More to Lawyering than Lawyering

How many hats does a modern lawyer wear? When you graduate, you'll wear one central hat that shows off your foundational substantive knowledge (think Rule of Perpetuities and the elements of a battery) and practice skills (think statutory interpretation and oral advocacy). You may want to make room for a few more hats.

Modern lawyers may "mix" into other disciplines and skill sets to become **cross-disciplinary lawyers**. Some already do, many more face pressure to do so. Legal advice doesn't exist in a silo as much as it has in past generations. A successful 21st-century lawyer will strive for a healthy dose of complementary, non-expert understanding of a range of things that impact their clients and practice area. Step out of your lawyer shoes and into a client's shoes. Suppose you are CEO of an insurance company and have an issue with how thousands of company contracts are organized and managed (or how they are not). Would you want a single helpful source to discuss and brainstorm innovative improvements with your lawyer, or would you want your lawyer to tell you they'll draft contracts but anything beyond that is beyond their purview? If I was that client, I know which lawyer I'd prefer—a creative problem solver willing to help me see the big picture.

Remember the T-shaped graphic in Figure 2A as you read this book and start to shape your career. The bottom of the "T" is the expertise you've achieved in law school. I hope it's just the beginning of what you'll learn as a modern lawyer. Aim to maintain a strong bottom to your "T"—the vertical base of foundational legal expertise and skills. But be willing to try to obtain a wider, albeit shallower, breadth of knowledge and cross-disciplinary competencies—the horizontal top of the "T"—including competencies like technology, data analytics, and process improvement, all introduced in this book.

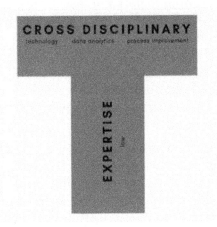

* Figure 2A: T-shaped lawyer.[9]

Your Need to Know here is that a collaborative and multi-disciplinary approach to solving a problem may trump narrow legal expertise. Not always, and not for every lawyer, but often. Consider yourself warned that future clients might expect you as their lawyer to have baseline familiarity with, for example, project management or business fundamentals. Perhaps your law school offers courses on some of these topics. The American Bar Association has urged law schools to provide students opportunities to study "entrepreneurship, innovation, the business and economics of law practice, and other relevant disciplines."[10] I've heard the concept described as a "NewLaw" mindset—professionals who embrace a more holistic approach to legal services. By the end of this book, I hope you'll consider yourself part of that group.

## Need to Know #8: All the Buzz About Artificial Intelligence (AI)

You've heard the phrase **artificial intelligence** (AI). But are you really in the know with it? I'm not always sure that I am. This isn't a software engineering book. It's not an advanced robotics manual. I'm not a computer expert and I promise not to dive into the weeds of things like neural networks or cognitive computing. But the concept is important enough to deserve a few minutes of thought beyond our daily personal life context— whether that's listening to personal assistants such as Alexa and Siri, reading an article about a computer beating a human in a game of chess, or wondering if our phones are eavesdropping on us after sweatshirt ads pop up on social media accounts hours after chatting with friends about fashion trends. Moving beyond the popular media buzz about AI—even if slightly—is important because technology captured under this broad umbrella impacts a lot of new legal practice technologies.

What's AI? Entire books are devoted to it and have been for decades. For our purposes let's keep it simple; a quick online search offers hundreds of varying definitions. AI is more a category of technologies than it is one technology itself.

---

**LIT TIP**

Artificial Intelligence: a computer program's ability to complete tasks in a way that replicates how a human would do them.

---

What does it mean when a machine "acts" or "thinks" like a human? Let's use a simple example. Imagine someone shows me pictures of different shapes and tells me to point to all the triangles. I can use my knowledge of shapes to do that and find patterns. If someone creates a set of instructions (also called an algorithm) for a computer as to what a triangle is, then the computer software can find the same shape triangle pattern just like I did. Sometimes AI technology like this is called an expert system (a phrase we'll review in chapter 6): a step-by-step program that mimics human decision making through different Yes/No type of steps, like a decision tree. Using our triangle example, I might ask if are there three straight sides. If yes, it's a triangle. If no, it's not. I can program a computer with the same set of rules to ask those same questions and make those same decisions.

Beyond expert systems, AI captures technology based on machine learning. This is where things get more complicated. Now the computer doesn't need you to write a rule for it to follow to perform a task like identifying triangles. It can simply "observe" what someone or something else does with information and mimic and continue those patterns. Put another way, now the computer can create its own step-by-step guide to a particular task. AI can get thorny because the software aims to create the same output as a human would but doesn't always use the same process. This is where we see a good amount of distrust around the so-called mystery of AI systems because of the uncertainty in what process a system uses to decide or create something. One prime example of this is criminal sentencing algorithms, which can exhibit bias based on a defendant's race. If a piece of software learns different patterns and changes its approach based on factors and information invisible to us (or information from only one particular source), how can we trust it with such important matters such as the length of a defendant's jail sentence? It's a hard question with no easy answer.

This introduction to AI is oversimplified. Applications to legal innovation and technology are complex and widespread. Lawyers and clients have a lot of information and pairing AI technology with enormous amounts of data can create powerful opportunities and new solutions. More complex machine learning networks are called "deep learning"—the technology behind things like self-driving cars and facial image recognition. This is when simple patterns become complex ("deep") ones that a computer follows ("learns"), spread out, for example, over millions of pages of contractual documents or hundreds of thousands of court decisions.

I hope this baseline Need to Know about AI helps you understand why there's buzz about it in the legal profession and beyond. This quick-blink introduction gives you context for upcoming chapters when we examine AI technology fueling advances in areas such as editing software, data analytics, contract management, document automation, electronically stored information (ESI), and many others.

---

**LIT TIP**

"The bottom line is that it is essential for lawyers to be aware of how AI can be used in their practices to the extent they have not done so yet. AI allows lawyers to provide better, faster, and more efficient legal services to companies and organizations. The end result is that lawyers using AI are better counselors for their clients. In the next few years, the use of AI by lawyers will be no different than the use of email by lawyers—an indispensable part of the practice of law."[11]

American Bar Association Resolution 112

---

## Need to Know #9: LIT in the Midst of Societal Shifts

It's difficult to write a book about a topic that will never stay the same from one day to the next. The modern legal profession is part of our modern world. In this complicated world, things move fast and are unpredictable. "Innovation" and "technology" are words that often signal change, and change doesn't exist in a bubble for anyone—lawyer or client or otherwise. For example, I planned this book project well before the Covid-19 pandemic began in the late winter of 2020, amid the explosion of the Black Lives Matter movement and battle for Democratic or Republican control of United States Congress and the White House. I finished it in 2022 after Russia invaded Ukraine and the United States hit its highest inflation rate in decades.

We shouldn't pretend major shifts in the world such as a great recession, a war, financial crisis and bank collapses, or a global pandemic are irrelevant to industry advancements, whether in law or otherwise. They are relevant. The world changes, and smaller pieces of it such as the legal profession try to keep pace. Regarding Covid-19, many LIT topics related to lawyers long before we were forced to social distance. But the pandemic accelerated the pace of change; most notably, development of remote lawyering communication solutions that helped lawyers, law firms, courts, agencies, and legislatures keep the system chugging along once face-to-face conversation and shared physical workspace became impossible.

A modern lawyer won't view their profession as a static time capsule insulated from changes (both good and bad) in our global society. Professional skills evolve alongside whatever unprecedented "thing" comes next. For example, today's clients face new demands and opportunities related to Environmental, Social, and Governance (ESG) factors in their businesses or new expectations and needs for their efforts related to Diversity, Equity, and Inclusion (DEI). Those acronyms didn't exist for lawyers of past generations. They do for you. Societal shifts, big and small, impact what society needs from lawyers and affect what lawyers demand of themselves. An openness to innovation and technology may be one small piece. Need to Know #5 was Access to Justice. Consider how new post-pandemic communication practices might help the justice system serve more clients in need. Or how data analytics patterns might help the legal profession recognize its shortcomings and better reflect the diverse population it serves.

The question isn't whether a societal shift will affect your career—it's which one, when, and how. Technologies welcomed in one country might be shamed in another; innovation feared in one corner of the globe might be celebrated in another. This book doesn't have everything you'll need to keep your skills "modern" as the world turns. The only constant is that society will keep spinning. I hope you'll move right along with it.

---

 *Expand Your Knowledge*

➢ Heidi Frostestad Kuehl, *Technologically Competent: Ethical Practice for 21st Century Lawyering*, 10 CASE W. RES. J.L. TECH. & INTERNET 1 (2019).

➢ THOMSON REUTERS INSTITUTE, ALTERNATIVE LEGAL SERVICE PROVIDERS 2021 1 (2021), https://www.thomson reuters.com/en-us/posts/wp-content/uploads/sites/20/2021/07/ALSP_2021-Report_FINAL-1.pdf [https://perma.cc/Q3 WY-PMHP].

➢ LEGAL SERV. CORP., THE JUSTICE GAP: MEASURING THE UNMET CIVIL LEGAL NEEDS OF LOW-INCOME AMERICANS 1 (June 2017), https://www.lsc.gov/sites/default/files/images/TheJusticeGap-FullReport.pdf [https://perma.cc/4D4Q-8S KA].

# Endnotes

[1]  MODEL RULES OF PRO. CONDUCT (AM. BAR ASS'N 2020).

[2]  MODEL RULES OF PRO. CONDUCT r. 1.1 (AM. BAR ASS'N 2020).

[3]  *James v. National Finance LLC*, No. CV 8931-VCL, 2014 WL 6845560, at *12 (Del. Ch. Dec. 5, 2014) (internal citations omitted).

[4]  MODEL RULES OF PRO. CONDUCT r. 5.4 (AM. BAR ASS'N 2020).

[5]  MODEL RULES OF PRO. CONDUCT r. 5.5 (AM. BAR ASS'N 2020).

[6]  LEGAL EXEC. INST., ALTERNATIVE LEGAL SERVICE PROVIDERS 2019 1 (2019) https://legal.thomsonreuters.com/content/dam/ewp-m/documents/legal/en/pdf/reports/alsp-report-final.pdf [https://perma.cc/T5RX-FTWA].

[7]  WORLD JUSTICE PROJECT, RULE OF LAW INDEX 7 (2020) https://worldjustice project.org/sites/default/files/documents/WJP-ROLI-2020-Online_0.pdf [https://perma.cc/8RLD-SG6C].

[8]  Harvard Law School, *Access to Justice Lab*, https://a2jlab.org/ [https://perma.cc/2QSH-NMVY].

[9]  Alyson Carrel, *Legal Intelligence Through Artificial Intelligence Requires Emotional Intelligence: A New Competency Model for the 21st Century Legal Professional*, 35 GA. ST. U. L. REV. 1153, 1174–75 (2019).

[10]  AMERICAN BAR ASS'N, REPORT ON THE FUTURE OF LEGAL SERVICES IN THE UNITED STATES 1 (2016) https://www.americanbar.org/content/dam/aba/images/aba news/2016FLSReport_FNL_WEB.pdf [https://perma.cc/5RF6-YT64].

[11]  AMERICAN BAR ASS'N, RESOLUTION 112 (Aug. 12, 2019) https://www.american bar.org/content/dam/aba/directories/policy/annual-2019/112-annual-2019.pdf [https://perma.cc/ER5R-V6GN].

# Chapter 3

# DOCUMENT PROFICIENCY

*Core Concepts*

| | |
|---|---|
| *document structure* | *keyboard shortcuts* |
| *document templates* | *document collaboration* |
| *electronic navigability* | *tracked changes* |
| *e-briefs* | *document metadata* |
| *digital typography* | *legal editing software* |

*Knowledge Kickoff*

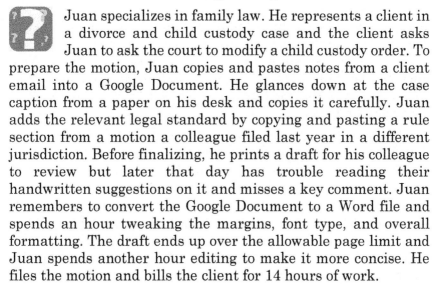

Juan specializes in family law. He represents a client in a divorce and child custody case and the client asks Juan to ask the court to modify a child custody order. To prepare the motion, Juan copies and pastes notes from a client email into a Google Document. He glances down at the case caption from a paper on his desk and copies it carefully. Juan adds the relevant legal standard by copying and pasting a rule section from a motion a colleague filed last year in a different jurisdiction. Before finalizing, he prints a draft for his colleague to review but later that day has trouble reading their handwritten suggestions on it and misses a key comment. Juan remembers to convert the Google Document to a Word file and spends an hour tweaking the margins, font type, and overall formatting. The draft ends up over the allowable page limit and Juan spends another hour editing to make it more concise. He files the motion and bills the client for 14 hours of work.

Which statement best captures Juan's approach to creating this legal document?

a) It was great that Juan reused sample legal documents; copying and pasting past work product is an efficient fool-proof approach to document creation.

b) Juan probably overbilled and may not have produced excellent work product in the most competent way, given that he used no standardized templates, struggled with effective collaboration with his colleague, and overall relied on piecemeal manual steps that risked sloppy errors.

c)   It was safest for Juan to do the document creation and editing work himself, even if time-consuming, because relying in any way on technology for formatting and editing isn't smart—a careful lawyer does that themselves.

d)   It's not Juan's fault his law firm didn't train him better—creating a document involves many stages, and the spots for potential error like missing handwritten edits are an inevitable part of the process.

---

We begin with something familiar. Something simple, at first glance: documents. Electricians use wires, hockey players use sticks, nurses use stethoscopes, lawyers use documents. Yes, lawyers also talk, negotiate, argue, and present evidence. But documents are the medium through which a lot of modern lawyering happens.

We think of the word "document" based on life experience—things we create with words. Handwritten notes to a friend, class notes, college term papers, law school application essays. That definition isn't wrong but it's narrow. The word "document" comes from the Latin words *doceo* and *instrumentum*; *doceo* meaning to instruct, inform, or show something and *instrumentum* meaning an instrument, tool, or equipment. Legal documents are the broad category of instruments a lawyer creates to communicate.

This chapter introduces how technology (new tools and tools we've used for years) impacts a modern lawyer's work behind the scenes: planning, creating, drafting, editing, and collaborating with others on legal documents, and then sharing and securing them. We'll focus on the form of documents and save for another day concern over the underlying substance. You'll have plenty of time to wonder whether your interpretation of statutory law is correct or whether it is helpful to include a thesis introduction paragraph in a court filing. Beyond important decisions about the substance of a document are equally important ones about its form. Today's lawyer ensures **document structure** is sound. Ensures the *instrumentum* doesn't interfere with success of the *doceo*. Ensures the medium doesn't mess up the message—it enhances it.

The title of this chapter includes the word "proficiency." That's the goal. Above-average competence creating modern legal documents. Legal tasks like "writing" and "creating" come in many shapes and sizes. You've done case briefs, office memoranda, persuasive briefs, and e-memos. But lawyers also "write" spreadsheets, presentation slides, forms, and letters. And they "create" these instruments using tools of our trade in many ways. How a lawyer works on a document can be just as crucial as what the document says.

Build careful attention to document creation into the start of your career as a modern lawyer. While I try to convince you of its importance, I encourage you to reflect on how you already use document tools—and whether you do so in the most effective and efficient way possible. Spoiler alert: you probably don't.

---

**LIT TIP**

Based on the experience of Casey Flaherty, founder of Procertas®, a legal technology assessment company, only about one-third of law students are likely to be able to complete basic functions in Microsoft® Word[1] most relevant to legal practice such as accepting tracked changes, formatting fonts, inserting hyperlinks, and applying and modifying document styles.[2]

---

Legal writing will always be critical, whether done with a feather quill pen on parchment paper or with a sleek laptop keyboard. But modern legal documents are more than just words. Much more.

## First Stop: Choosing What Type of Document to Create & What Tools to Use

Before technology impacts *how* you create a document, you must decide what type of document you want to create and what tools you'll use. Lawyers today have a menu of choices for what type of communication fits any one scenario, as well as what document software to use (and on what type of operating system or device to use it). Modern lawyers take full advantage of this variety. A purposeful choice is critical. The document may forever be lasting proof of your careful (or sloppy) lawyering.

Let's give some thought to the choice about what type of document to create—assuming you've determined a phone call, text message, or quick office hallway chat won't do the trick. Take a hypothetical lawyer Alex. Alex works for the Securities and Exchange Commission recommending enforcement actions against public companies that are in hot water for illegal accounting practices. After months of work, Alex is set to present to their local internal SEC team urging the team to bring an action—like a civil lawsuit—against Company X for misrepresenting information in its shareholder report.

What type of document(s) should Alex create for the presentation? Alex could use none, though that's risky if we presume the report is complicated and the goal is a robust communication to support an informed decision. And messy handwritten notes photocopied from a yellow legal pad aren't the best option for anyone.

Here are some of Alex's options:

- ✓ Circulate the analysis in a 10-page single-spaced memorandum typed in Microsoft® Word or WordPerfect.

- ✓ Create a new document in Google using an old Chromebook that a roommate still uses at home.

- ✓ Type the information in an email, even if team members' thumbs would be sore from scrolling down their phones to read it all.

- ✓ Convert the Google Document or Microsoft® Word file into a PDF to send to colleagues.

- ✓ Offer a stack of spreadsheets of thick financial data prepared with Microsoft® Excel or Google Sheets.

- ✓ Export information into a simple graph and share it visually using presentation slide software such as

Microsoft® PowerPoint, Google Slides, or Apple Keynote.

This chapter will not tell you which type of document Alex should create to achieve their goals. It will, I hope, teach you that they should think carefully about the decision. From a technical viewpoint, there's no one correct approach. From a practical and professional viewpoint, Alex will make the best decision they can. The end choice of what document to create is less important than the open-minded decision-making process that gets you there. "I'm a lawyer—I don't do spreadsheets" will not cut it. Becoming open to choosing different mediums for communication depending on the context and audience will start you on the path to document proficiency—a path that will keep winding as technology keeps modernizing. Thirty years from now, the common legal documents we have today—word processed documents, presentation slides, spreadsheets, emails—may seem as antiquated to future lawyers as typewriter pages seem to us. Perhaps the physical, static format we still picture when we think of a document will be long gone. Future lawyers may:

- ✓ prepare work via multi-author recorded audio files
- ✓ submit drone footage of 3D environments at trial instead of a still photograph
- ✓ upload multimedia presentations for an arbitrator instead of written statements
- ✓ file interactive, dynamic, and cloud-based complaints in court (more on the cloud later)

Beyond the type of document, modern lawyers give thought to the tools they'll use to create it. You may not pay much attention to this in your personal life—perhaps it's the software pre-installed on your laptop or the suite of tools offered for free at your university or workplace. You may have done a lot of work as a student within the Google family of tools—whether bundled as Google Apps, G Suite, or Google Workspace. You may be more comfortable within a MacOS (operating system) compared to a Windows-based PC (personal computer) platform. I suspect many Millennial and Gen Z readers consider themselves happy members of Apple's Mac "family" and are accustomed to Apple

Pages, for example, to create documents. Although the divide between MacOS and PC was deeper in past generations, today many software products, including Microsoft® Office, are available for MacBooks, iMacs, and PCs.

Why does this matter? When I look around law school classrooms, I see a lot of MacBooks but require my students to submit documents in Microsoft® Word format—not Pages. The point isn't that one software or operating system is better than another but that modern lawyers might use different ones depending on variables such as their team, clients, audience, or jurisdiction. While most classrooms are Apple-heavy, most people in the legal profession today still regard Microsoft® Windows as the most-used operating system, Microsoft® Office as the most-used program, and Microsoft® Word as the most-used word-processing software for legal documents. For example, many state and federal courts around the country require documents in Microsoft® Word file format, such as with this local rule from the Eastern District of California:

---

**LIT TIP**

"Effective October 1, 2013, the United States District Court for the Eastern District of California is a Microsoft Word only court. All documents required to be submitted to the court in word processing format pursuant to Local Rules 137, 163 and 281 (proposed orders, jury instructions and pretrial statements) must be submitted in Word format (.docx)."

United States District Court, Eastern District of California[3]

---

This could change with the next generation of modern lawyers. Past decades marked a slow transition from WordPerfect word-processing to Word (I'm sure most readers today have never even heard of WordPerfect!). What will the next decade bring? More lawyers today use MacBooks. More use cloud-based platforms like Google, which we'll discuss in this chapter. But for now, keep in mind that Microsoft® Office (Word, Outlook, PowerPoint, Excel) is still the primary document comfort zone for many lawyers, clients, businesses, and judges with whom you'll work. So that's where we'll focus. If you are a diehard user of different software to create documents, stay open minded and proceed with caution. In your quest for document proficiency, don't let software speed bumps make you the lawyer forced to say this in an embarrassing motion:

---

**LIT TIP**

"Come now the Plaintiffs . . . request that this Court allow Plaintiffs to file their responsive brief one hour late . . . Plaintiffs have employed a team of lawyers to prepare their responsive brief. During the course of preparation, Plaintiffs' counsel have encountered numerous technical incompatibilities in the software versions between Google Docs and Microsoft Word resulting in editing difficulties and text problems."[4]

*Gohmert v. Pence*, No. 6:20-cv-00660-JDK (Tx. 2021)

---

We aren't setting out to be software-specific experts. This chapter's goal is familiarity and awareness of principles behind sound document work—not technical expertise. If you want to become a master at Excel, design the world's most exciting presentation slides, or memorize hundreds of keyboard shortcuts, I wish you well. Check out Continuing Legal Education (CLE) courses, local bar association and library trainings, LinkedIn Learning programs, and good old YouTube videos. There's no shortage of resources to lead you in more technical directions on your own beyond what this chapter can cover.

## Structuring & Starting Documents from Scratch— or Not

Ever baked a cake from scratch? You need eggs, butter, sugar, flour, milk, and vanilla extract. Dry and wet ingredients get combined in a certain order in a certain way for a delicious, finished product. Perfection every time, right? Wrong. Starting from scratch every time means a lot of opportunities for things to go wrong. Even an experienced baker gets distracted and forgets an egg or uses one cup of flour instead of two. One cake might be moist, the next dry; one smooth, the next lumpy.

Before you get too hungry, think of starting a legal document like baking from scratch. The more variables, the more opportunity for variation and error. Yes, the end product could be perfect after years of baking (or writing) experience—but also after enormous amounts of time and attention to every little detail. Bakers (and writers) with a consistent, methodical, organized, and structured approach will fare better than bakers (and writers) who change things up on the fly or recreate processes with every new occasion.

Today's technologically competent lawyer is like a boxed cake mix baker. Modern lawyers create **document templates**: basic backbones to documents (the boxed cake mix ingredients) that remain constant. Atop that basic structure, a lawyer then customizes a document particular to a case, jurisdiction, or scenario—just as a baker might customize a boxed cake mix to, for example, add coconut for one celebration or chocolate chips for another.

Consider the downsides of the alternative approach. Fast-forward a few years and imagine yourself as a lawyer who prepares professional legal documents of all types. Suppose every time you create a new document, no matter the type, you are a baker starting from scratch. You:

- ✓ select the font to use (even if it's the same font a local court has required for years)

- ✓ set the margins (even though they're the same margins you've preferred for years)

- ✓ type the word MEMORANDUM atop each office memo you draft (even though the word MEMORANDUM in bold, all caps has been atop every memo you've drafted for years)

- ✓ tweak presentation slides to the precise shade of light blue your supervisor prefers with every slide deck (even though they've preferred the same shade of blue for years)

- ✓ type the words *Attorney Client Privileged* in large, italicized font on the bottom of every client email you send (even though you've sent thousands)

- ✓ manually type out numbers 1, 2, 3, 4 for listed contract provisions (even though you'll need to change them once provisions get added, deleted, or moved)

Starting from scratch in these examples makes no sense. What if future you forgets to adjust the font one day and a court filing is rejected for non-compliance with local rules? What if future you includes an embarrassing typo in the email disclaimer because you rushed to type it for the 879th time? What if future you bills a client thousands of dollars for time spent fiddling with presentation slide design? What if future you creates an ambiguous contract provision because the contract refers to Section 3 when, because of edits, no such section seems to exist?

There must be a better way, and there is. Start thinking about a more "set it and forget it" approach to structuring documents. Time is a lawyer's most precious commodity; accuracy their most desired document characteristic. A one-off, "manual" approach to document structure jeopardizes both. We'll focus not on shiny new technology tools but using existing tools better:

✓ word-processing

✓ presentation software

✓ spreadsheets

✓ email

The document structure tips that follow are introductory. I don't provide a screenshot of every technique, nor do I give step-by-step and click-by-click directions for every task. It will take time for you to practice and master document creation best practices with whatever software you use. These techniques will vary from project to project, case to case, client to client, document to document, and computer to computer (I aim to offer both PC and Mac commands). A starter set of options in your toolbox and familiarity with some terminology are important first steps.

###  Word-Processing

Lawyers use word-processing software for everything and anything: office memos, outlines, discovery or due diligence requests and responses, letters, corporate agreements, transactional formation documents, contracts, and court filings. Modern lawyers work to create everyday documents in better ways—and a better process can equal a better work product.

✓ Create your own bank of reusable templates. A template is like our boxed cake mix mentioned earlier—standard, reliable, predictable, and ready to go. Choose from Microsoft's® online library of templates in Word or create your own for documents you may create on a frequent basis such as pleadings, letters, contracts, or memoranda. Save any work product file as a template for later use by choosing Word Template when you save as and then select file type. Later, when you need that template, instead of creating a new document from scratch simply select New > Custom (or Personal) and browse through your personalized template library.

✓ Use the Styles feature for consistent, predetermined formatting such as text size or font type. Styles are like a bundle of formatting choices all wrapped up for you. They help create the "bones" of a document you can view in the navigation pane of Microsoft® Word (like a personal table of contents for the document). You might, for example, choose a particular style for how you prefer to format point headings in a persuasive brief. Always enable the navigation pane under the View tab for a birds-eye check of your content. You can confirm your ideal organization or drag and drop different parts from just within navigation.

✓ Set custom, default formatting items in line with local rules, office practice, or personal preference. Prefer Arial as a font but get frustrated every time a new document starts off in Times New Roman and you change it? Sick of fiddling to set margins? Do it in less than a minute in Microsoft® Word (and Google Documents) by adjusting format, choosing the category such as font type or size, and then specifying preferences. Click Default > Apply for all documents, and voilà! Set it and forget it.

✓ Create automatic numbered lists in affidavits, complaints, indictments, statements of fact, or any memo, letter, contract, or brief. Don't manually tab, use the space bar, or keep pressing Return to indent or type the numbers 1, 2, 3, etc. with each new listed item. Modify your multilevel list to fit your preferences with indents, spacing, and position (distance from the margin). Then sit back and enjoy as your lists automatically readjust each time you add, reorder, or delete an item.

✓ Experiment with text expansion: typing a few characters that software recognizes to "trigger" a longer word or phrase (like smartphones do for us when texting). Find AutoCorrect Options in Word and check Replace text as you type. For example, next time you want to type the Americans with Disabilities Act for the 15th time, set it up so you can type Amer . . . [space bar] and the entire statute name will appear.

✓ Try out Quick Parts in Microsoft® Word. It's your own electronic clipboard of sorts on which you store frequently used building blocks to insert into documents. Think of it as a gallery of recycled generic text you might use often, such as a Certificate of Service for a filing or boilerplate contract provision. Picking and choosing from a Quick Parts "bank" is safer than copying and pasting from old sample documents—where you risk making sloppy errors such as copying a former client's name into a new client's document.

## Presentation Software

You've navigated hundreds of presentation slides from the audience perspective of a student. Now think of the software as the creator. Presentation slides or slide decks, as they're often called, can be a great option for a more attractive, dynamic legal document that communicates information in a concise way. Lawyers need not be graphic designers but can save time and ensure a consistent, professional presentation.

✓ Choose pre-built templates from your software's library to get started in the right direction and minimize errors. Presentation software tools offer free templates you can fill and edit.

✓ Customize a template for repeat audiences. Having a unified design instead of something new per slide provides consistency. Microsoft® PowerPoint has a Design Ideas tool for layout and formatting options.

✓ Instead of manually changing repetitive slide details like font and color one at a time, set a change once. Your top thumbnail slide is usually your master slide or you can View > Master Slide. Changes you make to it will apply to the rest of your slides, such as adding a logo once instead of copying and pasting to individual slides.

### Spreadsheets

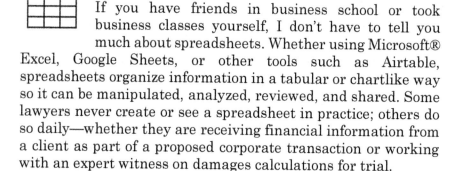
If you have friends in business school or took business classes yourself, I don't have to tell you much about spreadsheets. Whether using Microsoft® Excel, Google Sheets, or other tools such as Airtable, spreadsheets organize information in a tabular or chartlike way so it can be manipulated, analyzed, reviewed, and shared. Some lawyers never create or see a spreadsheet in practice; others do so daily—whether they are receiving financial information from a client as part of a proposed corporate transaction or working with an expert witness on damages calculations for trial.

✓ Templates are a great starting option for spreadsheets, too. Create a standard template for each family of projects you return to often, such as billing invoices, case budgets, or damages projections.

✓ Spreadsheets can "do" math, but resetting formulas (the calculations the software completes) manually takes time and risks error. Set up a reliable spreadsheet by copying a formula across cells to ensure consistency.

✓ Use a format painter tool instead of manual changes to format spreadsheet data. Select the portion with the preferred formatting, click Format painter in Excel (Paint format in Google Sheets), and then select the new group of cells, row, or column where you want to apply the preferred formatting.

### Email

 There are more than 4 billion global email users, and billions of emails are sent and received each day. Email can be a lawyer's best friend and greatest enemy. You can imagine the time modern lawyers spend on email: communicating with clients, corresponding with opposing counsel, drafting substantive and procedural e-memos to colleagues, contacting potential clients for business development, and planning and negotiating business transactions. If there's one document creation task where time equals money, this is it.

---

✓ Standardize emails by starting simple with a signature block and any attorney-client privilege or work product disclaimer applicable to your practice (more on email signatures in chapter 10).

✓ Email templates are available in almost every email platform you might use. Compose and save an email as a template; then choose, insert, and customize it in the future. A solo practitioner might, for example, structure a marketing business development email notice in similar fashion for distribution every Friday afternoon, or an in-house general counsel might send updates in the same form via email to the company's shareholders at the end of every month.

✓ Take advantage of Quick Steps or Quick Parts functions if using Microsoft® Outlook. Suppose you often end emails to clients by typing "Please let me know if you have questions or would like to talk further. I'd be happy to connect by cell at your convenience." Save that excerpt to your autotext gallery and next time you type "Please," the saved text will pop up as a suggested autocomplete. Maximize time; minimize errors.

---

No matter what legal document you repeatedly create, stick with standard ingredients just like a boxed cake mix. Maximizing technology to help structure a document is a win/win. It:

1) frees up time later after initial upfront effort

2)   reduces likelihood of error

3)   supports optimal navigation by digital readers and improves universal accessibility

4)   facilitates smooth collaboration among different authors of a document

5)   keeps form from overshadowing what lawyers really care about: the substance

## Designing Documents for the Digital Reader

Shift perspective from you as the author to your reader. Successful lawyers design documents for today's modern readers. Just as we "consume" documents electronically in our personal life, so too will legal readers. Technology changes how writers write and how readers read. You know this—at least you do if you've read a happy birthday email on your phone (not a handwritten card from the mail carrier) or scrolled through a magazine article on your tablet (not a crinkly one from the coffee table). Paper is two dimensional; digital is multidimensional. Think about how and what you read. I bet you've gone digital—or, if you haven't, you're on your way, and so are countless members of the legal profession.

---

**LIT TIP**

"Legal writers need to think beyond just their words and legal authority. They need to think about how their writing looks. More and more, judges and their clerks read briefs and exhibits on iPads and other digital readers. I have for years and I appreciate documents that make my job as a reader easier so I can focus on digesting complex legal arguments. Designing briefs and other materials with this in mind is just smart legal advocacy, and every advocate of the future should be thinking about it."

United States District Court Judge William E. Smith[5]

---

From litigation to transactions to everything in between, digital readers are here to stay. In legal writing courses, you learn to consider how audience impacts organization, content, form, style, and tone. One faulty move undermines your credibility with the reader, perhaps jeopardizing our "ethos" as a central pillar to persuasion (along with logos—logic—and pathos—passion). Today's 21st-century lawyers must consider where the documents they build are likely to land—in their reader's lap or on their screen?

## 1)   Electronic Document Navigability

Erase the image of a stapled office memo on 8.5 × 11 paper dropped on a colleague's desk, or a stack of corporate governance papers being wrapped with a rubber band to bring to a negotiation. Readers of the past flipped through pages, used sticky notes to flag key portions, turned to a front cover table of contents, and carefully scanned each page, top to bottom, line by line, before physically turning to the next page.

Meet today's digital legal reader. Many readers of this book grew up digital and have never known a nondigital world. You might be reading this book electronically. Legal readers often skip, skim, link, annotate, fast-forward, go back, lose focus, regain focus, and interact with a document like never before. They want information the same way many of us get ours because of ingrained screen habits and preferences: quick and convenient. Our modern brains are conditioned to accept—even crave—bite-size pieces of the information we want when we want it.

**Electronic navigability** means a reader can actively engage with a document. For example, in the word-processing context, lawyers should insert navigational bookmarks in longer documents such as a contract or appellate brief. This is critical for any final PDF formatted document filed with a court. Bookmarks work with hyperlinks and cross-references to help readers jump to certain spots in a document instead of flipping pages (or endlessly scrolling up and down). For example, suppose you are working on a 100-page contract for a manufacturing company with a heading STORAGE OF GOODS on page 5. The contract mentions this storage provision frequently. Designing for a digital reader means you insert cross-references back to that provision so when the word "storage" appears later, the reader can smoothly skip back to that main provision instead of scrolling up and down trying to remember where that main text was located. Digital documents are something modern readers can actively *use*—not just passively read.

> **LIT TIP**
>
> "Survey results show that one hundred percent of justices like briefs that are thoroughly bookmarked."[6]
>
> Blake E. Hawthorne
> A Guide to Creating Electronic Appellate Briefs, Supreme Court of Texas

Designing electronic briefs, or **e-briefs** as they're usually called, is not just interesting—in some jurisdictions it's required. For example, in federal court lawyers are expected to convert documents to PDFs for e-filing. This allows the lawyer to use PDF tools in programs such as Adobe Acrobat to create electronic navigation such as by bookmarking and adding headers. A lawyer who simply saves an unstructured Microsoft® Word document as a PDF or scans a paper document to create a PDF file for filing does not give their digital reader convenient options. Worse yet, that lawyer might be violating local filing rules.

## 2) External Hyperlinking

A prime spot where digital design helps a lawyer's substantive communication is linking to sources beyond a document's four corners. The time and effort for a digital reader to access sources in an electronic document pale in comparison to paper readers of old. A great example is court filings. Decades ago, if a lawyer cited an old executive regulation, most readers wouldn't go through the effort of tracking that volume down from their local law library to review. Today, if we do our job at the outset, readers enjoy a seamless and interactive back-and-forth between our textual document and many things we can direct them to with a quick tap or click in support of our position such as record exhibits, prior docket entries and filings, statutes, case decisions, videos, regulations, and any other guidance, picture, source, or website we deem worthwhile context to include.

---

**LIT TIP**

To insert a hyperlink, copy the URL of the link you want to add. In your underlying document or email message, select the text you want to apply that link to (sometimes called the anchor text). Then Insert > Hyperlink or right-click and select hyperlink, or use the shortcut
*Control + K* (PC) or *Command + K* (Mac).

---

When adding external hyperlinks to a legal document, be aware of paywalls and dead links. A paywall is a virtual wall restricting access unless the reader pays. Sending your reader to a hyperlinked source behind a paywall causes frustration and prevents them from accessing the source you hoped they'd consider. For legal authority, consider avoiding pricey legal research database sources and instead linking to free, public sources such as:

✓   CourtListener

✓   FindLaw

✓   Justia

✓   Google Scholar

Even more frustrating than a paywall is a dead link, taking the reader to a "404 Page Not Found" or similar error message. Websites change, get taken down, and moved. Modern lawyers can avoid "link rot" by using Perma.cc to archive internet sources, "freezing" the hyperlinked information as it appeared when cited. The Perma.cc tool (free, at least when I wrote this book) is gaining momentum as a best practice for hyperlinking by creating a new, unique URL that won't change or disappear.[7]

3)   Accessibility

Documents are effective only if accessible. A full discussion of this topic is beyond the contours of what this chapter can tackle but audience is a lawyer's most important consideration. Sometimes readers with disabilities need to interact with documents in a different way, whether due to a visual, hearing, cognitive, or some other impairment. Consider these scenarios:

✓   A lawyer includes a demonstrative visual in a presentation for a client meeting and circulates the slides to team members in advance. Readers reliant on screen reader software wouldn't be able to understand the graphic if the author neglected to include an "Alt-text" tag with the image (something that takes about 10 seconds to do by right-clicking on the image and typing descriptive words).

✓ A lawyer emails a document that gets "scanned in" using an all-in-one copier/printer/scanner. Such a machine scans the contents and creates a snapshot of the page. In electronic form, that attached document snapshot might never be readable if the intended reader uses assistive technology requiring OCR (optical character recognition) conversion to access the text.

The ins and outs of digital design as it relates to audiences with disabilities or audiences with language barriers who use translation software is complex—but it's something modern lawyers pay close attention to.

4) Digital Typography & Visuals

Which version of the following legal rules would you prefer reading when scrolling down through a lengthy document on your tablet screen?

| | |
|---|---|
| A battery as defined by Massachusetts law is the intentional touching of the body of another person in a harmful or offensive manner, without consent. *O'Leary v. O'Leary*, 432 Mass. 12 (1986). | A battery requires:<br>1. Intent;<br>2. Touching;<br>3. Harmful/offensive without consent.<br>*O'Leary v. O'Leary*, 432 Mass. 12 (1986). |

We all have our preferences. Studies suggest screen readers prefer a right-side column, as in this tort rule example, to best digest content from a digital document. Certain typography decisions help or hurt delivery of your message. By **digital typography**, I mean how the body of a document generated using computer software looks—things like font type, font size, line length, and white space. Good lawyers consider typography with paper documents; great ones make even more purposeful decisions for their digital readers.

What are some of these decisions? For starters, electronic readers like white space. A lot of it. Our eyes don't appreciate long blocks of heavy, single-spaced text in any context but especially on a screen. Give your digital reader's eyes a break by, for example, using navigational visuals like bulleted or numbered lists as we did with the tort rule example (and, in fact, as I've tried to do throughout this book). Ensure adequate spacing between "breaks" in a legal document such as headings in a brief or provisions of a contract. Digital readers likely take a more jumpy and less linear approach to reading text: stopping at things that catch their eye, skimming a few lines and focusing down the vertical left side of the screen for key topic sentences, headings, or titles (known as an "F pattern" of reading). In modern typography for a digital screen reader, less is more.

Modern lawyers also consider moving beyond text and exploring visual design: images, charts, timelines, graphics, tables, graphs, and color. Consider a trademark dispute, when one company alleges another company's mark infringes (copies) their own. A lawyer could explain the similarities between the two marks in a long, detailed paragraph to persuade the reader of likelihood of confusion. But as in Figure 3A's example from a complaint brought by In-N-Out Burger against Puma for allegedly copying and profiting from a small palm tree design on shoelaces, a picture might be worth a thousand words:

\* Figure 3A: *In-N-Out Burgers v. Puma N. Am. Inc.* complaint image.[9]

Modern lawyers that format and insert visuals can create dynamic legal documents more likely to engage their digital readers. This is true beyond litigation.

Contracts, for example, are notorious for being long, dense, and not user-friendly. One survey in the commercial business context showed only 1 in 10 responders agreed that contracts were "easy to understand."[10] Besides cutting the word count, modern lawyers might explore use of visuals, infographics, and color to communicate contractual concepts.

Figures 3B and 3C are examples from the global energy company Shell for a contract provision in its marine division involving risk and title during delivery. Just by giving each a quick glance, which would you rather try to read and understand?

### Risk and Title

Delivery will be completed and title and risk will pass to you either:

9.1.1      for bulk Deliveries, when the Marine Lubricants pass the flange connecting the delivery facilities with the receiving facilities provided by you; or

9.1.2      for Delivery in containers:

9.1.2.1      when delivering to a quay or other point on land, when the goods are landed from the delivery vehicle to the ground;

9.1.2.2      when delivering by a barge operated by us and using our barge's lifting equipment, when the goods are landed on the deck of the vessel;

9.1.2.3      when delivering by barge or vehicle and using lifting equipment provided and operated by you, when the goods are lifted off the deck of the barge or off the vehicle; or

9.1.2.4      when delivering by barge, and you have contracted with a third-party service provider or operator to provide pump ex-IBC service, immediately before the pump ex-IBC service.

\* Figure 3B: Shell visual contract Text; reprinted with permission Shell.[11]

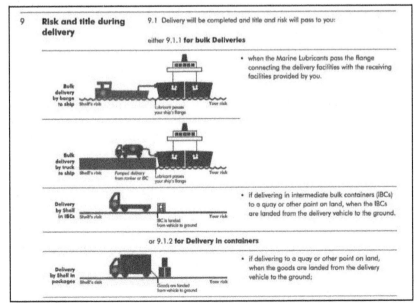

\* Figure 3C: Shell visual contract images; reprinted with permission Shell.[12]

Whether bookmarking within a document, hyperlinking to external resources, or using colored graphs to summarize data, designing a legal document for today's digital reader takes forethought and effort. It also offers the modern lawyer new opportunities to improve what all lawyers strive to do better: deliver information in a clear and concise way.

---

**LIT TIP**

"[T]urning the traditional, linear, text-based brief into a multidimensional e-document is a key example of how the medium changes the message and suggests that it is time to rethink that classic legal document."[13]

Professor Ellie Margolis
Temple Law School

---

## No Shortcuts to Success (or Are There?)

Everything we buy today seems to come with bells and whistles, most of which get ignored. Your television remote has 30 buttons and features; you use the same 4. Your clothes dryer has 6 cycles and 4 heat settings; you've never changed them once.

And so it goes with lawyers and document software. In some ways, knowing the minimum for day-to-day needs saves us the time it takes to learn new things, prevents us from getting overwhelmed, and keeps us in our comfort zone. What busy lawyer has time to experiment with Microsoft® Word hacks or fiddle with advanced features of Microsoft® Excel? You do! OK, not every night or all the time. But a modern lawyer recognizes the importance of some upfront investment with core tools to save time later—saving energy, frustration, and their client's money paying for work that their lawyer could have done quicker.

Most lawyers scratch the surface with everyday document tools. Modern lawyers strive to do better. From adjusting settings in Microsoft® Outlook to **keyboard shortcuts** for PC and Mac users to tips in the Google Workspace, we could fill an entire chapter. Generally (but not always), you can "translate" popular PC commands into Mac commands by using the Command key instead of the Control key. For now, we'll stick to a few key tips—

with the caveat that as your career advances, so too should your sophistication with tools you use.

If you can save precious minutes or even hours with the documents, spreadsheets, presentations, and email tasks throughout your career, that adds up to real time over the days, weeks, and years ahead. What will you do with that extra time?

 ## Word-Processing Shortcuts

✓ Don't scroll through or "eyeball" a document for a certain word or corrections. Use *Control + F* or *Command + F* to locate what you need, or *Control + H* to quickly "find and replace" something old with something new throughout a document.

✓ Avoid scrolling and highlighting large portions of text with your mouse while editing (many a lawyer has forgotten a line or two of text doing that!). Place your cursor in the paragraph and triple-click (x3) to select the entire paragraph, then *Control + C* to copy, *Control + X* to cut, or *Control + V* to paste. Beware of whether you keep old formatting from what you copied or cut into its new spot, or whether you want to select the option to merge formatting to match its new spot in the document.

✓ Create custom additions to your word-processing dictionary. In Microsoft® Word, under Office > Commands > Proofing > Custom Dictionary edit your word list to include, for example, a company's unique name on a matter you'll work on for years. On a Mac, choose Preferences > Spelling & Grammar.

✓ Set up clean page breaks in a long document with *Control + Enter* for a break at your cursor spot.

✓ Avoid spending time with manual formatting adjustments of things like underlining and bold. *Control + [spacebar]* clears formatting of a section in one swoop.

**Presentation Software Shortcuts**

✓ Avoid fiddling with spacing of text or images on a presentation slide. The Align tool in Microsoft® PowerPoint creates equal spacing between objects.

✓ Copying and pasting text from one slide to the next? Even better, copy text with formatting between slides by clicking *Control + Shift + C* on your formatted object, select what you want that formatting pasted to, and then click *Control + Shift + V.*

✓ Tired of boring bullet point lists in your slides? Avoid tedious manual adjustment and click on Convert to SmartArt after highlighting your list—then choose a design already done for you.

 **Spreadsheet Shortcuts**

✓ Navigating spreadsheets starts with seeing them. Standard column width is often narrow. Instead of dragging your mouse ever so sightly to resize, double-click while hovering your cursor over the column you want to expand.

✓ Using keyboard shortcuts to select rows or columns is safer than clicking and scrolling your mouse across spreadsheets and overshooting by an extra row or missing a column. Use *Shift + [spacebar]* to select a row; *Control + [spacebar]* to select a column (same for PC and Mac).

✓ Add or delete new rows or columns quickly. Select any row or column, press *Control + Shift + [+]* and a new row or column will appear to the left (column) or above (row) your original selection. To delete, select it, press *Control + [-]*, and it's gone!

**Email Shortcuts**

✓ Half the battle with email is organization and distraction. To avoid interruption, in Microsoft® Outlook deselect options for Message Arrival such as sounds and those small but distracting rectangle "pop-up" alerts at the bottom of your screen.

✓ Triage your email inbox by setting up different rules or conditional formatting. For example, using View Setting > Conditional Formatting or Automatic Formatting in Microsoft® Outlook, apply bold red font to all emails from a particular client. Or, under Home > Rules > Manage Rules and Alerts, create a new rule that moves emails from a supervisor to a designated folder.

✓ Hundreds of keyboard shortcuts (hot keys as they're called) are available in email software like Microsoft® Outlook and Gmail (if first enabled in Gmail Settings). For example, in Microsoft® Outlook, *Control + R* replies to an email, *Control + Shift + G* flags an email for follow up, *Control + 5* switches you to the Notes feature, *Control + 2* takes you to calendar, and the life-saving *Control + Z* is a magic eraser to undo earlier "clicks" and actions.

Shortcuts get a bad reputation. No lawyer should cut corners with careful organization, critical legal reasoning, and attention to detail. But shortcuts for uncreative, lower-level small aspects of legal document work are terrific. The key isn't to learn every trick imaginable. It's to be aware they exist and stay motivated to learn which ones are relevant to your daily work.

---

**LIT TIP**

"Lawyers using Microsoft Word don't need to be perfect but they do need to be competent. When a lawyer spends billable time manually performing easily automated tasks or fruitlessly fiddling with word processing software because they haven't learned styles or tracked changes, then that fee is not truly earned. Billing clients for this busywork looks a lot like systematically collecting unearned fees, which is tantamount to stealing. A pattern of technologically incompetent work—by accident or design—violates Model Rule 1.5, which could lead to fee disgorgement. Even if a lawyer won't become an advanced user, they should be aware that additional functions are available and look for improvements in areas where they tend to waste the most time or experience the most frustration."

Ivy B. Grey
Legal Tech Entrepreneur
Vice President of Strategy & Business Development
WordRake, LLC

---

## The More, the Merrier

Better together, the saying goes. Such is often the case with excellent legal documents. Lawyers rarely work alone. They collaborate within internal teams and across external ones—whether drafting a brief, negotiating a deal, or preparing a joint stipulation. **Document collaboration** usually leads to a better end work product, but along that path a modern lawyer collaborates with caution. We'll fast-forward past the last place option of handwritten changes and instead consider two flavors of collaborative work: traditional "versions" and cloud-based collaboration.

By version work, I mean the back-and-forth, table-tennis type of creation of different documents by different authors at different times on different computers. In my practice, I recall seeing a file name like this for a summary judgment brief:

**SJbriefclientfinal.finalupdated.finaltoday.dyaneolearyv.28.doc**

Version 28? Final, final? Or was the most up-to-date version the final, updated one? Was it the file I stored on my computer, or the one emailed and then saved on a colleague's desktop?

Confused yet? You can imagine the risk of confusion, error, overlap, missed changes, forgotten additions, overlooked edits— not to mention time and stress wondering if the team had too many cooks in the kitchen, or if we were spending time working on a document that was yesterday's old-news version.

A different collaboration path growing in popularity is cloud-based collaboration. This is something readers may be familiar with from well-known tools like Google Drive, Dropbox, or Microsoft® 365 OneDrive—services that allow simultaneous access by different authors to one synchronized central document stored on the internet. Many firms and organizations use cloud-based document sharing platforms to manage every day document work (more on this in chapter 7 when we turn to law practice technology).

Whether skipping between back-and-forth versions or offering comments to a single document in the cloud, collaboration brings risk with both substance and form. Where did that great argument go that I added on page 12? Why are the first 10 contract provisions bold but the next 5 italicized?

Worst case: Critical content is deleted or privileged comments remain in the final version.

Second worst case: The document looks mismatched and sloppy.

Best case: The document is unified and consistent, and the reader has no idea it was the product of a team approach.

Modern lawyers learn and use document collaboration best practices. Let's review tips within a hypothetical settlement negotiation. Suppose you represent an individual plaintiff settling a negligence tort claim against a manufacturing company, ABC Product. ABC Product's lawyer sends you a draft settlement agreement created in Microsoft® Word. You review the document and have questions for a senior products liability lawyer with whom you work. So, before you send it along, you enable a **tracked changes** editing feature such as Word's Track Changes tool on the Review tab and add internal notes and changes (a similar option in Google Documents is called "Suggesting" mode). Lawyers often call this "redlining" a document because the tracked changes additions and deletions by default usually appear in red font:

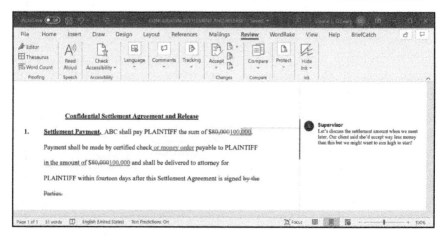

\* Figure 3D: Example of Microsoft® Word Track Changes in Confidential Settlement Agreement and Release.[14]

Always double check username settings before using collaborative software. These show the author of changes and you'll want to ensure the name or initials displayed are appropriate and what you prefer (feel free to change the color, too!). This isn't an issue if one or two lawyers redline a document. But tracked changes from dozens of anonymous users make it impossible to know which comment belongs to which contributor.

Back to our hypothetical. You receive a redlined document version 2 back from your supervisor. They've accepted some of your tracked changes, deleted others, and answered questions with notes in electronic comment bubbles alongside the right-hand margin, as we see in the preceding image. Best practices at this stage might include:

- ✓ deleting, resolving, or hiding electronic comment bubbles

- ✓ setting your Review tab to "All Mark Up" to ensure you see all electronic changes

- ✓ reviewing, rejecting, or accepting suggested changes one by one

- ✓ disabling tracking with any later changes for a final new document to distribute

Think back to chapter 2's Need to Know #3 about the ethical duty of technology competence. Suppose an electronic comment from your supervisor on the draft agreement said, "Our client said she'd accept way less money than this but we might want to aim high to start."

Yikes! That privileged internal communication in the drafting of work product would *not* be something you'd want ABC Product or its lawyer to see. Disclosing it would be a serious ethical violation of the rule protecting client confidentiality and may call into question the lawyer's general competence under Rule 1.1. Electronic behind-the-scenes changes and comments become part of a document's metadata, a concept we'll turn to next. Before sending the revised settlement agreement back to ABC Product's lawyer, you'd delete all comments and confirm there is no remaining visible record of electronic changes.

Two days later, suppose ABC Product's lawyer sends back a new version of the agreement. To ensure careful and thorough representation of your client, you would need to understand what ABC Product might have changed, kept, deleted, or added from the prior version. Instead of printing the old and new versions and reading them side by side, modern lawyers collaborating on documents use a Compare feature in word-processing software (also called legal blacklining) to get an efficient visual representation of any differences between two versions.

Finally, you'll reach the "enough is enough" stage. To ensure a final version, a lawyer can "lock down" the document to restrict further editing. For example, the Protect Document feature in Microsoft® Word (File > Info > Protect Document or in the Review menu on a Mac) offers options such as password-protecting the document, marking as final, and restricting editing and access. In other words, at this stage others can look at the document but not touch it.

---

**LIT TIP**

Electronic collaboration tools are in the Review tab in Microsoft® Word. Complete tasks like add or delete or respond to comments, skip through and reject or accept Track Changes, compare versions, or restrict other users' interaction with the document. A cloud-based tool such as Google Documents offers similar features like Insert > Comment (*Control + Alt + M*) and preferred review modes (Edits, Suggestions, or View only). While collaborating, insert a Watermark to remind readers it is DRAFT or CONFIDENTIAL or any other custom mark you create (often under the Design tab in Word).

---

Collaborative drafting isn't going anywhere for the modern lawyer, especially as we increasingly "go remote" and work with others from different devices and different locations and at different times (more on remote lawyering in chapter 8). Lawyers often look to specialty third-party cloud-based vendors to help store documents and support collaboration. This creates its own unique set of hurdles, such as security and confidentiality and potential restrictions on what lawyers or law firms can or can't do with the confidential or private information that lives within legal documents. Stay tuned for this discussion about cloud computing and security in chapter 9.

## Metadata: Behind the (Document) Scenes

Wait! You aren't done yet. Even if you've examined every visible line, comment, or change in your electronic document, you still might be missing something.

**Document metadata** is information about files invisible to you "on the screen." Data about the data. Digital baggage in different forms that is "stored" such that it follows a document along its path.

> **LIT TIP**
>
> <u>System (directory) metadata</u>: information about a file that your computer's operating system provides (e.g., Microsoft® Windows creates the "Modified" date for a contract you're drafting)
>
> <u>Application (file-level) metadata</u>: information about a file that a particular computer application provides (e.g., Microsoft® Word tracks contract revisions you make)

If you prepare a complaint to start a lawsuit with Microsoft® Word on your laptop, the metadata might include:

- ✓ the date and time the file was last modified
- ✓ file author or authors
- ✓ electronic comments and redlined tracked changes
- ✓ the time and date the file was first created
- ✓ the number of times the file was revised or number of versions
- ✓ the file's electronic location such as a particular group directory or folder

Metadata touches all documents, not just word processing. If you create a spreadsheet using Microsoft® Excel to summarize financial information in an offer by your client to buy a competing company, the metadata might include:

- ✓ the name of the person who last edited the spreadsheet
- ✓ the date it was created
- ✓ cells with confidential data you "hid" instead of deleted that can reappear

| Properties ⌄ | |
|---|---|
| Size | 419KB |
| Pages | 25 |
| Words | 7032 |
| Total Editing Time | 147 Minutes |
| Title | Add a title |
| Tags | Add a tag |
| Comments | Add comments |

**Related Dates**

| | |
|---|---|
| Last Modified | 1/9/2022 4:54 PM |
| Created | 1/5/2022 2:35 PM |
| Last Printed | 1/8/2021 10:09 AM |

**Related People**

| | |
|---|---|
| Author | DL Dyane L. O'Leary |
| | Add an author |
| Last Modified By | DO Dyane O'Leary |

\* Figure 3E: Sample Microsoft® Word metadata fields.

Document metadata is often boring . . . and of little interest . . . until it's not. Metadata is like a price tag on a fancy new shirt—useful when you're browsing in a store deciding what to buy, but awkward and problematic if you forget to cut the tag off and everyone notices it at your next party. Would metadata be boring in these scenarios?

- ✓ Your tracked changes reveal to opposing counsel that your client engaged a third-party industry expert consultant to offer advice on a civil complaint before filing.

- ✓ Opposing counsel reads an insult about them you wrote in an electronic comment bubble and learns that you worked on 14 prior versions of a joint stipulation before sending a draft.

✓ A company your corporate client is interested in purchasing learns that your client tried to buy a competitor company last year after noticing metadata details from a financial disclosure spreadsheet that had been created months ago.

✓ You included on a client bill a charge of $300 for two hours of editing but the client viewed document metadata showing total editing time of 18 minutes.

A lawyer's duty of confidentiality under Model Rule 1.6 captures everything about a legal document, visible at first glance or not.

Another common "invisible" pitfall with legal documents is redaction. Redaction is when a lawyer removes snippets of information from a document; for example, removing a Social Security number from a public document filed with the court or removing personal private bank account information in a document produced in a merger negotiation. Believe it or not, lawyers once used thin strips of sticky white tape to physically cover up redacted portions of hard-copy documents before photocopying or scanning them. Some still do! Today's software options offer redaction tools that make redactions easy and safe—that is, if we know what we're doing. If not, the original text may still be viewable.

Thankfully, a technologically competent lawyer can take steps to guard against inadvertent disclosure of metadata. Here are a few to get you started:

✓ In the Microsoft® suite of tools, use the Document Inspector tool to get at your behind-the-scenes document data (Inspect Presentation for slides and Inspect Workbook for spreadsheets). Beware that "old" metadata follows a document along so be extra careful if reusing a sample or document from a previous matter. Choose File > Info > Check for Issues > Inspect Document. After reviewing the inspection results, the safest bet is to Remove All.

✓ Consider converting a Word, Excel, or PowerPoint file to a PDF document before sending it. PDF files still have metadata (often in the Description tab), but it's more

> limited and will help "erase" old metadata from the original file type. Think of a PDF as more of a picture snapshot of a different original file type. Common PDF software like Adobe Acrobat offers security options for metadata.
>
> ✓  Ask if your employer subscribes to or might reimburse you for the cost of metadata "scrubbing" software for an additional layer of peace of mind.

A final note about metadata: it's a double-edged sword in that it can be a *good* thing. We'll unpack this in chapter 5, when we turn to electronically stored information (ESI). The flip side of protecting your document metadata is discovering someone else's—perhaps someone represented by a lawyer not as technologically savvy as you! Metadata can be helpful substantive evidence. You could discover electronic comments in documents exchanged in a breach of contract dispute that help establish the element of intent or knowledge. A modern lawyer also must be cautious *not* to remove metadata when it's not appropriate to do so. While you might want to remove metadata to protect client confidences and attorney work product in documents you as a lawyer create, the ethical duty to preserve evidence might prohibit you from scrubbing it in other situations (such as with underlying documents your client produces in response to a discovery request or subpoena).

---

**LIT TIP**

"[A] lawyer is responsible for acting competently to safeguard information . . . [c]ompetency in relation to metadata requires a lawyer utilizing electronic media for communication to maintain at least a basic understanding of the technology and the risks of revealing metadata or to obtain and utilize adequate technology support."[15]

Oregon State Bar Association Opinion 2011–187

---

## Signed, Legal Writing Robot, Esq.

Document proficiency involves two things: technology and you. The lawyer. The user. The human brain. One without the other does no good. The same holds true for when technology becomes a tool that helps with the style and substance of writing—not just its form.

Yes, the style and substance of writing: complaints, motions, letters, deal documents, leases, wills, contracts, you name it. We've focused on electronic formatting tools but we'll finish this chapter with tools that go beyond that. New **legal editing software** tools impact the words we write and decisions we make to best craft our communication. I've often heard that creative thinking should be done by people but leave everything else to machines. Let's test that out as it relates to some hypothetical document work.

Suppose you are drafting a motion to dismiss an employment discrimination case on behalf of a large hospital. You are on a tight deadline. If you're anything like me, you want to spend time and energy on the fun stuff: what case precedent to use, what key facts to include, what persuasive phrasing to use for stand-out point headings, what policy argument to lead with, what punchy way you can distinguish adverse authority on which your opponent relies. We sometimes hear this as a lawyer practicing "at the top of their license." It's the hard stuff you spent so much time and effort learning and practicing in law school.

If that work is at the top of your law license, what's at the bottom? You may not enjoy time spent on "lower-end" writing tasks such as:

- ✓ checking for spelling
- ✓ reviewing for proper punctuation
- ✓ ensuring you have one space after each period at the end of a sentence instead of two (or whatever local custom or rules require)
- ✓ wrestling with grammar decisions such as whether to use "which" or "that"
- ✓ double-checking you haven't used your favorite word "however" at the start of a sentence too many times
- ✓ omitting common clutter and build up phrases such as "hereinbefore mentioned"

The problem is lower-end writing tasks still contribute to the quality (or lack thereof) of our overall work product. Done well, they enhance communication. Done poorly, they distract the reader and undermine our credibility.

Enter the modern lawyer's Legal Writing Robot assistant. It's not that dramatic. There are no robots—just computer software. Software is getting more sophisticated—dare I say smarter? Lawyers have new options for tools that can edit, suggest deletions, and recommend changes. For those of us accustomed to spellcheck or auto-complete when we draft text messages, the concept isn't earth shattering. These tools are often grouped under the umbrella title of "artificial intelligence" (AI), a concept we introduced in our earlier Need to Knows. For now, think of writing software as a series of thousands of instructions whereby software is trained (taught) by many earlier samples. If a software developer tells a program to always suggest deletion of the clutter common legal writing phrase, "it is important to note" then the tool continues to spot that phrase with every new document and make the same suggestion.

Before exploring new editing software, we should use familiar tools better. Microsoft® Word and Google Documents have editing features you know about—spellcheck, for example, giving us that helpful red line to catch typos and misspellings. But it's worth a few minutes to check whether you're using existing features to their full capabilities for aspects of writing lawyers should pay close attention to. For example, spellcheck often by default is not set to apply to words in ALL CAPS such as point headings in a brief or titled contract provisions. One quick click can change that, but only for the modern lawyer careful enough to confirm. Microsoft® Word's Spelling & Grammar tools offer a menu of other editing reinforcement choices you can select beyond basic spellcheck. Speaking of editing, consider having your computer read your document to you with "read-aloud" tools. Hearing words through text-to-speech rather than seeing them on your screen can offer a helpful new editing perspective to catch errors.

---

**LIT TIP**

Adjust and confirm your preferred editing settings in Microsoft® Word or other software. In Word, go to Options > Proofing. Under Writing Style > Grammar & Refinements (depending on your software version you may see Style > Settings. Select or unselect choices relevant to effective written legal communication such as:

- ✓ single or double space between sentences
- ✓ passive voice
- ✓ wordiness
- ✓ gender-neutral pronouns
- ✓ contractions
- ✓ sentence structure
- ✓ clarity

---

Beyond familiar word-processing features are some new players. Over the last decade, there has been a growth in popularity of software that lawyers can layer on top of traditional document processing and in email communication, too. For example, Grammarly markets itself as a "writing assistant" to help with clarity, proofreading, and grammatical mistakes. It works with writing you do in your word-processing, email, or any app on your smartphone (no lawyer wants a typo in their LinkedIn profile, as we'll turn to in chapter 10). Other products such as WordRake and BriefCatch are designed specifically for legal writing. WordRake is a general editing tool for concision and brevity and BriefCatch is geared toward common pitfalls with persuasive writing to a court. For transactional work, tools such as Definely and Donna market themselves as technology to help with contract drafting and proofreading, such as spotting missing definitions or eliminating duplicative contract provisions.

New legal editing tools don't just point out general errors. Basic spellcheck is old news for the modern lawyer. Writing software is more substantive and more individual than it's ever been. By that, I mean the tools flag style and tone decisions such as readability, clarity and accessibility of language, wording patterns, and whether sentences begin effectively. This software is based on human decisions about what is or is not good legal writing and may not always connect with your own style. But most writers who care about improving their craft in an efficient way welcome tools that offer a replacement or correction with an explanation to consider, accept, or reject. As seen in Figure 3F, legal editing software is like a personal expert editor drafting alongside you. The tools aren't free and, depending on where you work, access to them might come out of your own pocket. But if given the opportunity, wouldn't you want one-click access to more than 11,000 possible edits so you can benefit from examples such as the one shown in Figure 3F based on a renowned Supreme Court Justice's legal writing style?

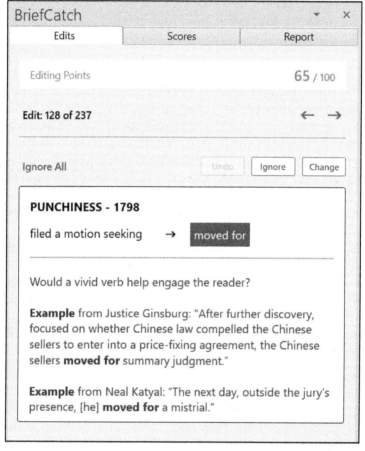

* Figure 3F: BriefCatch example; reprinted with permission by Legal Writing Pro/BriefCatch™.

Writing and editing software won't create fresh new works on a blank page, at least not yet. In the next chapter on legal research, we'll turn to one tool that starts to look a bit like software creating legal documents. Our virtual legal writing robot assistants are only as good as the input we give them. Garbage in; slightly better garbage out. Software won't think abstractly, won't create policy arguments, won't make analogies, and won't analyze concepts the way you've learned to in law school. But if our goal as modern lawyers is to create excellent work product in the most efficient fashion, and we're aware of the limitations of writing software, then have at it. Good work product in; even better work product out.

---

**LIT TIP**

"Writing software for lawyers is an exciting space. It's evolved from automating rote proofreading tasks to giving lawyers on-demand access to the secrets of the profession's star writers."

Ross Guberman
President of Legal Writing Pro LLC
Creator of BriefCatch 3.0

---

\* \* \* \*

Now that you've started down the path to achieving modern document proficiency, you'll need equally excellent, cutting-edge legal research skills to go with it. In many ways, the distinct and separate line between online research platforms and document creation tools is getting blurry. Lawyers are craving more of a one-stop-shop approach to creating work product with everything at their fingertips in an integrated, customized research and writing platform. Curious as to what that looks like? We'll turn to it next in chapter 4.

---

 *Review Your Knowledge*

1) A law school classmate spots you reading this chapter and asks for a one-sentence summary about the optimal

approach a modern lawyer takes when creating an electronic legal document. You tell them it's to:

a) maintain an open-minded decision-making process at the outset of a document project and ensure sound document structure.

b) learn every available technological shortcut with a tool before you can be comfortable and able to work most efficiently.

c) include visual designs on every page of a document to engage the reader.

d) stick with favorite cloud-based document tools such as Google for document work if that's what a lawyer is comfortable with, even if others they work with use different software—they'll be able to figure it out.

2) Laura is a real estate lawyer helping Pat with documents to sell his house. Laura needs to submit sale paperwork. She has created thousands of similar documents during her career and finds herself crunched for time with Pat's closing. She uses a document prepared in the past for a different client. The document was submitted to the same registry of deeds in the same jurisdiction as Pat's sale so it complies with the rules. Pat's situation is similar so all Laura needs to do is change the names and monetary amounts and "save as" a new document. Instead of scrolling through and "eyeballing" the document, Laura uses the keyboard shortcut *Command + F* on her MacBook to find and replace names and monetary amounts. Unfortunately, the old document had misspellings and typos and Laura didn't catch the old client's name and monetary amounts in a few spots. Was Laura's approach sound?

a) No, because use of sample documents is a form of plagiarism and cheats Pat out of ethical and competent legal representation.

b) No, because keyboard shortcuts like *Command + F* instead of reading a document carefully are too risky— lawyers shouldn't use them for formal work product like real estate paperwork.

    c) No, because with every new legal document project Laura should have started from scratch and typed a new document to ensure more polished, mistake-free work.

    d) No, because even though a "find and replace" tool can help, the soundest approach for Laura would have been to start by using a standard document template.

3) Sienna is working on a deal agreement on behalf of a limited liability partnership (LLP) buying a startup company. She drafts in Microsoft® Word and emails the file as an attachment to Carlo, the lawyer for the startup company. Carlo enabled Word's Track Changes feature to add internal notes and changes before emailing it to his client Dana, one of the startup founders. Dana emailed back the redlined document to Carlo with an electronic comment bubble saying, "If this LLP won't agree to this admittedly high price for my company, I have 8 other offers from folks who will!" Before Carlo sends the revised agreement back to Sienna, he no longer views Dana's comments on his screen—but Carlo's word-processing Review settings were set to show No Markup. Thus, he believed Dana's privileged comment bubbles were gone for good. They weren't. Tech-savvy Sienna, curious about who worked on the revised agreement and when, opens the revised draft attachment to show All Markup. She reads Dana's comments and reviews the file's metadata. As to the electronic comment bubble, Carlo:

    a) fulfilled his ethical duty of competency because his intentions were good and lawyers can't be expected to be proficient in every word-processing function.

    b) didn't fulfill his ethical duty of competency because he must "scrub" the metadata from every document transmitted using the most advanced metadata scrubbing software on the market.

    c) didn't fulfill his ethical duty of competency because he should have taken additional steps to ensure the revised document did not disclose privileged communication, such as checking Review settings, creating a PDF file, or consulting with someone more knowledgeable if he was not experienced with electronic collaboration tools.

d) fulfilled his ethical duty of competency only if he explained to his client Dana that there was inherent risk of disclosure if she insisted they use electronic collaboration tools.

4) Rossi must submit a 20-page summary judgment brief to Charlestown Court in a week. The brief cites regulatory sources not easily located in traditional casebooks or statute volumes. The brief has four sections, two of which have subsections. Charlestown Court requires electronic upload instead of paper copy filing but the rules state that scanning a paper document to create a PDF file for e-filing is adequate. Rossi knows about PDF files with a navigable table of contents and electronic bookmarks that help a reader skip around sections, along with hyperlinks to difficult-to-find cited sources that might increase the chance that a reader reviews them. Rossi's supervisor tells him not to take the extra time to create that "type" of brief because the client won't pay for it, and instead just scan a printed paper copy. Rossi's navigable PDF file approach:

a) makes sense if he can get a sense of whether the Charlestown Court presiding judge reads digitally, and if he is familiar enough with the methods to create the e-brief in a reasonable amount of time without passing on significant "learning curve" costs to this client.

b) isn't necessary because the local rules allow scanning a paper document, so submitting a brief with electronic navigability tools would likely confuse the judge or clerk.

c) makes sense even if Rossi needs to spend significant on-the-job time learning how to do these methods in an e-brief, all of which he bills to the client.

d) isn't necessary because as a junior lawyer, Rossi should follow the practice of his supervisor and not risk his reputation by doubting the firm's existing methods.

5) Highpoint, LLC is a small biotech corporation. Lucas is Highpoint's in-house counsel and its corporate secretary. One administrative duty is preparation of presentation slides for Highpoint's CEO to present at Highpoint's annual shareholder meeting. For weeks, Lucas works on the slides, many of which include numbered lists for topics such as strategic goals. At the last minute, the CEO sends him edits to include on the slides. Lucas works the changes into the lists on different slides but doesn't realize that because he manually typed #1, #2, #3 for every list item, many lists are now out of sequence or duplicative (two #2s) after the CEO's hasty additions. At the shareholder meeting, there is confusion when the CEO references different listed items during his remarks that don't match up to the numbered lists shareholders see on the slides. Lucas is embarrassed. Highpoint's CEO:

a) shouldn't be frustrated because Lucas couldn't have anticipated last-minute edits and lawyers don't have the chance to proofread everything in time-pressured situations.

b) has every right to be frustrated because Lucas should have set the numbering on slide lists to automatically renumber with changes, and applied that custom style to slides to ensure consistency, notwithstanding last-minute tweaks.

c) shouldn't be frustrated because Lucas's daily work includes large deal documents using word-processing tools and email correspondence, so there's no reasonable expectation of familiarity with less common tools such as PowerPoint.

d) has every right to be frustrated because Lucas was ethically obligated under Model Rule 1.1 (Competency) to create every legal document free from any and all errors and Lucas failed to do that.

*Practice Your Knowledge*

## Exercise #1: Set It & Forget It

Create a document template using Microsoft® Word for something you've done a lot of and may do a lot more of: case briefs. Preview available templates or set up your own from an existing case brief file in a format you prefer. Review the styles and settings thoroughly because you'll be "stuck" with them when you go to save your document as a template (File > Save As > Word Template). Practice creating a new case brief from your personalized template and never manually type out "Procedural History" at the top of a page again!

## Exercise #2: Document "Safety" Inspection

Choose a Microsoft® Word document you have saved "locally" on your computer. Aim for a file that's long; even better if it's one you've worked on with other people or at different times. Check the document's metadata (usually File > Info). Review Properties and Advanced Properties and note the types of metadata you see. Find the Inspect Document tool to uncover potential invisible data. Protect the document by creating a password (Protect Document > Encrypt with Password) and marking it as a final version (Protect Document > Mark As Final). Covert your new "cleaned-up" document to a PDF file and rest assured with a "safer" document than you started with.

 *Expand Your Knowledge*

➢ Ivy Grey, E-book: *The Lawyer's Guide to MS Word Training and Resources*, Intelligent Editing (Jun. 22, 2019), https://legal.intelligentediting.com/blog/free-e-book-the-lawyers-guide-to-ms-word-training-and-resources/ [https://perma.cc/F3AC-QH8P].

➤ Jonah Perlin, *Making Your (Power)Point: An Introductory Guide to Digital Presentation Design for Lawyers*, 18 LEGAL COMMC'N & RHETORIC: JALWD 81–131 (2021).

➤ Bryan Sims & Nerino J. Petro, Jr., *PDFing for Lawyers*, TechShow2021, https://www.techshow.com/2019/01/pdfing-for-lawyers/ [https://perma.cc/A7DS-JECL].

*Answers & Explanations*

*Knowledge Kickoff*

b) Juan's overall approach to creating this legal document was inefficient and ineffective. Because he started with no standardized approach or template, he ended up down a road of using different sources and methods to build content and format. Switching between manual typing of a caption off a piece of paper and copying and pasting from a filing in a different jurisdiction carries a significant risk of error and takes time that this client would not be pleased to learn she paid for. Juan should use a "trust-but-verify" approach not to ignore document formatting and creation and blindly trust technology but work alongside more efficient techniques—whether his law firm trains him to do so or not.

*Review Your Knowledge*

1) a) There are many choices and possibilities around what type of electronic document a lawyer should create; it depends on the situation, the audience, available software and tools, the reader's preferences (if known), etc. A technologically competent lawyer will be thoughtful about what document communication tool (spreadsheet, slides, email, word-processing, etc.) fits a situation. No lawyer must learn every technological shortcut on every different document creation tool. Stick with what you use and do the most. Learning shortcuts takes time during your career—not a crash course. Typography options like visual designs are just that—options. And while you've used cloud-based tools before, not everyone you work with may. Be aware of what others use and ensure that the way you create your document produces fewer headaches for those with whom you work—not more.

2) d) A standard template with preset provisions for a document Laura frequently uses in practice would be the most proficient approach here and a better option than tweaking a past sample. Templates are blank,

standardized, and ready to be filled in. Samples include prior case information. Here, even with her efficient find-and-replace approach using a relevant keyboard shortcut, Laura failed to replace prior case information. Misusing a sample leads to sloppy work product or disclosure of confidential information. Laura could have created a reusable document template with the standard sale provisions but without past client information. Creating a brand-new custom document from scratch every time costs Laura and her client time and money.

3)   c)   If electronically collaborating on legal documents, lawyers need to be aware of the technological risks and take reasonable steps to safeguard against inadvertent disclosure of confidential or privileged information. Carlo didn't need to be an expert but a basic familiarity with this tool would have prevented the disclosure. Good intentions can't hurt but don't always matter. The steps to take with metadata of electronic legal documents are situation dependent. Scrubbing software might be appropriate at times but an obligation to scrub every document a lawyer ever transmits is overbroad. Being a technologically competent lawyer doesn't mean obsessing about metadata—it means understanding it and being aware of when more heightened measures might be necessary.

4)   a)   Exploring new technology features is a balance. While the extra time to create a more reader-friendly and persuasive document might be worth it eventually, it's probably not ethical for Rossi to bill one client for hours and hours of experimentation and YouTube videos learning new tricks and tips. As long as local rules don't prohibit it, there's no reason Rossi can't submit a brief above and beyond what is customary. As a junior lawyer, Rossi should offer reasonable suggestions to the lawyers he works with about how technology can enhance their zealous advocacy for clients. He'd just need to be prepared to do some of this

learning and "fiddling" with the technology on some non-billable time.

5)   b)   A technologically competent lawyer doesn't always create perfect legal documents but does use technology to minimize the chance of substantial errors. If a lawyer uses presentation slides, they should take advantage of basic best practices this chapter introduced such as formatting numbered lists instead of typing the numbers manually. Last-minute edits are what lawyers might expect in any given situation. Proper document structure at the outset of a project helps the bones of a document keep shape as later work continues. Faltering with tools we're less familiar with may be understandable, but no modern lawyer wants to rely on that excuse.

## Endnotes

[1]   Microsoft, Excel, Office, OneDrive, PowerPoint, and Word are trademarks of the Microsoft group of companies. All other trademarks are the property of their respective owners. The book *Legal Innovation & Technology: A Practical Skills Guide for the Modern Lawyer* is an independent publication and is neither affiliated with, nor authorized, sponsored, or approved by, Microsoft Corporation.

[2]   Darth Vaughn and Casey Flaherty, *Tech Comes Naturally to 'Digital Native' Millennials? That's a Myth*, LEGAL REBELS (Oct. 13, 2016), https://www.abajournal.com/legalrebels/article/tech_comes_naturally_to_digital_native_millennials_thats_a_myth [https://perma.cc/2FCU-VU66].

[3]   UNITED STATES DISTRICT COURT EASTERN DISTRICT OF CALIFORNIA, MICROSOFT WORD FORMAT (Oct. 1, 2013), https://www.caed.uscourts.gov/caednew/index.cfm/attorney-info/word-format/ [https://perma.cc/WLE4-E6Y9].

[4]   *Gohmert v. Pence*, No. 6:20-cv-00660-JDK (Tx. 2021) (plaintiff's motion to file responsive brief late) https://storage.courtlistener.com/recap/gov.uscourts.txed.203073/gov.uscourts.txed.203073.26.0.pdf [https://perma.cc/R954-P77E].

[5]   Judge William E. Smith, United States District Court, District of Rhode Island (2002–present).

[6]   Blake E. Hawthorne, *A Guide to Creating Electronic Appellate Briefs*, Supreme Court of Texas (June 6, 2019), https://www.txcourts.gov/media/1443805/guide-to-creating-electronic-appellate-briefs-2019-adobe-acrobat-pro-dc.pdf [https://perma.cc/J3QK-USF5].

[7]   https://perma.cc/.

[8]   MATTHEW BUTTERICK, TYPOGRAPHY FOR LAWYERS (2019).

[9]   *In-N-Out Burgers v. Puma N. Am. Inc.*, No. 19-0413 (C.D. Cal., filed March 1, 2019), available at https://heitnerlegal.com/wp-content/uploads/In-N-Out-v-PUMA.pdf [https://perma.cc/4CC4-GUAM].

[10]   Kristian Foss, Why Are Agreements So Hard To Understand?, WORLD COMMERCE & CONTRACTING (Apr. 18, 2019), https://journal.iaccm.com/contracting-excellence-journal/why-are-agreements-so-hard-to-understand [https://perma.cc/CE56-C2FV].

[11] Shell Visual Contract; reprinted with permission Shell, image available at Visual Contracts for Shell (illustration), IIDAWARD (2020), http://iiidaward.net/index.php?pg=4&ab=0&awardpage=2630&suchekat=Corporate%20designänd%20communications&suchename=&suchetext= [https://perma.cc/M27D-8PLX].

[12] Shell Visual Contract; reprinted with permission Shell, image available at Visual Contracts for Shell (illustration), IIDAWARD (2020), http://iiidaward.net/index.php?pg=4&ab=0&awardpage=2630&suchekat=Corporate%20designänd%20communications&suchename=&suchetext= [https://perma.cc/M27D-8PLX].

[13] Ellie Margolis, *Is the Medium the Message? Unleashing the Power of E-Communication in the Twenty-First Century*, 12 LEGAL COMMC'N & RHETORIC: JAWLD 1 (2015).

[14] Copyright Microsoft®; reprinted based on allowed use of Microsoft® screenshots available at https://www.microsoft.com/en-us/legal/intellectualproperty/copyright/permissions.

[15] OREGON STATE BAR ASS'N OPINION 2011–187 (Revised 2015), https://www.osbar.org/_docs/ethics/2011-187.pdf [https://perma.cc/2EBP-GXZY].

CHAPTER 4

# NEXT GENERATION
# LEGAL RESEARCH

*Core Concepts*

| | |
|---|---|
| *AI legal research* <br> *predictive search* <br> *research + document* <br> *integration* <br> *document builders* <br> *document analyzers* | *data-driven research* <br> *legal analytics* <br> *docket* <br> *data visualization* <br> *legal news tracking* |

*Knowledge Kickoff*

Samantha is a lawyer at Greater Atlanta Legal Services providing civil legal aid to low-income individuals. She is working on a federal class action lawsuit against the Atlanta Transportation Authority, seeking improved access to public transportation services for individuals with disabilities. Facing a motion to dismiss, Samantha researches the issues of standing and mootness. First, she reads the motion. Second, she types the citations into a research database and prints each authority to read. Third, she uses a citator service to update the law, taking notes on what she sees, printing additional sources, and creating a chart to understand the legal landscape in this jurisdiction. Fourth, after several unsuccessful terms and connectors searches, she talks with colleagues about their experiences in the federal district where the case is pending and creates a rough estimate for a budget and timeline. After fielding a client's phone call about the likelihood of settlement, Samantha responds, "Your guess is as good as mine!" Samantha then asks a paralegal to spend five hours manually checking each citation. Later, as she's relaxing and scrolling through her phone, Samantha sees a news headline about a class action settlement by a Florida public transit company. Interesting, she thinks, before fading off to sleep without ever reading the article.

Which statement best evaluates Samantha's research approach?

a) It's thorough and sound—Samantha followed traditional research steps carefully and reviewed every piece of legal authority in a methodical way, as a good lawyer should.

b) It's thorough and sound—by doing every manual research step herself and outsourcing some tasks to a paralegal, Samantha can keep costs down and perform research more efficiently.

c) It's flawed and imperfect—Samantha's decision to start with her opponent's motion won't jumpstart comprehensive research because it's written persuasively from one viewpoint.

d) It's flawed and imperfect—Samantha spent a lot of time and energy on individual, one-off research tasks and random conversations instead of taking advantage of tools that could boost the efficiency and quality of her research and work product.

---

Innovation and technology are fueling the next generation legal research tools. Just ask hypothetical lawyer Sasha how her "then" in 2003 compares to her current day "now":

 The year is **2003**: Sasha is a second-year associate at a mid-size law firm in San Francisco. Exhausted at her desk, Sasha puts her head in her hands in frustration. She has 12 tabs open on her computer and is hard at work drafting an opposition to a motion for summary judgment in a construction contract dispute (she represents the plaintiff, a developer). One tab is an "all cases" search from Lexis®; one tab is Westlaw™; one tab is her draft opposition in Microsoft® Word; one is an email to the firm's librarian asking whether a local practice guide is available in hard copy; one is her firm's internal document management system where she'd typed the keywords "construction motions" into the search field, returning a bunch of files dating back to 1994. On her desk lay (1) her Bluebook® citation guide; (2) the motion; (3) a reminder to call the client with her best prediction of whether they'll withstand the motion and an estimate of billable hours; and (4) a stack of cases she found after using the terms and connectors search of *construction /p contract! and summary judgment.*

The year is **present day**: Sasha is co-managing partner of the Los Angeles office of a major law firm specializing in intellectual property litigation— specifically, patent law. Comfortable at her desk, Sasha reviews a draft opposition to a motion for summary judgment an associate prepared in a patent case. Having asked the associate to keep costs down, Sasha is impressed with the supporting case law the associate obtained by first uploading a PDF file of opposing counsel's motion into a legal research brief analyzer (which suggested three cases their opponent failed to cite). The associate also ran natural language searches and used a visual scatter plot tool to confirm the clusters of most relevant authority. The draft opposition is structured well, with point headings the associate created efficiently using research/ document integration software—working seamlessly within one tab instead of 12. Sasha prepares for a client meeting with a chart showing judicial trends in the Eastern District of Pennsylvania, including a timeline of how long it takes the presiding judge to rule on motions for summary judgment. Sasha prepares notes as to the projected budget for the matter (based on internal firm data from patent matters of similar scope), how often cases go to trial in this jurisdiction, and the number of times opposing counsel has litigated, won, lost, or settled in this district.

Sasha laughs at the memories of her old associate days getting lucky (or not) with her trial-and-error, manual, and expensive search term approach, running out of staples after plodding through clunky stacks of irrelevant case law, and communicating far too many vague gut instincts to her supervisors and clients.

My, how times have changed.

Legal research is no stranger to change. Decades ago, lawyers researched "in the books" by sifting through case reporters, digests, statutory indexes, practice guides, and treatises. Today, most don't. You probably haven't in law school. Giant online legal research databases Lexis® and Westlaw™ (sometimes lumped together and termed "Wexis") prompted the steep decline in paper research. Given your early experience with online research, would it surprise you that this advancement horrified some lawyers? Concerned traditionalists and naysayers objected. How would lawyers understand the ins and outs of precedent if they couldn't touch and feel the crisp pages of the cases? How would lawyers learn to analyze levels and types of authority if they take the easy way out and copy and paste from the first result that pops up on their search screen?

The skeptics were wrong. A poor legal researcher is a poor legal researcher, whether paper or online. A good legal researcher is a good legal researcher, whether paper or online. Online research did not signal the demise of thorough lawyering. Like so many topics in this book, our focus is *how* lawyers use innovative new approaches and technology—not whether tools themselves are inherently "good" or "bad."

From paper to online and now from manual to machine. If the transition away from paper was the first big wave of research change in the profession, the second is here—and it's been building for years. Broadly speaking, we'll capture the concept "from manual to machine." It's not just about being online—it's about what those online tools can now do for lawyers. Artificial intelligence (AI) is a term we touched on as a Need to Know in chapter 2. Its impact on legal research is significant.

Until recently, search engines like Lexis® and Westlaw™ were built, operated, and used manually. Human lawyers (and others) at research companies added vast amounts of information to databases and created headnotes; human lawyers then searched the vast amount of online information by exact keywords and sought to make connections. Sometimes it worked; sometimes it didn't. For example, if back in 2002 our hypothetical associate Sasha searched for patent cases by entering keywords "duration of infringement" and a binding decision instead discussed "*time* of infringement" she'd miss that important case. If she searched for "car" she'd miss a statute involving "automobiles." If she searched for "gun" she'd miss an article about "weapons." Her research wasn't poor; it was less efficient with a trial-and-error approach. The machine was just not smart enough to make those connections for her.

Now it is. We can use technical descriptors like machine learning and natural language processing, but let's be honest. Do we truly understand the ins and outs of what those computer programming terms mean? Perhaps a few do, but most students don't. Most lawyers don't. That's OK. The simplest way to think about this **AI legal research** technology is that it can now understand not just our search terms but their meaning and context. Research databases rely on sophisticated algorithms that train software with complicated sets of instructions. The tools now "think" more broadly along the lines of how humans do, aware of variations and concepts instead of only linear, exact matches in terms. We know this from using search engines like Google in our personal life. If I'm ready for dinner and type "Boston pizza" into my Google search bar, the top results are things like "where to find the best pizza in Boston" and "25 Essential Pizzas in the Boston area." I didn't tell Google I was looking for recommendations on where to go for the best or most popular pizza—it just knew. In other words, its algorithm, as impacted by search engine optimization efforts, has trained the system to understand that's what my terms likely meant.

Lawyers look for legal information, not pizza. But advances in the way we find things aren't too different. Innovative search technology using AI has combined with business and financial market enthusiasm to create exponential growth in legal research techniques. More data combined with more ways to search it equals more opportunities to get information in an easier, faster, and less expensive way. Investment and interest in research technology has grown in recent years. The playing field is no longer just "Wexis." It's companies such as Fastcase®, Bloomberg Law®, and Casetext.

This is great news for the modern lawyer. Innovators aren't stuck on outdated notions of what legal research is. They are considering what it could be. In the past, legal research has meant primary and secondary legal authority and basic corporate information in the context of transactional lawyering:

✓   cases

✓   statutes

✓   regulations

✓   practice guides

✓   treatises

✓   publicly available corporate disclosures

Why stop there? Research in the 21st century is broader. The traditional phrase "legal research" is stretching to capture many new avenues and angles. For example, this chapter explores data-driven decision making based on analytics—making meaningful connections with large amounts of information to inform strategy. Next generation research captures not just legal authority but underlying information that matters just as much—if not more—than traditional precedent upon which lawyers customarily rely. Examples of this "new" information that can inform case strategy and offer a competitive advantage include:

✓   judicial decision trends by jurisdiction or individual judge

✓   probability of motion outcomes by plaintiff/ defendant side

✓   lawyer/law firm performance by jurisdiction

✓   jurisdictional comparisons

✓   time until resolution by case type

✓   average time to trial by case type

✓   active cases pending by judge/jurisdiction

That's a bird's-eye view of what the "Next Generation" title of this chapter means. We'll cover AI search techniques, document and research integration, data analytics, data visualization, and real-time news currency. As we do so, keep two key concepts in mind: patterns and context.

Lawyers look for patterns, such as what cases have been persuasive or what arguments have failed. That's not changing. It's just that now there are infinite more patterns to look at, and they are easier to find (whether because of the better search inputs research systems now help us create, or the better aggregate visual pictures of the patterns we now enjoy).

Research is context specific. That's not an invitation for the modern lawyer to ignore the next generation of advancements under the "well, that probably won't apply to me" theory. It's true that a solo practitioner doing real estate title exams and residential home sale closings in one county may not have a need for advanced analytics. There are many areas where research advancements don't seem all that helpful at first glance. But maybe they are. Maybe they should be. Maybe they apply to your client. Maybe they apply to your opponent. Maybe they apply to a regulator, competitor, insurer, or vendor. Legal research is a broad concept with cutting-edge ideas and features that will far outpace future editions of this book—make sure they don't outpace your efforts to stay aware, interested, and willing to learn.

## Not Your Average Q&A Search

Let's start with how modern lawyers craft search queries, and how legal research software gives answers. It's so familiar to most readers that you might take it for granted. In the big picture for the legal profession, it's actually quite new. We can think of search advancements in legal research within a simple context I suspect readers are familiar with: a text message chain that goes something like this:

> *Mom: honey, what time will you be here for our fancy dying?*
>
> *You: dying?*
>
> *Mom: urgh, dumb phone—I mean drying.*
>
> *You: drying, mom?!*
>
> *Mom: URGH again. dining! I hope you're hungry—it's take out:)*

What do these frustrating and often sometimes funny autocorrects have to do with crafting careful searches as a legal researcher? They embody a new way of getting information we want. In the past, terms and connectors manual searching was like searching for exact words and phrases in a thick phone book or dictionary—we needed precision to tell the machine exactly what information we sought. We relied on some luck finding the needle in the haystack of authority. Today, it's the other way around. Machines tell us what we want. Software is one step ahead, bringing the needle to us.

---

### LIT TIP

"The AI [ordinary people] use in products like their smartphones . . . is largely invisible to them. They don't have to choose to use it; it's just part of the product. It's the same with legal research; for decades now, AI techniques have made their way into legal research products, and lawyers have been leveraging that technology, often without being conscious that it's AI."[1]

Noah Waisberg and Dr. Alexander Hudek
Founders, Kira Systems

---

Let's call this **predictive search** technology something other than the mind reading we often think of it as. You might hear it described as predictive text, Smart Compose (with Google Documents), or type ahead. Software takes past patterns and common characteristics (search history) and uses them to predict future action (search terms and results) in real time based on the inputs we type or tap. This technology applies whether we're texting on a smartphone, writing words in a Google Document or other word processor or email, or typing search queries in a web browser. In our personal lives, a text message I start with "what . . ." prompts my phone to suggest "whatever." Typing "Feel free . . ." in an email prompts my software to suggest "Feel free to let me know if you have questions." Tapping "can you put . . ." into an internet search engine prompts it to suggest many things, some more helpful ("can you put tin foil in the oven?") than others ("can you put Neosporin on a dog?").

Research innovators use similar technology to make basic search queries more efficient. I suspect it's something you've taken for granted as a rookie researcher. But the capability of systems to intuitively capture and phrase the issue we're searching for is a relative newcomer in the decades of online legal research. Just as with our personal lives, the technology is terrific when it works—saves time, gets us where we need to be, prompts us to consider new angles we were missing. But just like my mother's autocorrected text message about dining, so too can it be frustrating, misdirecting, and distracting if we fail to bring our own caution, patience, and discerning legal brain.

Take for example my search below on Lexis+®:

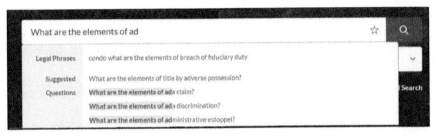

\* Figure 4A: Predictive Search of adverse possession elements; reprinted from LexisNexis with permission. Copyright 2022 LexisNexis. All rights reserved.

The software predicted I wanted the elements of adverse possession. Assume that I did—the suggestion is helpful. Assume that I didn't—I would ignore it and not get sidetracked. In this example, though, the database returned more than 10,000 results since I never pre-filtered the database by jurisdiction and level of court. Like most research tools, predictive search works only if I work.

That's enhanced predictive searching but what about predicting what lawyers really care about—the answers! Westlaw™, Lexis®, and others use AI technology to suggest not only a lengthy list of resources that *might* contain answers but often the answers themselves. Revisit for a moment our broad Need to Know introductory definition of AI from chapter 2—software that recognizes patterns based on past training to give information based on a lot of data. Research systems now aim to offer one-stop shopping, using the same family of advanced machine-learning technology as an internet search engine that suggests the best local pizza place. Modern legal research databases mine millions of cases and other legal authority to bring suggested substantive answers to the forefront.

Our answer to my adverse possession question, assuming I narrowed my jurisdiction to Massachusetts cases, might look something like Figure 4B on Westlaw Edge™:

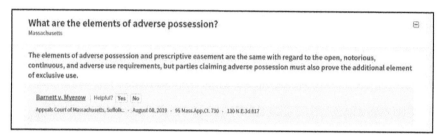

**What are the elements of adverse possession?**
Massachusetts

The elements of adverse possession and prescriptive easement are the same with regard to the open, notorious, continuous, and adverse use requirements, but parties claiming adverse possession must also prove the additional element of exclusive use.

Barnett v. Myerow ｜ Helpful? Yes No
Appeals Court of Massachusetts, Suffolk... · August 08, 2019 · 96 Mass.App.Ct. 730 · 130 N.E.3d 817

\* Figure 4B: Westlaw Edge™ search for elements of adverse possession; screenshot reprinted with permission from Thomson Reuters.

I've heard enhanced answer features described as software "understanding" a researcher's question. Maybe. Maybe not. It feels too good to be true, and sometimes it is. But sometimes the technology is that good and gives modern lawyers a direct answer that has a decent chance at being accurate.

Of course, good lawyers don't rely on decent chances. With any fast track-ish approach, there are cautions (just as with not assuming the top search result for the best pizza must be, in fact, the best). Selecting a "one-stop-shop" answer without digging into underlying sources is like going to the first-listed pizza place without reading any reviews. What if the reviews said each pizza cost $50? What if the reviews said customer service was horrendous? In our personal lives, we've learned not to always take a top search result at face value. A healthy dose of human skepticism goes a long way. Answers based on AI technology are often a great starting line, but not always the finish. The same goes for advanced research features that tempt us into thinking they can do all the work. They're doing a lot of it, but we need to do some too.

## Research + Document Integration: Document Builders & Document Analyzers

The shorthand title for this subsection of chapter 4 might be the "1 tab or 20?" discussion. We've all been there. On average, I might have 10 or 15 tabs open at any one time. Often I toggle between a word-processing document and legal research screens. Work on document; jump back to research. Review research; jump back to document. I probably have a basic search engine tab open, too. Find something relevant; jump back to include it in my document. Review a sample brief from a previous matter; copy and paste from it and jump back to research tab to update that case law. Find updated case law; jump back to my document to work it in. Repeat.

The workflow makes me tired just thinking about it, but it's all too familiar. Legal research doesn't exist in a vacuum. Lawyers research with and for other deliverables, whether an email memo, notes for a client meeting, appellate brief, trial court motion, draft license agreement, or any other work product. Innovators have wondered if they can create a better way for lawyers to create work product that involves law (research) and documents (writing). Today's advances in technology have transformed that back-and-forth process (research, write, research, write) into a more seamless integration of these two vital lawyering tasks. Instead of 2 (or 20) tabs, might lawyers be able to work in just one?

We'll cover innovative **research + document integration** tools in two categories: (1) Document Builders; and (2) Document Analyzers.

| LIT TIP | |
|---|---|
| Document Builders | Document Analyzers |
| research IN; document OUT | document IN; research OUT |
| tools that can speed up and inform document creation by first offering substantive research guidance "along the way" as a user builds written work product | tools that can speed up and inform substantive research guidance by first analyzing existing written work product a user submits |

1)   Document Builders (research 1st ➡ document 2nd)

**Document Builders** are a family of new tools that help lawyers create legal documents by providing substantive law and suggested language. That's a broad definition, and these tools come in different shapes and sizes from basic transactional form templates to more sophisticated "brief building" software that creates document language for you. Document Builders in the research context fit within the broader category of Document Assembly (or Document Automation) we'll tackle later in chapter 6.

Let's use you as the next hypothetical modern lawyer to explore how Document Builders work. Suppose you have a sister Natalia moving to New York City to get a graduate degree. She has never rented on her own before. An acquaintance has a studio apartment near Central Park that is perfect. They aren't requiring a lease, but for peace of mind Natalia wants one. She asks you for help.

Your "20-tab" approach to researching and then building an apartment lease might look something like this:

1)    open a new word processing document

2)    type RESIDENTIAL LEASE at the top

3)    pause, realizing you know next to nothing about property law or lease creation

4)    open a tab for legal research—one tab that will quickly become 5 or 10

5)    spend hours reading about laws in New York

6)    copy and paste different provisions and reminders for yourself

7)    bounce in and out of your draft document

That's inefficient. Remember our boxed cake mix example for efficient document structure from chapter 3. Lawyers rarely want to work from scratch and in this scenario it would be best to find a template, or form, from which to start. But even if you found a sample, would you understand the law behind it? Would you know why certain provisions are included? How would you learn what to delete, add, modify, or negotiate?

Enter Document Builders. Forms, checklists, templates, and drafting tools have been around for a while but they are better and more enhanced. By enhanced, I mean that software now pairs basic templates and forms with substantive "know-how." This is the legal authority a lawyer needs to craft a document with confidence, in real time alongside their draft—not what they happen to find with a few quick internet searches.

For Natalia's apartment, you might use a Document Builder tool like Lexis+ Practical Guidance® to search for residential lease agreements in New York and get something that looks like this:

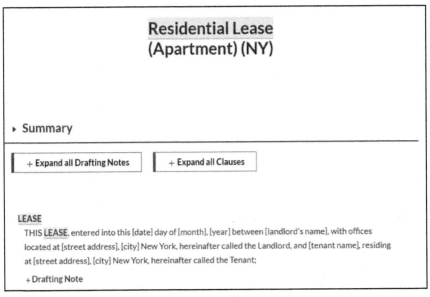

* Figure 4C: Residential Lease Practical Guidance®; reprinted from LexisNexis with permission. Copyright 2022 LexisNexis. All rights reserved.

Here's where the real research + document integration happens. Throughout the lease template are "Drafting Notes" and "Alternate & Optional Clauses" where the software provides substantive law to shape document decisions. For example, in creating Natalia's lease you'd probably want to specify her monthly rent. In doing so, the software provides an optional clause about written notice and New York statutory law about a landlord's obligation to notify a tenant of rent default:

> – Optional Clause
>
> **Optional Paragraph 3.(c):**
>
> (c) If the rent is not received in full by the 5th day of the month, the Landlord shall send a written notice to the Tenant, by certified mail. Such notice shall state that the Tenant has failed to pay rent in full as of the 5th day of the month.
>
> – Drafting Note
>
> **Drafting Note to Optional Paragraph 3.(c)**
>
> This provision creates an affirmative obligation on the landlord to provide notice to the tenant of a rent default which continues past the fifth day of the month. It may be included based upon preference. However, the landlord's failure to provide such written notice may be used by a tenant as an affirmative defense in an eviction proceeding based upon non-payment of rent. See NY CLS Real P § 235-e(d).

\* Figure 4D: Optional Clause & Drafting Note; reprinted from LexisNexis with permission. Copyright 2022 LexisNexis. All rights reserved.

Optional clauses and drafting notes are a starting line for the modern lawyer—not a finish. Templates and forms within databases such as Lexis+® usually offer the option to open the form as a new word-processing file, offering a more immediate document creation but not a finished product tailored to a client's situation. We're back to the "use new tools with caution theme." Document Builders may be more efficient than a back-and-forth "20-tab" disjointed approach, but they're only as good as the careful lawyer using them.

Beyond transactional form work, lawyers explore Document Builder tools for litigation writing too. They're sometimes called Brief Builders and have the same goal: to integrate the research and writing process into a more cohesive workflow. For example, Compose© by legal research company Casetext is an "all-in-one" tool that offers research and drafting together in one platform.[2]

Let's explore a Brief Builder using another hypothetical with Natalia. Thanks to your residential lease drafting, she's enjoying graduate school in New York City until she comes to you for more help. She invented a new temperature gauge for clay oven kilns, patented it, and now claims an art supply company in Pennsylvania copied it. Another lawyer helped her sue in New York federal court for patent infringement, and now she faces the Philadelphia company's Rule 12(b)(2) motion to dismiss for lack of personal jurisdiction. You have no experience with patent litigation.

Embracing a "trust but verify" approach with technology and unfamiliar areas of substantive law, you might explore a Document Builder tool such as Compose©. Compose© is a brief automation platform linked with Casetext's underlying library of millions of legal authorities and its CARA A.I. search technology (Casetext's proprietary legal research engine). The tool started with federal law and practice but has expanded into state law and other areas such as products liability. A lawyer drafts a brief using the software (or by adding it to their Microsoft® Word toolbar) but alongside Casetext's legal resources specific to case type, jurisdiction, procedural context, and even the side of the case a lawyer is on.

For example, here's how Compose© would help build an opposition to a motion to dismiss for lack of personal jurisdiction. First, you'd select which side you are on:

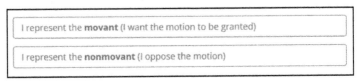

* Figure 4E: Compose© image; reprinted with permission; Compose© by Casetext, available at https://compose.law/.

You'd select nonmovant on Natalia's behalf. Then, you'd select the court, enter party names (note the **Opposition to Pennsylvania Copying Company's Motion** title that automatically populates the document at the top right of Figure 4F). The software populates your brief (on the right-hand side in Figure 4F) alongside a library of potentially relevant research authority (on the left in Figure 4F). Sandwiched in the middle is a menu of argument statements and supporting legal standards from which to choose, favoring both the moving and non-moving parties based on binding and non-binding authority:

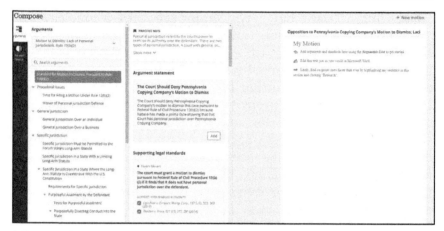

\* Figure 4F: Compose© full image; reprinted with permission; Compose© by Casetext, available at https://compose.law/.

Document Builders can jumpstart projects for lawyers unfamiliar with a subject or procedural context or help more experienced lawyers create documents in a streamlined way. A tool like Compose© is like an ice cream sundae bar for lawyers creating a legal document. It doesn't map out the full recipe but it offers ingredients to get started. You might want chocolate chips; you might not. You might want whipped cream; you might not. You choose the amounts, the combinations, the flavors. A modern lawyer chooses their arguments, organization, and supporting precedent. Document Builders avoid the messy scatter of ingredients and instead lay them out for you in an organized and descriptive way. The result? A delicious ice cream sundae (or excellent opposition brief for Natalia) based on careful and informed selections.

2)    <u>Document Analyzers</u> (document 1st ➡ research 2nd)

**Document Analyzers** (also called Brief Checkers or Brief Analyzers) work in reverse. If the Document Builders we just discussed give you research to help create documents, Document Analyzers take your documents to help give you research. Instead of starting with a blank page, now we're starting with a blank search box. Document Analyzers create and perform searches by contextualizing and "understanding" the content of documents you feed into the software.

Let's use some more family drama to see how a Document Analyzer might help. Your hypothetical sister Natalia is all set but your brother Dario has a problem. He's a songwriter in New York who works with bands and other musicians. He was enjoying the ride in the music industry until Musicians R Us sued him for copyright infringement, alleging he copied song lyrics from singer and performer Taylor Swift. Your brother emails you a PDF file of the complaint filed in federal court in the Eastern District of New York. You're not experienced in copyright law and have no idea where to begin.

You could start your research by uploading the complaint to a Document Analyzer such as Westlaw Edge's™ Quick Check© tool. Document Analyzers rely on a software's underling advanced AI search technology to analyze the citations, text, headings, subheadings, and contextualized arguments and legal propositions in the document submitted and generate a report of relevant authority. Figure 4G shows the Quick Check© option where you would upload the complaint (or a past memo, opposing filing, other sample work product, or just about anything else).

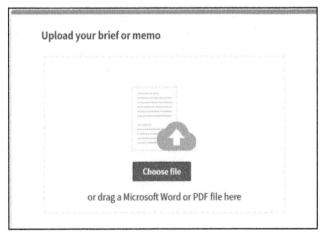

Upload your brief or memo

Choose file

or drag a Microsoft Word or PDF file here

* Figure 4G: Westlaw Edge™ screenshot; reprinted with permission from Thomson Reuters.

The key with Document Analyzers is that you enter terms to narrow the purpose of your search (for Dario, we could specify "copyright infringement") but never get more specific than that.

If, for example, on behalf of Dario, you uploaded the complaint about infringement of song lyrics, the software would return authority involving copyright infringement and song lyrics or music cases. You never told the software the legal issue was in the context of song lyrics; it contextualized that from the content of the complaint and was able to "push" the most factually relevant authority forward.

Modern lawyers use results from Document Analyzers in different ways such as:

- ✓ a starting point for a high-level research report in an unfamiliar area of law

- ✓ an additional step in their overall research process

- ✓ a final "gut check" before finishing research and submitting a document such as uploading a draft summary judgment brief before filing

- ✓ a way to dissect an opponent's brief to try to find authority other lawyers may have missed or omitted

- ✓ a way to compare several documents on the same subject (such as Westlaw™ Quick Check© Judicial tool where a researcher—often a law clerk or judge, but really anyone—can upload multiple documents to compare citations, reveal overlap, or suggest authorities neither document included)

Are Document Analyzers secure? We'll turn to security in chapter 9 but readers may have paused at the thought of uploading attorney work product to a third-party provider. Does that ruin the privilege? The short answer is probably not, but it's a great question to ask and to my knowledge at the time of writing this book there's been no decision or formal bar guidance on the ethics of using these systems. Research companies with Document Analyzer tools report that the tools encrypt uploaded files, do not store them after processing, and delete all inputs. Many compare the level of security used to that of a bank. In chapter 9, we'll drill down on questions to consider when considering whether to use a third-party service in connection with work product or confidential information.

So what's next? Integration and customization are getting a lot of attention. Modern lawyers are recognizing the improved efficiency when research and writing platforms together can work with and alongside their own work product and document sets. This means you can create a personalized, custom research experience by integrating outside research tools and techniques with your (or your law firm's or law department's) own internal work product bank, taking advantage of millions of legal authorities and advanced search technology—all within your own templates, work product, and preferences. Research options will continue to become "plug-ins" and "add-ons" to word-processing tools for a more streamlined workflow. The collaborative single hub approach such as with the tool Clearbrief (2022 Legalweek New Law Company of the Year winner) and with Lexis® for Microsoft Office shown in Figure 4H helps a lawyer keep focus on one centralized document work screen with one application for research, fact checking support, and writing instead of switching across different tabs and tools.

\* Figure 4H: Lexis® for Microsoft® Office Ribbon Toolbar; reprinted from LexisNexis with permission. Copyright 2022 LexisNexis. All rights reserved.

## Legal Analytics: Data-Driven Decision Making

Modern lawyers now have more—much more—information on which to base their judgments than the traditional sources you've learned about such as statutes, cases, and regulations. Now they have data, too. No, you don't have to become a data scientist before you graduate law school. But you should understand and leverage data as it may relate to your practice not as a replacement for traditional sources but as a complement to them. Legal sources and factual **data-driven research** work together. Data can complement (or even replace) a lawyer's gut instinct or hunch. Informed prediction plus human judgment is a powerful combination.

> **LIT TIP**
>
> "It's no longer the case that data analytics is only for large firms with data scientists on staff . . . [f]irms may expect that only the most sophisticated clients want data-enabled decision making from their law firms. That may have been true in the past, but it isn't true any longer."[3]
>
> Ed Walters
> CEO, Fastcase®

"Big Data" pops up at different spots in this book, such as in chapter 5 electronically stored information (ESI). Analyzing large amounts of data is not unique to the legal profession. Capturing information and using it to create predictive models to guide decision making applies to almost every industry and aspect of society: buyers' retail shopping trends, stock market patterns, insurance premiums, viewer entertainment streaming preferences, or sports performance and draft pick value in the major leagues. Even the local weather forecast is infinitely better today because it's based on far more historical information and patterns than a week of information combined with the forecaster's instinct that it gets sunny after a stretch of rain. How often have you chosen a hotel or restaurant not because of rumors but because you saw a 5-star rating? That's basing a decision on data.

Let's rewind to the hypothetical lawyer Sasha from the start of this chapter. Compared to decades ago, the current-day Sasha prepared for a client meeting with a chart showing judicial trends in the Eastern District of Pennsylvania, including a timeline of how long it takes the presiding judge to rule on motions for summary judgment. How could she know that? Did she interview the judge? Work with a paralegal to pull records from that courthouse clerk's office for every past motion? No. This data always technically existed but it's been next to impossible to capture in a manual, one-off way. Until now.

**Legal analytics** means culling information from large amounts of data relevant to different aspects of a proceeding, such as clients, attorneys, case expense, case strategy, pricing, the likelihood of outcomes, judges, judges' tendencies, and case timelines. Besides the substantive underlying law that impacts a matter, think of this as the real-world nuts and bolts of everyday lawyering decisions. Research that helps inform if you should:

- ✓ File a complaint in Texas or Michigan as the more advantageous venue?

- ✓ Settle or fight a motion to dismiss in the District of Massachusetts?

- ✓ Advise a client to expect a court decision in weeks or months?

- ✓ Expect $3000 in damages or $3 million?

- ✓ Allow a junior associate to argue a matter or take it on yourself, depending on your opponent's experience?

- ✓ Seek approval for a class action in Delaware or in New York?

Modern lawyers won't make decisions in a single-case isolated vacuum. They'll do so with insight from a bigger and less anecdotal picture. Competitive intelligence, so to speak. Data-driven, quantitative guidance instead of qualitative guesses. Depending on the case, this flavor of information might be just as important if not more than traditional precedent, especially for client pitches or tactical strategy decisions.

Legal analytics research tools first need to get at the underlying data. This data usually comes from a **docket**. A docket is a log of the complete history of a single case. It has a unique number or number/letter combination, and docketing format varies with jurisdiction and court. Often a docket includes abbreviations for the presiding judge or court and the year, looking something like these:

**2:14-10-12422-TZ    4:19-cv-00221-RH-MTP    IPR2018-1241**

Docket data isn't binding legal precedent. It's the bones behind a case: a chronological recap of everything filed, decided, stayed, disputed, and resolved. Dockets can be pending for current cases, or past dockets for cases already filed and resolved years or decades prior.

Docket data isn't always easy to get. Dockets are generally maintained by the court clerk where a matter is filed. A case might have different docket numbers depending on the level of court (an original trial court docket, for example, but then a different one with appeals in different appellate courts). Some state court systems are still paper-based and that makes collecting state court docket information tricky. This is especially so at the trial court level or at more particularized courts such as housing or probate. Many analytics tools have as their primary focus federal dockets, because companies can access millions (probably billions) of electronic federal court records through a platform called PACER (Public Access to Court Electronic Records). PACER captures all the case documents filed online in electronic form through the federal judiciary's CM/ECF docketing system (Case Management/ Electronic Case Files).

Analytics aren't just for trial courts. In 2022, the legal analytics platform Lex Machina (owned by LexisNexis) launched Appellate Analytics with comprehensive coverage (hundreds of thousands of cases and appellate briefs) covering federal courts of appeals from all 13 federal circuits.[4] Lawyers can use this tool to, for example, research timing of appellate rulings, favorable appeal outcomes by judge or circuit, or appeal wins and losses for certain law firms, lawyers, and parties.

Modern legal research systems also often capture analytics from other non-court information such as from the Patent Trial and Appeal Board (PTAB) or the United States International Trade Commission. Legal research companies such as Lexis®, Westlaw™, and Fastcase® use advanced technologies to get at underlying docket information and allow lawyers to "slice and dice" it however it helps inform their research.

Let's return to the example of Sasha preparing for a client meeting about pending patent litigation. The Westlaw Edge™ Litigation Analytics shown in Figure 4I offer a view of judicial information relevant to motions for summary judgment in the Eastern District of Pennsylvania.

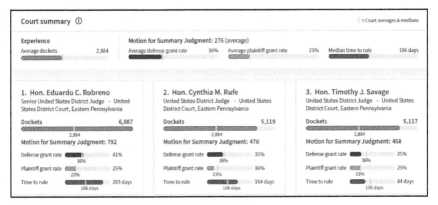

* Figure 4I: Westlaw Edge™ Litigation Analytics screenshot; reprinted with permission from Thomson Reuters.

Analytics tools allow lawyers to filter with granularity across different categories of docket data by, for example:

✓ jurisdiction

✓ case type

✓ judge

✓ date

✓ experience of lawyers

✓ expert witness challenges and areas of expertise

✓ experience of judges

✓ damage awards, amount, and type

✓ case outcomes

✓ motion types

Imagine Sasha's case was pending before Judge Timothy Savage in the Eastern District of Pennsylvania and Sasha was interested in advising a plaintiff client facing a defendant's motion for summary judgment. She may review analytics such as those shown in Figure 4I to see that Judge Savage has the shortest time to rule (84 days) compared to the average in the district (106 days) and a slightly lower defense grant rate (25%) compared to the average in the district (36%). Would those percentages be remarkable for her client? Probably not. Others might be. Not all analytics data is earth shattering. It's a piece of the overall research puzzle.

Most lawyers won't stop at just the surface docket percentages and numbers—they want to and should dive deeper into the substance. Many research tools offer access to the underlying docket documents, such as Judge Savage's past decisions on summary judgment using the Figure 4I example. Or if underlying documents aren't easily already available in electronic form—as is often the case with state courts—some research companies invite lawyers (or any user) to request the pleadings, motions, or other docket documents that the research company can "fetch" as part of its service.

Analytics paired with underlying docket documents means lawyers have yet another tool in their tool belt for client counseling and advocacy. Suppose hypothetical lawyer Sasha learned from her analytics review that Judge Savage routinely cited the authority of *Canal v. Dials Manufacturing* for the proposition that summary judgment in a patent dispute is rarely appropriate before the patent claim construction phase. Her client wants to make that same argument—why wouldn't she cite the *Canal* case with which the judge (or their law clerks) may be familiar?

A modern lawyer makes these calls with caution and in context; citing this precedent to Judge Savage in our example does not guarantee a slam-dunk victory. But if the choice is between a relevant case a presiding judge may have never included in a written decision, or a relevant case they've cited favorably in similar context hundreds of past times? I know which one I'd choose.

Analytics aren't just relevant in the traditional "who will win?" court system. For example, they can offer a treasure trove of information about lawyers, law firms, and companies relevant at different stages and in different context throughout your professional career. For example:

✓ Looking to make a move in the job market and interviewing with a new contact? Filter analytics by attorney to get a sense of their practice area and recent cases.

✓ Thinking of outsourcing legal work as in-house counsel to an outside law firm? Explore the types of active cases a law firm has, where they most often practice, how often they win, lose, or settle, whether they more often represent plaintiffs or defendants, or how diverse (or not) a law firm is as to gender or race.

✓ Preparing a pitch to get business from a potential new corporate client, or doing research about a company that has just sued, threatened to sue, or expressed interest in buying or merging with your client? As with the example in Figure 4J using the large public company Johnson & Johnson, Party Analytics available through Fastcase®'s Docket Alarm feature (other platforms such as Monitor Suite from Thomson Reuters offer company analytics as well) reveal insights such as:

   ✓ how many new proceedings per month a company has

   ✓ what type of cases the company is involved in

   ✓ whether a company is more often a plaintiff or defendant

   ✓ what law firms a company employs

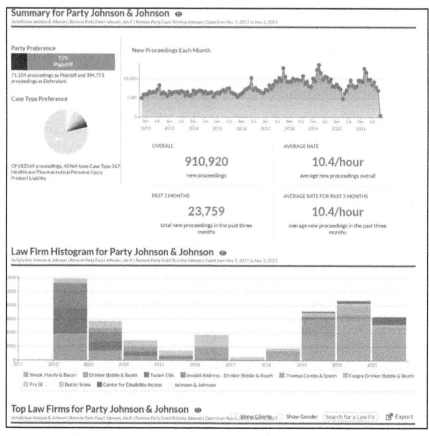

* Figure 4J: Party Analytics through Docket Alarm; reprinted with permission Fastcase®.

A modern lawyer doesn't need to be a data expert but the data spigot isn't shutting off anytime soon. Innovative technology + data is a powerful combination. Practical information will keep coming in faster, different ways. The question is whether you'll be ready to welcome and leverage it. Instead of telling clients, "I'm not sure, it depends, we'll have to wait and see," tomorrow's lawyer may consult analytics to inform a prediction (along with other relevant variables). Past analytics don't make future results certain; they are a worthwhile piece of the modern lawyer and client decision-making puzzle. Instead of "wait and see," clients may prefer and expect to hear statements such as "There's been a 20% chance of success in this jurisdiction at this juncture over the past three years and no similar case has ever survived a motion to dismiss. That data supports being open to an early settlement."

---

**LIT TIP**

"When I was a lawyer, clients would sometimes ask: "If we were to file a Motion to X, what are the odds of us winning? Like most lawyers, I would start with "In my N years of experience" and then explain chances using words like "decent," "pretty good," or "not bad." Those imprecise words are cold comfort to a data-driven client. Litigation analytics allow lawyers to give data-driven, actionable responses like:

In <DISTRICT>, judges grant <MOTIONS_TO_X> at X%.
But <JUDGE> is much worse, granting <MOTIONS_TO_X> at only Y%.
And for <AREA_OF_LAW>, that number drops to Z%.

That's data-driven lawyering. And it's the present, not the future."

Damien Riehl
Managing Director, Fastcase®

---

## Data Visualization: A Picture Is Worth . . . a Lot

Deep looks into vast amounts of information are intriguing. But not if we can't understand what we're seeing. Lawyers need to grasp patterns, trends, and take-aways without substantial time and effort. We don't want individual trees—we want the full forest, in context. Enter **data visualization**.

This general concept isn't new. Infographics and visual displays are everywhere in society bringing often dull information to life, from a simple sign on a bathroom door letting us know "no shoes, no shirt, no service" to a colorful map on the news letting us know state-by-state election results. Major news companies and newspapers have employees dedicated to visualization. No matter the level of sophistication, the goal is simple: get the message across.

Back to lawyering. In chapter 3 we touched on visuals to enhance modern document creation. As a researcher, you want your information simple and clear. You might have understood this point while reading this chapter. My description of analytics in a wordy paragraph in the section you just finished reading was just OK. I hope it hit home better when you saw the bar graph screenshot or other visual examples of analytics. A picture is worth a thousand words. Research results are no longer just words on a page. A technologically competent modern lawyer understands this and stays open to visualization tools as an effective and efficient way to turn information into patterns into sound legal advice. In 5, 10, or 15 years, it might be hard to imagine lawyers ever received research results from a boring, basic bulleted list of authorities.

One spot where innovative visualization improves the research experience is in the depiction of relationships among cases. Earlier we looked at a basic search for the elements of adverse possession. A list of cases is fine, but it's time consuming to weed through and decide what cases matter and what cases are the leading precedent. Platforms like Lexis+® offer visual displays of authority, often with a simple formula for understanding like in Figure 4K: the bigger the circle, the more we pay attention because it's been cited the most:

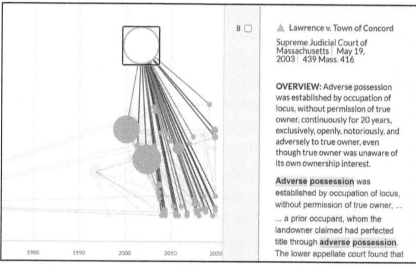

* Figure 4K: Ravel™ View; reprinted from LexisNexis with permission. Copyright 2022 LexisNexis. All rights reserved.

Visualization maps such as Ravel™ View on Lexis+® offer a way to grasp citing relationships between authorities and one way to get at what any good legal researcher craves: the big picture. In this example, when a researcher hovers over the top, largest bubble, the system gives the case name with a quick synopsis. In Figure 4K, the leading case is *Lawrence*. So rather than stumble upon the *Lawrence* case on adverse possession as a needle in the haystack of hundreds of other Massachusetts cases (or see it at the top of a numbered list and wonder if that means it's a key case), a researcher can immediately grasp its significance as influential precedent. Ravel™ View also uses displays of different color lines to indicate positive or negative case treatment. Hovering over the smaller bubbles would continue to complete the landscape of Massachusetts precedent in this area of law. From just one visualization map, a lawyer can grasp relevance, top cited cases, and a chronology or evolution of precedent across years or decades.

Visualization is one aspect of next generation research. Data is only as good as our ability to see it and combine it with our other traditional lawyering tools: precedent, creativity, careful analysis, problem solving, critical thinking, intuition, and experience. Stay abreast of future opportunities for research tools to *show* results instead of tell.

## Good News Travels Fast

A final piece to next generation research is less about how we search for information or how software gives it to us. It's about how fast it's coming.

Flashback to lawyering decades ago. Lawyers researched in the books, learned about key practice area developments through conferences, conversations, networking receptions, newspapers, or a national nightly newscast on cable television. Sometimes this new knowledge would come days after legal news, sometimes months. Fast-forward to today (and tomorrow). The information cycle is immediate. Staying "current" means current: yesterday's news is old. Clients might expect their lawyers to track trends, appeals, decisions, corporate public filings, case filings, the stock market, regulatory changes, enforcement actions, statutory amendments, executive guidance, lobbying efforts, or draft legislation. Sources of information are exploding—so too is the expectation that modern lawyers keep up and stay current.

There are many ways lawyers stay current with **legal news tracking**, just like we do in our personal lives. You follow a chef you love on Twitter if you're interested in new dessert recipes. Or you subscribe to a blog about your city's sports teams and enjoy constant feeds to your email inbox. You get real-time text alerts for a stock you have your eye on or allow "push notifications" for breaking news from your preferred news service. Modern lawyers should be proactive and take advantage of simple and strategic ways to stay "in the know."

Here are some tips to start off:

✓ Set your internet browser start (home) page to kickstart your day with preferred sources of information. Experiment with personalized dashboard tools to set up several news and research briefings alongside your email or calendar.

✓ Use networking social media platforms like Twitter or LinkedIn as sources of news and legal information from lawyers or journalists in your area of interest (more on this aspect of your online presence in chapter 10). Follow and connect with law firms, bar associations, trade groups, bloggers, legal publications, lawyers, clients, clients' competitors, public interest groups, or local organizations. Use tools like Twitter Lists to organize and prioritize tweets you see by category.

✓ Subscribe to industry e-newsletters (or similar content from lawyers in your practice area) that digest news on a topic and curate valuable content for subscribers.

✓ Set up customized alerts tailored to areas of interest through Google or as part of a paid service such as Westlaw's™ Daily Docket daily legal news summaries, Thomson Reuters Westlaw Today alerts, or Reuters Legal News.

✓ Customize a Google Alert by clicking Show Options after you've typed your search term and filter the sources you'll get, how many results, the geographic scope, and how often you want notifications. Consider a daily digest summary option instead of instant alerts.

✓ Narrow large quantities of Google Alert results to more authoritative sources by using search modifiers such as *filetype:pdf* (only returns PDF documents, often giving more robust treatment of an area of law) or *site.gov* (only returns materials from an official government website).

✓ Transactional lawyers or lawyers interested in public companies can subscribe to alerts through the United States Securities and Exchange Commission's EDGAR database, which collects submissions that companies file with the SEC. Advising a start-up company or negotiating a corporate transaction? Do your "due diligence" with an advanced investigation tool such as Tracers to explore connections among corporate entities.

✓ Take advantage of docket and legislative tracking tools that monitor activity for a case, statute, or other matter like a patent application. Customize docket checks (daily, weekly, etc.) and get alert emails with links from tools such as Lexis® CourtLink®, Westlaw™ Alerts, or Fastcase® Docket Alarm.

✓ Explore other free services to round out your research routine. Top tools lawyers use for free research (often accessible at no cost for bar association members) include Findlaw®, Cornell's Legal Information Institute, Fastcase®, government websites, Google Scholar, and CourtListener.

Information brings knowledge. Knowledge brings power. Power brings confidence. But the downside of all this information is too much of a good thing. This has the potential to be a real thorn in the modern lawyer's side because information will keep coming at a lightning pace. It's easy to get a lot of information. It's not easy to read, digest, manage, curate, and communicate it. While no good lawyer wants to miss the next big thing that relates to their practice, no good lawyer spends all day every day reading news feeds, blog posts, and Twitter chatter. Filtering scope, managing frequency, and limiting news by source, region, and type of publication can prevent information overload. So too can being purposeful about your approach, whether that's setting aside 20 minutes every morning to review current developments or using commute time to skim updates and alerts.

\* \* \* \*

We started this chapter with hypothetical lawyer Sasha doing legal research back in 2002 and fast-forwarded to her present-day approach. We'll end by reflecting on how innovation and technology will impact research in the next decade, from the topics this chapter covered to whatever exciting new development is next. Research is changing fast. As a modern lawyer looking for the best information, you're ready to change too.

---

 *Review Your Knowledge*

1) Ada's friend tells her that Chris is searching for representation in a pending malpractice case against a hospital involving injuries to his newborn son. His initial lawyer withdrew due to a conflict of interest. Chris is considering several new lawyers and Ada sets up a meeting. Ada has minimal medical malpractice experience and has never appeared before either the assigned magistrate or presiding judge. Ada seeks to grow this area of her civil litigation practice and wants to impress Chris. To prepare for the client meeting, what should Ada do?

   a) Consult with data scientists to analyze likelihood of settlement or a high monetary jury award in this jurisdiction.

   b) Look up past medical malpractice cases against any company in this jurisdiction on a case management system such as PACER and weed through hundreds of dockets to search for relevant motions and decisions.

   c) In addition to reviewing precedent, use analytics research tools with data from the jurisdiction and these judges as a starting point (maybe even this specific hospital defendant).

d) Rely on her experience and instincts alone because clients deserve personalized advice and statistics won't ever help.

2) Kenneth is a tax attorney helping a friend with a divorce. Because Kenneth has no family law experience and has never filed for one or created a settlement order, he uses an online Document Builder research tool: he filters to family law/divorce/settlement agreement, types the court (Essex County Family Court), and types spouses' names. The tool creates a divorce agreement in a Word file, and it looks to have a lot of necessary information with authority. Kenneth can't believe his good luck and how easy the process was. Is Kenneth ready to submit the divorce agreement to complete competent representation of his friend?

a) Yes, since Kenneth filtered by jurisdiction, advanced research tools ensure the agreement will comply with local rules.

b) No, because Kenneth should have used a Document Analyzer tool instead of a Document Builder to create this unfamiliar new work product.

c) No, because to be competent, Kenneth must combine use of a Document Builder with his own substantive review of the unfamiliar area of law.

d) No, because Document Builders are limited to litigation documents like motions and aren't for repetitive transactional work product.

3) Harcot Publishing is sued in Indiana for violating the Americans with Disabilities Act for its policy requiring mandatory office attendance. Employees claim work from home allowances are a reasonable accommodation for their disabilities. You are new to employment law. After reading the complaint, you type "is working from home a reas . . ." and the database shows this image from Figure 4L:

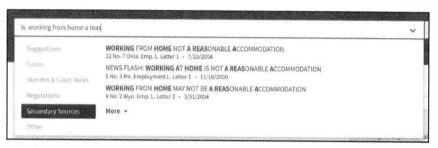

\* Figure 4L: Westlaw Edge™ screenshot; reprinted with permission from Thomson Reuters.

The problem is that:

a)    you didn't pre-filter by jurisdiction so predictive search suggestions with sources from Oklahoma, Maine, and Wyoming are not helpful.

b)    you must think critically about what software suggests you search for—that's why you went to law school and the software didn't.

c)    the predictive search algorithm jumps you to secondary sources, which aren't as helpful as the primary sources you would have found if you had used a "drag-and-drop" Document Analyzer tool instead.

d)    answers (a) and (b) are both correct.

4)    Myriah is the CFO of SecurityUSA, Inc., which develops videoconference security software. The company is well-known and is entertaining interest from larger public companies that want to buy it. Myriah is overwhelmed with the idea but wants to consider it in the future. She asks you as SecurityUSA's outside counsel to evaluate the market and to research and track potential buyers before negotiations begin. Your workload is already stretching you thin and you aren't sure how to fit this in or where to start. Your best approach might be to:

a)    use the list of companies Myriah provides and set up email notifications from the Securities and Exchange Commission (SEC) for every public filing any of the companies make, and ensure those come to your email inbox to review daily.

    b)   set up SEC email notifications for the companies, but only for key annual documents that offer real insight, such as a Form 10-K annual report.

    c)   combine SEC notifications of key filings with a general search engine alert to capture additional market insight research and news-clipping services, and set up an automatic email rule to filter it to company-specific email folders you create to avoid inbox clutter and stay organized.

    d)   continue your general practice of spending weekend time reading the major newspapers and magazines in the financial and security software space, and be careful to pay attention or take notes if you get lucky and spot any of the companies Myriah is tracking.

5)   Decker is a general practitioner at a medium-size law firm in New Jersey. He receives a panicked call from a former client. They are worried about whether they may be on the hook for injuries stemming from a drunk-driving car crash yesterday after an intoxicated guest left a party they hosted. Decker promises to do some quick research and call back that same day. Decker searches "social host liability in New Jersey" online and skims a few practice guides and blogs for the general rules but wants to double-check key case law. He notices a chart at the bottom of his screen that appears to give a visual, scatter-plot type of map of the most important cases. It shows three primary clusters circling around three recent cases from New Jersey's highest court. The best next step for Decker to take is:

    a)   review the three cases and call the client for a preliminary discussion, so long as the cases reinforce his understanding of social host liability from secondary authority.

    b)   ignore the case visualization because he is still at the early stage of research and visualization and case mapping tools only apply as a final "check" near the end of the research process.

    c)   review the three cases but manually update them and review many other cases too, given that Decker must think critically and can't be fooled into relying on an algorithm's visual indications of what the key sources might be.

d)   screenshot the visualization chart and email it to the client to keep costs down and get them the information fast.

---

 *Practice Your Knowledge*

## Exercise #1: Pick a Judge Analytics

Experiment with an analytics tool on any legal research platform you can access. Select a federal district court judge in your home state or state where you attend school. Search for that judge and filter the available analytics in different ways. Do some digging. Pretend you are preparing for a new client meeting in that district with a case pending before that judge. Prepare a few bullet points of information about the judge, such as time to resolution for certain types of matters or granting tendencies for pretrial motions.

## Exercise #2: Legal News Alerts

Set up two different legal news-tracking tools from the tips in this chapter for an area of law or subject that interests you or is relevant to a class, job, internship, application, or interview. Give some attention to ways to narrow, curate, and organize the content such as a daily feed instead of instant email notification.

---

 *Expand Your Knowledge*

➤   Sean La Roque-Doherty, *Not All Litigation Analytics Products Are Created Equal*, ABA Journal (2020) https://www.abajournal.com/magazine/article/analytics-products-offer-different-results-depending-on-data-sources-quality-and-the-types-of-analytics-and-reports-they-provide [https://perma.cc/4JNZ-YHSZ].

➤ Paul D. Callister, *Law, Artificial Intelligence, and Natural Language Processing: A Funny Thing Happened on the Way to My Search Results*, 112 LAW LIBR. J. 161 (2020).

➤ *Data in Court*, HARVARD LAW (2022), https://thepractice. law.harvard.edu/article/data-in-the-court/ [https://perma.cc/ R7BQ-9PXQ].

*Answers & Explanations*

*Knowledge Kickoff*

d) Samantha's approach is imperfect. It's not outright wrong, but she doesn't execute her tasks in the best way. While every legal research project need not always involve latest-and-greatest technology at every stage, in this example Samantha's approaches don't take advantage of any advanced tools such as Document Analyzers, enhanced natural language search technology, or legal analytics. A modern lawyer with full awareness of advanced research technologies could likely achieve similar substantive results with less time and ad hoc effort and greater reliability and confidence.

*Review Your Knowledge*

1) c) A modern legal researcher need not become or consult a data scientist but shouldn't ignore data as part of the process. One-off review of docket information from this court would be unnecessarily time-consuming and costly. Experience and instincts are relevant but can be combined with verifiable data. Individual advice can still be data-driven. Using analytics to inform strategy and help predict things like damages, settlement, motion practice, or budget is Ada's best approach to impress Chris.

2) c) Kenneth's use of a Document Builder tool for a transactional document is a fantastic start—but even the most tech-savvy modern lawyer can't 100% outsource a task to this tool. Kenneth must pair the "nuts and bolts" of a draft file that his software creates with his own foundational understanding of divorce law. Technology is only as good as its user. A research tool gives Kenneth basic ingredients but he should do more to ensure the agreement is sound and tailored to the client's situation in this jurisdiction.

3) d) Predictive type-ahead search features in real time are a helpful modern research tool to find information fast and consider ideas you might not have first thought of. But like many new tools, they're only as good as the

approach you take. Fundamental research basics (such as pre-filtering your jurisdiction and starting with secondary sources instead of narrower primary sources) don't get abandoned just because AI-enhanced search technology makes the process look more seamless than it is.

4) c) Staying current means different things for the modern lawyer, but receiving daily email alerts of every filing into your inbox would be overbroad and annoying. It would also make it more likely relevant information gets overlooked and lost in the shuffle. Targeted news and filing alerts from a variety of online sources is the best approach, especially when paired with an efficient email rule that keeps them organized. Casual weekend news skimming won't impress Myriah when she asks to discuss these companies.

5) a) Sometimes things are as easy as they seem, and data visualization of research results often are. For general rules and leading principles, case mapping visuals can give a modern lawyer what they need fast. It's not a shortcut; it's an efficient starting line. If this matter moved forward, Decker would dive into the precedent and factual nuances. Reading lots of potentially irrelevant cases would not be a good use of Decker's time for the immediate task at hand. Healthy skepticism is always welcome, but so is an appropriate level of trust. Using at-a-glance tools at the outset can replace hours of expensive effort that would bring you to the same research place.

## Endnotes

1   NOAH WAISBERG & DR. ALEXANDER HUDEK, AI FOR LAWYERS 116 (Wiley, 1st ed. 2021).

2   COMPOSE, https://compose.law/ [https://perma.cc/3365-5LM7].

3   ED WALTERS, DATA-DRIVEN LAW: DATA ANALYTICS & THE NEW LEGAL SERVICES 5 (Auerbach Publications, 1st ed. 2018).

4   Legal Analytics for Federal Appellate Litigation, LEX MACHINA, https://lexmachina.com/practice-areas/federal-appellate-litigation/ [https://perma.cc/KGQ9-66 B8].

CHAPTER 5

# ELECTRONICALLY STORED INFORMATION (ESI)

*Core Concepts*

| | |
|---|---|
| *custodial-level data* *enterprise-level data* *electronic discovery reference model (EDRM)* *legal hold* *technology assisted review (TAR)* | *predictive coding* *redaction* *privilege log* *metadata* *fact management software* |

*Knowledge Kickoff*

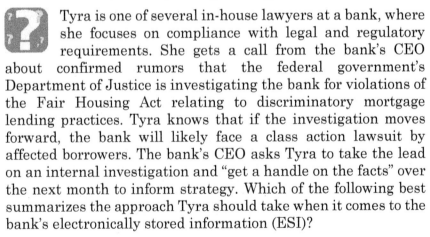 Tyra is one of several in-house lawyers at a bank, where she focuses on compliance with legal and regulatory requirements. She gets a call from the bank's CEO about confirmed rumors that the federal government's Department of Justice is investigating the bank for violations of the Fair Housing Act relating to discriminatory mortgage lending practices. Tyra knows that if the investigation moves forward, the bank will likely face a class action lawsuit by affected borrowers. The bank's CEO asks Tyra to take the lead on an internal investigation and "get a handle on the facts" over the next month to inform strategy. Which of the following best summarizes the approach Tyra should take when it comes to the bank's electronically stored information (ESI)?

a) Tyra should talk to key bank employees but there is no immediate duty to preserve electronic evidence; the bank can wait for a formal DOJ action or civil lawsuit to avoid a premature and expensive collection.

b) Tyra should talk to key bank employees and instruct each one to send her via email any data potentially

  relevant to the allegation, but only data stored on a
  bank-issued computer or device.

c)   Tyra should outsource this to experts and immediately
     hire a third-party vendor to take over the investigation
     by interviewing key bank employees and locating and
     reviewing potentially relevant data.

d)   Tyra should promptly issue a legal hold notice to any
     employee or department likely to have potentially
     relevant information (whether on a bank-issued or
     personal device), interview custodians about facts and
     the location of data, and work alongside a third-party
     vendor to ensure preservation, collection, and review of
     ESI.

---

The world creates a lot of information. By world, I mean all of
us. Around 2.5 quintillion bytes of data every day, if we're
getting specific. If you wonder how much a quintillion is, so do I.
There are 18 zeros in the number. It's big. And it's getting bigger.
And it's electronic. You've probably heard of gigabytes of
electronic information—today we're talking zettabytes of
electronic data in our world. Sure, children still fingerpaint
pictures on a poster and I still take notes with a pencil on a
yellow legal pad sometimes. But the overwhelming amount of
society's data comes with every email, text, message, file, tweet,
picture, post, video, recording, spreadsheet, voicemail, and
calendar entry we (and our billions of computers) create.

ESI touches almost every modern lawyer in some form. Lawyers
need information for hundreds of reasons, such as to:

  ✓   prove a fact at a civil trial

  ✓   prepare a witness for deposition or testimony (or
      prepare to cross-examine)

  ✓   advise a client on a proposed business transaction

  ✓   gauge whether a corporation committed a financial
      crime

✓   decide whether to advise a client to take action or settle

✓   determine whether someone violated a client's intellectual property rights

✓   persuade a regulator that a merger doesn't run afoul of antitrust laws

✓   provide a criminal defendant their constitutional right to a defense

This chapter summarizes what ESI looks like and the contexts in which modern lawyers navigate it. A subset of ESI is e-discovery. E-discovery is a key phrase you've probably heard before, and we'll spend some of this chapter on that topic. But a discussion of e-discovery in the traditional plaintiff v. defendant litigation context is too narrow. Broaden your mindset to the concept of ESI more generally. ESI is relevant in countless legal and business matters. I'll start a brainstorming list but we could add hundreds of scenarios:

| | |
|---|---|
| ✓  internal corporate investigations | ✓  incident response |
| ✓  subpoena responses | ✓  risk management |
| ✓  privacy disclosures | ✓  cybersecurity data breach analysis |
| ✓  criminal prosecutions and defense | ✓  information governance |
| ✓  compliance | ✓  corporate negotiations and transactions |
| ✓  FOIA (Freedom of Information Act) records requests | ✓  government inquiries, investigations, reviews, and approvals |

ESI presents opportunities and challenges. We'll address the topic from many angles and with hypothetical examples, taking a workflow/timeline approach:

1) First, what is ESI? What are the types? How and where is ESI stored?

2) Second, why do lawyers need it, and how do they help others preserve, collect, review, and do something with it?

3)    Third, are there rules that apply to the exchange of ESI? Who do lawyers ask for help with ESI, and what tools do they use to review and produce it all?

4)    Finally, what are the common pitfalls and traps to watch out for with ESI?

That's a lot to tackle in one chapter. Your school might have an entire course on e-discovery; we'll try to cover ESI in a handful of pages. It's an overview. You aren't becoming an ESI expert. You're becoming more confident and aware of how it's likely to touch your future law practice. At the end of this chapter, you'll understand basics about these introductory questions and be well positioned to gain more knowledge, experience, and skill with ESI as your career advances.

## What's ESI?

Let's start exploring ESI with a real investigation many readers might remember from the news. In 2021, a United States Congressional Committee started an investigation into the January 6, 2021 demonstrations and violent attacks at the United States Capitol in the aftermath of the presidential election between Joe Biden and Donald Trump. The Congressional Committee used its subpoena power to seek information from many individuals and companies in the form of documents, materials, and communications. But what exactly did it want? What exactly do those broad categories mean in today's modern world?

It wanted ESI. Not too long ago, businesses and people relied on things like filing cabinets and manila office folders to store information. Today, millions of pages from a filing cabinet could be stored on a computer drive the size of my thumb. I probably have more data on my own smartphone than an entire small company might have had 15 years ago. As the volume of ESI and the speed at which we create it explodes, so too does the number of different types of this documentary evidence (as opposed to oral testimonial evidence). In the congressional investigation example, ESI might be in any or all of these sources from companies and individuals:

| | |
|---|---|
| ✓ emails, calendars, memos, summaries | ✓ records from virtual collaboration tools such as Zoom, MS Teams, Slack, and Google Meet |
| ✓ video communications | |
| ✓ texts and instant messages | ✓ records from social media companies such as Twitter and Facebook |
| ✓ digital time stamps and other metadata for media | ✓ cell phone GPS location data |
| ✓ photographs | ✓ smart device history such as from an Apple Watch or home personal assistant |
| ✓ call logs, recordings, voicemails | |
| ✓ ephemeral data like "snaps" from Snapchat | ✓ web search history and activity |
| ✓ unmanned aerial vehicle data (drones) | |

These examples come to life in our real-life congressional investigation scenario: what if GPS cellular location data from a key political official put them near the United States Capitol Building on that day? What if two individuals used a messaging system that revealed surprise at what was occurring? What if incoming and outgoing call logs shed light on communication failures or who knew what and when? What if a video posted to social media revealed an individual suspect was at home that day, far away from Washington D.C.?

Collecting legal information in the 21st century doesn't involve searching through a file cabinet or stack of printed emails. Society is electronic; relevant legal facts are too. Let's define ESI as any information stored electronically. That's simple, but the ins and outs of where lawyers find ESI is not.

Start thinking about ESI by the two primary levels where it might exist: the custodial level and the enterprise level. **Custodial-level data** means something created, obtained by, and stored by a person—a custodian—whether on their computer, mobile device, in the cloud, or removable media such as a USB flash drive. An individual custodian with traditional ESI has control over their files such as emails, spreadsheets, word-processing documents, and presentation slides. In contrast, **enterprise-level data** is everything "behind the scenes" that users might share in an organization or business group. Examples include ESI such as billing or customer records, internal records management documents, or anything else generally under the control of organizational management instead of individual users. Individual custodians with custodial-level data often have no idea what additional ESI exists at the broader enterprise level. Sometimes data can be a bit of both; for example, internal organizational messaging services like Slack let users store messages locally on their computer but are also typically managed and tracked by an organization's information technology (IT) department. Or you might have emails saved locally on your computer, but an organization could use backup tapes that automatically back up your system every day to an enterprise storage network location—or more commonly today, in the cloud. Pause here to think of an organization you might have worked at before or during law school—in your day-to-day work, you created and stored custodian data, but chances are good that you also created or accessed enterprise data stored as part of a larger business unit.

---

**LIT TIP**

<u>custodial-level data</u>: ESI a person creates, obtains, possesses, or stores (e.g., the data custodian of an email is the owner of the email mailbox)

<u>enterprise-level data</u>: ESI that is "behind the scenes" and centralized that might be shared by users in an organizational or business group level (e.g., entries in a sales database accessed by hundreds of employees)

---

Now that we've reviewed ESI sources, think about why it can overwhelm lawyers. How much ESI there is in a legal matter will vary but the trend is a clear upward trajectory. Even when society moved beyond hard-copy paper documents decades ago, the early days of ESI started off slowly. An individual custodian working at a company 10 or 15 years ago might have had about 1 gigabyte of ESI. In terms we might understand from experience with our own device data storage plans, that might mean a few hundred thousand messages or emails, a few hours of video, a few hundred streaming music files, and maybe a few thousand pictures. Today, though, an average individual custodian with ESI has far more, closer to 20 gigabytes. Larger organizations will have terabytes of ESI—1 terabyte is equal to 1,024 gigabytes, and a few terabytes of electronic data is the rough equivalent of several million pages stored in over 100,000 cardboard boxes. I'm not sure we can grasp exactly how much that is, but it's a lot. We create all these emails, texts, pictures, videos, files, and messages using more platforms than ever before: computer, smart device, mobile phone, mobile tablet, mobile applications, mobile wearables, etc. Types of ESI data and their source locations are skyrocketing.

Not only do we create more data and use more platforms to do so, we also enjoy an easier time storing it all. Stockpiling vast amounts of ESI used to be expensive and tedious. Would you advise a client to pay expensive monthly warehouse rent charges to store boxes and boxes of paper documents for hundreds of different matters? But today, anyone who has signed up for an iCloud account or other cloud-based storage tools knows it's easier and less expensive than ever to empty that file cabinet or thick photo album and hold on to mounds of electronic information. Think of every email you've ever written or received—if you printed out a gigabyte worth of email, you'd likely fill the bed of a pickup truck!

Companies face pressure to get a handle on this big data. Instead of having different departments such as IT or records management working in silos, there is a trend toward consolidated and cohesive information governance. Clients need lawyers to be proactive and forward-thinking about managing and reducing overwhelming volumes of ESI—not only for traditional litigation or investigation purposes but for other aspects of business such as compliance obligations, records retention requirements, or responsiveness to potential security breaches and data loss (more on this in chapter 9).

With that general introduction to what ESI is and why society has so much of it, how does a lawyer think about collecting it?

## ESI Holds & ESI Requests

Lawyers play defense and offense with ESI. By defense, I mean lawyers help clients identify, preserve, and produce their own ESI to others. By offense, I mean lawyers seek ESI of others. Both get referenced under the loose umbrella term "discovery," but that varies with different scenarios. No matter the terminology, a modern lawyer needs a foundational understanding of how to get ESI and communicate with others about it.

Let's examine ESI exchange using another hypothetical, this time in the traditional plaintiff v. defendant context. You represent a public transportation company that operates city subways and buses. Suppose a tragic accident involves a subway train and a person standing near the tracks who gets severely injured. That person sues your client and a month later requests electronic information related to things like subway operations, past mechanical issues, 911 calls, and employee communications before and after the accident. In this context, you're at the starting line of discovery: the pretrial process of obtaining evidence. Discovery is about getting information that will shape the path a case takes, whether that information is from a client, an opposing party, or a third party you've subpoenaed.

Today, all discovery is e-discovery. In this hypothetical negligence lawsuit, a lawyer would need to seek ESI from others (the injured plaintiff) but also help hold, collect, review, and produce it from the transportation company. We're just at the starting line but seeing the big picture of this traditional path of ESI in a matter is important.

One well-known visual overview of the different stages of this process seen is Figure 5A is known as the **EDRM: Electronic Discovery Reference Model**.

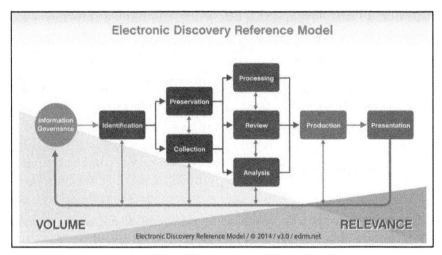

* Figure 5A: EDRM graphic; reprinted from edrm.net with permission under Creative Commons 4.0 License.

The EDRM visual lays out context for what actions a lawyer might take and the people, services, processes, and tools that may be necessary along the way. As a modern lawyer likely to work with ESI, you might do so at each of these EDRM stages in order, at only one of them, or at all of them at different times in a different order. Maybe a client engages you at the outset of a matter to identify potentially relevant ESI, or engages you at the end to help with final presentation of the facts drawn from ESI.

Back to ESI defense and offense. Let's start with defense. In our hypothetical, you would collect ESI from the transportation company to help answer critical questions such as whether anyone knew of mechanical defects, whether there had been prior complaints, whether the train's "black box" system recorded speed, or whether the driver admitted to misconduct. Before you collect, though, you must help your client avoid losing ESI. This critical first step is known as identification and preservation. Lawyers work with clients to identify where potentially relevant ESI is and where it might be. As you might imagine, who has what ESI, and where, ranges widely. It might be a handful of individual custodians' computers, or 30 individuals' phones, tablets, cloud storage, and computers, or an entire company's internal network of data storage. In our transportation company lawsuit, you'd work with the client's internal IT employees (and likely the company's internal legal team, too) to understand how ESI is kept and by whom.

After identification comes the duty of preservation. This is a critical ethical obligation. If you held physical evidence in the palm of your hand, most readers would realize it would be unethical to throw it in the trash. The same is true of ESI. While we can't "hold" a client's ESI in our hands, lawyers must treat it with similar care and prevent its destruction or loss. This duty kicks in once a lawyer knows of, or reasonably should anticipate, litigation (or an investigation or subpoena, as the case may be in other contexts).

The duty to preserve is akin to pressing the pause button. Lawyers do this by way of something called a **legal hold**.

---

**LIT TIP**

A legal hold is a formal notification to a person, entire organization, or certain individuals instructing recipients not to delete ESI (or destroy paper documents). A legal hold may also be referred to as a litigation hold, hold order, preservation order, preservation notice, or document preservation demand.

---

Legal holds preserve the status quo because identifying and collecting ESI takes time. They seek to find a middle ground between holding onto every piece of ESI on the one hand, and continuing deletion and other routine business practices that dispose of ESI in the normal course on the other hand. For example, legal holds don't mean a custodian can't ever delete a text message from a friend about the latest sports score in a big game or a funny personal email chain. The duty of preservation allows a lawyer to focus custodians on broad categories of data that might relate to a matter. In our hypothetical, individuals at the transportation company could go about their daily business but be instructed either by outside lawyers or an in-house legal team not to delete ESI involving things such as mechanical train operation, communications about the accident, and complaints.

Legal holds aren't a one-and-done, set-it-and-forget-it task. Throughout the life of a matter, lawyers must work with their clients to:

- ✓ monitor compliance with the hold
- ✓ require custodian acknowledgments of the hold
- ✓ issue regular reminders and updates
- ✓ communicate with IT professionals about potential new sources of data
- ✓ update the hold to add new custodians, document categories, or topics as a matter develops
- ✓ consider reaching out to third parties for ESI that isn't necessarily under a client's control but may be discoverable and relevant, such as social media or other app-based messaging tools custodians use to communicate

Navigating legal holds is not a light undertaking. A lawyer might have multiple clients with multiple custodians under multiple legal holds from multiple matters at any given time, who use multiple tools for their daily work. That's a lot of multiples!

---

**LIT TIP**

A lawyer's duty to preserve ESI does not require them to ask clients to retain "every shred of paper, every email or electronic document, and every backup tape[,]" but extends to "those employees likely to have relevant information—the 'key players' in the case." Once the duty to preserve kicks in based on the reasonable anticipation of a legal matter, lawyers must advise clients to issue a litigation hold and "suspend [their] routine document retention/destruction policy" to ensure relevant documents are preserved.[1]

*Zubulake v. UBS Warburg* (groundbreaking ESI decision)

---

Sounds daunting, right? It can be, but lawyers rarely go at it alone unless it's a straightforward hold with one or two custodians. For larger clients and matters, a lawyer will often work with IT professionals to weed through technical details of where and how ESI is stored and how to stop potential destruction of it. For example, if a corporation routinely deletes electronic backup tapes of its files at the end of every week, a lawyer would need to uncover that practice and discuss whether it needed to be modified or suspended. Other lawyers might have the benefit of specialized e-discovery attorneys and technologists at their own firm or organization. Lawyers aren't the IT experts. That's OK. But they do need to know enough to work with those experts. A technologically competent modern lawyer must recognize when a legal hold of ESI is necessary and be motivated to ask the right questions of the right people to prompt the wheels to move in the right direction.

If legal holds are the defense, the offense is ESI requests. This is when lawyers seek ESI from someone they don't represent. To do so, they must be familiar with what ESI is and where and how it might be kept. In the transportation company hypothetical, this might be requesting ESI from the injured patron or ESI from a third party such as a store with security video footage. Playing offense for ESI isn't always adversarial. You might request ESI from a company your client is considering licensing its intellectual property to. You might request ESI from a company that is negotiating a potential merger with your client. You might request ESI in the context of agreeing to damages as a condition to a civil settlement or criminal plea bargain.

Litigation requests for ESI come in the form of Requests for Production of Documents ("RFP") sent to the opposing client and lawyer. RFPs define "documents, materials, and communications" broadly to encompass all types and sources of ESI. In a different context such as a proposed business transaction, a lawyer might call this a Due Diligence Request ("due diligence" is a catch-all term describing fact investigation and "digging" done before entering into a transaction, such as reviewing someone's finances before forming a business partnership). In another context, the government might issue a subpoena for documents in an investigative proceeding. In all of these situations, the goal is to cast as wide a net as possible.

The next LIT TIP offers an example of how the Securities and Exchange Commission might define the term "document" in one of its subpoenas—it leaves little to the imagination!

> ### LIT TIP
>
> "The term "document" in the context of a production responsive to a subpoena includes, but is not limited to, any written, printed, or typed matter in the possession, custody or control of the subpoenaed entity or individual including, but not limited to all drafts and copies bearing notations or marks not found in the original, letters and correspondence, interoffice communications, slips, tickets, records, worksheets, financial records, accounting documents, bookkeeping documents, memoranda, reports, manuals, telephone logs, telegrams, facsimiles, messages of any type, telephone messages, voice mails, tape recordings, notices, instructions, minutes, summaries, notes of meetings, file folder markings, and any other organizational indicia, purchase orders, information recorded by photographic process, including microfilm and microfiche, computer printouts, spreadsheets, and other electronically stored information, including but not limited to writings, drawings, graphs, charts, photographs, sound recordings, images, and other data or data compilations that are stored in any medium from which information can be retrieved, obtained, manipulated, or translated."[2]
>
> United States Securities and Exchange Commission

ESI requests like the one from the SEC are broad, but they aren't open fishing expeditions. No party, government or private, is entitled to anything and everything they might want from someone, no matter the expense or burden in obtaining it. Lawyers requesting and providing ESI must remember two key considerations: proportionality and reasonableness. Preservation, collection, review, and production of ESI is no small feat. It's expensive, time consuming, distracting, and burdensome. Both proportionality and reasonableness involve a cost-benefit analysis by lawyers, clients, regulators, courts, and just about anyone who might be involved in a matter with ESI. This analysis balances the needs of the case and potential importance of the ESI with the burden and expense in finding, reviewing, and producing it. Some ESI may be easy to get but of minimal relevance. In contrast, some ESI is difficult to get but of paramount importance.

Modern lawyers discuss ESI at the outset of a matter and aim for agreement as to their obligations. Courts are hesitant to get involved in this party-driven process, but there is no shortage of guidance and suggestions. For example, in the federal court system, Fed. R. Civ. P. 26(f) requires attorneys to meet and confer on "issues about disclosure, discovery, or preservation of [ESI], including the form or forms in which it should be produced." Fed. R. Civ. P. 26(b)(2)(B) specifies that a party "need not provide discovery of [ESI] from sources that the party identifies as not reasonably accessible because of undue burden or cost." Many state rules have similar provisions.

Parties routinely negotiate and enter into agreements and protocols about exchanging ESI. Some courts even supply model stipulated ESI orders for parties to modify. Government agencies and local Attorney General offices often have standard templates and guidance documents for ESI requests. The United States Department of Justice Antitrust Division, the Federal Trade Commission, the Internal Revenue Service, and the SEC all issue public materials relating to ESI. There's even a well-known working group project called the Sedona Conference, started back in 2002, which continuously publishes foundational guidance, principles, and best practices. Many modern lawyers recognize Sedona Conference materials as one go-to source for everything ESI.

ESI agreements set expectations. They spell out what will—and what won't—be preserved, prioritized, and collected, as well as how it will be reviewed, produced, redacted, withheld, labeled, and quality-checked. Such agreements usually also include how the parties will treat confidential or privileged ESI or what they will do upon inadvertent disclosure. Most parties agree to some sort of "clawback" provision mandating return of mistakenly produced ESI and no resulting waiver of the attorney-client privilege.

Done well, ESI agreements ensure consistency and proportionality and keep expenses predictable (remember the entire EDRM workflow timeline might last not weeks but months or years). Not done well, these agreements become the subject of dispute (usually in pretrial demand correspondence and motion practice) and courts are forced to break up the logjams.

**LIT TIP**

"The discovery of [ESI] provides many benefits such as the ability to
search, organize, and target the ESI using the text and associated data.
At the same time, the Court is aware that the discovery of ESI is a
potential source of cost, burden, and delay . . . an attorney's zealous
representation of a client is not compromised by conducting discovery in a
cooperative manner. Cooperation in reasonably limiting ESI discovery
requests on the one hand, and in reasonably responding to ESI discovery
requests on the other hand, tends to reduce litigation costs and delay."[3]

United States District Court Northern District of California

We aren't done yet. After a lawyer discusses ESI obligations with their client, other lawyers, third parties, investigators, or regulators, and then communicates holds and makes requests, then the real work begins to figure out what the ESI reveals.

## Team Detective: Collect, Process, Review, Produce—Repeat

In 2016, weeks before the presidential election between Donald Trump and Hilary Clinton, allegations came forward that then Secretary of State Clinton used a private email server for government work. The FBI reviewed about 650,000 emails in less than one week. The FBI didn't do that by having Secretary Clinton print out emails and deliver them in boxes. It didn't have federal agents thumb through each one and take notes on a legal pad. It didn't have a group of agents sit in a conference room 24 hours a day clicking through every individual file or doing random, manual keyword searches.

What the FBI *did* do is use the best technology available to it at the time to streamline its review of this ESI. Technology and ESI go hand in hand. Today, advanced AI tools designed for ESI help lawyers make sense of millions of electronic pages and files. While we can't dive too far into how these tools work in just one chapter, some foundational awareness of this critical stage of work with ESI is a must-have.

Warning: this stretch of the Electronic Discovery Reference Model (EDRM) timeline is quite technical. That's why I term this "Team Detective." Lawyers rarely do this work alone; there is no one-size-fits-all approach. There are hundreds of different e-discovery providers and vendors who support ESI processes. It's a multibillion-dollar industry and growing. Some smaller clients or law firms will outsource this process and pay a third-party vendor to assist with ESI processing, review, and production. Other clients and law firms may keep it "in house" and buy or license software designed to help users process, review, and produce ESI. Some clients and lawyers might do both at different times and for different matters, depending on the complexity and ESI volume (or lack thereof). No matter the approach, a common thread is that you as a modern lawyer will be involved and keep a lead role. Vendors, e-discovery specialists, IT professionals, and other technologists are vital to a lawyer's success navigating ESI—but they don't replace your constant involvement, supervision, and high-level direction and strategy.

First off, ESI must be collected and processed. Lawyers need to get it in a usable form. Sometimes this is simple—like having a custodian do a keyword search of emails and computer files and save potentially relevant documents to a network server (this self-collection method is common but rife with opportunities for error and not the soundest approach). Often it's much more complex. Lawyers work with technicians and experts to "image" ESI (copy it). This is called forensic collection and involves specialists with sophisticated tools that can, for example, uncover deleted data, reveal evidence that ESI has been tampered with, or get at otherwise hard-to-find "hidden" files. Then the data needs to be processed, meaning run through software that extracts metadata about the ESI and converts it into a format that allows it to be loaded into an application or some digital space where ESI gets "hosted" and, ultimately, analyzed and reviewed.

After collection and processing comes review. This is often known as "document review" but we know ESI includes more than traditional documents. In the EDRM workflow, ESI review usually takes lawyers the most time and costs clients the most money. It's not a spot to cut corners. Comprehensive review of ESI to determine what it reveals is critical. Remember, you might review your own client's ESI before producing it to someone else (pre-production review) or also review someone else's ESI that has been produced to you. Reviewing ESI is difficult because so much can be irrelevant "background noise" that nonetheless gets captured in broad collection efforts.

Approaches to ESI review take varied paths. Years ago, the traditional approach was a page-by-page review by human lawyers. That was and still is expensive, slow, inaccurate, and challenging. Human review is still alive and well in many contexts but modern lawyers take advantage of assisted technology to explore ESI. These tools create a big digital sandbox for lawyers to sift through large volumes of data. For example, ESI software can help:

- ✓ organize thousands of documents into chronological order

- ✓ "de-duplicate" files to narrow down volume and eliminate the burden of reviewing copies of the same file

- ✓ filter data to "hits" of key search terms, custodians, date ranges, and file types

- ✓ skip between file types such as from a text message to an email, then to a spreadsheet

- ✓ run advanced search term reports and bundle categories of documents

- ✓ keep "file families" together, such as an email (the parent) and its attachments (the children) or a single-conversation email "thread"

- ✓ track review and production progress so lawyers can budget, plan, and gauge completion

- ✓ reveal data gaps that might signal mistakes (such as zero documents from a key custodian or zero documents from a significant time period)

Different vendors offer tools to aid ESI review. One such tool is DISCO e-discovery, from Austin, TX-based CS Disco, Inc. Figure 5B is a screenshot of the tool in action: the center of the screenshot shows the "Fw: Super Bowl Story" file a lawyer is reviewing (note at the top this is document #1 of 36,746 files). To the left when viewing the document, you'll see category decisions a lawyer uses in review, such as Non-Responsive or Responsive. To the right of the document is document data such as whether it has other "family members" (such as an attachment), the file's custodian, when the document was sent and received, and even the file path where the file was stored at the time of collection:

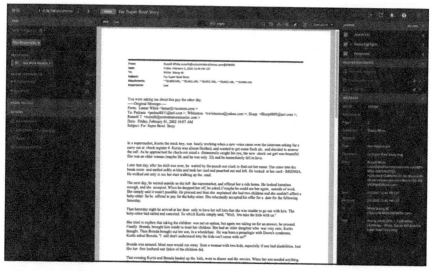

\* Figure 5B: DISCO e-discovery review; reprinted with permission. © 2012–2021 CS Disco, Inc. All rights reserved.

ESI review helps lawyers make sense of a large volume of material, find evidence, decide what to produce, and get at the truth of a set of facts. Lawyers use different electronic systems you might think of as virtual sticky notes to organize and classify using certain designations. The first and most important designation is often a Responsive/Non-Responsive choice, where Responsive means responsive to a particular request (also often called Relevant/Not Relevant). Lawyers also review, mark, and "tag" documents using basic or custom classifications such as:

- ✓ Needs Further Review
- ✓ Privileged/Non-Privileged
- ✓ Attorney Work Product
- ✓ Redaction
- ✓ Confidential/Non-Confidential

✓ "Hot" Document

✓ Content Type

✓ Notes for key custodians or legal issues

Like many spots in this book, ESI review brings modern AI technology into play (remember Need to Know #8 from chapter 2). **Technology Assisted Review (TAR)** algorithms to help with ESI have been around since about 2010 and they keep getting better, faster, smarter, and more common. TAR is computer software that helps categorize documents akin to how a human would. There are two basic variations, TAR 1.0 and TAR 2.0.

TAR 1.0 is tied to the phrase **predictive coding**. A human lawyer with knowledge of the case works with a small set of ESI by marking ("tagging") whether files are Responsive/Non-Responsive, Privileged/Non-Privileged, etc. Based on those choices, the software learns to identify Responsive/Non-Responsive documents and can help predict responsiveness for the rest of the large volume of ESI. Think of TAR 1.0 as a predictive ranking system: it scores the likelihood of responsiveness for each document on a scale of 0 to 100, and a lawyer decides from that point whether to review only documents above a particular "cut-off" score, or review only a particular subset.

TAR 2.0, the newer variation, is known as "continuous active learning." It also relies on tagging from human lawyers, but as its name suggests, it is based on ongoing input rather than a lawyer tagging a static set of documents and then using that to predict responsiveness for the whole as with TAR 1.0. TAR 2.0 typically involves a larger group of lawyers tagging documents for responsiveness. As they do so, the algorithm continually evolves and refines its identification of responsive documents, "pushing" a smaller subset of ESI front and center for the lawyers to review first.

This is an oversimplified summary of very complex technology. The key is that lawyers aren't outsourcing entire ESI reviews to machines. They're working with them. Lawyers make important legal decisions at every step to ensure the defensibility of the process they, and their clients, use. Besides the initial training, lawyers must still track, test, quality-control, and validate the entire process. The more lawyers train and improve an algorithm in an ESI tool, the better it "understands" what's relevant. Many standard Discovery Orders and Joint Protective Orders discussed earlier include provisions about the use of TAR; for example, what statistical recall and precision rates need to be met or at what stage parties may forgo manual review of documents that software has coded as responsive. Turning over thousands or millions of client files after reviewing only a portion of them probably sounds risky; think of the entire review process and the use of TAR as a balance. It's much riskier (plus unduly burdensome and expensive) to have big groups of different error-prone human—often junior—lawyers take months to glance at every file in a review set and make inconsistent and sometimes wrong decisions about whether to produce. With careful safeguards and a modern lawyer ready and willing to ask for help and rely on expert technologists, advanced AI technology for reviewing ESI is here to stay.

---

### LIT TIP

"Technology Assisted Review—whether it's TAR 1.0 predictive coding or TAR 2.0 continuous active learning—is critical to a lawyer's ability to get at the key evidence in any case and to fulfill discovery obligations. The proliferation of data in the last 10 years makes traditional document-by-document review impractical, if not impractically costly, in many cases. I've used TAR for massive multi-district litigation, internal investigations, data breaches, and pre-merger diligence. Every attorney, regardless of their specific practice area, should have some understanding of it."

Jessica Tseng Hasen
Senior Counsel, E-Discovery Services & Strategy
Perkins Coie LLP

---

The usual final step in the ESI life cycle is production. Clients and lawyers must do something with the ESI. If not already the subject of an agreement, lawyers must decide in what file format to produce responsive documents (usually .pdf, .tiff, or "native" type). Native file format is the original format in which it was first created; for example, a Microsoft® Word document by default has a .docx file extension. A .tiff file extension means the file is in a tagged image file format, more akin to a picture.

Lawyers can face dilemmas about what to do with problematic file types that don't print well (spreadsheets are a common one) and ensure organization of files with unique identifiers for each (Bates numbering is the traditional term for identifying produced files). Production of ESI is often "rolling." That is, lawyers negotiate a schedule for different custodians or sets of data at different times instead of doing one large "data dump." This can be strategically advantageous over the course of a long matter and helps lawyers identify and remedy ESI production problems sooner rather than later.

Finally, production helps you and your client, too. Yes, you are giving away relevant ESI from your client to someone else as you may be obligated or want to do. But advanced technology helps lawyers make internal sense of their final sets of ESI to better understand and structure a case, settlement position, strategy, plea deal, or other response. For example, platforms can help lawyers build a detailed case chronology or predict which electronic documents may be most relevant for exhibit sets or witness preparation. In this sense, effective management and final production of ESI is a win-win for the modern lawyer: you fulfill your client's external production obligations (whether civil, criminal, regulatory, or transactional) and you (digitally) wrap your own hands around key information, too.

Beyond case substance, advanced ESI tools help the modern lawyer with aspects of matter management and planning such as staffing and budgeting. Popular platforms such as Relativity© and the one shown in Figure 5C from CS Disco, Inc. offer advanced metrics to track the pace and "burndown" rate of ESI review, helping users gauge progress and time to completion.

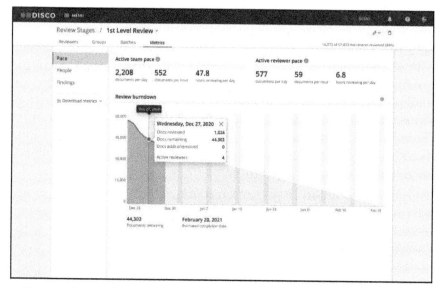

\* Figure 5C: DISCO e-discovery 1st Level Review metrics; reprinted with permission. © 2012–2021 CS Disco, Inc. All rights reserved.

## ESI in the Cloud

Many technical aspects of the EDRM workflow are moving to cloud platforms instead of on premises at a law firm or client (known as "on prem" software). The macro concept of cloud computing is something we explore in different chapters of this book. As to ESI and the cloud, there are two angles for a modern lawyer to consider:

First, what happens when a client's ESI is stored in the cloud and needs to be collected?

Second, what happens if you want to use a cloud platform to review ESI?

---

**LIT TIP**

Cloud computing refers to services and software that operate with secure access via the internet instead of locally on a computer or client network. Photos backed up to iCloud are stored in—where else? The cloud. But a file you create and save to a desktop folder on your laptop is not.

---

We first touched on legal work in the cloud in chapter 3 with document collaboration using cloud-based word-processing tools, when you change a document on a computer at home and then pick back up where you left off later when you're working on a different computer at a local coffee shop. Picture the Google Drive or Amazon Cloud Drive folders you might be familiar with in your personal life but now make those tools bigger, faster, stronger, and more sophisticated such that they can support ESI storage for clients that might have thousands of employees or hundreds of physical locations around the world. We'll explore more ways lawyers use cloud-based systems in later chapters on law practice management and remote lawyering.

First, what happens when a client's ESI is stored or located in the cloud? There's a great chance it will be. Most people, and most clients, have some form of ESI in the cloud (think of your own pictures, email, documents, social media information, etc.). Information governance, at least for larger entities, is trending toward cloud storage at the enterprise level, that is, company-wide level. A preliminary question for a lawyer navigating cloud-based ESI is whether a client is considered to have that ESI in its possession, custody, or control even if it uses a third-party cloud vendor for storage of that data. Yes. ESI in the cloud presents some wrinkles but it does not mean a client can hide its ESI in the cloud and avoid its legal obligations. As we'll dive into in chapter 9, how do clients and their lawyers know the ESI is secure with a third-party vendor? Could it be lost to a breach? What if that service loses or deletes a client's ESI? Today's lawyer must have enough of a foundation of these principles to work alongside modern clients who will use the cloud to store and manage large volumes of ESI.

The second key concept is moving ESI processing and review tools from "on premises" at a physical law firm or office location to the cloud. For example, the "on prem" popular platform Relativity© released a cloud-based option called RelativityOne©.[4] The decision between "on prem" and cloud-based ESI tools will be specific to the law firm, department, office, client, and matter; some will use a combination of both. Having your own e-discovery "on prem" platform can be a heavy burden, whether because of expense, security concerns, continuous necessary upgrades, or the need to train and maintain knowledgeable staff for technical support. Transitioning to cloud-based ESI tools should be a careful decision for a modern lawyer with consideration of infrastructure and resources, ease of access, expense, security, and technical support.

* Figure 5D: Cloud e-discovery comic; reprinted with permission, Jim Gill and Brittany Lang; creation for IPRO Tech LLC.

With the nerve-racking idea of client data "just floating around" like in Figure 5D's comic strip, lawyers proceed with caution when considering cloud-based ESI services. For example, if you are involved with this decision in your career, you'll be ready to do more research and realize the importance of asking cloud service providers thoughtful questions we'll cover in chapter 9 about topics such as their security processes, experience with large amounts of ESI, and response and "disaster" plans in the event of a security incident.

With any reward comes risk. Whether ESI storage and ESI tools exist at a physical location, in the cloud, or in a hybrid combination of both, and whether you need to use them all the time or only "on demand" when a matter requires it, as a forward-thinking modern lawyer you'll be ready to support clients by asking the right questions and making the most ethical and informed decision you can.

## ESI Pitfalls & Cautions

All this data; all these steps along the EDRM workflow. Organize. Preserve. Negotiate. Hold. Collect. Process. Review. Produce. Repeat. What could go wrong? Quite a bit. A lawyer not well versed in the ins and outs of ESI or a lawyer not aware enough to seek guidance from others will find themselves in hot water at some point (plus get their clients in it, too). The introduction in this chapter will help you take steps to *not* become that lawyer. Just in case, let's review some potential pitfalls and trouble spots. This isn't meant to instill fear or freeze you with apprehension of career-ending malpractice claims, crippling monetary sanctions, or bar punishments. Most lawyers navigate ESI with success. I hope these pitfalls and cautions remind you of your obligation to stay up to date with the technology relevant to ESI tools you, your clients, and others work with. This chapter nudges you in the right direction; it's your job to keep moving.

ESI pitfalls and cautions fall into four general categories:

1) Ethical ESI Obligations

2) Privileged ESI

3) ESI Metadata Messes

4) ESI Orders, Sanctions, & Bar Discipline

1)  <u>Ethical ESI Obligations</u>

The EDRM workflow is rife with ethical risks. "Ignorance of the law is no excuse" the saying goes. A lack of basic competency with ins and outs of ESI is no excuse for a lawyer who does not fulfill their professional obligations. We touched on one key ethical rule back in our Need to Knows in chapter 2 when we learned that Comment 8 to Model Rule 1.1 Competency instructs that a lawyer stay abreast of the benefits and risks associated with relevant technology to fulfill the ethical duty of competent representation.[5] This overarching rule dovetails with other rules governing a lawyer's conduct in certain matters such as the Federal Rules of Civil Procedure. While ethical and rule compliance may include some delegation and technical support with ESI, it does not mean a lawyer simply leaves things to the

IT professionals or a third party and washes their hands of any further obligation.

Beyond competency, two other ethical duties arise relevant to a lawyer's ESI work: the duty of candor and the duty to avoid spoliation of evidence. Model Rule 3.3 prohibits false statements of fact and requires lawyers to make complete and accurate representations to a court about ESI-related topics such as:[6]

- ✓ particulars of a client's legal hold such as automatic deletion policies

- ✓ a client's ability or inability to locate or collect ESI

- ✓ contents of a particular production such as file types and custodians

- ✓ the plan for ESI review methods such as using keyword searches or predictive coding and TAR

If a modern lawyer is in a position to discuss ESI with a court (such as in requesting a Protective Order, attending a court-mandated ESI conference, or defending a Motion to Compel Production filed against their client), the lawyer must have a fundamental knowledge of their client's ESI and related processes to support any factual assertions they make.

Spoliation of ESI is a topic no modern lawyer wants to think about. Spoliation means ruining or destroying something, like food left out on the countertop that "spoiled." With ESI, it means hiding, deleting, or losing data. Model Rule 3.4 prohibits lawyers from obstructing access to evidence or altering, destroying, or concealing "material having potential evidentiary value."[7] At the start of the EDRM workflow, lawyers could violate Rule 3.4 by not taking reasonable steps to preserve ESI. Undercollection is a common ethical and discovery violation related to ESI, whether it be an inadequate legal hold or some other deficiency such as not collecting from key custodians or failing to identify a relevant data source. A lawyer who willfully destroys ESI or knows of, but does nothing about, a client's destruction of ESI violates Rule 3.4.

> ## LIT TIP
>
> "If electronically stored information that should have been preserved in the anticipation or conduct of litigation is lost because a party failed to take reasonable steps to preserve it, and it cannot be restored or replaced through additional discovery, the court . . . upon finding prejudice . . . or intent to deprive . . . may (A) presume that the lost information was unfavorable to the party; (B) instruct the jury that it may or must presume the information was unfavorable to the party; or (C) dismiss the action or enter a default judgment."[8]
>
> Federal Rule of Civil Procedure 37(e)

Feeling shaky about an ESI situation? Unsure of the technical details? Worried you aren't satisfying ethical obligations? Ask for help. The ethics rules in many state jurisdictions and countless bar guidance opinions and court decisions echo one of the driving themes behind all the technology we discuss in this book: as a modern lawyer you don't need to have expert knowledge about everything—but if you don't, you must work with someone who does.

## 2)   Privileged ESI

Privilege issues with ESI could fill an entire chapter. You have learned or will learn that in most legal matters (at least in the United States legal system), parties can assert attorney-client privilege or attorney work product protection. With testimonial evidence, this means refusal to answer a question. With documentary evidence like ESI, this means refusal to give something. Protecting privileged ESI from disclosure and knowing when and how to assert privilege is a serious obligation.

The high volume of ESI is what makes identification of privileged ESI difficult. If you had one or two boxes of hard-copy documents 30 years ago, it would be easy to flip through them and flag memoranda between lawyer and client, settlement notes, or other strategy or work product. In cases with large volumes of ESI, identifying privileged information can be another needle-in-the-haystack effort. Thankfully, just as TAR helps lawyers review ESI to determine responsiveness and relevance, it also helps lawyers streamline privilege reviews. ESI software does not replace a lawyer's nuanced judgment about whether information qualifies as privileged, but it can help by targeting ESI that is likely privileged. How could software know what is likely privileged? Based on things like a list of known attorney names and other indicia of privilege (like the phrase itself on a document, *Attorney-Client Privileged*). Lawyers can then review and "tag" a document to withhold from an ESI production.

Privileged ESI brings up **redaction**. When only part of a document is privileged, lawyers use redactions to "hide" a portion of a file, whether a select paragraph in an email or a few seconds of a recorded voicemail. If some of a file is privileged but some is not, lawyers produce the non-privileged portion but redact and withhold the privileged part. The same goes for when part of a document contains private or confidential information like a Social Security or bank account number or password, but the rest of the document is relevant. As privacy laws many companies face around the globe expand and evolve, careful redaction of ESI to comply with obligations surrounding personally identifiable information (known as PII) will be paramount (more on data privacy and confidentiality in chapter 9).

Believe it or not, in the old days of hard-copy information, lawyers manually redacted one-off documents by sticking adhesive white tape over the portion to redact. ESI software helps modern lawyers with redaction across large data sets. When used with caution, these tools help save enormous effort and costs.

Figure 5E shows a step in the ESI redaction process when using the DISCO e-discovery platform; the tool supports an attorney choosing to redact and withhold a spreadsheet column of numbers as Confidential:

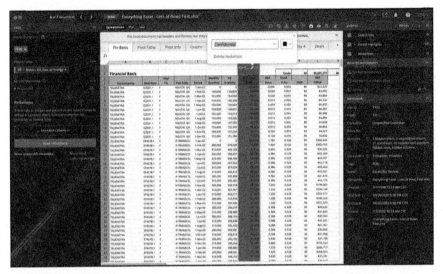

\* Figure 5E: DISCO e-discovery Excel redaction; reprinted with permission. © 2012–2021 CS Disco, Inc. All rights reserved.

Lawyers make designations of privilege and redactions throughout the review and production process. In doing so, they must balance on the fine line between describing the basis for withholding ESI without disclosing the actual privileged content. Lawyers do this in a **privilege log**: a document that tracks and describes materials withheld from a production. In the past it was tedious, manual, and loathsome for lawyers (often the junior ones!) to create a table or chart with fields such as document type, Bates ID number, date, to/from/cc, and description that looked something like this:

| ID# | BegBates# | EndBates# | Date | Basis | Description |
|-----|-----------|-----------|------|-------|-------------|
| 324 | 7148 | 7150 | 3/15/21 | A/C | Email from L. Lawyer to C. Client re: settlement |

Here too innovations in technology help. Privilege logs are easier to create, organize, review, and produce because ESI tools expedite and automate the logging process. Think of this as an automatic, extra-large spreadsheet that leverages known metadata about your privileged documents to help create and customize, collecting your privilege decisions and redactions and presenting them in a logical and organized fashion. ESI privilege issues are not one size fits all. Parties have wide leeway to negotiate aspects of the exchange of ESI such as inadvertent production of privileged materials not equating to a full waiver of the privilege (called securing a "no questions asked" 502(d) order in federal court) or agreeing to a "clawback" method for return of privileged ESI. A technologically competent lawyer will prompt discussion of these topics at the outset of the EDRM workflow.

---

**LIT TIP**

Modern lawyers who understand different options for ESI privilege logs can determine which approach makes the most sense for a particular matter or client and negotiate and plan accordingly:

custom log: lists each individual file withheld with
a tailored description of each

categorical log: lists specific categories withheld
instead of a per-file approach

metadata log: lists only ESI metadata with no detailed descriptions

---

3)   ESI Metadata Messes

In chapter 3, we learned about **metadata** and the risk of mistakenly disclosing behind-the-scenes information about a single legal document. We called metadata "data about data." Now we think about metadata not just for a single document but for thousands or millions of them in the context of ESI and things get tricky. Lawyers working with ESI need baseline knowledge about what metadata is, when it gets generated, how it might be accessed or removed during the EDRM workflow, and how it can create the risk of inadvertent disclosure of privileged material.

ESI metadata travels with the file to which it relates throughout the life of a matter and can be a lawyer's best friend or worst enemy. It can be your friend when tiny fragments fit together to help a lawyer navigate large volumes of ESI, authenticate sources, and investigate certain pieces of information with answers to questions such as:

- ✓ who authored a document?
- ✓ who forwarded an email?
- ✓ who accessed PowerPoint slides and when?
- ✓ on what computer was a spreadsheet created?
- ✓ what are the GPS location coordinates to a digital photograph?
- ✓ how long did an individual spend browsing a particular website?
- ✓ how many minutes was a phone call?
- ✓ how many direct messages did someone receive, and on what dates and times?

The evidentiary value of ESI can be clarified and improved through metadata. That's the best friend. But remember that metadata can also be a lawyer's enemy. Metadata about certain files that appears hidden can be damaging when produced and revealed to someone on the receiving and reviewing end.

Metadata obligations with ESI production vary greatly. There is no one bright line rule. Lawyers must approach the topic with a broad understanding, ready to communicate about it or negotiate as necessary. By default, unless otherwise specified, most rules require ESI to be produced as a client or person ordinarily maintains it. This means often ESI is produced with metadata intact. It's not off limits per se. It can be fair game for an opposing party or regulator or prosecutor to dive into the metadata in produced ESI. Some refer to this practice as "data mining." Depending on the context and absent other agreements, a lawyer can't always decide to "scrub" metadata or convert files into different forms for production if doing so would destroy potentially relevant metadata.

As with most aspects of ESI, parties can make their own rules for metadata. For example, if parties produce documents in a non-native format (such as .tiff or .pdf files), metadata does not necessarily come along for the ride with those image files as it does with native file production. In that instance, if the parties don't reach agreement, or if a party alleges non-compliance, the subject of metadata can become the topic of dispute. Parties can agree not to produce any metadata or negotiate to produce only certain types likely to be meaningful in a particular matter, such as file dates for ESI in a contract dispute that might show knowledge or intent (creation, last modification, or last access). Parties that receive a request from a government agency or a subpoena will often receive those entities' preferred production format and metadata details and can discuss and, in some instances, negotiate. In all these contexts, reasonableness and proportionality come into play. A technologically competent lawyer thinks about ESI metadata early by discussing it with their client and a requesting party at the preservation, collection, and discovery conference stage. Advance effort and explicit communication help the modern lawyer avoid unnecessary expense, effort, conflict, and ethical traps.

4)    ESI Orders, Sanctions & Bar Discipline

Adverse discovery orders, discovery sanctions, and bar disciplinary actions have lurked in the background for lawyers for decades, long before innovations in technology. While we need not dwell on them, today's complicated ESI landscape means even more trouble spots and risk for the unaware lawyer and client. The following examples give a glimpse of a few among thousands of scenarios where lawyers (or their clients) have been taken to task.

Orders & Sanctions:

> ➢ *Apple v. Samsung*, No. 11-01846 (N.D. Cal. July 29, 2014)[9] (sanctioning Samsung and its attorneys for failing to ensure confidentiality of a patent license Apple produced) ("A junior associate missing one redaction among many in an expert report is not exactly a historical event in the annals of big-ticket patent litigation. Even if regrettable, these things can happen, and almost certainly do happen each and every day. But when such an inadvertent mistake is permitted to go unchecked, unaddressed, and propagated hundreds and hundreds of times by conscious—and indeed strategic—choices by that associate's firm and client alike, more significant and blameworthy flaws are revealed.").

> *DR Distribs., LLC v. 21 Century Smoking, Inc.*, 513 F. Supp. 3d 839, 942 (N.D. Ill. Jan. 19, 2021) (granting sanctions, finding violations of rules of professional conduct, and ordering over $1 million in attorneys' fees and costs and completion of mandatory legal education where defendant counsel failed to take reasonable steps to preserve ESI, failed to timely disclose ESI, and contributed to spoliation of email and chat messages due to failure to disable the auto-delete feature) ("It is no longer amateur hour. It is way too late in the day for lawyers to expect to catch a break on e-discovery compliance because it is technically complex and resource-demanding.").

> *Measured Wealth Private Client Grp. v. Foster*, No. 20-80148, 2021 U.S. Dist. LEXIS 62143 (S.D. Fla. Mar. 31, 2021) (ordering appointment of a forensic expert to create images of smart devices after the defendant failed to produce relevant iMessages and SMS text messages).

> *Waskul v. Washtenaw Cty. Cmty. Mental Health*, No. 16-10936, 2021 U.S. Dist. LEXIS 209859 (E.D. Mich. Oct. 31, 2021) (imposing sanctions for the defendant's "stubborn and meritless insistence that they need not produce basic electronic discovery" and for refusing to cooperate in search term testing and negotiation of proportional searches or seek aid from and partner with knowledgeable e-discovery liaisons).

Bar Discipline:

> *In re Attorney X*, Case No. BD-2017-048, Massachusetts S.J.C. Order of Term Suspension entered by Justice Lenk on May 10, 2017 (attorney suspended for one year and one day for failure to create a privilege log).

> *In re: Attorney Y*, Illinois Supreme Court Commission No. 2019PR00053 (public censure of an attorney for failing to take reasonable remedial measures after learning that a client submitted material false evidence to the court relating to the spoliation of documents in litigation against the client's former employer).

> ➢ *In re: Attorney Z*, Massachusetts Board of Bar Overseers, No. 2013-21 (public reprimand for recommending that client scrub confidential information from his laptop, constituting unlawful obstruction of the other party's access to evidence).
>
> ➢ *In re: Attorney A*, Bar No. 025177 PDJ-2013-9003 2013 WL 3486674 (Arizona Disp. Com.) (four-year attorney suspension for, among other things, causing relevant evidence to be lost or destroyed).

## Putting ESI to Good Use: Fact Management Software

Let's not forget the big picture. Technical steps aside, what's the point of all this ESI? ESI provides information. Facts. Evidence. Proof. Leverage. Strategy. After the process, lawyers must get at the substance. Modern lawyers take advantage of tools that help transform gigabytes and terabytes into real stories for real audiences—whether snippets of digital evidence for a courtroom visual aid at a criminal trial, a timeline for a presentation to an in-house general counsel, or one of a hundred exhibits for a witness deposition. Of course, lawyers did this long before advanced technology—flipcharts, notepads, presentation software, spreadsheets, word-processing outlines, binders, and, above all, their brains! Lawyers still use those things. A central theme of this book is that manual approaches aren't wrong but might be better and faster at times with technology.

Available tools in this space are called **fact management software**. Some ESI vendors offer their own case and fact management software; others are standalone products (and usually cloud-based, accessible for team collaboration). For example, CaseMap (owned by LexisNexis®) and its latest iteration CaseMap Cloud are leading tools in case and fact management. These tools help modern lawyers:

✓ organize evidence

✓ analyze fact details

✓ visualize and craft strategy

- ✓ plan for witness preparation and testimony
- ✓ plan expert needs
- ✓ understand relationships between entities and people
- ✓ create interactive and engaging timelines
- ✓ plan and create helpful visual aids

Ever watch a detective television show where the detectives tack pictures to a large bulletin board with lines drawn among suspects or victims, and then stand and stare at it to make sense of the situation? Fact management software for lawyers is like that, but on a larger and more complex scale to capture the many moving parts of a matter. These programs bring ESI into the context of real case decisions—for example, where does an email chain fit? Who needs to authenticate a spreadsheet? Which text message will prove a key disputed fact? Who said, copied, made, knew, saw, or heard what—and when? The names of vendors and services for fact management will change as your career takes shape. Technology to help lawyers use what's buried deep within ESI is here to stay.

* * * *

More future challenges and opportunities are on the horizon during your career when we think of ESI. You may have heard the concept of society being in the midst of "4IR"—the fourth Industrial Revolution, disrupting traditional industries and our everyday way of life with fundamental shifts at an exponential rate to machine-based smart technology. This megatrend chatter is somewhere between overblown and understated. But it's not all fiction. One certainty is that our ESI digital footprints will keep getting bigger and more diverse. ESI will evolve from emojis, smart appliances, and geolocation data in the early decades of the 2000s to whatever might be next:

- ✓ internet browsing data from Web 3.0
- ✓ virtual reality metaverse activity
- ✓ "smart" robots and personal assistant data
- ✓ blockchain transaction data

- ✓ facial recognition database images
- ✓ object location-tracking tool information from devices like AirTags
- ✓ personal digital implants, wearables, and biometrics
- ✓ augmented reality headsets, glasses, and other devices that track eye activity

Data is called the "new oil" because it's a commodity everyone wants. And it's only going to get more difficult to capture and use throughout your career because:

- ✓ sophisticated encryption methods will offer greater protection
- ✓ those who have data will limit disclosure based on increasing privacy rights
- ✓ people creating data will do so from more locations and with more shared tools
- ✓ data will be created in new and different file types and formats
- ✓ more data by design will disappear seconds or minutes after creation (called ephemeral or transitory data)
- ✓ more data will be moved across state and international borders in our global economy, teeing up inconsistencies among jurisdictions regarding how data is stored and when and in what form parties must provide it (not to mention hurdles reviewing foreign-language documents)

ESI won't exist on an island. As a modern lawyer, you'll be expected to navigate it in the broader context of a client's overall business, personal practices, expectations, financial pressures, confidences, and challenges. No single ESI situation will be like any other. That's a good thing. Instead of being intimidated by the thought, be confident. By working through this chapter, you've started your approach to ESI with the caution, understanding, and ethical awareness that will serve you well as you begin your career.

*Review Your Knowledge*

1) Hayden is a solo criminal defense attorney representing a local businesswoman alleged to have conspired with others to bribe a congresswoman. The client has been criminally indicted in federal court and the prosecutor suggests a "meet and confer" session with the attorneys who represent each of the alleged co-conspirators to discuss the volume and mechanics of electronic discovery (prosecutors generally have a duty to disclose evidence before trial, although the particulars vary). Hayden thinks the indictment of his client is ridiculous and refuses to cooperate. Months later, Hayden receives an electronic production of evidence against his client that includes body camera footage, GPS tracking and cell location data, messaging data among the conspirators, and thousands of other digital files. Hayden runs a small defense practice and is overwhelmed by the ESI. He calls the prosecutor and jokes that he (Hayden) is "digital data illiterate" and the voluminous production threatens his client's constitutional right to a fair and speedy trial. Hayden threatens formal motion practice in federal court. If Hayden moves forward with that strategy:

a) he's in a good position because the problem of storage and management of ESI is a big one in our digital society, and courts are likely sympathetic to a solo criminal defense attorney with limited resources.

b) he's not in a good position because it's his fault he didn't meet and confer to discuss and agree on the "nuts and bolts" of the production format in advance, and as a criminal defense attorney who must deal with ESI and digital evidence he should learn or engage third-party services who can help him.

c) he's in a good position because proportionality and reasonableness are key with ESI, and a court will likely order the prosecutor to produce easier new file formats to ease Hayden's burden before trial.

d) he's in a good position because no agreement was made so Hayden has full discretion to dictate the particulars of how the defendant is entitled to receive the ESI.

2) SAPC Motor, Inc. is an automotive manufacturing company in a large contract dispute in state court with its supplier, Venso Corp. At the outset, SAPC and Venso negotiate a lengthy 17-page document entitled "Joint Stipulation Regarding E-Discovery." In it, they agree: (i) to limit discovery to 12 individual custodians a side; (ii) not to include ESI from mobile devices in their productions; (iii) to each designate an ESI liaison to discuss discovery issues; (iv) to produce most files in .tiff file format; (v) to negotiate in good faith pre-production search terms and use TAR 2.0 software to perform some aspects of the review. Can the parties do this?

   a) No, an applicable state rule of civil procedure would govern these detailed ESI topics to ensure the benefits of the exchange of ESI outweigh the likely burden of production on both sides in a case.

   b) Yes, but such an agreement means the parties are stuck with it and cannot seek a superseding court order or adjustment as the litigation continues, even if new information is learned or additional issues come to light.

   c) Yes, if both lawyers have enough knowledge of ESI processes and advanced technology assisted review to have an informed discussion with clients about the advantages and disadvantages with these ESI particulars.

   d) No, because technology assisted review is not yet widely approved for use with ESI and a lawyer who outsources any aspect of careful human review to AI software violates the ethical duty of competency.

3) Massive online retail company Azamon has negotiated a deal to merge with another online service provider, Shoogle. Under federal antitrust law, parties to certain large mergers must notify the Federal Trade Commission and turn over business data that informs whether the FTC challenges the deal. Part of Azamon's pre-merger submission to the FTC

includes hundreds of spreadsheets with sales and financial data relevant to the merger—but several spreadsheets include columns with attorney-client privileged notes from Azamon's attorneys about other past proposed mergers that never moved forward. In its production to the FTC, Azamon's attorney should:

a) withhold the entire set of spreadsheets as attorney-client privileged, because if any single part of a set of documents is privileged, the entire document and "family" of related ESI is too.

b) produce the spreadsheets and carefully redact the privileged columns, but only after reviewing the FTC's specifications for electronic productions to ensure use of a proper production format and permissible type of privilege log.

c) produce the spreadsheets in their entirety with no redactions because attorney-client privilege designations and privilege logs only apply in court cases.

d) move for a protective order to avoid an overbroad request for privileged ESI that will be expensive and unduly burdensome to produce to the FTC.

4) Your first position out of law school is as a designer and customer solutions professional at a technology company building out a comprehensive new ESI tool and looking to gain traction in the legal technology market. You are tasked with designing and planning the ESI review interface. Which of these tools or features would a modern lawyer likely look for in advising a client whether to pay for this new third-party ESI service?

a) The ability to gauge how many documents in a set remain unreviewed, and sort that by file type and individual custodian to predict likely completion date.

b) The ability to customize review "tags" and search filters for different matters, save search history, and annotate documents with internal electronic "sticky notes."

c)  The ability to perform redactions and automate support for creation of privilege log entries.

d)  All of the above.

5)  Landry (pronoun they/them) is a scientist at a pharmaceutical company. They have a falling out with management after complaining of a hostile work environment. Landry quits and is sued months later for theft of trade secrets. The company alleges Landry copied confidential trade secrets onto a personal thumb drive on their last day of work. Months later, Carl represents Landry at his deposition and during a break Landry whispers to Carl, "I hate this company. Joke's on them because the files on the thumb drive aren't all I took. The real insider chemical data that I stole I deleted from my personal laptop before my deposition Ha!" Carl had already produced files from Landry's personal laptop to the company as part of the litigation. He says nothing. The company later suspects spoliation of evidence from Landry's personal laptop, and a computer forensics expert determines Landry's laptop was scrubbed with a file-wiping program the week before Landry's production of documents and deposition. Carl:

a)  can't be expected to police his client's every move and could not be expected to have the same technical expertise as a computer forensics expert.

b)  likely violated the ethical duty not to assist someone else in altering or destroying material with evidentiary value as well as the ongoing ethical duty of candor when he did not try to disclose or correct Landry's blatant failure to preserve ESI.

c)  may take a hit to his reputation, but the mishap will not affect the substance of Landry's underlying case with sanctions or an adverse inference.

d)  did not commit an ethics violation because although he stayed silent after Landry's admission, Carl himself didn't unlawfully destroy or conceal evidence he knew to be relevant.

*Practice Your Knowledge*

## Exercise #1: Meet & Confer ESI Checklist

Do some (free) online research to find and review different sample ESI model orders and stipulations for parties to consult and use (the Western District of Washington, Eastern District of Michigan, and Central District of California are a good starting point). Create a one-page outline or checklist for a supervisor getting ready for an early case meet and confer meeting with lawyers on a large corporate contract dispute litigation. Take a broad approach to topics you think the lawyers would need to discuss at the meeting, using the content of the model orders and stipulations as a guide to prompt some ideas.

## Exercise #2: Legal Hold ESI Categories

Return to the knowledge kickoff question at the start of this chapter with in-house bank attorney Tyra. Suppose you work in the bank legal department too and are asked to draft the description of the categories of ESI to include in the forthcoming legal hold notice, given the likely DOJ investigation. Draft a paragraph or two broad enough to capture the different types of data the bank would probably ask its employees to preserve such as emails or word-processing documents—but don't stop there!

*Expand Your Knowledge*

➢ *The Sedona Conference Glossary: eDiscovery & Digital Information Management, Fifth Edition,* 21 SEDONA CONF. J. 263 (2020) [https://perma.cc/TY44-BJ5U].

➢ Scott J. Etish, et al., *Fools Rush In: The Importance of Negotiating Comprehensive ESI Protocols,* Gibbons (April 12, 2021), https://www.gibbonslaw.com/resources/publications/fools-rush-in-the-importance-of-negotiating-comprehensive-esi-protocols [https://perma.cc/W5YX-TQ YE].

➢ Marc Fulkert, *Using eLitigation Tools to Advance Your Case*, 69 DOJ J. FED. L. & PRAC. 13 (2021).

*Answers & Explanations*

*Knowledge Kickoff*

d)   Knowing when ethical obligations with preservation and collection of ESI start is more an art than a science and there is certainly gray area. But here, the bank executive confirms the existence of the DOJ's investigation and that triggers the duty to take reasonable steps to preserve relevant evidence. Put another way, the bank can't delete relevant ESI under the idea that the DOJ hadn't actually issued or filed anything against it yet. Although Tyra's task is to complete an investigation, she can't pick and choose what ESI to preserve and collect only for internal review. She needs the full story, so to speak, whether for internal review or otherwise. Therefore, the bank in this instance must use a legal hold notice and work with Tyra and, if necessary, outside counsel and third-party vendors to make a complete preservation, collection, and review plan in anticipation of an impending legal matter.

*Review Your Knowledge*

1)   b)   Exchange of ESI as a part of the civil or criminal discovery process is generally regarded as a private matter subject to negotiation between the parties. Hayden should have met and conferred with the prosecutor to discuss production of the evidence and prepare for how he would review it (or negotiate a different preferred format). If he isn't experienced or knowledgeable about ESI, he needs to consult with a third party or someone else who is. Presuming the prosecutor's production was not in a format too far beyond the usual bounds, Hayden's after-the-fact broad complaints of being overwhelmed aren't likely to receive sympathy from a court hearing a motion for a protective order or motion to compel re-production of ESI in a different format.

2)   c)   Parties may negotiate specifics of ESI even if it means limiting to fewer custodians or less data. Doing

so makes it more difficult to cry foul or ask a court for modification, but the door to do so always remains open (for example, if SAPC Motor amended its complaint to include a new claim that teed up a different source of potentially relevant ESI from Venso). Technology assisted review using AI software has grown in popularity over the years, especially in cases with large volumes of ESI. If clients stay informed and lawyers have sufficient foundational understanding or support from expert consultants, TAR is an acceptable (indeed, often preferred and popular) approach.

3)    b) Privileged designations must be specific and narrow, even in large ESI productions. Azamon's attorney can't ethically withhold an entire spreadsheet just because one column includes privileged or confidential information. Just as parties in litigation negotiate joint discovery agreements and discuss ESI parameters, so too may parties and government entities in the transactional context, to set expectations and keep costs down. Broad categories of requests often capture privileged ESI and necessitate privilege logs—that alone does not make them overbroad or unreasonable.

4)    d) A modern lawyer may need to advise clients on whether to use ESI tools and, if so, what tool or tools are best. The decision is context-specific; one client with deep pockets and hundreds of matters will require different support than a smaller client with fewer matters and smaller ESI volumes. No matter the context, you don't get what you don't ask for—and clients will expect their lawyers to stay abreast of improvements in ESI technology when necessary to advise and decide what "bells and whistles" are worth paying for.

5)    b) Although Carl didn't himself delete evidence, he had an ethical obligation to try to obtain and produce the deleted files after learning of Landry's misconduct. Navigating a client relationship in the context of ESI is tricky because for many, our devices, files, and

communications feel and are very personal. But that's no excuse for spoliation of evidence or discovery misconduct, and neither is the fact that Carl isn't as sophisticated as an expert computer professional. The duty to preserve ESI is ongoing and if a lawyer comes across an ESI mishap of any sort, failure to act will have serious consequences for both the lawyer and the underlying case. Here, Landry could face spoliation charges or, if the case continues, face an adverse jury instruction permitting the assumption that the deleted laptop files were stolen trade secrets.

## Endnotes

1    *Zubulake v. UBS Warburg*, 220 F.R.D. 212, 217–18 (S.D.N.Y. 2003).

2    SECURITIES AND EXCHANGE COMMISSION, ENFORCEMENT MANUAL 1 (2017) https://www.sec.gov/divisions/enforce/enforcementmanual.pdf    [https://perma.cc/73TU-6L27].

3    U.S. DISTRICT COURT NORTHERN DISTRICT OF CALIFORNIA, GUIDELINES FOR THE DISCOVERY OF ELECTRONICALLY STORED INFORMATION 1 (updated Dec. 1, 2015), https://cand.uscourts.gov/filelibrary/1117/ESI_Guidelines-12-1-2015.pdf    [https://perma.cc/9GUB-MRVM].

4    RELATIVITY, https://www.relativity.com/ediscovery-software/relativityone/?utm_source=google&utm_medium=ppc&utm_campaign=BrandedNA&utm_term=relativityone&utm_content=relativityone&gclid=CjwKCAjwgr6TBhAGEiwA3aVuIQ7JHVhk jbId119OLT1xugbm7zskrZ_QhBUl7KxP2smER5sJ0niUXBoCfh8QAvD_BwE    [https://perma.cc/D4SZ-SW49].

5    MODEL RULES OF PRO. CONDUCT r. 1.1 CMT. 8 (AM. BAR ASS'N 2020).

6    MODEL RULES OF PRO. CONDUCT r. 3.3 (AM. BAR ASS'N 2020).

7    MODEL RULES OF PRO. CONDUCT r. 3.4 (AM. BAR ASS'N 2020).

8    FED. R. CIV. P. 37(e).

9    https://perma.cc/KAR2-VGV4.

# CHAPTER 6

# INNOVATION IN DELIVERY OF LEGAL SERVICES

*Core Concepts*

| | |
|---|---|
| legal process improvement<br>legal operations<br>productization<br>automation<br>expert system | document assembly<br>guided interview<br>contract lifecycle management (CLM)<br>self-help legal services<br>unauthorized practice of law |

*Knowledge Kickoff*

Theo is an in-house lawyer at Spacial, LLC, a commercial real estate company in New York. Spacial's business has grown fast. It represents landlords seeking to fill commercial office space, as well as tenants seeking to find new space or negotiate a new lease. When brokers initiate a transaction, they email Theo a bulleted list of information for a draft lease or drop hard-copy materials on his desk. Theo works on several hundred leases each year. The information he receives from the broker is almost always incomplete, requiring him to go back and forth with the broker and client until he gets relevant information like square footage and base rent. It can take weeks or months to finalize the leases, as every broker Theo works with has a different process. The final contracts end up in brokers' email inboxes and Theo's desktop. Spacial's CEO wants to start a blog highlighting Spacial's booming commercial real estate work in the New York City market. She asks Theo to summarize Spacial's transactions for the past 18 months, broken down by different lease and market metrics.

Which of the following options represents the best approach Spacial (and Theo) could have taken in the past that would have made Theo's contract summary task easier?

a)   Spacial could have explored using a client-facing platform where landlords or tenants could get legal advice for commercial leases through a chatbot.

b)   Spacial could have invested in document assembly technology to automate creation of the leases so Theo didn't have to deal with any of this mundane contract work.

c)   Spacial could have taken steps to improve its overall processes, with brokers and lawyers working together to explore better workflows such as a more efficient information intake, a document assembly platform for streamlined contract creation, and a better database plan for managing contract content.

d)   There's not much Theo or Spacial could have done differently because keeping track of details for lease contracts and being able to summarize big picture contract metrics are the responsibilities of the real estate brokers, not Theo.

---

Days before I drafted this chapter, the fast-food giant McDonald's® announced use of voice recognition technology for robots to take orders at an automated drive-through. Weeks later, I vacationed with my family and checked in at the airport terminal using a self-service kiosk instead of waiting to talk with the one available employee. On the drive to our destination, we zipped through highway tollbooths with the transponder in our rental car instead of slowing down to toss quarters into a basket or wait for a toll collector to give us change for the $20 bill we found under the driver's seat. Once I returned home in December, I set up holiday light decorations with a smart plug and set a timer from an app for the lights to turn on at dusk. After receiving a defective coffee maker as a holiday gift, I requested a replacement on the manufacturer's website by typing answers to questions from a chatbot "assistant" at the bottom of the screen. After a "thumbs up" emoji from the bot— voilà! My new coffee maker was ordered in minutes.

No matter your age, you too have hundreds of examples of everyday aspects of life you do differently than in the past. For other generations, changing processes were embodied in things like the invention of vending machines to make snacks more accessible and cash registers replacing individual clerks calculating the amount of change due. For today's generation, pause to consider the way you might:

- ✓ complete forms online before a new doctor's appointment instead of sitting in a waiting room with a pen and clipboard

- ✓ make a bank deposit from your smartphone instead of grabbing an envelope and waiting for the bank to open

- ✓ return new clothing that doesn't fit to an online retailer with a few clicks and a drop of a package outside your door instead of driving 30 minutes to the mall

- ✓ get a lift home with a ride share service instead of wondering about a taxi cab's cost or whether you'll find one

- ✓ enjoy custom-ordered food delivered to your door in minutes with a few taps on your tablet instead of walking to your takeout spot and hoping they have your favorite on the menu that day

Changes like these are so entrenched in culture you might not think of them as "new" or reflective of big change. But with a wide-lens view of time, these changes are very much new. And they're often quicker, easier, more reliable, less frustrating, and—let's be honest—they often require less effort and patience from us consumers.

This chapter introduces how innovation and technology are changing delivery of legal services. They're doing so through improved processes, greater efficiency, automation, prepackaged productization, self-service legal online tools, and many other approaches or some combination thereof. By necessity, this chapter is on the longer side compared to others and takes a very broad brush. These umbrella concepts cover many other topics in this book, from automated legal writing software in chapter 3 to new document management law office technology in chapter 7. These developments in legal practice didn't occur by magic or happenstance. They came from human initiative, creativity, technology, collaboration, and communication. After all, what good is an airport kiosk if users have no idea where it is or how to use it? Other chapters are heavy on the technology; this is heavy on innovation. The latest and greatest AI software might get the wheels of a certain idea turning but technology has a short shelf life. People and ideas don't.

This chapter is not about cutting-edge technical details. It's about a modern lawyer's mindset.

---

LIT TIP

"The real problem is not whether machines think but whether [humans] do."[1]

B.F. Skinner
American Psychologist (1904–1990)

---

Here's a road map as we tackle these broad topics:

1)   First we glance backwards at the approaches we might be improving upon—what legal service "problems" need solving?

2)   Then we explore historical hurdles to changing processes within the profession and introduce terminology for the patterns, types of approaches, and tools of change we'll cover:

---

Process Improvement * Productization * Automation * Expert Systems * Document Assembly

---

3)   We'll then spotlight contract lifecycle management as an example of innovative technology improving how lawyers work with some of their most important documents.

4)   Our second spotlight example examines how legal know-how gets repackaged in "self-help" legal

services to
the Access to o

5) We conclude with th... used to help address
Providers (ALSPs) play Need to Know #5).
prohibitions against unau... ive Legal Service
ethical considerations, and e... #4), and how
reform impact future work. ...ctice of law,
...egulation

Remember the goal. It's not for you to code a ne...
app. It's not for you to memorize every automation tool mobile
market. It's not for you to understand the inner workings day's
contract analysis technology. It's not to scare you into thinking
automation signals the end of your job prospects. It may change
and expand job prospects but it won't end them. Rather, the goal
is to ignite thinking about what aspects of legal services are well
positioned for a fresh approach and inspire you to realize the
power of your own legal know-how.

## Improving What?

The word "improvement" in the chapter title prompts the
question: what needs improving?

Modern lawyers consider improved efficiencies, technologies,
and concepts like automation to improve legal service delivery.
But what's the underlying problem? Are the so-called old ways
of doing things that bad? Yes and no. Problems are context
specific. Plenty of lawyering tasks are chugging along just fine.

But other aspects of everyday lawyering are ripe for
improvement. Start with the traditional model of a lawyer as a
one-on-one counselor. We are a service industry serving clients
with individual problems in a specific, bespoke, and custom way.
Ethical duties travel directly to those clients, such as duties of
competency, zealous advocacy, and confidentiality. Think about
this: when you go to the hair salon or barbershop for a haircut,
do you close your eyes and let your stylist pick from several "off-
the-shelf" stock cuts or colors? Likely not. You want style and
service designed just for you. Legal clients do too.

Here's the thing: not every aspect of lawyering for a client is
unique. Many are not. Think of the hundreds of leases

e kickoff question. With their
LF can find significant overlap from
o the next with repeated, routine
ogy in chapter 2 of the boxed cake mix
om scratch every time. If Theo creates
cument files a year, he need not start from
le. Not starting from scratch isn't just about
ation. It applies in a substantive lawyering "know-
xt, too. Suppose a veteran legal aid lawyer works with
ho seek restraining orders to protect themselves from
vio.nce or harassment. The lawyer knows the statute like the back of her hand, and with each client she asks the same questions and goes through the same steps: she asks if the client is in immediate danger and should call 911. She asks where the client lives. She asks if children are involved. The intake goes on and the answers shape the path of advice. While the eventual application for a restraining order is custom to that client's situation, the steps the lawyer takes are not. The client's problem is unique; the way the lawyer gets at the legal issues is not.

The "problem" to be solved here is more an opportunity to be seized. The hypothetical legal aid lawyer's process is not wrong. Could she do it better? Could she:

✓ do it faster but still ensure each new client feels comfortable?

✓ serve more clients in need, instead of the 10 she's forced to turn away at the door each night when she leaves?

✓ package up her approach such that if she takes a leave of absence, her colleagues can use her knowledge and continue to serve clients?

✓ avoid burnout from the monotony of her daily legal aid intake work and be re-inspired in her career by focusing on the nuanced and creative aspects of lawyering that she loves?

Not every legal task needs an overhaul, but some do. This book prepares you for that decision; it can't make it for you. Tension spots vary and so too will a modern lawyer's solutions. Some examples in this chapter are brand-new approaches—big changes that turn the "old ways" upside down. Others are small tweaks to small processes that go a long way. Innovation and technology aren't all-or-nothing concepts. They may work alongside lawyers' one-on-one creative client problem solving but they don't replace it. That's where our real value as counselors will always be.

## Historical Hurdles to Change

My backdrop might paint too rosy a picture suggesting the legal profession is jumping to change its ways. It's not—yet.

You've heard the phrase "think outside the box." Let's go outside the lawyering box to consider the hurdles and roadblocks. Bringing about change—with or without technology—is rarely easy. It's harder still when impactful and on a large scale. We could fill pages with examples, from my grandmother across the country who sends handwritten notes because she refuses to videoconference, to folks in the early 1900s who clung to the hope of horses pulling their buggy faster and worried about the dangers of gasoline from Henry Ford's new Model T automobiles. Even small process changes having nothing to do with technology wreak havoc. Years ago, my child's preschool asked parents to check in at the director's office before visiting a classroom instead of walking down the hall to a classroom, as the policy had been for years. It was as if they had asked me to check in on the Moon. I appreciated the underlying rationale but just plain didn't like the new approach.

Back to lawyering. "Technology is nothing without people" is an overused phrase in legal innovation and technology circles (of which you should now consider yourself a part). So is "people first, tech second" and "process first." These refrains are overused but true. You might have amazing technology hidden under your bed, but if you don't know it's there or aren't willing, able, or motivated to try it out, it's worthless.

Setting aside the fading reputation of the profession as a collection of Luddites who resist change, it easy to see why altering lawyers' mindsets could be an uphill battle. By training, lawyers look backwards. We use precedent and facts to inform decisions. We crave reliability and consistency. We are risk averse. In contrast, process improvements and innovation ask lawyers to take risk by looking forward, being creative, and imagining how to complete tasks "better"—whether cheaper, faster, smarter, for more clients, more satisfying, more impactful, or something else. That's outside many lawyers' comfort zones.

Law firms especially get a bad rap. Most people don't perceive firms as innovative, and they've had trouble shedding the image of conservative "this is the way it's always been done" lawyers. Aspects to traditional firm life such as the billable hour, partner/associate model, high attrition rates, and a "work first at all costs" burnout mentality contribute to this reputation. The traditional, one-on-one lawyer to client service mentality and business model, which has been ingrained in United States law firms since the 1700s, remains atop the pedestal for many. Changing ways requires broad buy-in from not just lawyers but other important law firm stakeholders such as paralegals, knowledge management experts, IT professionals, and support staff. Worthwhile change requires a perfect combination of many not-so-perfect variables such as:

| | |
|---|---|
| ✓ motivation | ✓ culture |
| ✓ expertise | ✓ client demand |
| ✓ purpose | ✓ market pressure |
| ✓ money | ✓ collaboration |
| ✓ leadership | ✓ feedback and assessment |

Even firms, legal departments, and organizations that put money and resources toward legal innovation often realize a disconnect between good intentions and real results.

Though an uphill battle, some lawyers do clear the hurdles and embrace (or at least accept) this so-called industry disruption. In small pockets, modern lawyers are experimenting and implementing real change, as we'll see in the examples throughout this chapter. Take these large law firm examples to start:

➤ Baker McKenzie has an innovation program termed Reinvent that "brings together all [the firm's] change initiatives in support of better client outcomes . . . Reinvent captures our commitment to apply clever solutions to meet our clients' challenges and most strategic goals."[2]

➤ Wilson Sonsini launched a software platform called Neuron that aggregates and automates routine legal needs of startup company clients in its emerging companies practice group, helping the firm in 2022 become the first-ever law firm named to a "World's Most Innovative Companies" list.[3]

➤ Davis Wright Tremaine is recognized as a top innovative law firm and has a dedicated innovation and research arm De Novo® where lawyers, project managers, technologists, and others work on client-specific solutions such as a streamlined intake process to help a client triage its high volume of third-party subpoenas.[4]

So beware of the hype but ready to hurdle. "Innovation" as an overused buzzword dampens the credibility of lawyers interested in real change. Short-term pain points can cloud long-term benefits. The legal innovation and technology space is crowded, noisy, and confusing. Some lawyers roll their eyes and think it's a distracting waste of resources. They've heard shouts for years about competitive disruption to the market and remain skeptical and without motivation for real change to the way legal services get delivered. Historical hurdles will remain, but they'll be kicked down a few notches throughout your career as change creeps in and pressure mounts from technology companies, clients, Alternative Legal Service Providers (Need to Know #4), and forward-thinking modern lawyers like you.

## Patterns, Types of Approaches & Tools of Change

Work hard or work smart? Both. Figure 6A offers five concepts we'll use to capture some key patterns, types of approaches, and tools lawyers work with to reimagine delivery of legal services.

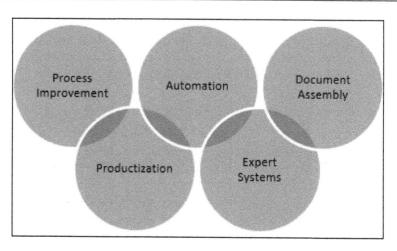

* Figure 6A: Innovation concepts in law.

This is not an exhaustive list. These concepts work alone but also together with a lot of overlap. It's a starting framework, not a finish line. For each, we'll start with a definition and turn to explanation and examples. Focus more on the broad ideas and less the specific approach, software, or demonstrative product. While many examples include AI technology, which we introduced in Need to Know #8, don't let that impede your understanding of the bigger picture. It's tempting to shy away from these concepts because "AI technology is complicated and I don't understand it." Lawyers (and others) do this all the time. You need not be an expert with the technologies—become the expert thinker behind the scenes instead. Flavors of AI technology will evolve in the years to come. Product names and features will change. Legal technology companies will be bought, sold, acquired, or fall by the wayside. This chapter showcases what's happening today so you'll be ready for what's going to happen tomorrow.

1) Legal Process Improvement: Operations, Project Management & Design Thinking

No tech is where we start. Human thought driving change—not sparkly technology. Before we do tasks better, we must recognize status quo spots needing attention. Think about the last time you boarded an airplane. It probably wasn't perfect but imagine no rhyme or reason to the process: no seat assignment, no phased boarding by zone, no priority for those in need of assistance, no baggage limits, no delay announcements, no window/middle/aisle seat ordering or priority. Today's hindsight makes that seem like a confusing disaster. At some point, someone sat down, thought critically, defined the problems, considered affected stakeholders, mapped out a better way, and then assessed whether that better way was, in fact, working out better.

---

### LIT TIP

"If we try to automate rubbish, we, at best, get automated rubbish . . . [t]here are few quick tech fixes. We must pay down the process and cultural debt first and then find tech fit-to-purpose. But the inverse is exceedingly common. We are inclined to start with tech, assuming we will work out our process along the way. That is a terrible plan that tends to end poorly."[5]

Casey Flaherty
Co-Founder & Chief Strategy Officer, Lex Fusion
Co-Founder, Procertas
Former Director of Legal Project Management, Baker McKenzie
Former Corporate Counsel, Kia Motors America

---

The umbrella phrase **legal process improvement** embodies the ideas in the airplane boarding example: thinking critically, defining problems, and mapping out a better way. This connects to related concepts like legal operations ("Legal Ops"), legal project management ("LPM"), and design thinking. Legal Ops, LPM, and design thinking aren't unique to law and aren't new. These departments and roles exist in businesses, government entities, educational institutions, manufacturers, and the military. They might be small scale (me as the "back office" operations manager running my busy household) or large scale (a corporate Operations department with an enormous budget such as at a company like Toyota or Verizon).

Legal process improvement refers to examining and streamlining processes to deliver quality work more efficiently, often bringing advantages such as lower costs, better client service, and greater profitability. Professionals in this area are involved in bringing high-level strategy and goals down to the day-to-day tasks. A fundamental misconception is that these positions are lower-level administrative roles. They're not. In a law department or law firm setting, **legal operations** professionals (often using process improvement principles) might work with lawyers and others to:

- ✓ introduce project and case management fundamentals

- ✓ forecast law firm growth and financials and create timelines

- ✓ improve knowledge management (KM) systems (more on KM in chapter 7)

- ✓ set practice group or organization goals and priorities

- ✓ roll out new technologies or systems

- ✓ research and implement cost control or cost cutting measures

- ✓ design trainings for lawyers and staff

- ✓ help manage work with outside vendors

- ✓ gauge return on investment (ROI) across different organizational sectors

- ✓ find internal "data-mining" opportunities to collect and analyze firm information such as caseloads, demographics, billing metrics, and remote work practices

As a broad field, Legal Ops has taken off over the past decade, especially with in-house legal. It's likely to continue to do so. The Corporate Legal Operations Consortium (CLOC) is a global group of lawyers and professionals focused on more effective and efficient business-driven approaches to practice. A 2021 report described Legal Ops as a "major component of an increased focus on legal department management" and found 80% of those surveyed agreed, up from 56% in 2017.[6]

---

### LIT TIP

Giant international energy company Shell is an example of in-house legal process improvement and legal operations driving internal change. Its Global Law Department created a new legal operations center, consolidated its number of outside law firms, standardized contract management processes, centralized and streamlined creation of NDA contracts (non-disclosure agreements), and implemented new methods for extracting data about the company's thousands of patents into a searchable dashboard. According to Shell's leader of these initiatives:

"We strive to create a culture where bold, creative thinking is encouraged and nurtured. One way to develop a culture of innovation is to have talented people with diverse experiences and skills collaborate on ways to rethink what work should get done and by what means. I challenge my team to be 'outside the box' thinkers. In my experience that requires having a box that includes more than lawyers."[7]

Donny Ching
Legal Director, Shell

---

Another concept for the modern lawyer interested in improved processes is design thinking. This is another topic widespread in non-legal business settings where folks are looking to innovate. A handful of law schools offer specialty electives in design thinking (if yours does, I recommend it, along with a course such as Process Improvement or Project Management). Lawyers and design thinking experts swap out their legal pads and laptops for Post-it notes, whiteboards, mind maps, and creativity. Design thinking is a bit of an intentionally unique worldview— a new lens through which to approach something. It represents a user-centered approach to innovation whereby lawyering inefficiencies get improved through a series of hands-on, discrete, and concrete steps, such as:

- ✓ discovering new problems
- ✓ understanding an issue
- ✓ defining the problem
- ✓ brainstorming solutions
- ✓ creating, testing, and implementing prototype solutions

That sounds big. Sometimes it is. It doesn't need to be. Improvements in delivery of legal services may start with one small defined problem and an equally small but purposeful solution. The modern lawyer's mentality isn't about settling on one "best" solution to a big problem and sticking with it forever. It's about the value of a more iterative approach to both big and small aspects of your lawyering, and a constant effort towards "better" designs for how we do what we do.

2)   Productization

From no tech we inch forward to a more "low tech" category— although as a concept it often pairs with technology. **Productization** means capturing some or all of a traditional lawyering task and repackaging it as something that can be provided to others. You might hear this idea described with related terms such as "scaling" or "unbundling" a legal service or parts thereof. We might express the concept as:

> *legal knowledge + repeated patterns / discrete tasks =*
> *opportunity to capture service*

First, the knowledge. Chapter 2's Need to Know #6 Law as a Business Product introduced my neighbor's food and nutrition business. She transitioned from one-off, repetitive visits to friends' homes to a prepackaged service for many more people— skyrocketing revenue and freeing up her time for more personalized cooking sessions. Her expertise was the impact of too much sugar. Your expertise is the law. This book is about practical skills, but here's where substantive legal knowledge (think bar exam and core law school doctrinal classes) comes into play. It's an asset. *Your* asset. Maybe it's the United States tax code. Maybe it's how to incorporate a business in Nevada. Perhaps it's what to include in a repair demand letter to a landlord in Maine. Or maybe you know the statutory requirements for a valid zoning appeal in a local county in Georgia like the back of your hand. Whatever the area of law, if you know something, and you use that knowledge a lot in largely the same way, perhaps you can use it more efficiently—or allow others to use it themselves.

How do you use substantive knowledge in the same way? Repeated patterns and tasks. Our brains are trained to look for patterns in our personal lives but we often miss them in our professional work. Take the weather. If we see dark clouds, we expect rain and grab a jacket and umbrella. We might do this all the time with little custom thought or nuanced decision making. It's our automatic pattern. When a lawyer asks clients the same intake questions hundreds of times a year, many lawyers still view that as a unique service for that one special client. It's not. The client is special; the questions—the pattern—may not be. At least not to start.

The sum of productization is the opportunity to capture service and deliver it in an easier way or deliver it to more users, often at less cost but with similar quality. Like all the concepts in this chapter, avoid the all-or-nothing approach. If an entire task such as creation of a will for estate planning can't be replicated at scale, often a small communal piece can. Modern lawyers might consider productizing some aspects of service, not necessarily all.

I like productization as a category of change because it comes in many shapes and sizes. Most of the self-help tools we'll turn in this chapter are an example of a productized legal service. Before we move on to more "tech-ish" tools lawyers might use to productize, here are simpler examples to jump-start your thinking:

| Routine Task | Productization Idea |
|---|---|
| Answering the same questions from prospective or existing clients about billing and communication procedures. | Creating and providing a Frequently Asked Questions (FAQ) document or link for your clients with general answers. |
| Instructing clients about the same financial documents to bring to a meeting. | Creating a simple checklist to share in advance. |

| Summarizing important recent regulatory changes or case decisions for one or two clients. | Drafting a newsletter, pamphlet, or blog, or posting the summary to your firm's website to capture and showcase expertise to others (remember this tip for chapter 10 and online presence). |
| --- | --- |
| Reviewing your junior colleagues' calculations regarding alimony payments in family law cases. | Drafting a step-by-step guide for the jurisdiction or a more tech-ish alimony calculator to help minimize error. |

Productization won't always replace individual client counseling but works alongside it. Consider it a hybrid approach to modern lawyering, combining something packaged or automated (our next topic) with traditional, client-specific advice. Not all substantive legal knowledge is ripe for this approach, and law-as-a-product is not without risk. There could be poor design that misses substantive provisions, complacent approaches that don't stay current, or products offered without useful communication such that clients feel alienated—that they're missing out on the lawyer-as-counselor personalized experience they might expect. A modern lawyer understands the concept of productization, stays open to its applicability in some contexts, and trusts that by packaging up "small stuff" they'll be putting their legal talent toward the "big stuff."

---

**LIT TIP**

"[A] productized service isn't necessarily a tech tool. For example, turning a complicated process, like filing a patent application, into a series of easy-to-follow checklists is a productized service. Nor is there necessarily a profit motive behind every productized service. For example, volunteers at CALI's A2J Author created guided online interviews that automated thousands of forms laypeople once struggled to complete on their own. There are all kinds of productized services."[8]

Professor Gabriel H. Teninbaum
Author, Productizing Legal Work: Providing Legal Expertise at Scale

3)   Automation

**Automation** is an enormous umbrella covering many new processes, systems, technologies, and approaches to delivery of services—for legal and for thousands of workplaces and businesses today. It's a simple idea that's been around for a long time. Machines replacing human labor in factories during the last century is automation. But in other respects, automation is evolving and has an exciting future. Self-driving cars are an example of automation. So are "robot" vacuum cleaners and automatic home heating systems that turn on in the morning. Remember my airport kiosk example from the start of this chapter? That's automation. The airline took a high-volume, manual, and repeated task (a person saying hello to thousands of passengers, asking for flight number, asking security questions, scanning a credit card, printing a boarding pass) and created a way for a computer to replicate the work.

A broad definition of automation is machines or software that replace human action. It is technology that does a high-volume, repeated task that a person used to do, or technology that does some of a task and thus minimizes the human effort needed to accomplish something (though the human designing and implementing automation tools behind the scenes is anything but minimal).

Automation ranges from incremental and "low tech" to significant and highly technical. Document word-processing templates, discussed in chapter 3, are a form of automation. So is a simple configuration of email software to automatically send monthly marketing emails or a generic welcome message when someone visits a website. More advanced forms of automation use AI technology such as machine learning to complete tasks that people sometimes call "higher-order" work. Now we're automating not just small tasks but entire workflows at scale. As technology improves so too does the sophistication of what we automate. You might hear these concepts called "smart" automation or "hyperautomation."

Consider a familiar example: a garage door. One hundred years ago, humans used their own strength to manually raise and lower garage doors with a door handle. Then, technology improved and humans used electric transponders to press a button and open or close doors. Fast-forward, and smart home technology now means door systems can connect to a Wi-Fi network to control and monitor the door activity. You might connect one to a voice assistant like Google Assistant and announce your arrival or set a home security camera to record if the garage door opens after midnight. Automation means the repeated task works well with little effort or thought on your part 99% of the time, and you save your arm and back muscles for those few rare occasions where the door gets stuck or frozen shut with ice (that still happens in Boston where I live!).

Examples of legal automation are everywhere. We'll explore them throughout this chapter, but here are a few to get started, ranging from the administrative "business of law" context to completion of more substantive lawyering tasks:

- ✓ *Clio Scheduler* automates a law firm's client intake and lets clients book, pay for, confirm, and reschedule appointments.

- ✓ *DocuSign* allows users agree to digital contracts with e-signature tools or by checking a box with "clickwrap" automation technology.

- ✓ Onit, Inc.'s *Automate NDA* help lawyers minimize manual drafting and execution efforts with high volume standardized NDA contracts (non-disclosure agreements).

- ✓ *Rowan Patents* (formerly *TurboPatent*) offers software to support lawyers with automated creation of intellectual property documents like invention disclosures, patent drafts, and patent applications.

- ✓ The *Tubman Project* creates and shares AI-enabled tools with public defender offices to, among other things, assist in automation of documentation and filing.

- ✓ Companies such as *Incfile* offer state-specific business services such as automating creation of formation documents for an LLC or requesting a registered agent for a corporation.

Why automate? Lawyers do so for many reasons, whether to increase profitability, improve efficiency, serve more clients, or free up time and energy for creative higher-level legal analysis work. Just like productization, automation doesn't fit every situation. There is plenty of "one-off" legal work for tomorrow's lawyer that still depends on nuanced judgment and discretion. But the movement toward automation of routine standardized aspects of work lawyers do with (let's face it) minimal "brain power" is here to stay. So if you hear the tiresome phrase, "the robots are coming," what that really means is automation is coming. And you should welcome it. Automation helps you do more with less. It doesn't replace your work. It changes and improves how you'll do some of it.

## 4)  Expert Systems

**Expert systems** move into a more technical landscape of change. But let's start with something simple. Think back to your Civil Procedure course. You may have sketched out or seen a decision tree or flowchart that looked something like this:

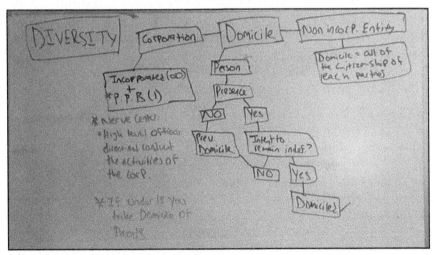

* Figure 6B: Civil Procedure student flowchart; image reproduced with permission by Jess Miers, Attorney, former student blogger at ctrlaltdissent. com.

Expert systems are like fancy flowcharts. Technology mimics the decision-making thought process of a human, often through "if-then" sets of rules in the most basic form. If we need to figure out domicile for a corporation, then this. If we need to figure out domicile for a person, then that. In the handwritten flowchart, the student captured Civil Procedure expertise through a series of steps and aimed to replicate it in a manner usable to others.

Return to a different example from the start of this chapter: the chatbot that helped with my request for a replacement coffee maker on the manufacturer's website. If a human customer service representative asked me my request, and I typed, "replacement," then that person would be trained to ask for my product order number. If I typed "shipping problem," they'd ask something else. Behind the scenes, expert systems capture these different nested decision paths to emulate the levels of reasoning a person uses, and then interact with a user in some back-and-forth sharing of information and answers. On a larger scale, think of an expert system tool like TurboTax (a massive decision tree of state and federal tax law) to prepare taxes or WebMD's online Symptom Checker (a massive decision tree of health care information) to investigate possible medical issues.

Starting simple is helpful, but expert systems combined with enhanced AI technology in almost every industry have evolved at a blistering pace, well beyond the simple binary "if-then" approach in our Civil Procedure decision tree. As machines get smarter and humans give them access to more and more data, the facts, patterns, decisions, inferences, "if-then" calls, and classifications expert systems can make get more complex.

Expert systems can be valuable but aren't perfect. On a positive note, they help lawyers (and others) ask the correct questions and obtain necessary information—skipping over unnecessary or irrelevant details to save time. In the Civil Procedure example, that means we wouldn't waste energy asking about a minor's living situation because the fact that a party to litigation is a minor would lead us to the conclusion that we should examine the parent's domicile instead. But what happens if the underlying framework changes, such that the Q&A flow of an expert system no longer works? What if Congress passed a law creating new standards for diversity jurisdiction in federal court? The flowchart would need to change. Asking questions that obtain information relevant to an outdated diversity jurisdiction statute would be useless. Expert systems are only as good as the persons creating, maintaining, and using them.

---

**LIT TIP**

"Expert systems in law deliver self-help—efficient, scalable answers to relatively routine legal questions at high volume and low cost. Can I do this? What are the risks if I do that? What are the procedures I need to follow in order to do X, Y, or Z? In a cost-conscious world, being able to answer those relatively routine questions in an automated way is a compelling story to government agencies, corporate legal departments, and law firms, as well as other legal service providers."[9]

Michael Mills
Co-Founder & Chief Strategy Officer, Neota Logic

---

Expert systems often form the back-end runway to innovative legal services tools today. Keep that in mind with self-service examples. They capture a discrete area of knowledge in many steps and simulate expertise without traditional one-on-one consultation. Expert systems transform legal know-how into a digitized decision-making process someone else can use, whether that's sharing knowledge with another lawyer for that person to use in serving their own clients or sharing it directly with individual clients for them to use themselves.

Creating an expert system takes time, patience, hard work, expertise, and continuous follow-through to ensure accuracy. This is so even with low- or no-code options in today's legal marketplace, although more lawyers are starting to dabble in the world of coding. The process isn't easy, but the technology offers exciting opportunities for how tomorrow's modern lawyers deliver services and how the public consumes them.

Expert systems hold great promise, especially for the way legal services may get to those who need them the most (remember chapter 2's Need to Know #5 Access to Justice). Imagine a world where we could capture the expertise of the most excellent and thorough family law lawyer in a specific jurisdiction and bring that knowledge and guidance to individuals who need it most, and who otherwise might never have the chance to get it. That's powerful stuff.

---

**LIT TIP**

**To Code or Not to Code?**

A common question in the context of automated legal tools and expert systems is should today's modern lawyer know basic computer programming language to design (or help design) software? Those who say yes point to increased employability and the ability to organize complex information to build simplified solutions. Those who say no point to coding being too "in the weeds" and an unproductive use of a lawyer's time, energy, and substantive knowledge. Find a middle ground where you grasp the basics and are open to working with technologists, inventors, or software developers. You'll decide if becoming a "lawyer-coder" or learning beginner basics—or none at all—is what's best for you.

---

## 5)   Document Assembly

**Document assembly** is also called document automation. It puts the idea of automation in the context of creation of documents that are identical except for some defined variables. Imagine you were tasked with sending fundraising letters on behalf of a charity you support. Would you draft the same letter 75 times? I hope not. You'd use the same letter but input different variables such as the name and address of the prospective donor and amount of their past donation. Document assembly is another flavor of the "don't bake from scratch" boxed cake mix example of work that can be standardized. We touched on a basic document assembly idea in chapter 3 with reusable Quick Parts and the idea of a library of repeated components to documents from which you can choose as you create new ones.

---

**LIT TIP**

Document assembly supports creation of customized, near-polished drafts of routine legal documents that include the same fields or general content. Some examples include contracts, wills, letters, trusts, bills, forms, invoices, corporate merger agreements, real estate forms, license renewals, prenuptial marital agreements, public filings, board resolutions or minutes, and trademark applications.

---

Document assembly tools are sometimes split into two categories (although some tools offer features that could fit both): *document first* or *document second*. Document first is a more basic approach wherein a tool starts off with an "empty" document shell with standard fields and variables that a lawyer completes and customizes, replacing the blank field with a custom name, monetary amount, location, etc. This approach is a little bit like doing a "find and replace" of certain parts of a document (or fill-in-the-blank).

Document second tools are often viewed as more sophisticated. Users start with no document. Information first gets collected, often through a chatbot or web-based guided interview Q&A. The tool generates a custom document that comes "second" as an output, with the inputted data included.

A **guided interview** is an expert system approach whereby broad questions take more narrow and diverse paths depending on the answers to eventually reach conclusions or end points. Answers become inputs to documents. It could be as simple as inputting a client name and court address for a letter, or it could be more in-depth legal variables and issues for something like forms and motions for a pro se tenant facing eviction. Lawyers use software that creates guided interviews to mimic the questions they would ask sitting across from a client to prepare a legal document.

Well-written guided interviews take time to create a sound behind-the-scenes framework. They must be comprehensive, accurate, up-to-date, and clear, such that they capture correct information in the correct location. If questions in a guided interview are the wrong ones, the information is wrong. If the information is wrong (or in the wrong place), the document is wrong.

Figure 6C is a simple example of a document second assembly tool for a Marriage Without Delay form. A user in Massachusetts can create, download, and file it as a request to waive the usual three-day waiting period for a marriage license. The tool first gathers simple information relevant to the form such as name and address through a series of Q&A like those shown in Figure 6C.

\* Figure 6C: Suffolk University Court Forms Online MassAccess sample address intake form; software copyright 2020 Legal Innovation & Technology Lab.[10]

Using inputs, the tool populates necessary fields and creates a form for a user to download as shown in Figure 6D:

\* Figure 6D: Suffolk University Court Forms Online MassAccess sample marriage without delay form; software copyright 2020 Legal Innovation & Technology Lab.[11]

Lawyers use document assembly in different ways. Address intake for a short court form is a simple example. The same principle of specific inputs creating content applies to complex legal topics and longer documents, too. Some lawyers create high volumes of documents in their practice in an efficient, consistent way. Other lawyers package document assembly tools with aspects of innovation we've discussed to produce a service that faces "outward" whereby others enjoy the lawyer's expertise and create documents themselves, with little or no individual consultation (such as in the Court Forms Online example).

Figure 6E is another example of packaging legal knowledge using guided interview document assembly principles. Upsolve is a nonprofit technology company helping individuals in the United States understand and file for bankruptcy. Besides a community messaging forum and substantive explanations of bankruptcy law, Upsolve's online questionnaire and form generator was named one of *Time* magazine's best inventions of 2020.[12] It uses guided screening questions that a user answers at their own pace to generate bankruptcy forms in PDF format for that user to file.

* Figure 6E: Upsolve My Bankruptcy Filing Tool; copyright Upsolve; reprinted with permission.

Hundreds of document assembly tools are on the market for businesses and services of all types today—not just in law. Some popular platforms lawyers use with robust document assembly features include:

- ✓ Docassemble
- ✓ A2JAuthor
- ✓ Fidu Legal
- ✓ Documate
- ✓ Rally

Document assembly isn't a quick fix or instant win. There is a reason I used the phrase "near-polished" documents in my definition and not "polished" or "final" or "perfect." Trust this technology but verify it. That's a modern lawyer's best approach to ensure that competency and client satisfaction remain paramount.

To recap, we've summarized 5 innovation themes for a modern lawyer to think about:

| Process Improvement * Productization * Automation * Expert Systems * Document Assembly |
| --- |

You'll come across some or all of these in different pockets of your career. Take a proactive approach instead of waiting to react to problems or inefficiencies. Lawyers welcoming of new methods of delivery of services and purposeful about their application may:

- ✓ reduce costs
- ✓ minimize errors
- ✓ soften frustrating inefficiencies
- ✓ serve more clients
- ✓ support profitability
- ✓ improve access to legal services
- ✓ free up time for more nuanced lawyering

   ✓   enjoy less mundane work and an enhanced work-
        life balance

Lawyers not so welcoming of these approaches? They might be
fine. Or they might find themselves left behind in the back of the
pack—like the driver still searching under their seat for a $20
bill at the automated tollbooth or the traveler refusing to use the
airport kiosk and standing in line for hours to speak with the
one service agent left.

For a finer point on how these broad concepts play out, we'll
spotlight two exemplary categories of innovation: contract
lifecycle management and "outward" repackaging through self-
help legal services.

## Innovation Spotlight #1: Contract Lifecycle Management (CLM)

There's a reason every first-year law student takes a Contracts
course. The black letter law for the bar exam has looked the
same for decades (mailbox rule, anyone?). Contracting in the real
world has too, right?

Far from it. Society's day-to-day commercial transactions have
become digitized, fast-paced, and widespread. Consider a
massive company such as Visa, ExxonMobil, or Johnson &
Johnson. How many contracts do you think each executes in
year? Hundreds? Thousands? Tens or hundreds of thousands?
Contracting touches supply, manufacturing, employment,
intellectual property, consumer rights, real estate . . . we could
go on. Tapping the "I agree" box on a tablet or agreeing to a user
agreement using facial recognition on a smartphone are two
everyday examples of how contracting has changed. Today's high
volume of contracts can be an inconsistent mess. Or that high
volume could become a treasure trove of information. Past
lawyers may have been complacent with the mess. Modern
lawyers like you won't. How can we (or our clients) manage what
we can't even measure?

Enter contract tech. It's a hot topic in legal operations and legal
technology circles; it's an umbrella term linking several concepts
we've covered. Contract tech tools help lawyers and other

professionals take a fresh look at improving conventional contract processes, both leading up to a contract (pre-execution) or after the fact (post-execution). You read cases about contract disputes in law school, but a contract timeline is a much bigger picture:

*Request* ➡ *Negotiate* ➡ *Create* ➡ *Approve* ➡ *Execute/Sign* ➡ *Store* ➡ *Classify* ➡ *Extract Useful Data*

Contract tech tools help lawyers and those with whom they work:

- ✓ understand and ensure consistency of substantive contract provisions

- ✓ automate outdated manual workflows of contract negotiation and formation

- ✓ digitize contract execution and signature processes

- ✓ secure centralized organization and digital contract storage

- ✓ extract valuable information post-execution at scale across high volumes

One popular pre-execution concept is **contract lifecycle management**, known as CLM. CLM tools are popular with lawyers inundated with a high volume of contracts. CLM tools help lawyers, salespersons, and countless other business professionals involved in contracting organize and manage the ins and outs of the contracting lifecycle.

Imagine the many steps of the contracting lifecycle done by different people, in different locations, in different ways, with different tools, and then stored in different electronic locations. That's messy. CLM tools can offer a better approach. You might consider them a master centralized contract hub—a dashboard library of sorts to track contracting steps across an organization or legal department, pulling standard language from clause banks, or automating creation without reinventing the wheel for each new agreement. CLM tools often include approval and e-signature features, making execution far more efficient than junior lawyers dashing around with a pen and mounds of hard-copy papers. Lawyers will also look to CLM tools to help with storage. Instead of random files, folders, or drives, modern lawyers crave a convenient repository that's organized, searchable, shareable, and secure.

---

### LIT TIP

"You've probably enjoyed a Clif Bar or two, but you probably didn't think of the thousands of contracts fueling the baking of those energy bars. At Clif Bar & Co., our contracts team worked with a great pairing of the Thomson Reuters Contract Express tool and contract automation advice from external United Kingdom legal technology consultants, Skye (award-winning leaders in the legal tech world), to automate our contracts lifecycle processes. Our company grew quickly, and legal processes needed to keep up. For example, we hardwired the signoffs and workflows in the system so that along the way everyone knew all the boxes had been checked by all the right functions and who checked the boxes. We also empowered self-serve agreements that did not require any touch points with legal or accounting because of this embedded governance system. This meant Clifsters could do what they loved best— creating and selling yummy, sustainable food."

Marjorie Goux
Chief Legal Officer, Rodan + Fields
former Chief Legal Counsel, Clif Bar & Company
former Chief Counsel, The Clorox Company

---

Post-execution, the work's not done for a modern lawyer. A big-picture view transforms contracts from individual documents to valuable holistic data. Remember in-house commercial real estate lawyer Theo from this chapter's kickoff question? Leases at his company Spacial were everywhere, formed by all different one-off methods. It's no wonder Theo would have trouble understanding, summarizing, or gleaning meaningful data from them. Modern contract repositories give lawyers and clients deeper insight to answer the "if we only knew what was in there" question.

For example, digital contract management company Ironclad's Dynamic Repository, captured in Figure 6F, shows the result of contracts loaded into a platform that lets users do things such as filter, search for contracts up for renewal at a certain future date, or export spreadsheets of groups of contracts for further review.

\* Figure 6F: Ironclad Dynamic Repository; reprinted with permission.

Manual capture of the sort of contract information shown in Figure 6F such as Contract Value or Agreement Date was and still is in theory possible. But the cost and effort are often prohibitively high. Consider the following hypothetical requests from future corporate clients. Would lawyers be able to competently respond to such requests if contracts were scattered, inconsistent, and going in a thousand different directions? Doubtful.

Dear Modern Lawyer:

    ✓    Can you tell us which of our contracts are affected by changes to Europe's General Data Protection Regulation (GDPR) privacy laws, or the December 31, 2021 expiration of LIBOR (London Interbank Offered Rate) as the benchmark in place for years for contractual loan interest rates?

    ✓    Can you help us learn what past contracts reveal about a company we're performing due diligence review on as part of a proposed corporate merger?

    ✓    Can you help us create a comprehensive summary of our employment agreements only for employees in South America and Africa to gauge exposed risk in those jurisdictions and discover any inconsistencies across agreements?

Those are hard questions. Contract tech makes answering them not easy but easier. A modern lawyer isn't satisfied with estimates and gut instincts, just like we touched on in chapter 4 with research analytics. For these and thousands of other detailed inquiries, manual review falls short. It's expensive, time consuming, difficult, and risky.

Advanced AI analytics is a growing aspect of contract tech. These tools apply sophisticated technology to the data set (all the contracts) and spot patterns that help the software "understand" contract content. Picture software doing what it would take a human lawyer years to do if eyeballing, reading, and taking notes on thousands of pages of contracts. Here's an oversimplified summary: contracts are loaded into software; the software is trained to find hundreds of different contract provisions (either generically preset or customized to a client's needs); the software finds (or doesn't find) provisions; the software provides user-friendly summary results and reports to describe what's in the contract data. It's not magic; it's visibility.

This spotlight is a non-technical teaser into the very technical world of contract tech. Contracts questions on the bar exam have not changed much; contracts in action have. They're another form of "big data" and the possibilities are endless. In the past and probably still today, some people considered it unethical for a lawyer to rely on technology to create, manage, and understand contracts. In the future, it might be unethical for a lawyer *not* to.

## Innovation Spotlight #2: Self-Help Legal Services

Our second spotlight of innovation in delivery of legal services pivots from large-scale, often private business contracting to everyday people. Real people with real legal problems in need of real help. How might a modern lawyer reimagine services in this important context? Here the theme is less about profits or corporate improvements based on big data and more about implications for the justice system. Can new ways of delivering legal services in the space known as "justice tech" really help "democratize" the law for everyone?

It's tempting to label new approaches to legal services delivery as a "bonus"—a convenient new mobile app, interesting database, and nice-to-have-but-not-really-necessary tool that captures substantive legal knowledge. But sometimes legal services are very necessary—necessary even as in life or death. Legal services impact a person's family, education, living situation, health, livelihood, privacy, and safety. Automating thousands of business contracts is great. Automating a single form that saves someone from losing their home is another level of great.

Remember the Access to Justice gap, Need to Know #5. Many middle-class and low-income people in the United States get inadequate legal aid or no legal aid at all. Often A2J is expensive and difficult and historically unequal, with certain groups such as white, wealthy people having greater access to services compared to racial and other minorities. As I did in chapter 2, I urge you to explore the A2J crisis in greater detail, whether in the context of innovation and technology or a substantive area of law that interests you such as criminal defense or immigration.

Can **self-help legal services** help solve this problem? They can chip away at it. Accessibility of knowledge through technology has made many of us "DIY" (do it yourself) experts in all sorts of ways. Last time my shower drain clogged, I watched a few YouTube instructional videos and fixed it myself instead of calling a plumber, waiting to schedule a service call, and paying them for their time and labor. Navigating solutions to legal problems is far more complicated and intimidating for most than unclogging a drain. But maybe it doesn't have to be.

The concept of self-help legal service isn't new. LegalZoom is regarded as the parent (maybe now the grandparent) of self-service legal automation. LegalZoom was founded in 2001 and went public in 2021, valued at over $7.5 billion. Its online platform and mobile app epitomize large-scale productization and automation, offering flat-fee legal document creation for things like estate planning, intellectual property protection, or business formation documents, along with an option for attorney advice. Rocket Lawyer is another well-known online legal services company, announcing to users of its mobile app: "Legal made simple. What can we help you with today?"

---

**LIT TIP**

In 2021, LegalZoom handled approximately 10% of LLC formations and 5% of all corporation formations in the United States— 378,000 new companies.[13]

In 2021, Rocket Lawyer was valued at around $1 billion with more than 25 million registered users enjoying access to more than 1,000 different legal documents.[14]

---

LegalZoom and Rocket Lawyer were early players, but the field has expanded. Companies are zeroing in on how to deliver services for the routine and frequent legal issues people have. Save the most complex, high-level legal issues for the bespoke traditional lawyering of old but approach less complex, lower-risk matters in a different way. This is possible as the public becomes more tech-savvy and able to use mobile devices and access the internet (although not all—equal access to reliable Wi-Fi is still a real concern). Slowly but surely, we're getting comfortable with the idea that every legal issue doesn't need custom one-on-one attention. High cost can become lower flat-fee cost, which can become no cost. Instead of traditional legal "advice" from a lawyer, there are many options for how the public obtains knowledge and guidance (often from a location and at a time of their choosing):

- ✓ People visit legal websites and forums for direct help from lawyers, such as the American Bar Association's Free Legal Answers.

- ✓ Referral services and online pro bono portals connect lawyers looking to help with vulnerable individuals navigating issues like unemployment or eviction.

- ✓ Bar associations and nonprofit organizations like the Legal Services Corporation (LSC) partner across the country to create legal help guides for the public, such as the Michigan Legal Help website, which connects people to lawyers, e-filing information, court rules, and substantive guidance on topics like immigration and traffic crime.[15]

✓ Court systems around the United States offer self-represented litigants access to information and resources, such as with a protection order kiosk in a courthouse lobby (where an individual answers questions and receives an assembled application for a restraining or protective order).

✓ Consumers enjoy web and mobile tools to guide them through personal legal issues such as a divorce, like the Hello Divorce platform shown in Figure 6G, which offers the options of a free download of a "Divorce 101" guide, a free 15-minute introduction call, a quiz to determine whether the online service might be right for the user, and different service plans with set costs and varying levels of service such as filing the forms for you or serving forms on your spouse.

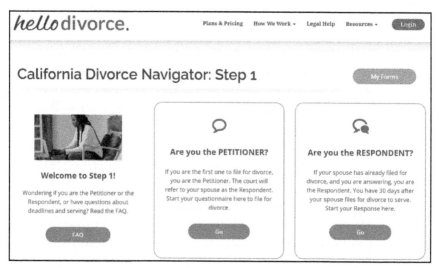

* Figure 6G: Hello Divorce California Divorce Navigator; reprinted with permission Hello Divorce.[16]

Discussion of self-help legal is incomplete without mention of the Covid-19 pandemic. Using technology to deliver legal services to those in need existed before 2020, but like several book topics, the pandemic prompted renewed attention on the issue once individuals couldn't visit courthouses or legal aid offices in person. One terrific example: lawyers partnered with the Massachusetts state court system and launched a Court Forms Online website with an assembly line of user-friendly, mobile court forms for people to complete and file remotely after an online guided interview Q&A. Forms such as a motion to stay to prevent eviction from one's home or a request to change a restraining order against another person were created to be available in different languages and accessible at a sixth-grade education level. Individuals needing to find and file court forms online during the Covid-19 pandemic (or after) could browse by categories such as Housing or Family Law, or, as shown in Figure 6H, even describe their problem in everyday language ("What seems to be the problem?") so the system's natural language issue spotter could point them in the right direction:

**Find and file court forms online during the emergency**

This site offers a way for you to reach the court during the COVID-19 crisis. It provides court forms and self-help materials for areas of urgent legal need. Describe your issue here, and our issue spotter will look for helpful resources. You can also browse forms below by category.

**What seems to be the problem?**     0 words

Share your story here

Reply should be at least 5 words long. Longer replies get better results. Do **NOT** include identifying information like your name or address.

☑ Use my reply to help people facing similar issues. Learn how

Find Help

* Figure 6H: Suffolk University MassAccess Court Forms Online homepage.[17]

True story: during the Covid-19 pandemic, a Massachusetts citizen used this tool to create a motion to stay an eviction when they were being evicted from their home—as in, when a constable was physically at their home removing their belongings! The person answered all the questions and the online form was filed with the Appeals Court. The court granted the motion, meaning the eviction stopped and the person was able to bring their belongings inside and stay at home at least for another day. If that's not proof of the power and promise of technology in the hands of individuals who need legal help, I'm not sure what is.

Self-help is simple in theory but difficult in execution. The cost of creating these tools isn't small, nor is the effort to build them, maintain accuracy, and communicate their existence to users. Modern lawyers will explore ways to share information and technology not just with individuals needing services but with other lawyers also trying to help. If a terrific expert system and document assembly tool is built based on Michigan landlord/tenant law, and Pennsylvania law differs only slightly but has no such tool available to tenants, forward-thinking lawyers in the A2J space will, I hope, continue to work to share that resource. What does more quality tools in more lawyers' hands in more jurisdictions mean? It means more legal services for more people in need.

## "Unbundling" Opportunities, Regulatory Roadblocks & Future Concerns

I said the goal of this chapter was not for readers to learn cutting-edge technologies but to focus on a modern mindset amid so-called disruption in traditional legal services. As we conclude, I'll plant the seed for future thought about opportunities, roadblocks, and concerns likely to creep up as the profession's status quo shakes up.

Starting with the positive, a modern lawyer has the opportunity to divide up discrete aspects of work with others who can take on those tasks. Our discussion of productization mentioned the term "unbundling." Picture your entire legal service as a bundle of sticks. What if you didn't need to hold all of them? What if your client didn't want you to? You and your client choose the best ones to be handled in the best ways, by the best person or third party, at the best time. I once heard the analogy of the modern lawyer more like a football quarterback managing the overall game plan instead of a one-stop shop for all aspects of a matter. Lucky for us, as we saw in chapter 2's Need to Know #4, entire companies exist that are ready and willing to share the bundle of sticks: Alternative Legal Service Providers (ALSPs). Not ready to sort through hundreds of client contracts? Hire someone else. Dreading a complicated internal investigation with large volumes of ESI? Enjoy a third-party vendor's expertise. This is an oversimplified summary, but remember:

more ALSPs and more cost-effective, expert approaches means more clients will explore unbundling. As a modern lawyer, you should too. Keeping a tight grasp on the entire bundle of sticks might not be the best move in the future for you or your client.

Now some caution when we think about innovative change. You'll take (or you've completed) a legal ethics class in law school. When I showed one student the Hello Divorce tool from Figure 6G, she remarked, *"Are lawyers really allowed to do that?!"* Her question got at the wrinkly issue of whether innovative delivery tools and platforms such as LegalZoom and Hello Divorce are ethical:

- ✓ Do these tools constitute formal legal advice?

- ✓ Do the lawyers building them have an ethical obligation to do so competently?

- ✓ Are tools that a lawyer builds restricted geographically by where that lawyer is licensed to practice?

- ✓ Are tools built and managed by lawyers together with non-lawyers allowed?

- ✓ Do these tools, websites, and apps engage in the **unauthorized practice of law**, as Model Rule 5.5 forbids?

You won't be surprised by the answer: it depends and it's complicated. As lawyers and others explore innovative ways to offer services, others cling to the existing ethical rules that can dampen such efforts. As much as today's sophisticated technology like AI is new (well, newer), anxiety around unauthorized practice of law and non-traditional paths for legal advice is not. In 1930, it was concern about judges on a radio show giving listeners advice. In 1998, it was concern about hard-copy legal self-help books in Texas until a state law eventually exempted the books on the condition of fine-print disclaimers that they didn't contain legal advice. Today, it's concern about websites, mobile apps, and chatbots. Tomorrow? Maybe it's concern about an avatar lawyer in the metaverse!

---

**LIT TIP**

In *Florida Bar v. TIKD Servs. LLC* in 2021, the court in a 4–3 decision granted a request to enjoin a mobile app designed to connect people with lawyers to fight traffic tickets, holding that the startup company engaged in the unauthorized practice of law under state rules because it gave advice beyond pure administrative and service functions:

"We fully acknowledge that TIKD appears to have found a profitable business niche that capitalizes on an unusually high rate of traffic citation dismissals, resulting in a very "good deal" for most of the corporation's legal clients . . . [i]t could be argued, therefore, that TIKD in some ways increases affordable access to our justice system. However, irrespective of any benefits arguably created by TIKD's unique, and perhaps temporary, niche, we cannot address the access to justice problem by allowing nonlawyer corporations to engage in conduct that, under this Court's sound precedent, constitutes the practice of law. We recognize that advanced in technology have allowed for greater access to the legal system through readily available legal forms, which represent the commoditization of legal work products that at one time were only readily accessed by hiring lawyers. Although continuing advances in technology could offer similar opportunities, those issues should be explored through this Court's rule making process . . ."[18]

---

LegalZoom is still in business, and so are other tools this book introduces. That alone gives you a sense of how state-by-state challenges to online legal services companies and technology providers have fared. But the roadblocks are there. Lurking in the background is criticism that these ethical rules and regulations created decades ago (by lawyers themselves) have more to do with protecting lawyers' financial interests and insulating them from competition than they do with protecting the public. Recall chapter 2's discussion of Need to Know #4 Legal Services Without (or Alongside) Lawyers. Modern lawyers will wrestle with thorny issues like what happens when a user of a tool is physically located in a state where the attorney who created the tool is not licensed, or how Model Rule 5.4's prohibition against non-lawyers having an ownership interest in a law firm jibes with renewed calls for change in delivery of legal services and creative approaches to solving the A2J problem. Other countries such as the United Kingdom embrace lawyer and non-lawyer co-ownership (that's why large accounting firms around the globe can pair legal advice with financial services, for example, as noted in Need to Know #4).

Innovative legal tools using AI also swirl up intriguing questions such as:

- ✓ In what jurisdiction is a so-called robot lawyer licensed to practice?

- ✓ Who, if anyone, is on the hook for potential malpractice if (when?) AI legal tools don't work well or make errors?

- ✓ Should ethics rules treat AI tools different from anyone or anything else a non-lawyer (such as a paralegal) may do today, so long as supervised by a lawyer?

- ✓ Are AI tools an extension of a lawyer's duty of confidentiality or duty to ensure reasonable security with client information submitted or shared with an AI system?

These questions haven't been answered during my career; I'm not sure they'll be answered anytime soon during yours.

This chapter is about change. Efforts at regulatory change are in full pursuit. As summarized in our Need to Know #4, regulatory sandboxes (or movement towards them) are underway in several jurisdictions in the United States such as Utah and Arizona. A "sandbox" means a safe, approved opportunity for states to experiment with temporary trial periods for new lawyer/non-lawyer business models and non-lawyer limited "practice" of law (such as licensed paralegals). Sometimes it's one step forward and two steps back, but wheels are in motion. The regulatory framework insulating the legal profession has existed for generations, and change should be slow and careful. It's not going to happen overnight. I can't promise the ethics rules of the profession will modernize just like the underlying services they govern are. No matter what, a modern lawyer will stay abreast of regulatory developments as they impact the pace and breadth of innovative change.

---

**LIT TIP**

"As a lawyer-entrepreneur, one of my jobs is to help narrow the justice gap. I strongly believe we can do well and do good. There are certainly legal service business models that could make a lawyer more money quicker and easier—but that lowers our impact and it's not a trade-off I'm willing to make. The Hello Divorce tool is an example of 'justice tech.' For now, justice tech must operate within existing regulations of law practice where there's significant interest in maintaining the status quo. Despite that challenge, lawyers must look beyond their lawyer point of view and think through systems and structures from the point of view of their legal customer. There are innovative opportunities for frameworks that can better bridge the A2J gap and result in positive outcomes for both the consumer who needs help and the lawyer delivering help to them in a creative way."

Erin Levine
Founder & CEO, Hello Divorce

---

\* \* \* \*

Take this new mindset for change with you. Next, we'll turn to how law practice management and the administrative business of lawyering have changed with new and improved client-centered processes. No matter your practice area, the profession will see new shake-ups, new realities, new challenges, and new opportunities. The demand for legal expertise in our complex world is increasing; so too is the demand that lawyers deliver it in a client-centered, efficient, and convenient way. Whether termed part of the "online gig economy," the "Uberization" of the legal industry (as in what Uber did to taxis), or an aspect of the so-called creator economy trend, the question is this: will you be motivated to stay involved in the game or be content to watch from the sidelines?

---

 *Review Your Knowledge*

1) *DoNotPay* was invented in 2015 in the United Kingdom as an online tool for individuals to contest parking tickets.[19] It expanded to a subscription-service "legal assistant" in other

areas for consumers such as cancelling a subscription service, applying for a tuition fee waiver, receiving a refund for an Uber Eats order, or creating a document for use in suing a utility provider such as Comcast or Verizon in small claims court. Based on this description, the tool is an example of what principle or principles relating to innovative approaches to delivery of legal services?

a) Document assembly only, because users build and file forms and documents.

b) Unauthorized practice of law, because lawyers aren't permitted to involve themselves in mobile apps that offer legal advice.

c) Productization, expert system, automation, and document assembly, because the platform captures human know-how and creates interactive Q&A where inputs from users help create outputs like documents, forms, and draft emails.

d) Legal Operations, because it involves many people doing transactions.

2) Brooklyn is a budding legal techie in her final year of law school. Her mother is a solo practitioner focused on estate planning services. She wants to design an expert system and document automation tool to help her mother create wills and trusts. Brooklyn is familiar with the software she can use to build the tool and feels confident she can convince her skeptical mother that she can complete her work more efficiently. The most important thing Brooklyn should do as she starts out is:

a) select only one or two legal documents to focus on first.

b) talk to her mother to understand how she usually collects client information and builds the documents.

c) learn nuances among the different jurisdictions where her mother's clients live and need the estate planning materials.

d) all of the above.

3)  Suppose an experienced lawyer in Tennessee created an unemployment benefits online toolkit with state-specific information about what the benefits are and how to apply for them. He was passionate about closing the Access to Justice gap and wanted to help individuals who were out of work and in need of support. He worked with a law student intern on the project, and the advice was comprehensive and detailed—although it also contained its fair share of legalese and heavy legal citation. They even tracked the number of visits the site received and over the course of a year were disappointed to learn the site had fewer than 100 visitors, and fewer than 40 people who actually used the toolkit. Part of the problem with this effort at a productized legal tool might have been:

a)  they should have worked with more unemployment benefits experts to ensure the substantive law was accurate.

b)  they should have focused on user design and the accessibility of the content because it could have been too complicated.

c)  they captured expertise but might have failed to communicate about it and share the tool in an effective way, such as by working with community legal aid offices, shelters, or courthouses to post flyers.

d)  answers b and c could both be part of the problem.

4)  After working in the insurance industry for decades, Enrico went back to law school to earn his JD in a part-time program. His partner was diagnosed with cancer and Enrico slowed down his practice to support his treatment and care. Years later, with his partner in recovery, Enrico realizes all he's learned navigating the insurance and health-care system in the context of a person surviving cancer and volunteers to give lectures and workshops with local nonprofits, cancer centers, and hospitals. People are grateful for his help and he has never felt more professionally fulfilled. Is Enrico's specialty a good candidate for productization of a legal service?

a)  No. Cancer is a very personal topic and technology will interfere with the human-to-human compassionate experience.

b)  Yes. Enrico could package his know-how and interest in this niche area with a low-tech platform such as a monthly podcast to bring guidance to more people.

c)  Yes. Enrico could package his know-how and interest in this niche area but only if he stops all individual legal representation of clients.

d)  No. Enrico's specialty is too narrow a field to be a good candidate for productization.

5)  Gabrielle is a new lawyer at a medium-size law firm in Los Angeles specializing in residential real estate. The other real estate lawyers in the firm have done their work the same for years, with traditional paper and "wet ink" in-person signatures on documents such as the purchase and sale agreement. Sitting in freeway traffic for hours returning from a closing at a client's new home, Gabrielle is frustrated at the inefficient and slow workflows. Later, she starts to explore new e-closing remote options for the firm to consider but knows it will be a tough sell to her veteran colleagues. Which of the following statements is true?

a)  Gabrielle should stress that the initial time, investment, and effort is worthwhile in the long run because e-closing options with e-signatures offer the office and clients more convenience, enhanced security, better consistency, and quicker processes (not to mention more eco-friendly than large reams of paper).

b)  E-closing remote options in the residential real estate context probably won't work because clients will expect an in-person approach at their home.

c)  Implementing new e-closing workflows and software will be quick and easy, with a minimal learning curve for Gabrielle's veteran colleagues.

d)  E-closing remote options are great for "self-service" legal so the office should develop a mobile app for residential real estate customers to do everything themselves.

 *Practice Your Knowledge*

## Exercise #1: Process Improvement One-Pager

Think of any process or procedure that frustrates you anywhere: your school, internship, workplace, fitness center, grocery store, bank, doctor's office, etc. Draft a "mini" process improvement one-pager. First, define and explain the problem, mapping out the process as best you know it. Second, list interested stakeholders and other people you'd need to talk with before any changes. Third, brainstorm redesign solutions that consider the end user and purpose of the process: how could it be improved? Finally, note how the change would have to be implemented and assessed. Change is difficult for one small everyday process—no wonder it's hard for a profession of millions of lawyers!

## Exercise #2: Document Assembly at Work

As the tech-savvy new associate, you've been asked by a senior lawyer to investigate document assembly and meet with her to give some basics. Go online to learn more about and test out at least two document assembly tools. You may use something mentioned in this chapter or one that you find. Request a demonstration, sign up for a free trial, or experiment with a free tool. (This exercise does not require you to enter payment information; for example, one free and simple document generator in transactional lawyering to check out is Cooley GO https://www.cooleygo.com/.) Don't use real names or information. Fill out some forms or create some documents on different tools with different choices and inputs. Prepare overview notes for your meeting about your user experience, questions, frustrations, cautions, observations, and overall impressions.

*Expand Your Knowledge*

➢ John O. McGinnis & Russell G. Pearce, *The Great Disruption: How Machine Intelligence Will Transform the Role of Lawyers in the Delivery of Legal Services*, 82 FORDHAM L. REV. 3041 (2014).

➢ Marshall Lichty, *Design Thinking for Lawyers* (2019), https://lawyerist.com/news-articles/design-thinking-for-lawyers/ [https://perma.cc/8H54-FE3Y].

➢ LUCY ENDEL BASSLI, THE SIMPLE GUIDE TO LEGAL INNOVATION: BASICS EVERY LAWYER SHOULD KNOW (2020).

*Answers & Explanations*

*Knowledge Kickoff*

c) Technology is one tool for lawyers but alone it can't fix every problem or improve every inefficient workflow. This question encourages a broader view of how Spacial might rethink its lease formation processes at the outset, not just employ a document assembly tool to help lawyer Theo at one isolated spot in the overall process or an internet chatbot that would be inapplicable in this setting. Theo's negotiation for real estate clients and discussion with brokers are examples of higher-level lawyering with nuanced judgment; no simple Q&A automated process like a chatbot expert system should replace that. Manual review to get at the important contract data Spacial's CEO wants is unrealistic, both because of the time and effort required and the fact that Theo doesn't have a secure, standard, searchable repository for all of Spacial's brokered leases.

*Review Your Knowledge*

1) c) *DoNotPay* is an online legal tool that captures know-how and productizes it for consumers. With some very basic Q&A and expert systems (remember the Civil Procedure flowchart), the tool walks users through step-by-step processes to seek some result, often including an eventual output. It's not an example of Legal Operations because that is generally in a different context, most often a law firm or legal department and not an individual tool like this. *DoNotPay*'s website includes the disclaimer that it is not a law firm and is not providing legal advice and, to date, it has not been held to constitute unauthorized practice in any jurisdiction. If it does face challenge, it won't be because advice came via a mobile application—that medium alone does not raise red flags.

2) d) Remember the phrase "people first, technology second." Brooklyn should focus on her mother's practice and procedures before building a tool to capture the work. The idea is a good one but the project could be

derailed if, for example, Brooklyn took on too many documents at once without first confirming one of them worked well in execution, or if Brooklyn's tool failed to account for substantive differences in estate planning law across jurisdictions where clients lived. Brooklyn's tool will only succeed if she understands her mother's workflow and takes time on the front end to carefully capture the know-how and estate planning expertise.

3) d) Self-help and DIY legal tools are promising in theory but can struggle to get off the ground. They aren't a quick fix to society's need for affordable and accessible legal services. Modern lawyers with terrific intentions to productize and sell or make available their expertise alone aren't enough. Getting products and resources off the ground is hard work, and efforts at innovative legal services delivery methods to improve the A2J gap must be collaborative to ensure those in need can access, read, understand, and use the packaged service.

4) b) Enrico's niche specialty with insurance law and cancer treatments is a great candidate for a low-tech tool such as a podcast, social media video series, or newsletter to spread his knowledge to more individuals in need. Narrow expertise is often an advantage for productization, not a disadvantage. There's no reason Enrico can't pair a productized service with continued traditional representation of clients. Productization isn't an all-or-nothing option. While cancer is of course a personal topic, most legal issues are. Tools that productize can complement in-person client counseling—they need not replace it.

5) a) Real estate documents are a popular candidate for innovation. These paper transactions are slowly moving in the digital direction in some jurisdictions (often prompted by the Covid-19 pandemic). A mobile do-it-yourself approach isn't the best fit here, nor is it Gabrielle's goal to outright remove a lawyer's custom guidance from the sale process. Digital tools work alongside the real estate lawyer. While some clients

may be used to in-person support, the majority of legal consumers will likely appreciate the convenience of completing a transaction at a place and time of their own choosing.

## Endnotes

1 B. F. SKINNER, CONTINGENCIES OF REINFORCEMENT ch. 9 (1969).

2 *Reinvent*, BAKER MCKENZIE, https://www.bakermckenzie.com/en/expertise/solutions/reinvent [https://perma.cc/EYB4-H45X].

3 *Wilson Sonsini—1st Even Law Firm in Company's 'Most Innovative' List*, ARTIFICIAL LAWYER (Mar. 11, 2022), https://www.artificiallawyer.com/2022/03/11/wilson-sonsini-1st-ever-law-firm-in-fast-companys-most-innovative-list/ [https://perma.cc/P7ZD-GZRT].

4 *De Novo*, DAVIS WRIGHT TREMAINE LLP, https://www.dwt.com/about/de-novo [https://perma.cc/F7HY-BDTE].

5 Casey Flaherty, *Tech-First Failures—Value Story*, GEEKS AND A LAW BLOG (Dec. 13, 2021), https://www.geeklawblog.com/2021/12/tech-first-failures-value-storytelling-6.html [https://perma.cc/5UFG-NSR9].

6 *Legal Department Operations (LDO) Index 2021 (Sixth Edition): The Risk of Being Left Behind*, THOMAS REUTERS, https://legal.thomsonreuters.com/en/insights/reports/legal-department-operations-index-sixth-edition-2021/form [https://perma.cc/A5CE-4CFV].

7 Rose D. Ors, *In Practice: How Shell Maximizes the Value of Its Legal Operations Function*, REUTERS (Aug. 10, 2021, 2:17PM), https://www.reuters.com/legal/legalindustry/practice-how-shell-maximizes-value-its-legal-operations-function-2021-08-10/ [https://perma.cc/HKX7-VSYK].

8 GABRIEL H. TENINBAUM, PRODUCTIZING LEGAL WORK: PROVIDING LEGAL EXPERTISE AT SCALE (Wolters Kluwer 2021).

9 NOAH WAISBERG & DR. ALEXANDER HUDEK, AI FOR LAWYERS 148 (Wiley, 1st ed. 2021).

10 Reproduced under MIT License https://github.com/SuffolkLITLab/doc-assembly-line/blob/master/LICENSE [https://perma.cc/MJN5-UEBX].

11 Reproduced under MIT License https://github.com/SuffolkLITLab/doc-assembly-line/blob/master/LICENSE [https://perma.cc/MJN5-UEBX].

12 *Free Filing Upsolve*, TIME, (Nov. 19, 2020, 8:59 AM), https://time.com/collection/best-inventions-2020/5911367/upsolve/ [https://perma.cc/C36G-Q564].

13 LEGALZOOM, https://www.legalzoom.com/ [https://perma.cc/9GKZ-DAN9].

14 ROCKETLAWYER, https://www.rocketlawyer.com/ [https://perma.cc/9AX3-8KJX].

15 MICHIGAN LEGAL HELP, https://michiganlegalhelp.org/ [https://perma.cc/M5SX-CTBJ].

16 https://hellodivorce.com/ [https://perma.cc/48H5-6EJJ].

17 https://courtformsonline.org/ [https://perma.cc/FX8A-MR2F].

18 *Florida Bar v. TIKD Servs. LLC*, 326 So.3d 1073 (Fla. Oct. 14, 2021), https://www.floridasupremecourt.org/content/download/795189/opinion/sc18-149.pdf [https://perma.cc/M6CX-Y8ES].

19 DONOTPAY, https://donotpay.com/ [https://perma.cc/8VGJ-ZEAD].

# CHAPTER 7

# LAW PRACTICE MANAGEMENT

*Core Concepts*

| | |
|---|---|
| law practice management (LPM) software<br>client-centered experience<br>paperless law practice<br>knowledge management<br>document management | portals and dashboards<br>calendar integration<br>VoIP systems<br>e-payment<br>e-signature |

*Knowledge Kickoff*

Richard and his law school classmate Ariella opened a criminal defense law firm following years of work as local prosecutors. They specialize in DUI/OUI defense. Their small firm built up a strong client base over the first year through referrals and other connections. Richard and Ariella were excellent in the courtroom and developed a reputation for being savvy plea negotiators. Behind the scenes, to keep costs down, the firm had no administrative support. They used two phone lines with a basic voicemail option, a single shared office computer drive for files, and an occasional intern who mailed out client bills once a month. A whiteboard calendar on the front office wall kept deadlines. A few years into practice, the firm noticed business dropping off. Richard ran into a former client who explained that he didn't rehire him because Richard never returned the client's calls, never explained the firm's billing procedures, didn't accept online payments, missed a scheduled probation officer meeting, and couldn't locate court documents the client needed for a job application. Richard shared this with Ariella, who asked if they should rethink office practices such as a client extranet for communication and information sharing. A reasonable response from Richard would be:

a)   no, the firm shouldn't—phone tag is part of small-firm life and clients need to be patient because Richard can't call them all back right away.

b)   no, the firm shouldn't—a client portal poses too great a security risk and clients don't expect real-time, transparent access to case files.

c)   no, the firm shouldn't—one grand gesture of apology and the client will forget about the intermittent inconveniences.

d)   yes, the firm probably should—an upfront investment in better processes and technologies would improve client experience and in time make the lawyers' lives easier.

-----

Rewind a few years and consider this question: is law a profession or a business? If you answered this question at the start of your law school journey, most readers would probably choose profession. But after making it this far in the book, I hope you see it's a little bit of both. This chapter addresses the business and administrative aspects of law practice. In law school, you focus on what the law is and not as much on how it works. You learn substantive law and legal practice skills. Most students don't learn the "everything but" behind-the-scenes non-billable grease that keeps the legal advice wheels moving: the document management, timekeeping, invoicing, paper pushing, scheduling, record keeping, correspondence, and much more.

You're not most students, so here you are.

Client expectations for a modern lawyer are different today. Lawyers of past generations may have enjoyed more of a "lawyer's market" (like a "seller's market" in real estate) with more business than they can handle. But today's clients are consumers of legal services with more choice and greater expectations than ever before. Why? Because they get it everywhere else. Did you ever think to compare a law firm to a business such as Amazon, Uber, or Apple? We expect a lot from the modern businesses we use every day: convenience, communication, customization, advanced technology, and on-demand customer service (not to mention a high-quality underlying product worth our money). Why shouldn't consumers expect the same of their experience with a lawyer? They should; they do; they will.

This chapter helps prepare you to meet those expectations. It starts you on the path to ensure excellent behind-the-scenes service matches your excellent substantive legal advice. If you don't drive like you did 10 years ago, don't grocery shop like you did, don't pay your dog walker like you did, don't make a dinner reservation like you did, why should you handle the business of being a lawyer in the same old way? You shouldn't.

**Law practice management** (LPM) is the business of law. This chapter builds upon the last chapter, as many tools and improved LPM processes exist because lawyers and others have pursued innovative change. This chapter also sets up the next topic of Remote Lawyering (chapter 8), as sound LPM and administration "in the office" sets lawyers up for sound remote lawyering "out of office." Many ideas in this chapter have a mobile-access angle as lawyers head out of the office more than ever before. And although we'll discuss LPM in the traditional law firm setting, the general concept of excellent service using technology is transferable elsewhere—though the particulars will vary with different professional paths. So whether you're making every LPM decision at your solo practice or you're one of 200 lawyers at a large government agency, every modern lawyer understands that the administration of legal service to a client impacts the totality of their experience.

## The Modern Consumer Client

Let's start not with you as a lawyer but as a consumer client. You consume services at and from your school, dentist's office, music and movie-streaming service, city public transit network, and favorite retailer. But what's the product you're after? The product is what you get; the service is everything else about how you get it:

✓ The product you're after at the dentist is a root canal but the service is the helpful text reminder you get the day before, having forgotten about the appointment.

- ✓ The product from a retailer is a new stylish pair of boots but the service is the convenient one-tap payment linked to your online payment account.

- ✓ The product from your streaming service is a comedy series but the service is the email announcing the release date for season two.

- ✓ The product from Starbucks® is a coffee but the service is grabbing your drink from the counter with a quick mobile order instead of waiting in a crowded line.

As a lawyer, the product you offer is legal advice. The service experience can be more. Both should be excellent. In law school, you've "met" hypothetical clients (or you've been fortunate enough to enjoy a clinic with actual clients). The hypothetical law school client is someone you've interviewed, counseled, and advised. You've done research, drafted a contract, or prepared them for a mediation.

What you haven't done is manage service expectations. Outside of clinics, law school insulates students from the administrative burdens and opportunities of serving a client. It makes sense to focus on substantive law and practice skills. But daily practice of law is more than knowing a hearsay exception under the rules of evidence. The convenient aspects of business you enjoy as a consumer in your personal life won't disappear in your professional one—you'll just switch roles and give them instead of receive them.

Service has always been part of lawyering but innovation and technology impact what it means today. 60 years ago, clients were impressed with a comfortable leather sofa in a law firm waiting room or satisfied with a small index card to take for a reminder of their next appointment. I'm doubtful that today's clients would be impressed. Society is accustomed to conveniences that make our lives easier and shy away from things that don't, as with these examples:

✓ If the TaskRabbit website is down and no one responds to my request for same-day help painting my house, I'm moving on to another option.

✓ If I can't book a routine medical appointment online, I'm not thrilled about waiting on hold for 10 minutes or calling back during "business hours" or leaving a voicemail with an answering service.

✓ If I can't shop an influencer's Instagram site with a tap of my screen, I'm not buying the product they feature or I'm finding it somewhere else.

---

### LIT TIP

"Lawyers think of client value as the advice and counsel they're giving, or their work product, which is absolutely, hands down, one of the things that clients buy. But that's not the only thing clients are buying. If you are a pain to do business with, or you're just rude, or you're obnoxious, or you can't get a bill out on time, or your bills don't make any sense, sooner or later that client relationship is going to erode. You're providing negative value even though you may be the smartest lawyer there is."[1]

Professor Joshua Kubicki
Director, Legal Business Design Hub & Entrepreneurship Program
University of Richmond School of Law
Co-Founder, Bold Duck Studio
Former Chief Strategy Officer, Seyfarth Shaw LLP

---

Lawyers must meet consumer clients where they're at. Some do; some don't. Many firms and offices look like they've looked for years, maybe decades. Some use the same:

✓ manual client intake systems

✓ organization (or lack thereof) in the same filing cabinets and folders

✓ white "sticky" labels on papers for client and matter identification

✓ printers to print and mail monthly bills

✓ large desktop calendars (the real physical desktop on top of the desk!)

- ✓ letter openers to rip open envelopes and take out client payment checks

- ✓ legs to walk payment checks to the local bank for deposit

Some traditional LPM is fine. This chapter doesn't suggest every firm turn its framework upside down to become the Airbnb or Amazon of law firms. As we learned last chapter, change is difficult and expensive and that's just as true with business aspects as it is with delivery of substantive legal advice. Decades into the 21st century, many law firms see that "fine" might not be good enough anymore. Consumers crave predictable, simple, and reliable aspects to services. Lawyers that supply a positive, effortless experience will draw in more business, just like popular streaming services draw in more subscribers. Lawyers that don't offer a **client-centered experience** may see those clients take their legal needs elsewhere. Which group will you belong to?

## Delegation & Administrative Support

Why bother with all of this business "stuff"? Won't someone else take care of it? Nope.

Many readers have experience working in a professional office setting with dedicated staff to take care of aspects of behind-the-scenes service. Many settings where lawyers work include both lawyers and many other professionals: law firms, for example, may include paralegals, litigation assistants, and administrative support. As law firm size increases, so too does the number of professionals working alongside lawyers, whether they're intellectual property specialists or criminal detectives or accountants or roles we've discussed in this book, such as Legal Operations Manager or E-Discovery Specialist (many of whom have JD degrees and are licensed lawyers themselves). It's a mistake for the modern lawyer to breeze past tasks such as billing, document management, or calendaring because of a misconception that they'll stick to lawyering but leave the rest to someone else.

Generations ago, that "someone else" existed. Lawyers dictated spoken words to support staff. Today, the thought of a lawyer dictating a word-processing document or asking someone to print emails sounds archaic. It is (although it still happens!). One-on-one secretarial support is fading (most environments I've been in, worked with, or visited no longer even use that term). Administrative support is context dependent but staffing is trending leaner. A small law firm may have a dedicated assistant or a large law firm may have a centralized pod of assistants at a firmwide hub located thousands of miles away from where you work. Technology has changed and replaced many tasks "someone else" did generations ago.

So be ready to use available support when it makes sense, is efficient, and is appropriate. Just be equally ready to display individual LPM competencies on your own when it's just as efficient—if not more—to do so.

## Going Paperless

Besides being a law professor, I'm a parent of a hockey player. I remember when my son joined a new team and I had to order a hockey uniform and equipment, and was asked to print and complete the paper order form and fax it to the hockey club office. FAX? It was an actual LOL moment. But that's how the club operated. I completed the form with my pen, drove to a local library, and paid $1.99 a page so my son would get his gear.

Chances are you've never used a fax machine. Lawyers used to use them all the time (virtual fax software exists, so the art of faxing isn't dead!). This chapter's introduction stated that some law firms have operated the same way for decades. The largest and most widespread change has been moving away from paper to digital law practice. Some move faster and farther than others, but the majority are heading in that direction. Many LPM tools hinge on the everyday currency of a lawyer's practice being more electronic than paper.

A **paperless law practice** doesn't mean 100% virtual. Paperless-ish may be more accurate: law firms or offices with a physical location that use paperless procedures and workflows to convert most paper files to digital documents. Going paperless might be light on the paper but it's heavy on the process. Whether for 2 or 2,000 lawyers, a broad transition in how a practice operates won't work without project management and intentional, well-communicated workflows (remember from chapter 6—people first, tech second).

The ins and outs of going paperless vary but at minimum a modern lawyer heading down that path will consider the following:

1) <u>Hardware</u>: A high quality document scanner to convert existing paper documents to digital and then a document shredder to destroy the paper. Remember from chapter 3 that some scanning machines don't include optical character resolution (OCR) and thus might not make digital documents searchable like you'd want them to be.

2) <u>Software</u>: What good are digital documents in formats such as PDF if an office does not use software, such as Adobe Acrobat Pro, to work with those formats.

3) <u>Digital Storage & Organization</u>: Where will all the digital information "live" and how will lawyers access it? An internal shared drive? A cloud-based platform?

Changing the backbone structure of any practice, business, or organization is no small feat. But it will be difficult—if not impossible—for a law firm to thrive and meet client expectations if it clings to paper folders, whiteboard calendars, billing envelopes, and stamps. I can't think of too many disadvantages of going paperless but there are plenty of advantages:

- ✓ enhanced security (if done well—something chapter 9 covers)
- ✓ improved understanding of what data exists and where if a disaster or data breach occurs
- ✓ organization that facilitates collaborative and remote work compared to paper
- ✓ convenient accessibility
- ✓ more environmentally friendly policies

✓ long-term time and cost savings (after up front effort and investment)

---

**LIT TIP**

"The legal industry may be resistant to change, but technology is slowly and surely shaping the field. The pandemic exacerbated this in some regards, but attorneys are always making decisions on what technology works for them, which ones don't, and which ones to bring into their firm. These decisions could be just as important as whether or not to take a case or what motion to make—a case is often won or lost in the preparation of it. Do these technologies aid in that preparation, or do they represent unnecessary hurdles to jump through to get the relevant information you need? Every attorney will answer that question for themselves, but in doing so they must weigh their own comfort level with technology versus the risk of getting left behind as the technology grows more popular or becomes obsolete."[2]

Alexander Paykin
The Law Office of Alexander Paykin, P.C.

---

## LPM: Managing Knowledge, Documents & Tasks

There's a reason LPM includes the word "management." Lawyers manage a lot. You might juggle 5 classes; lawyers and law firms might juggle 15, 50, 500, or 5,000 matters. Before you think about managing business as a lawyer, consider how you manage your business as a student. You might have scattered case briefs from different classes stuck in a notebook. Maybe you use desktop or shared drive folders and subfolders. You might track assignments or reminders in a Notes app on your phone or with sticky notes on your kitchen table. As a student, you manage broad categories of tasks (resume drops, networking events, student bar association activities) with the narrower pieces too (course registration deadlines, assignment due dates, study group meetings).

We can think about approaches to LPM in two categories:

1) ad hoc

2) all-in-one

An ad hoc approach means a firm uses different individual tools for different things. For example, a firm might use one document management system to manage documents and email, and then a separate software for calendaring, and then a separate accounting system for billing and payment. In today's legal marketplace, there are many vendors and software providers developing and marketing new tools to firms for aspects of LPM covered in this chapter such as calendar/docket integration, time tracking and billing, and client communication. Lawyers taking a more ad hoc approach to LPM need to be cognizant of how their tools work together and "speak" to one another.

An appealing option for the modern lawyer might be more of an all-in-one approach. Some LPM products aim to put a law firm's needs into one place. You might think of this like how you use technology from a single service platform like Apple or Google to manage your calendar, email, notes, music, documents, photos, and texts. LPM tools can become a centralized hub of a law firm—a single ecosystem.

Clio is one leading, well-known comprehensive LPM platform for law firms. Clio is a Canadian company that has grown its suite of tools to client intake, opening and closing of cases, conflicts checks, case management, document management, billing, contacts management, accounting, calendaring, online payments, time tracking, and client portal communication. Clio can also integrate with other "stand alone" practice tools such as for legal research or document assembly such that it truly becomes "all-in-one."

Figure 7A is a sample view of a Clio case management main dashboard page. Note the vertical and horizontal all-in-one "menu" options through which a user can toggle, ranging from calendaring and contacts to documents and communications, and the visual cues and reminders of important matter management details such as budgeting and time billed.

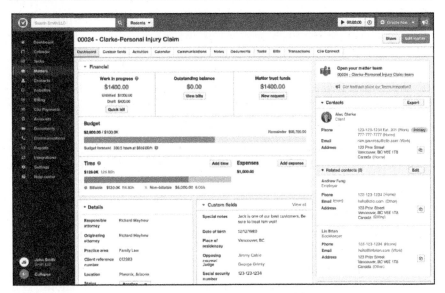

* Figure 7A: Clio Case Management LPM dashboard.[3]

Other popular all-in-one comprehensive LPM tools on the market when this book was published include:

✓ MyCase

✓ PCLaw: TimeMatters

✓ PracticePanther

✓ Rocket Matter

✓ Smokeball

A big goal of any LPM platform or approach is keeping track of what's what. We'll focus on three ways modern lawyers do so most relevant to their individual work product:

> Knowledge Management (KM) * Document
> Management * Task Management

## 1) Knowledge Management

**Knowledge Management** (often termed KM) is what it sounds like: how do lawyers manage and share everything they know?

Understanding what a collective group of lawyers knows, where that knowledge is, and how to access it is critical to success.

Contrast this approach with the "old" scattered and siloed way of doing things, though still alive in many places. If you are working on a products liability action in Delaware, and your colleague a few doors down worked on a products liability action in Delaware last year, wouldn't their legal research be helpful? What about a brief they filed with the same presiding judge? The stronger the KM, the stronger the legal advice may be.

KM gets tricky when lawyers use multiple software tools to do the same thing (you use Microsoft® Word; your colleague uses Google Documents; you use Microsoft® Outlook; your colleague uses Gmail). There might be multiple places where the same documents exist (you keep time records for billable clients in a folder on your desk; your colleague keeps them on his desktop). Everything lives in a different, independent, and often random place. The problems here are aplenty. It's hard to find what you need. It's tedious to get case details or discover conflicts. It's impossible to gauge big-picture aspects of the firm's caseload. It's risky from a security and confidentiality viewpoint because work product and confidential or private information is not under one digital roof but under hundreds or thousands. And it's hard for lawyers to efficiently share their most precious commodity: knowledge.

KM might be as small as one piece of software at a solo lawyer's office. Or it might be the effective capture of decades of experience at a corporation using different outside law firms in different geographic regions. If you are an in-house lawyer at a large northeastern corporation that gets sued in Alabama, would you want to guess at who you should hire for local counsel in Alabama? No, you wouldn't. KM can be as big as a dedicated group of KM lawyers and professionals under a Director of Knowledge Management who work with thousands of lawyers across the globe under one law firm. KM is a broad term that means many different things to many people. The goal of this introduction is that you make sure it means something for you in future practice.

2)    Document Management

A common LPM spot in a lawyer's life is **document management**, whether part of an all-in-one platform such as Clio or an ad hoc document management tool. As chapter 3 discussed, legal documents are a central tool to a lawyer's work. Some might think of document management as traditional productivity software like Microsoft® Office, on-site file servers where lawyers all save documents (an office shared drive), or a cloud-based service such as Microsoft® OneDrive, Google Drive, Box, or Dropbox. Many lawyers use a folder and subfolder document management approach, cloud-based or not, that looks something like the example shown in Figure 7B.

| Name | Date modified | Type |
|---|---|---|
| Case X v. Y | 1/11/2022 11:07 AM | File folder |
| Client ABC | 1/11/2022 11:08 AM | File folder |
| Legal Research | 1/11/2022 11:08 AM | File folder |
| Motions | 1/11/2022 11:08 AM | File folder |
| Transactional deal 123 | 1/11/2022 11:08 AM | File folder |

* Figure 7B: Sample traditional document folder organization.

That's a step in the right direction, but it's not true document management. Yes, foldering documents through these services can help organize things. But they are a poor substitute for a true document management tool—especially when lawyers don't work alone (as is often the case). True document management technology lets lawyers "track" documents, often by assigning them unique numerical IDs. The universe of documents within a law firm, organization, courthouse, or in-house legal department becomes searchable using advanced techniques, leading to greater KM and sharing of resources. For example, a document management tool might include a tag for the type of document so a lawyer could search for all documents marked "Motions for Preliminary Injunction" across an entire body of past work. Document management tools, such as the popular one NetDocuments, help lawyers:

✓ restrict access to documents

✓ mark favorites for active cases

✓ track and keep a history of who has looked at documents, and when

✓ carefully control versions

✓ ensure documents are "checked in and checked out" to avoid lost or duplicative work

✓ use advanced features like annotation and e-signature with documents

✓ enjoy basic and advanced search capabilities to extract information and insight from documents

Modern document management goes beyond keyword searching in desktop folders with ambiguous names or skimming through hundreds of pages in a binder on your colleague's desk hoping you get lucky and find what you need. That's the old way; you're interested in the new—and better—way.

3)  Task Management

A third key spot where technology keeps work running smoothly as part of LPM is task management. Most of us keep some "to do" list in our personal lives, whether on sticky notes or with a simple task manager in a tool such as Google Tasks or Apple Things. Keep watch for modern professional task management options that are more advanced, collaborative, cloud-based, and accessible from anywhere. Effective task management among groups or large teams of lawyers (across departments, across offices, across continents) is often a part of the legal process improvement efforts chapter 6 discussed. If a chosen all-in-one LPM software doesn't include task management (which it probably does), here are others to consider (don't worry—there's no requirement for modern lawyers to use a task manager that starts with the letter T!):

✓ Todoist

✓ Trello

✓ Toodledo

✓ Timely

LPM is a big picture. Stay focused on creating your own purposeful approach to KM, document management, and task management. Doing so offers advantages for you as the modern lawyer and your modern consumer clients.

---

**LIT TIP**

The majority of surveyed law firms adopted technology "to a level never before seen in legal during the pandemic":

85% were using software to manage their firms
83% were meeting clients virtually
79% were storing firm data in the cloud
73% accepted online payments
62% supported electronic documents and e-signatures

2021 Clio Legal Trends Report[4]

---

## Escaping the Inbox: Portals & Dashboards

Legal knowledge, documents, and tasks are too often hidden instead of managed. Hidden in email. Millions of lawyers' inboxes have become rabbit holes that trap our thoughts, ideas, correspondence, research, strategies, concerns, and legal advice.

We touched on email shortcuts in chapter 3 but focus here on tools a lawyer looks to for organization and recall of information instead of email. Think of it as individual process improvement and project management instead of the macro big picture chapter 6 discussed. Email might work well at times for individual, internal work product, but think about what and who it leaves out. Traditional email:

- ✓ becomes lost or deleted
- ✓ gets foldered or organized wrong (or not at all)
- ✓ is chronological without user organization
- ✓ creates a high volume many users can't keep up with
- ✓ makes it difficult to discern importance and prioritize
- ✓ becomes confusing, with attachments lost or recipients dropped over time
- ✓ is decentralized because different pieces exist in different spots

✓    creates gaps of knowledge and inefficient inconsistencies (Q: Didn't you see that note about the witness? A: No, I wasn't on that email chain)

The email rabbit hole traps internal collaboration with colleagues as well as external-facing work a lawyer does with others such as clients, other lawyers, and experts. A lawyer who multitasks with email, attachments, files, records, and notes throughout their inbox on a particular matter at different times throughout the day wastes precious time and energy and leaves a messy information trail in their path. The best use of email is *not* as a knowledge, document, and task manager for the modern lawyer.

The move away from email drudgery is not unique to law. Our professional counterparts in business and financial sectors use real-time collaboration and messaging tools such as Slack to relieve some of the inbox clutter (although instant messaging and chat tools themselves can create a whole new rabbit hole where valuable knowledge gets stuck). The two tools we'll explore for the modern lawyer are client portals and lawyer dashboards.

---

**LIT TIP**

client portal: external-facing private website for lawyers and specific permitted users (such as clients)

lawyer dashboard: internal-facing law practice management platform for lawyers

---

1)    Client Portals

Client **portals** are like a private, secure website just for lawyers and clients. They are limited to authorized users but accessible like any internet site. They allow users to share secure information such as documents, receipts, news summaries, invoices, tasks, calendar updates, messages, and deal negotiation updates (in chapter 8 we'll dive into Virtual Data Rooms, themselves a type of portal). You might hear law firm client portals referenced within the general idea of CRM (customer relationship management), which is not unique to law and is common across different businesses and service industries. CRM systems maintain, organize, and manage customers and their data. You might also see client portals referenced within the concept of a law firm extranet—a similar password-protected website for lawyers, clients, consultants, specialists, transactional partners, experts, co-counsel, and anyone else in the information-sharing circle.

All-in-one comprehensive LPM tools such as Clio, Rocket Matter, and PracticePanther offer client portal options. Portals streamline communication and increase transparency so clients are engaged in administration of their case in a manner they otherwise might not be with email. Portals can also improve case management and coordination of matters across different jurisdictions, for example, or matters involving numerous legal teams or plaintiffs. They are more secure than emails flying back and forth to different people (more on security of these and other tools in chapter 9), and they automatically save correspondence and case "chatter" in one cohesive spot. Portals are a worthwhile tool modern lawyers can use to improve the client consumer experience.

## 2) Lawyer Dashboards

Lawyer **dashboards** are another feature of many LPM tools, akin to a personalized homepage. While some dashboards interface externally with clients more like a portal, we'll focus on internal dashboards that capture a lawyer's knowledge, document, and task management. Consider this scenario: you are a medical malpractice lawyer and a plaintiff calls to ask how many lawyers are working on her case. Or another plaintiff calls to ask about the bill for an expert witness she received before a mediation. After you scramble through emails, folders, and notes on your desk, you play phone tag with other lawyers and paralegals to finally track down the answers and respond days later (much to the client's dismay). Imagine if instead you had a reliable one-stop-shop for case information?

If you and your team used a dashboard tool, you probably could have answered those client questions in minutes. Dashboards help law practice administration come to life on a lawyer's computer screen. Think of this as the "data" of a lawyer's practice, accessible and current at any time instead of, for example, having to wait for monthly or year-end billing statements or search through thousands of archived emails.

Dashboards within LPM software can also integrate with a lawyer's other office systems such as videoconference platforms or billing systems. Think about the dashboard on a car. It lets you gauge if you're running out of gas, what the name of the catchy song playing on your playlist is, and whether you're driving too fast. It doesn't drive for you; it guides you along the way.

Chapter 6 urged the modern lawyer to focus on improving inefficient processes at a macro, big-picture level; lawyer dashboards help lawyers with a micro approach to their own project management:

- ✓ managing daily work
- ✓ collaborating with colleagues
- ✓ prioritizing tasks and timelines
- ✓ taking constant pressure off of their inbox

The market offers many tools in this space; for example, Monday.com is a popular workspace management tool for businesses, lawyers, organizations, or anyone looking to better plan, track, and execute work. Specific to lawyers, for example, the product Dashboard Legal, shown in Figure 7C, integrates with the Microsoft Outlook email system and layers on top of email to integrate email, documents, tasks, and chat in one unified spot. Case and Client Boards can appear as "Starred" or "Primary" to give a cohesive, real-time picture of a lawyer's workflow.

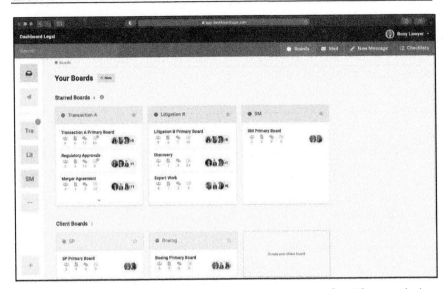

\* Figure 7C: Dashboard Legal Boards view; reprinted with permission Dashboard Legal.

Lawyers haven't abandoned email for good—not yet. And individual use of a dashboard or portal won't bring significant workflow improvements compared to widespread use by everyone at a firm or organization. So although email remains a part of LPM, a modern lawyer stays abreast of other options to ensure their behind-the-scenes work is client-centered and secure. And don't forget about the visual appeal. I don't know about you, but I'd rather digest information with a few purposeful graphs or charts and separated subtitled sections on my workstation desktop screen every morning instead of sifting through tabs, notepads, spreadsheets, and colleagues' messy file folders of dense information to get what I need.

## Scheduling & Calendaring Integration

Love them or hate them, these aren't the most exciting of law practice topics. But they are among the most impactful. Ask any lawyer what they did last week and they likely attended, scheduled, rescheduled, or canceled a meeting, or set, met, or requested an extension for a deadline. While every lawyer brings years of their own habits to these administrative tasks, stay open to technology tools improving them. Modern lawyers coordinate with teams of clients, lawyers, regulators, courts, experts, and others from across the country and across the globe. Effective use of technology for scheduling and calendaring is more than a matter of convenience. It's a matter of professional reputation and ethical competency.

---

### LIT TIP

"[A]dministrative errors—which include tickler system errors, clerical and delegation errors, lost file or document errors, and procrastination— account for 28.5 percent of reported [malpractice] claims . . . a failure to calendar is the fifth-most-common error . . . clerical and delegation errors include things such as simple clerical errors, errors in mathematical calculations, and work delegated to an employee that is not checked . . . with good time management skills and the proper use of tickler systems, administrative errors are probably the easiest to prevent."[5]

Daniel E. Pinnington
Legal Technology Specialist
President & CEO, LAWPRO

---

We're all familiar with the pains of scheduling from our personal lives—exchanging 29 text messages before deciding on a time to meet up with a family member, or 13 emails across a group of friends to decide on a date for a surprise birthday party. Or in the real old days, playing a game of phone tag. Scheduling meetings, calls, videoconferences, or more formal proceedings like a deposition or negotiation can be disjointed when everyone communicates at different times with no cohesion. In my practice, this circular process played out all the time. For example, a partner would tell me available times for a conference call, which I passed on to the client. By the time the client responded, the chosen time had been booked. Some lawyers used electronic calendars such as Microsoft® Outlook or iCal to help me gauge their availability; others used a daily planner and red pen, which was not helpful. Some lawyers added personal commitments to their work calendars; others didn't and often had to cancel last minute because I wasn't aware they left early on Thursdays to pick their child up at school. Repeat, repeat, repeat. Time consuming and frustrating. Not what I went to law school to do.

Today's scheduling tools can take the sting out of this legal admin, which often falls to more junior lawyers. Many LPM platforms offer standalone scheduling solutions (such as Clio Calendar) and other LPM software options focus on client appointment booking and intake (such as ClientRock). No matter the type, there is no shortage of tools from which to choose.

Scheduling connects to managing and calendaring deadlines. It's one thing to miss a meeting with a colleague and cause frustration; it's another to miss a court-imposed filing deadline or agreed-upon execution deadline between merging corporations and potentially cause professional disaster. This isn't a spot for lecture about the importance of deadlines to a lawyer—by now, as a law student, you know this. This is a spot to think about how lawyers can use technology to solidify calendaring processes and make them as foolproof as we can.

**Calendar integration** is one approach that helps the modern lawyer with scheduling and deadlines. "Integration" here means linking your calendar and the entity or source that sets the deadline or date—creating a more automatic process that cuts out the middle steps. A simple example is integrating a videoconference platform such as Zoom with a calendaring system, so meeting links and dial-in information automatically populate calendars when you share or schedule an entry. This means that instead of having to hunt down details somewhere else or copy and paste them into a calendar, details are where they need to be from the start.

So next time you set up a videoconference meeting, don't email meeting information or bury it in a Word document agenda. Create it using your group's email and calendaring system (such as the Zoom Microsoft® Outlook add-in shown in Figure 7D), invite your attendees, and be confident that everyone will have accurate calendar and meeting information where and when they need it.

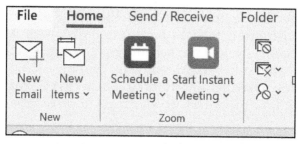

* Figure 7D: Microsoft® Outlook Zoom calendaring add-in.

---

### LIT TIP

Lawyers can take advantage of easy, everyday tools to schedule meetings and integrate meeting details into calendaring systems efficiently such as Doodle, Woven, Calendly, NeedToMeet, YouCanBook.me, Acuity, Microsoft FindTime, and Foogi. Choose a calendar tool that offers integration apps to schedule meetings right from the calendar, such as Google Calendar or Microsoft® Outlook. Automatic calendar integration with meeting information (whether physical location, videoconference link, or phone number) should be the default approach for an organized modern lawyer.

---

Sometimes the most important deadlines are the ones someone else sets. New tools help get those dates directly into a lawyer's calendar. Let's take a hypothetical scenario of Attorney Thompson with a case pending in federal court in Virginia. Remember chapter 3's discussion of dockets and the federal court PACER system. Suppose Thompson gets a PACER email notification of a deadline of Feb. 15 for filing of pretrial motions before trial. He might see that email, make a note in his personal electronic calendar, set an automatic week reminder, and tack a big Post-it note to his office bulletin board. But a lot can go wrong in that process. What if:

✓ Thompson's sticky note falls into the trash can (silly, but it happens)?

✓ Thompson records the wrong case docket number when entering it in his calendar, and gets confused between two cases?

✓ Thompson misses the initial PACER email and never knows about the deadline?

✓ Thompson gets sick and his colleague who takes over has no access to Thompson's personal calendar?

Eliminate manual "what-ifs" with integration tools that connect notifications more directly. For example, a tool such as ECFX Notice streamlines the court notice workflow and could send documents directly to Thompson's document management system. Or a tool such as CourtAlert acts as an "automatic rule" program to capture court notices and populate jurisdiction-specific docket deadlines into a lawyer's or their team's calendar. Modern intellectual property lawyers use subject-specific calendaring tools designed to organize a high volume of administrative submissions and filing deadlines from the United States Patent and Trademark Office.

Scheduling and managing deadlines will always be part of law practice. Lawyers have succeeded and failed for decades. Technology alone isn't a magic solution but it can help a modern lawyer avoid embarrassment or more public professional mishaps such as these:

> *Fox v. Am. Airlines, Inc.*, 389 F.3d 1291, 1294 (D.C. Cir. 2004) (describing counsel's argument that the electronic-filing system was to blame for failure to meet deadlines as "an updated version of the classic 'my dog ate my homework' line").

> *In re Tachner*, USPTO No. D2012-30 (Final Order Apr. 12, 2013) (United States Patent and Trademark Office suspending solo practitioner for missed client patent deadlines after manually tracking docket entries and deadlines with a whiteboard and single word-processing document with no back up).

> *Haddad v. Tri-County A/C & Heating, LLC*, 618 S.W.3d 380, 381 (Tex. Ct. App. 2020) (disagreeing with majority's earlier denial of counsel's motion for reconsideration based on argument that failure to meet notice of appeal deadline was due to law office's inability to conduct in-person calendaring meetings while working remotely).

> ➢ *Rollins v. Home Depot USA, Inc.*, 8 F.4th 393, 395–95 (5th Cir. 2021) (explaining an inexcusable "cautionary tale for every attorney who litigates in the era of e-filing" when plaintiff's counsel failed to oppose a summary judgment motion, claiming the docket notification inadvertently went to the firm's "other" email folder instead of the main inbox).

## Just a Phone Call Away

Email me. Text me. Those phrases are more common than "call me." But lawyers still call clients to give legal advice and clients still call lawyers to seek it. This aspect of LPM looks different today. A law firm's telephone landline might be as foreign a concept to you as a landline in your apartment or home that you would never use. Sure, some law firms still have large landline telephones with panels of red buttons that light up. But in many settings, voice over internet phone service (known as VoIP, Voice over Internet Protocol) has replaced traditional telephones. Law firms must still offer some professional phone option that consumer clients expect—just not one that's hardwired and sitting atop someone's desk.

**VoIP systems** allow lawyers to make calls over the internet instead of phone lines. This approach is cost-effective, convenient, and versatile, with providers offering tools for lawyers to accept calls or messages remotely. No client or prospective client would find it great service to be placed on hold for minutes or constantly redirected to voicemail greetings. Lawyers select from hundreds of service providers to ensure seamless phone communication. A modern firm chooses phone systems in the broader LPM context of service options such as:

- ✓ web chat
- ✓ call routing
- ✓ call history records
- ✓ call recording
- ✓ audio and videoconferencing services
- ✓ virtual receptionists

For example, Zoom Phone is a cloud-based product that supplies a single platform for all a firm's communication, whether video, voice, or chat.

We'll pick the phones back up in chapter 8 when we turn to mobile messaging. In the traditional phone call context, remember your privacy just as much as your client's. Many lawyers hesitate to share their personal cell phone number with clients or other lawyers or carry a separate phone just for work purposes, and with good reason, including security (chapter 9). Many VoIP tools and business communication systems such as RingCentral give lawyers the convenience of keeping personal and professional phone lines on a single device. Be careful to choose what works best for you.

## Pay up: Timekeeping, Billing & E-Payment

Admit it: as a student, you've thought about making money as a lawyer. No one in law school talks about how that works. Although more lawyers today explore alternative fee arrangements and flat-fee approaches to legal work, the billable hour model is still the usual approach in most law firms.

Lawyers have wide discretion in these LPM categories subject to a general reasonableness ethical requirement and other important rules such as not commingling lawyer and client funds. Effective use of technology to track billable time, create bills, and accept payment helps the modern lawyer ensure sound administration of these service aspects of practice.

---

**LIT TIP**

"A lawyer shall not make an agreement for, charge, or collect an unreasonable fee or an unreasonable amount for expenses . . . [t]he scope of the representation and the basis or rate of the fee and expenses for which the client will be responsible shall be communicated to the client, preferably in writing, before or within a reasonable time after commencing the representation, except when the lawyer will charge a regularly represented client on the same basis or rate. Any changes in the basis or rate of the fee or expenses shall also be communicated to the client."[6]

Model Rule 1.5

---

If I asked what you did at 10:27 a.m. yesterday morning, would you be able to answer? What about from 4:12 to 4:18 p.m. last Friday?

Capturing what lawyers actually do in increments of 6/10 of an hour, as is typical for the billable hour model, is difficult. Lawyers are responsible for making a contemporaneous record of their own time and it can be a time-consuming, manual process. Some lawyers might track time with handwritten scribbles or sticky notes copied over to timesheets. Worse yet, some try to recreate and remember work at the end of a long week or month.

Modern lawyers turn to technology to help capture time more efficiently and ethically. Timekeeping tools used to be simple "start-and-stop" mobile or desktop applications whereby a lawyer tracked time on their computer or phone, whether by color coding or naming different clients or matters. An organized stopwatch approach. Assuming a lawyer remembered to start, stop, and switch clients and matters on the timekeeping app throughout a busy day (and switch again . . . and again . . . and again), a basic tool like the one shown in Figure 7E can be effective and efficient.

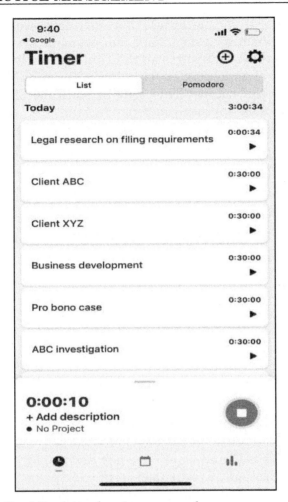

* Figure 7E: Toggl Track timekeeping app sample.

Timekeeping tools have advanced past simple stopwatches. Those still exist but tools are getting better and "smarter" by integrating with other platforms and doing more for the busy modern lawyer. Some timekeeping tools integrate across a lawyer's suite of LPM workplace tools and offer automation and AI technology (Need to Know #8), to do things like predict the client and matter to which the lawyer's time should be billed. For example, many timekeeping apps integrate with communication systems to automatically create a time entry based on a lawyer's phone calls or client portal activity. Or a lawyer might install time-capture software (alone or as part of an all-in-one LPM platform) that monitors work in other applications such as a document management system or legal research database. Software can then automatically create first-draft narrative time entries for a lawyer's review by tracking details from the source. This type of software offers a more passive real-time approach to time tracking. It's like your own AI billing assistant looking over your shoulder throughout the day to track what you're doing and help fill gaps when a busy day ends and what you did becomes a big blur.

Some timekeeping tools worth checking out include:

- ✓ Toggl Track
- ✓ LawBillity (formerly Timetracker)
- ✓ Harvest
- ✓ Time Miner
- ✓ Timewerks

Modern lawyers choose timekeeping technology wisely. Consider mobile accessibility (more on this in chapter 8), security (more on this in chapter 9), integration, and personal comfort. The goal is to find technology that complements your own work habits to ensure contemporaneous and accurate reporting.

Timekeeping doesn't magically turn your hard work into money. After time is tracked, recorded, and compiled, client bills get organized, issued, and paid. It's not always so simple. Like payment processes in consumer contexts, payment for legal services has modernized for many, though not all, lawyers. Manual processes are slow and tedious: an administrator (or lawyer) types out a client bill, mails it via snail mail (or even email), waits for a hard-copy check to arrive back, deposits that check with a bank, and records the payment. Modern clients now expect streamlined **e-payment** online options. Offering it is yet another piece to the overall client service puzzle.

Part of that service experience is to create bills (invoices) that are consistent and in a particular format. There is no one-size-fits-all solution; most law firms, small and especially large, have moved toward a standardized and automated practice, whether through simple document assembly tools or through all-in-one LPM software.

One concept to know in the e-billing space is LEDES: Legal Electronic Data Exchange Standard. LEDES is an open standard format for e-billing that large law firms and corporations use to keep things uniform and provide improved macro visibility on legal spend. For example, a LEDES invoice includes particular codes such as L310 Written Discovery or A102 Research. If you are a corporate in-house legal department receiving hundreds of different invoices from outside law firms each month, this consistency is invaluable. Many law firms (often those that serve large clients) must ensure that LPM or stand-alone billing software supports LEDES files.

After timekeeping and billing comes the money. Readers who enjoy the convenience of online payment as consumers can appreciate it from a lawyer's business viewpoint. Clients can pay quickly and easily on their own time, improving prompt collection by firms and avoiding frustrating bottleneck in manual processes. Law-specific payment software can offer law firms the opportunity to:

- ✓ automate billing notices and reminders
- ✓ use standardized, professional templates to minimize errors
- ✓ offer conveniences such as unique QR codes for clients to scan and be directed to a payment page
- ✓ track payment status and receive questions
- ✓ ensure security and confidentiality
- ✓ help lawyers comply with ethics rules such as the prohibition of commingling client and lawyer funds
- ✓ keep billing and payment data in one centralized dashboard

Figure 7F is an image from LawPay® online payment technology built for lawyers, showing a home dashboard view where, for example, a practice might track its total year-to-date payment volumes, number of transactions, average amount received, scheduled outstanding payments, and payment volumes received over time.

\* Figure 7F: LawPay® dashboard view; reprinted with permission LawPay® An AffiniPay Solution.

E-payments through a platform such as LawPay® or many others come in different forms, whether credit card (the most common), electronic check, wire bank transfer, and yes, even cryptocurrency (although still a niche novelty in the law firm billing world).

Cryptocurrency such as Bitcoin is a form of digital currency creating wrinkles for lawyers accepting it as payment. The emerging rules and ethical muddiness surrounding cryptocurrency are too varied to tackle in this chapter. A modern lawyer looking to accept this form of payment proceeds with caution to ensure use of a proper digital wallet and compliance with other regulations, including making sure fees are kept reasonable by promptly converting cryptocurrency to traditional currency (actual dollars) and being careful about who pays transactional or conversion costs.

---

**LIT TIP**

"In order to maintain the requisite knowledge and skill required of a lawyer, it is important for the lawyer to keep abreast of the risks associated with the technology used to transfer and hold cryptocurrency in his or her practice. Just like other client property, a lawyer storing cryptocurrency in escrow must use reasonable care to minimize the risk of loss to client's or third parties' property. More specifically, a lawyer is required to 'appropriately safeguard property' in a suitable place of safekeeping. There are several recommended methods to safeguard cryptocurrency held in escrow (e.g., cold storage wallets, encryption and back up of private keys, multi-signature accounts) that should be thoroughly researched and carefully considered by lawyers before accepting cryptocurrency. Additionally, a lawyer should inform clients of the apparent and inherent risks of holding and transferring cryptocurrency and explain the steps the lawyer will undertake to safeguard the client's property." (internal citations omitted)[7]

Ohio Bd. of Pro. Conduct Op. 2022-07 (2022)

---

From timekeeping to digital tokens, this chapter doesn't cover every in and out of how lawyers get paid. If you face these decisions in your career, you must familiarize yourself with context-specific variables such as:

- ✓ fees
- ✓ jurisdictional rules
- ✓ rules about interest on lawyer trust accounts (IOLTA)
- ✓ client demands and preferences
- ✓ third-party vendor security considerations
- ✓ integration opportunities and costs with other LPM tools
- ✓ ease and comfort of use

Timekeeping, billing, and e-payment tools will change faster than editions of this book can keep up. Your goal, as always, is to stay familiar with the breadth of options, become knowledgeable about the information you'll need, and remain committed to delivering a client-centered convenient service.

## Sign (or Click) Here

Signatures have always been part of law practice, whether on a letter, contract, pleading, filing, will, or trust. In the past, that meant printed stacks of paper, expensive packages for overnight delivery, and blue ballpoint pens. Today, it means electronic signatures lawyers carry out with the click of a button or finger swipe of a screen—just like you probably have on your computer, phone, or at most retail and service checkout counters. You don't think twice about this practice as a consumer but should consider how it fits as part of effective LPM. E-signature tools in today's paperless-ish world offer technologically competent lawyers (and clients) convenience, efficiency, and security.

**E-signatures** have been around for decades but have become widespread, and the supporting technologies have exploded. The legality of e-signatures is jurisdiction-specific and document-specific. At the federal level, the E-Sign Act of 2000[8] cemented the legality of e-signatures in the commercial context and most states either passed a similar law or adopted the Uniform Electronic Transactions Act,[9] which makes e-signatures valid akin to ink signatures. As prevalent as e-signatures are in the contracting world, there are still instances and documents where they won't work. For example, many states require estate planning documents to have wet ink signatures. Many jurisdictions enacted temporary e-signature allowances during the Covid-19 pandemic, such as allowing notaries to witness via videoconference a person's e-signing of a document. Acceptance of the practice continues to expand—though an inconsistent patchwork of rules remains among jurisdictions and among different tribunals and bodies before which a lawyer may appear, such as administrative agencies or specialized courts.

E-signatures (often called "dry" in contrast to "wet" from a pen) take different forms, from simple to more sophisticated. An e-signature could be:

- ✓ a person typing their name or using /s/ before their typed name, as is the custom for signing electronic filings in federal court

- ✓ a scan or picture image of someone's actual handwritten signature

✓ a version "handwritten" with a finger, mouse, or stylus pen

✓ a click on an "I agree" button or similar icon

✓ a signature through a third-party service that authenticates the signatory's identity and helps a lawyer send, track, follow up, and receive signed documents

Lawyers use stand-alone e-signature tools or those that are bundled into an all-in-one LPM platform. For example, DocuSign and HelloSign are two popular platforms lawyers use to upload documents that get emailed to specified individuals for online "signature." Lawyers use e-signature tools for hundreds of different types of legal documents such as real estate transactional forms, corporate deals and financing, litigation pleadings, medical and other record releases, corporate agreements, and many more.

E-signatures offer advantages for the modern lawyer and client. After upfront effort to get things off the ground, the tools are convenient and often result in reduced costs. They usually create a more streamlined process that avoids the bottleneck, back-and-forth of obtaining handwritten signatures. As a modern lawyer with a lot on your plate, would you want to spend three hours of your day driving to a client's home to obtain a wet ink signature if you could do it electronically in seconds? I doubt it. E-signature platforms are also environmentally friendly and jibe well with a more paperless workflow. Last but not least, e-signature tools from reliable and reputable vendors offer a more secure signing process. It might seem more secure to see a person signing a document in person, by hand, with a pen—until you realize paper documents can be lost, altered, or forged. As we'll cover in chapter 9, e-signature tools should include enhanced security measures to ensure documents remain confidential, personal signatory information remains private, and a lawyer gets a perfect non-paper "paper" trail to ensure full authentication of legally binding signatures.

\* \* \* \*

This chapter began with the idea that lawyering is as much a business as it is a professional consumer service. Your future consumer clients need legal advice. As a modern lawyer you'll compete for business just like everyday service providers compete for yours. Whether you practice at a law firm or not, give careful thought to your daily administrative tasks and how purposeful use of technology can enhance efficiency and effectiveness—all the while helping you deliver excellent legal service.

---

### LIT TIP

"For years, most lawyers were taught that better, faster, and cheaper was impossible in delivery of legal services and that they—and their clients— would have to settle for two out of three. But that old-school thinking no longer applies in today's world, where low-cost, easy to use law practice management technology enables lawyers to achieve that once unattainable trifecta. Automated law practice technologies allow lawyers to generate work product faster and at a lower cost. And technology such as a client portal is less costly than adding staff to respond to questions and provides superior client service instead of making clients call or email a firm and wait for a response. Law practice technology can create an overall better client experience because it creates transparency between lawyers and clients. At the end of the day, technology will never fully substitute for other capabilities a lawyer brings to a case. But it empowers them to deliver better, faster, and cheaper legal services. In my view, lawyers have an ethical obligation to explore and implement law office technology to best serve their clients."

Carolyn Elefant
Author, Solo by Choice, Third Edition: How to Start Your Own Law Firm and Be the Lawyer You Always Wanted to Be[10]

---

The LPM concepts in this chapter aren't everything to know— far from it—but they're a start. Build upon this foundation as you gain experience. Investing in modern tools and processes costs money, requires training and support, takes time, and feels risky. The real risk lies in not doing it.

Tomorrow's clients will have more choices than ever before. What will you do to ensure they choose you?

*Review Your Knowledge*

1) Marissa, Charmayne, Jasmine, and Matthew are lawyers at a boutique construction law firm. Each handles their own business intake. They've been at the firm for nine years and handled hundreds of cases using their own approach to document management. Marissa folders documents through Google Drive and saves local files on her laptop, where she has hundreds of folders and subfolders. Charmayne uses document management software to assign unique numerical IDs to every file under one central number for each client, allowing documents to be tagged, searched, and filtered. Jasmine keeps case files in storage cabinets with color-coordinated folders organized by case type and alphabetized by client last name. Matthew leaves his document management to his organized legal assistant and asks support staff to find a particular document whenever he needs it. Which lawyer has the best general approach to document management?

   a) Marissa, because cloud-based storage is inexpensive and she always has her laptop with her to access file folders.

   b) Charmayne, because her document management is organized, client-specific, and searchable by others with document tags she assigns such as "research," "pleadings," or "correspondence."

   c) Jasmine, because physical office folders are the most convenient and secure place for files so others in the office can access them if Jasmine needs help.

   d) Matthew, because delegating every aspect of administrative tasks such as document management is efficient and keeps Matthew's focus on billable work.

2) CareHealth Inc. operates a network of hospitals and is purchasing a children's hospital in Seattle. Morgan (pronoun they/them) is an associate at a law firm working

with a team of lawyers handling antitrust aspects of the deal. They set up a kickoff videoconference among 13 lawyers on both sides of the transaction and notify the group of the meeting date and time with an e-calendar entry invite that includes the Zoom link. Morgan receives notice that all attendees "accept" the meeting request. A month before the meeting, Morgan receives notice from the Washington Department of Health with extended deadlines for required hospital sale filings, so Morgan decides to push back the meeting a few weeks. They quickly send the group a separate new email with the new meeting date and delete the old meeting on their own Outlook calendar—but never send a notice of cancellation or change to those who accepted the original invite. On the day of the original meeting time, Morgan receives several calls and emails from frustrated colleagues and deal lawyers wondering why they've been waiting for Morgan as host to open the Zoom meeting room. Morgan explains that the meeting date and time changed, but is embarrassed that they wasted people's time. Morgan's biggest mistake was:

a) nothing; they made a good effort to use efficient e-calendaring tools and at some point, it's everyone else's responsibility to organize their own calendars and emails and keep track of their own schedule.

b) sending a shared e-calendar entry in the first place with the Zoom link, because they should have waited and sent the Zoom meeting information separately via email a few minutes before it was scheduled to begin.

c) not using the shared e-calendaring tool correctly. Besides a separate email notice of the change, Morgan should have updated the original shared meeting e-calendar entry to ensure a notice of cancellation and change went to all attendees to avoid this confusion.

d) not taking the time to open the old Zoom videoconference link on the original meeting day and time just in case attendees tried to join.

3) Amelia and Bianca own A&B law firm and focus on insurance law. They are the only two employees and often

share cases. Amelia took the lead on a recent matter for client Colleen. Months into the matter with little activity, Colleen reached out via email to the general firm email address. Bianca saw the message, in which Colleen asked for a billing clarification, a request for information about an upcoming calendar date, and a request to meet in person. Bianca ignored the email because she knew Amelia was lead on that case, assumed Amelia was copied on the email (she wasn't), and, even if Amelia wasn't, figured Colleen could just log onto A&B's client portal. Colleen calls Amelia a week later to complain about the lack of communication and information about her case and says she had no idea about a client portal. What more might Amelia and Bianca have done to avoid this scenario?

a) Nothing. Colleen should have used the client portal so it's her fault.

b) Bianca should have paid more attention to the firm's email inbox, realized Amelia was not copied on Colleen's email, and forwarded it to her when she got a free moment and remembered to do so.

c) Amelia and Bianca should not rely on a client portal because clients want one-on-one attention and an attempt to centralize communication might be off-putting.

d) Amelia and Bianca should have integrated the general firm email address with the client portal to ensure they viewed all messages and should have announced and explained use of the portal to every client.

4) Gene is opening a solo real estate law practice in Raleigh, North Carolina. He wants to create a modern and efficient firm and accept credit card payment. Gene's wife operates her own marketing consulting practice and has experience with a merchant account through a credit card processing company. She's had no problems for years, so Gene plans to copy her setup with the same company for his new law firm. The most important thing for Gene to think about in this context is:

a) doing research across different companies to make sure the one his wife uses has the smallest administrative processing fees to optimize Gene's profit.

b) the potential ethical issues with accepting credit card payments for legal services, because traditional credit card processors may not be set up to handle attorney trust account obligations with certain money received from clients.

c) that credit card payment might negatively affect business by bothering "old-fashioned" clients interested in paying by hard-copy check.

d) that he should instead accept cryptocurrency for payment, given that it's widely accepted by consumers.

5) Rosario is a lawyer at a small law firm specializing in estate planning and family law. She meets with individual clients, couples, and families to execute estate planning documents such as wills, power of attorney forms, and health care proxies. After an in-person or videoconference meeting, Rosario creates the documents, emails them to the client(s), and asks clients to sign electronically. Rosario's firm pays about $60 per month for e-signature software, which has made everyone's life easier. When Rosario gets notification through the software that her clients have signed documents, Rosario prints them on her office printer, scans them, saves a hard-copy file in a file cabinet organized chronologically by execution date, and ships via overnight mail an executed copy to the client's home. As to practice management, Rosario and her firm:

a) are doing great because they recognized an area of inefficiency with inconvenient in-person signatures and improved it.

b) shouldn't use e-signature software for something as personal and confidential as estate planning documents.

c) improved one area of inefficiency by using e-signature software, but should consider their broader workflow and improve related processes for post-signature paperless document management too (depending on applicable jurisdictional requirements).

d) shouldn't outsource any client service interaction such as obtaining signatures to unreliable third-party vendors.

---

   *Practice Your Knowledge*

## Exercise #1: Keep Up Your Time

Timekeeping is not an easy task but a key part of LPM. Track and record everything you do in six minute increments for about a half day during any "normal" day. First choose a no- or low-tech option such as a hard-copy notepad or single word-processed document or Notes app on your phone [example: *2–2:48 pm attend Evidence class; 2:50–2:56 pm use restroom and chat with friends; 2:56–3:08 telephone conference with dad*]. Then do the same on a second day using a different approach with one of the tools mentioned in this chapter (or another you find). Compare your two approaches and prepare some notes for discussion about advantages or disadvantages and what you preferred.

## Exercise #2: Experiment with E-Calendaring

Try out a free e-calendaring or scheduling tool beyond what you already use; for example, create an online "booking" page that integrates with a calendar (such as Google Calendar or iCal). Use a tool mentioned in this chapter (Calendly, NeedtoMeet, YouCanBook.me, Microsoft® FindTime, or Foogi) or do some research and select your own. Set up times you'd be available to meet during a day, week, or month. The goal is to create a link you could add to an email signature or send to colleagues, professors, or friends interested in scheduling a time to talk or meet.

*Expand Your Knowledge*

- ➢ JACK NEWTON, THE CLIENT-CENTERED LAW FIRM: HOW TO SUCCEED IN AN EXPERIENCE-DRIVEN WORLD (2020).

- ➢ *Paperless Law Office*, LAWYERIST, https://lawyerist.com/management/paperless-office/ [https://perma.cc/2ZAV-2P SB].

- ➢ CLIO, 2021 LEGAL TRENDS REPORT (2021), https://www.clio.com/resources/legal-trends/2021-report/read-online/ [https://perma.cc/2LSX-F6PA].

*Answers & Explanations*

*Knowledge Kickoff*

d) Richard and Ariella excel in their substantive courtroom practice but struggle with aspects of LPM. A modern lawyer needs both to thrive. While some delay and mishaps are part of a lawyer's busy life, the extent of Richard's former client's complaints suggest this was more than something simple apologies would cure (and likely part of why the firm has lost business). Client portals are one secure option to streamline information and help lawyers fulfill their ethical duty under Model Rule 1.4 to keep clients reasonably informed and promptly comply with requests for information.

*Review Your Knowledge*

1) b) Documents are a treasure trove of valuable information—if lawyers can access them. Excellent document management can be a game changer, and Charmayne's approach allows her (or someone with whom she works) to get at what she needs when she needs it. Having individual files across cloud applications such as Google Drive or hundreds of desktop folders is not true document organization, and physical office folders make efficient searching next to impossible. Tempting though it may be for a modern lawyer like Matthew to delegate all document management, they shouldn't. While a team-based approach to LPM is admirable, a technologically competent lawyer maintains some awareness of and involvement in their own KM and document management.

2) c) Morgan's intentions were great here to send an electronic meeting notice with an integrated Zoom meeting link, but they faltered a bit in execution. E-calendaring tools only work if lawyers use them correctly. If Morgan's approach relied on shared e-calendar Outlook invites, they should have seen it through, stuck with that approach, and ensured attendees received a notice of cancellation of the

original entry. It is true that lawyers are responsible for their own calendar but that doesn't mean Morgan bears no responsibility for the mishap. As an isolated occurrence, this miscommunication is annoying but not catastrophic. Perhaps Morgan should have opened up the meeting on the old date just in case, but that's not realistic on a larger scale. Multiplied over hundreds of scheduled meetings, calls, videoconferences, and deadlines over many days, weeks, and months, small calendaring mistakes wreak big havoc.

3)    d)    Client portals are only as effective as users use them. As this scenario shows, individual email communication can be risky—messages get missed, deleted, sent to the wrong person, etc. A&B's portal approach is good but only works reliably if the portal is used as part of the firm's overall systems. Direct communication with new clients to ensure they understand the plan for case communication won't solve every LPM blunder but it would have helped prevent this scenario.

4)    b)    As a modern solo lawyer, Gene should offer a credit card payment option. The benefits outweigh potential frustration by those few people today uncomfortable with online payment. Gene's most important consideration is the ethical obligations he has with payment in this fashion that don't apply to his wife's business. Model Rule 1.15 Safekeeping Property details a lawyer's obligation to hold certain client funds in trust accounts. Gene must ensure the company he uses handles lawyer and client funds appropriately so processing fees are not deducted from a client trust account (instead they usually get deducted from a separate firm operating account). Cryptocurrency could be an option if Gene's state jurisdiction permits it but it's not a "widely accepted" form of payment just yet.

5)    c)    Rosario's use of e-signature software to help improve efficiency clashes with the rest of her post-execution and paper-heavy practices. This question underscores the importance of LPM as a wholesale

concept: processes and practices working together, not just a lawyer using isolated technology here and there for small things. The benefits of secure e-signature software for Rosario and her clients are lost if Rosario then turns to slow, less secure, and more cumbersome document storage. Jurisdictional requirements are always key, and with documents such as wills there may be good reason for clients to keep an executed paper copy. But in the bigger picture, Rosario's firm might benefit from a process improvement view of how use of the e-signature technology integrates (or doesn't) with the rest of practice.

## Endnotes

1    JACK NEWTON, THE CLIENT-CENTERED LAW FIRM: HOW TO SUCCEED IN AN EXPERIENCE-DRIVEN WORLD 11 (2020).

2    Alexander Paykin, *2021 Practice Management*, ABA (Nov. 24, 2021) https://www.americanbar.org/groups/law_practice/publications/techreport/2021/pracmgmt/  [https://perma.cc/NS9Y-HA26].

3    Clio and the Clio logo are registered trademarks of Themis Solutions Inc. All other provided images and related intellectual property are provided under a limited, non-exclusive, non-assignable, non-transferable, worldwide, revocable right for use solely in connection with this publication. All usage must comply with Themis Solution Inc.'s Limited Brand Use License found here: https://www.clio.com/about/brand-assets/clio-limited-brand-use-license [https://perma.cc/J8WE-7S8L].

4    CLIO, 2021 LEGAL TRENDS REPORT (2021), https://www.clio.com/resources/legal-trends/2021-report/read-online/ [https://perma.cc/2LSX-F6PA].

5    Daniel E. Pinnington, *The Biggest Malpractice Risks*, 28 GPSolo: ABA 2, 18–19 (Mar. 2011).

6    MODEL RULES OF PRO. CONDUCT r. 1.5 (AM. BAR. ASS'N 2020).

7    Ohio Bd. of Pro. Conduct, Op. 2022-07 (2022), https://ohioadvop.org/wp-content/uploads/2022/08/Adv.-Op.-2022-07-Final.pdf [https://perma.cc/5778-27G7].

8    15 U.S.C. § 96.

9    15 U.S.C. § 7001.

10   CAROLYN ELEFANT, SOLO BY CHOICE: HOW TO BE THE LAWYER YOU ALWAYS WANTED TO BE (3rd ed. 2022).

# CHAPTER 8

# REMOTE LAWYERING

*Core Concepts*

| | |
|---|---|
| *remote lawyering* | *virtual courtroom* |
| *virtual law office* | *online dispute resolution* |
| *mobile document proficiency* | *virtual data room* |
| *mobile messaging* | *unauthorized remote practice* |
| *audio & videoconferencing* | *hybrid work model* |

## *Knowledge Kickoff*

Maria is a mid-level associate in the Financial Investigations group at a large firm. She works with corporate clients on internal investigations into white-collar misconduct. She juggles a lot and just recorded the most monthly billable hours in her career. She goes into her Philadelphia office two days a week, but otherwise works on her laptop, tablet, and phone from the couch in her small apartment. Last week, Maria logged into a videoconference with a forensic accountant and her client. Minutes into the session, she noticed the label on her Zoom "box" said, "*Awesome Roommate*" instead of her name. Furious at her roommate for the prank, Maria went for a jog to clear her head and received 29 texts from colleagues and clients. The "dings" on her AirPods interrupted her playlist with every step. At a stoplight, she quickly glanced down at her phone to respond to a few urgent requests and then texted "Will these people ever leave me alone ☹" to her mother—only she tapped the wrong message to reply to and inadvertently messaged the general counsel of her client instead. The next day, she made strategy calls about a pending DOJ investigation while still connected via FaceTime on her tablet with an old college friend (a news reporter) she'd been chatting with earlier. That night, a prospective client Maria met at a networking event emailed to request an in-person meeting. Instead of responding to the email, Maria texted the cell number on the email signature and suggested a videoconference. The client responded, "Thx but I prefer not to text re: business. I'm disappointed you can't meet me person." Embarrassed and burned out, Maria calls you as a friend for some advice. What would you tell her?

    a)   Maria's mistakes are understandable in today's busy mobile society, and no client will be concerned with these unprofessional mishaps.

    b)   Maria should slow down, reevaluate, and improve some of her remote work practices to better prevent these mishaps.

    c)   Maria's mistakes are catastrophic in that her professional reputation could be ruined for the rest of her career.

    d)   Maria should altogether avoid any remote lawyering and instead head back into the office on a full-time basis to prevent these mishaps.

---

Would you believe there's such a thing as "Kayak Court"? In 2021 in Utah, attorneys, social workers, assistants, and a judge started to take legal services down the Jordan River near Salt Lake City to contact and offer help to people experiencing homelessness and living in camps alongside the river.[1] About once a month weather permitting, state court Judge Jeanne Robison paddled with others in her kayak to find some dry land and, for example, recall a warrant or issue a community service sentence instead of jail time. It's a far cry from the physical courtroom but consistent with what every good lawyer and legal professional aims to do: meet clients where they're at.

Perhaps it's odd to start a chapter about remote (often called "virtual") lawyering in a book about technology with a story about services delivered next to trees alongside a river. But that's the point—it no longer matters from where legal services are delivered or from where people consume them. Society has transitioned to a point where the "where" is nowhere near as important as the "how," "why," and "when." Many aspects to remote lawyering were prompted, accelerated, or made mainstream by the Covid-19 pandemic. But many were in the works back when physical distance was a convenience rather than a necessity. Lawyers have been heading out of the office for years, using innovative approaches and technology to meet clients and others where they're at—whether that's alongside a river in Salt Lake City, on a sandy beach in Hawaii, or in a high-rise conference room halfway across the globe. The Covid-19 pandemic rewarded those modern lawyers and institutions already focused on providing secure and reliable remote services, and gave others the nudge they needed to head in that direction. The pandemic didn't create remote lawyering. It created widespread acceptance across different sectors of the idea that lawyering could be done remotely. And done well—maybe even better.

Remote work is obvious to today's generation of readers. Just like all discovery today is e-discovery, all lawyering is **remote lawyering**. As commonplace as remote communication is to our personal lives, in our professional lives it's more than editing documents on a smartphone. Longstanding institutions, proceedings, processes, and foundational aspects of practice that have remained stagnant for centuries are changing—from virtual law firms to virtual data rooms to online dispute resolution. Today's technologically competent lawyer understands these changes and stays abreast of the opportunities and growing pains that accompany them. For every convenience this chapter touches on, there's a corresponding security concern (more on that in chapter 9), potential inequity, or other caution to remember as your career moves forward.

Take the good with the bad. This chapter offers you the foundation to do so as you weigh the benefits and risks of working remotely.

## Virtual Law Offices (VLO) & the Virtual-ish Law Firm

We'll start by taking a concept from chapter 7 one step further. Chapter 7 discussed a paperless law firm with a physical office location that uses electronic business practices such as e-billing or client portals. Maybe that law firm allows lawyers the flexibility to work from home, a familiar concept for many of us. But does a law firm even need any central, physical location? No, it doesn't. Can a law firm exist entirely online? Yes, it can.

---

### LIT TIP

"The ABA Model Rules of Professional Conduct permit virtual practice, which is technologically enabled law practice beyond the traditional brick-and-mortar law firm. When practicing virtually, lawyers must particularly consider ethical duties regarding competence, diligence, and communication, especially when using technology. In compliance with the duty of confidentiality, lawyers must make reasonable efforts to prevent inadvertent or unauthorized disclosures of information relating to the representation and take reasonable precautions when transmitting such information. Additionally, the duty of supervision requires that lawyers make reasonable efforts to ensure compliance by subordinate lawyers and nonlawyer assistants with the Rules of Professional Conduct, specifically regarding virtual practice policies."

ABA Standing Comm. on Ethics and Pro. Resp., Formal Op. 498 (2021)

---

A **virtual law office** (VLO) is one with no permanent brick-and-mortar location. None as in zero, although employees may use shared office coworking spaces for occasional meetings. Occasional mobile out-of-office work doesn't make a law firm virtual. A true VLO is one that uses a secure client portal with a law firm website to interact with clients and colleagues in a secure and confidential way (including password protection and encryption—ideas we'll dive into in chapter 9). VLOs are a prime example of the innovative legal service delivery concepts introduced in chapter 6. Take for example Richard Granat, regarded as having started the first virtual law firm in 2003 in Maryland. Only Richard Granat isn't in Maryland—he practices from his home in Florida while his family law firm website offers client intake software, automated legal forms, and videoconferencing tools to deliver legal services.[2]

True VLOs exist but "Virtual-ish" law firms are more common. "Virtual" is not an all-or-nothing concept. A modern lawyer will experience different spots along the spectrum of virtual, whether at a law firm, government agency, legal department, legal aid office, nonprofit, or any other legal or business environment. Many workplaces are moving in a hybrid direction, mixing in-person and remote work and delivering services in a traditional in-person sense and others through online tools such as the LMP software introduced in chapter 7. This transition started well before the Covid-19 pandemic, but lawyers mix things up on a much greater scale now. Why? Because it's what modern consumers want. Consider the graph in Figure 8A, from Clio's Legal Trends Report, showing how many more consumers were open to working with a lawyer remotely in 2021 compared to just a few years earlier in 2018.

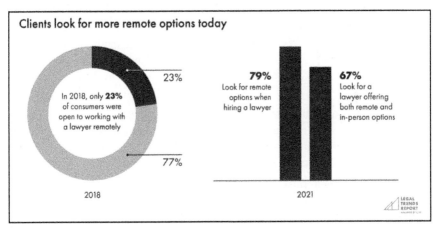

Clients look for more remote options today

23%

In 2018, only **23%** of consumers were open to working with a lawyer remotely

77%

2018

**79%** Look for remote options when hiring a lawyer

**67%** Look for a lawyer offering both remote and in-person options

2021

* Figure 8A: Remote Options; Clio 2021 Legal Trends Report Part 1.[3]

Virtual-ish practices aren't limited to law firms. A central physical location where most of the interaction with clients and colleagues takes place is likely to become less and less relevant, whether that's a courtroom or a office hallway at a government agency or nonprofit organization. Lawyers in any virtual-ish setting need a strong grasp of best practices to ensure competent service doesn't exit out the door just because they have. There's more to come throughout this chapter, but here are some basic remote work tips to start.

✓ Discuss, set, and confirm expectations, policies, and customs for remote work, especially if you are new to a particular group or office.

✓ Take time to get your work "hardware" and work environment in order, whether a laptop, desktop, document scanner, chargers, or second extra-large display monitor.

✓   Ensure you have a solid and stable internet connection (considering backup options such as a broadband Ethernet cable or portable Wi-Fi hotspot) and necessary data plan if applicable.

> **LIT TIP**
>
> Understand the method of connection your employer requires or prefers for remote work. Here are some approaches you might hear about:
>
> VPN (Virtual Private Network): VPNs give lawyers a secure connection "into" a private institutional (like an entire law firm) network, allowing them to access electronic files from an office or firm as if they were physically at that location.
>
> VDI (Virtual Desktop Infrastructure): VDIs give lawyers a way to work on an employer's computer but through their personal hardware device, using a virtual environment hosted with remote servers or cloud-hosted options an employer selects.
>
> Cloud Platforms: common web-based options, accessible from anywhere, that use no private network.

## 24/7 Mobile Lawyer

A notch down from virtual-ish lawyering is the simple idea of individual on-the-go mobile work when you aren't at a physical office location. Every person I know is a mobile person. Every law student I've met is a mobile law student. Every lawyer I've met is a mobile lawyer, and you will be too—whether a government employee, public defender, prosecutor, judicial clerk, in-house lawyer, small- or big-firm lawyer, or legal aid lawyer. It's impossible to capture in one section of one book chapter the countless things modern lawyers do remotely.

Lawyers work on tablets and smartphones. Data from 2021 suggests that 80% of attorneys in the United States use an iPhone in their practice, up from only 31% in 2011 (another 19% reported using an Android smartphone, bringing the total percentage in 2021 to 99%).[4] But you don't need data—you already know this. Many readers grew up using a mobile device every day, so *not* using one for work is illogical. Back in 2007 (not that long ago, in the big picture), many media outlets, technologists, and marketing professionals predicted that the iPhone would be nothing more than a luxury toy that would appeal to a select few. Well, they were wrong! Before the iPhone it was the BlackBerry device lawyers used in the 1990s and 2000s. Then it was the Apple Watch. Tomorrow will bring the next latest and greatest mobile device. The name will change, the features will improve, but the concept of productivity and accessibility from any location at any time is permanent. The prevalence of mobile devices means lawyers are less tied to any one physical location than ever before—a small fact with big meaning for how modern lawyers will work, communicate, and find balance between the blurry lines of their personal time and professional commitments.

We'll break down the many tasks in a 24/7 mobile lawyer's day into three categories:

> Mobile Document Proficiency * Messaging *
> Audio & Videoconferencing

1)    Mobile Document Proficiency

Picture yourself sitting on an airplane as a busy lawyer, frustrated at a long delay on the tarmac after boarding. With your laptop out of battery after you left the charger at your hotel, you receive a message on your phone from a colleague asking for a quick review of final changes to an employment contract for a client. Would you be confident in your ability to open the document on your phone, edit it, and send back the update?

**Mobile document proficiency** is a close cousin of the document proficiency explored in chapter 3. It might be as simple as making sure you have the necessary apps on your phone to do the work you need to do, within whatever programs you use in the ordinary course. For example, every lawyer who uses Microsoft® Office on their desktop or laptop (or Google Documents or any other word-processing tool) should ensure they have the mobile version on their phone (or at least the apps for individual tools such as Word, PowerPoint, and Excel). Almost every document management tool today—from general ones such as Google Drive and Dropbox to popular ones with lawyers such as iManage and NetDocuments—offers cloud-based mobile access through an app. So too do broader LPM suites of software such as Clio and MyCase, ensuring lawyers can access and work on documents when and how they need to.

Modern lawyers consider mobile capabilities beyond simple word-processing. For example, if you are working on a document on your phone (or in hard copy) and need to electronically file it before a deadline, you might need to quickly convert the document to a PDF file format. Remote lawyers make sure they know how to do so using, for example, a PDF converter app. Or, for hard-copy materials, many lawyers invest in a portable mobile scanner small enough to fit in a work bag or briefcase or download one of many mobile document scanner apps, such as:

✓ Scanner Pro

✓ TurboScan

✓ Genius Scan

✓ CamScanner

Mobile PDF annotation tools are another must-have on many lawyers' mobile devices. Besides the ability to create a PDF file on-the-go, lawyers often need to mark one up to complete tasks such as:

✓ providing comments to a colleague

✓ taking notes or making suggestions on a deposition or trial transcript

✓ giving feedback on a draft contract in PDF form

✓ annotating anything they're reading, whether work product or an interesting newsletter or article

A quick search of the App Store or Google Play Store for PDF annotation tools reveals a range of convenient options, including many that capture device screen handwriting with a stylus or smartpen and work well with screen protectors that can help make writing on a mobile device feel like writing on a piece of paper.

Notetaking, research, and dictation are three additional tools that can help a lawyer's on-the-go productivity. With no insult to notebooks and legal pads, loose pages to get lost in stacks of folders or left behind in a conference or airport. Lawyers use notetaking apps to speak, type, hand or take a picture of notes to ensure they are secure, synced, with other case materials, and often shareable with others.

Mobile access to legal research databases is another advantage for the mobile lawyer—a prime example is sitting in a courtroom when the judge or opposing counsel mentions a case with which you aren't familiar. Seconds later, on the spot from your phone, you're able to take a quick glance.

Finally, when a modern lawyer is truly on the go (as in hands-free driving or walking) or even when they are not, dictation apps capture spoken words and record information in an efficient, electronic, and convenient way. When a mobile device becomes a recorder and converts speech to text, busy modern lawyers can complete tasks without ever even touching it.

## 2)   R U Messaging?

In late 2021, the Securities and Exchange Commission fined a subsidiary of banking giant JPMorgan Chase & Co. $200 million for violating federal securities record-keeping laws.[5] Why? Because it had gone "offline." Managers, brokers, and employees used personal mobile devices, phone numbers, and email addresses to send texts, emails, and WhatsApp messages about sensitive company business among each another and clients— none of which was archived as federal law requires. If professional and secure messaging isn't a topic high on your list of considerations, JPMorgan could give 200 million reasons why it should be.

Years ago, I talked with students about pros and cons of legal "texting," that is, lawyers using their personal phone number to exchange texts with clients (and others). While traditional cellular phone SMS (short message service) texting is still relevant, **mobile messaging** has exploded into a broader category encompassing MMS (multimedia messages—digital images, emojis, videos, audio, etc.) and other types of internet-based, real-time communication through software most readers carry around on devices in pockets and backpacks: "DMs" (direct messaging such as on platforms like Twitter and Instagram),

...cial media messaging like WeChat, WhatsApp, group cha...Signal, business messaging services such as Slack iMessage...nd others within different LPM portals. or Zipwl...

Suffice...say there's a lot of messaging going on, and we'll take the go...with the bad.

Mobi...messaging requires the modern lawyer to keep a careful eye o...their habits—even the "digital native" generation whose men...ers have never *not* enjoyed this form of connection and co...nunication. Let's start with why messaging is so popular. In ge...eral, it's:

- ✓ quick
- ✓ inexpensive (or less expensive)
- ✓ real time
- ✓ convenient
- ✓ productive (people used to messaging are more likely to read and respond to a text than open and reply to an email)
- ✓ ideal for discrete pieces of information, such as scheduling confirmations, automatic billing updates, and status updates
- ✓ helpful

Just like you may appreciate a text reminder from your dentist or an update that flight is going to be delayed because of weather, messaging may help a lawyer meet the ethical obligation under Model Rule 1.4 to use "reasonable communication"[6] to keep clients reasonably informed.

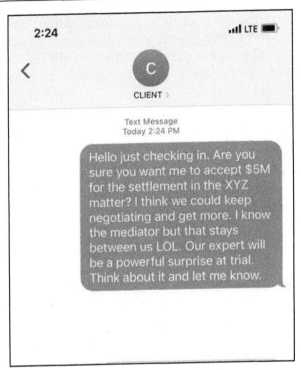

\* Figure 8B: Hypothetical attorney-client privileged text message.

Convenient, yes—but is it "safe" and smart to use messaging? That depends. The content in the hypothetical text message in Figure 8B is attorney-client privileged information. What about security? It's not a red flag to stop all mobile messaging, but a yellow one that urges caution (chapter 9 turns to security). Readers may not think about the security of everyday personal texts or social media instant messages. Key questions for the modern messaging lawyer include whether their employer has an applicable policy about messaging and what the lawyer can do to ensure confidentiality. No ethical lawyer would shout client confidences or work product strategy aloud on an airplane or leave privileged documents on a table in a coffee shop. Is transmitting information electronically from one mobile device to another that much better an option? Yes, sort of—so long as the modern lawyer takes reasonable steps like the ones outlined here and in chapter 9 and continues to stay abreast of changes with this perfectly imperfect communication technology:

✓ Communicate about communication: discuss messaging with clients to set parameters and gauge expectations. Consider whether to add information about messaging to a representation agreement, if applicable.

✓ Use a secure, reputable third-party messaging service or software with encryption instead of a personal SMS cell phone number.

✓ Disable the message preview feature on your smartphone or tablet's lock screen and remind clients to do the same, to avoid the wrong eyes viewing privileged information.

✓ Ensure your mobile device is password protected, including secure biometric authentication such as facial recognition or fingerprint scanning (more on password "hygiene" in chapter 9).

✓ Consider documentation, integration, record keeping, timekeeping, and billing: would you be able to document and archive mobile messages as part of a client's file? How will you account for billable time spent messaging?

✓ Avoid the temptation of informality and avoid messaging for complex discussions. Keep messages concise, professional in tone and style, and without typos, slang, acronyms, GIFs, or emojis. *IMO u got it :)!!*

Messaging and chat tools like Slack are an increasingly appealable option to avoid email drudgery. Even if you can use mobile messaging with clients or colleagues, should you? That's a different, important question. As convenient as the communication is a modern lawyer considers how messaging affects work-life balance, personal safety, stress, relationships, boundaries, privacy, and independence. This book prompts the questions; after careful consideration, you'll find your answers.

3) Audio & Videoconferencing

On-the-go lawyers communicate in writing. For many, that's not enough. We want to collaborate, see, hear, and talk with one another. "Zooming" became a household term amid the Covid-19 pandemic—as did "Zoom" classes and "Zoom" happy hours—but lawyers used **audio and videoconferencing** tools long before. Whether for a real-time "water cooler" quick chat with friends and colleagues, formal court proceeding (more on remote access to court next), or transactional negotiation, conferencing is and will remain the primary method for remote connection with others. Here too many of the same principles of mobile work apply, balancing convenience and productivity with security, integration, ease of access, and professionalism. We'll explore the ins and outs of security assessments of mobile communication tools in chapter 9, but it should be first on the list of things to think about before connecting via audio or videoconference.

Lawyers have no shortage of choice when it comes to conferencing tools. Some are stand-alone and others integrate as part of all-in-one LPM platforms. The bells and whistles of different tools aren't something we'll review because there are so many players in this space, such as Zoom, Google Hangouts, GoToMeeting, Slack huddles, Skype, Clubhouse, Webex, and Microsoft® Teams. Lawyers should be familiar with broad basics but experts with the platform(s) they use the most.

And use these tools you will. Videoconferencing saves massive amounts of time and expense. For some, it's a standard expectation and inconceivable (maybe even laughable) that clients were once charged thousands of dollars for a lawyer to fly across the country for a 20-minute court appearance that would clutter a lawyer's schedule for days. Relevant rules and expectations will change at courthouses, police departments, government agencies, offices, prisons, homes, and businesses across the world. The value (or lack thereof) placed on in-person, face-to-face communication will vary with every lawyer and client you meet, every matter you handle, and every situation you encounter. Just like with mobile messaging, there is no one-size-fits all approach to audio or videoconferencing and we'll turn more to security in the next chapter—but we can get going in the right direction:

  ✓ Stay aware of who joins a conference to minimize
     risk of hacking, sometimes known as "Zoom

bombing." Maintain up-to-date versions of conferencing software.

✓ Ask attendees of an audio-only conference (conference call) to introduce themselves at the start and ask that anyone joining do so too.

✓ Track attendees of a videoconference. Use a unique meeting password and meeting ID. Consider a "waiting room" feature to let only expected participants in. If available, use a "lock" feature to secure a videoconference after it begins, or ask attendees to introduce themselves.

✓ Practice best screen-sharing practices on your chosen platform(s). Close out of personal files or material from other matters to avoid disclosing confidential (or embarrassing) information such as personal photos or, better yet, screen-share individual files only and not your entire desktop.

✓ Avoid videoconferencing out of the office on a mobile device or home computer with lesser internet security and avoid public Wi-Fi connections.

✓ Know your surroundings regarding who might hear confidential audio or videoconference discussions, whether at home or on the go.

✓ Use extra caution with conference chat functions and be meticulous about mute/unmute settings to avoid unintentional disclosures.

✓ Ensure a professional remote appearance with proper lighting, accurate virtual name tag/label (including who you represent), eye-level camera, audible microphone or quality headset, and a minimally distracting background (or appropriate virtual background).

---

**LIT TIP**

Explore ways to foster connection and improve focus during videoconferences. We've all sat through a long remote session like a Zoom class where the host shares presentation slides and their face (and everyone else's) disappears, leaving us to stare at slides or a document. When I'm listening to someone explain material, I want to still see their face. Many platforms give the option to share slides or a document as a virtual background so the host speaker remains visible. For example, on Zoom, click Share Screen in meeting controls > Advanced > Slides as Virtual Background > Select File > Open. This option better mimics the in-person experience of a presenter speaking about material while attendees view both the material and the speaker. Added bonus: attendees may be less likely to get bored with background material if they can still see your engaging face!

---

## "See" You in (Virtual) Court

From individual, on-the-go and out-of-office mobile practices we turn to an institutional mainstay: courts. Historically, the phrase "go to court" made sense. Lawyers, clients, jurors, witnesses, parole officers, observers, news reporters, bailiffs, security officers, clerks, and judges *went* to court: they physically appeared in the building, whether to file a document or attend a proceeding.

Today, "going" to court means something else—not everywhere, but in a growing number of places—and not just during a pandemic. It's true that not every courthouse has traded its marble columns and grand stairway entrances for virtual waiting rooms and mute icons. Thousands of courthouses remain wide open for traditional business, shuffling people in and out of clerk's offices, witness stands, and courtroom gallery seats. But many aspects of the traditional courtroom experience are slowly creeping out of the physical courthouse, including operations turned upside down during the Covid-19 pandemic. For example, Texas was generally regarded as never having held any civil hearings by video before the pandemic, and now it has held many hundreds of thousands—if not more. And instead of limited public seating in its historical gallery as had been the case for centuries, in 2020 the United States Supreme Court welcomed hundreds of thousands of listeners "live" at its first-ever oral arguments held by telephone.

Some change has been huge; some incremental; some widespread; some isolated; some pandemic-related; some not. It's all significant for lawyers who practice in court and individuals who rely on court services, from criminal defendants to people resolving delicate family matters to Fortune 500 companies litigating complex contract disputes. Even if you don't envision walking up the courthouse steps during your career, every modern lawyer should recognize that the court system of the future is already here.

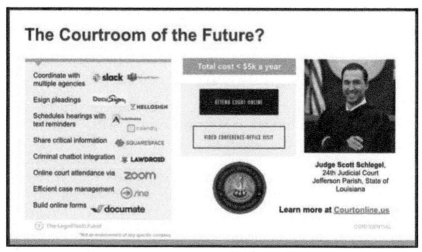

\* Figure 8C: Judge Scott Schlegel, The Courtroom of the Future? image.[7]

What do we mean by a **virtual courtroom**? Let's start by what it's not: e-filing/online dockets and courtroom presentation technology. Some courts, including the federal system, have offered e-filing and e-access to materials for decades. Others don't, and lawyers still walk into a clerk's office with hard-copy envelopes and filings that get date-stamped, copied, and put in a file drawer. Innovation in courtroom technology is another angle we won't address in this chapter: document cameras, computer monitors at the witness stand, counsel table, and jury box, projection screens for large display, and other multimedia presentation tools. The fact that lawyers display digital timelines on a screen to support their closing argument instead of marking up a large piece of posterboard on an easel is exciting, but it's not our focus.

Virtual court means court proceedings that occur with some or all participants appearing remotely outside of a physical courtroom. In some instances, court employees and a presiding judge are physically present in a courtroom but others—such as lawyers, clients, defendants, and witnesses—are not. While some courts conducted virtual proceedings before the pandemic, closing courthouse doors during quarantine prompted countless others to go remote with virtual discovery status meetings, motion hearings, grand jury proceedings, arraignments, and "Zoom trials," all done via videoconferencing.

Virtual court proceedings beyond the physical courtroom walls offer significant benefits and prompt serious concerns.

Among the many benefits:

- ✓ greater convenience for participants
- ✓ less expense for participants
- ✓ smoother scheduling transitions for busy court dockets
- ✓ improved ease of participants empowered from the comfort of their own home instead of an intimidating physical courtroom (after all, each "box" in a virtual setting on a computer screen is usually the same size!)
- ✓ continuity of service (not just emergency pandemics, but hurricanes, forest fires, or anything else that disrupts in-person work)
- ✓ improved transparency for public access (people might not travel to a physical courtroom to observe but may be tempted to do so virtually)

Virtual court proceedings have drawbacks; we're not just talking about a broken microphone. One huge concern is accessibility. The United States legal system seeks to ensure "equal justice for all"—not "virtual justice" or justice only for tech-savvy people, those fortunate enough to enjoy reliable internet access, and those with a high level of proficiency with the English language or enough money to buy and download the latest secure computer operating system or software. Sophisticated technology to support remote court proceedings is inspiring in theory, but a lost cause if the members of the public who need services the most can't access them. In the internet-connected environment of a law school or law firm, it might be difficult for readers to imagine people without high-speed internet access. But it is a real challenge, in particular for certain demographic groups and geographic regions with large rural communities. The same is true for individuals with certain disabilities who can't access the internet or navigate conferencing software as seamlessly as most judges and lawyers can. Technical difficulties, incorrect links, security breaches, or incompatibility with certain internet browsers or screen reader assistive technologies are all valid concerns as to whether virtual court proceedings are available to *all* who seek access to justice—not just a privileged subset.

Beyond accessibility lies an enormous mix of operational hurdles and substantive legal questions, too:

| | |
|---|---|
| ✓ sequestering witnesses<br>✓ ensuring attendance<br>✓ maintaining decorum<br>✓ supporting juvenile defendants or witnesses<br>✓ enabling pro se parties<br>✓ making credibility determinations<br>✓ securely distributing conference links and information | ✓ working through language barriers and translators<br>✓ integrating with prisons, police stations, probation offices, and community partners<br>✓ fostering constitutional confrontation rights<br>✓ guarding against witness tampering |

Consider these "what-if" virtual court scenarios:

- ✓ A judge becomes frustrated in an immigration proceeding and threatens to deport someone who seems uncooperative—when in fact the person's video had frozen and they had low audio quality because they couldn't afford a new microphone. Is that fair?

✓ A party requests a confidential "sidebar" in a virtual proceeding to share what they consider private, sensitive, and personal information. Can they do that?

✓ A party to a civil case conducted virtually moves to strike testimony upon suspicion of witness coaching, after overhearing an unmuted background comment and observing a witness looking off to the side of her screen and appearing to check her phone. Should the judge grant a motion to strike the testimony?

✓ A clerk administering an oath in a virtual proceeding asks a participant to raise their right hand and instead of raising their actual, physical right hand, they press the Zoom reaction icon and a small virtual hand image pops up above their head. Is that sworn testimony?

✓ A prosecutor in a domestic violence proceeding eliciting testimony from the victim in a virtual videoconference setting realizes that the alleged assaulter defendant is in a separate "box" on the screen but in the same physical location only a few feet away from the testifying witness. Should the prosecutor ask for a stay of the proceeding out of fear for the victim's safety? (This troubling example happened in real life.)[8]

Many courts in the United States and across the globe are modernizing processes for virtual court despite the speed bumps and doing innovative things with technology. For example, some offer "Zoom kiosks" at the courthouse to support virtual court appearances for individuals who do not have a reliable or safe method to appear in a remote session. Others set up automated text message systems to remind individuals of scheduled court appearances, helping avoid unnecessary defaults or rescheduling headaches from failure to appear. As court systems in the United States, Canada, and beyond move past pandemic-related emergency procedures and find their "new" normal, many players in these complicated systems recognize—and celebrate—that new approaches are inevitable.

LIT TIP

"It is clear that the use of virtual examinations will continue by this Court and will become the norm for the foreseeable future. Even when the pandemic is behind us, the comfort level we have all gained with this form of technology is such that it is likely to continue to be a strong option for parties, particularly where a witness is out of country, out of province or has mobility or health issues. Given the inevitable future of virtual examinations in the legal system, it is up to the judiciary, as its gatekeepers, to ensure that this tool is not abused nor seen to undermine our globally admired legal system."[9]

Justice Frederick Myers
Ontario Superior Court of Justice (Canada)

Virtual court proceedings in some shape or form are a given but the devil will be in the details for both civil and criminal matters. Many jurisdictions may turn to a hybrid approach, meaning both in-person and remote courthouse access depending on the nature of the proceeding, or hybrid in the sense of a mix of in-person and remote participants in the same proceeding (for example, a witness testifying virtually at an in-person jury trial). Individual counties, districts, judges, courts, officials, and state/federal systems will create their own rules, such as presumptions that shorter proceedings be virtual or prohibitions against virtual juror selection in jury trials. In civil matters, parties will craft agreements and proposed orders as to what aspects of a case they'll agree to conduct remotely, or squabble over whether and what proceedings should be remote, such as in some of these examples decided during the Covid-19 pandemic:

- ➢ *Guardant Health, Inc. v. Found. Med.*, Inc., No. 17-1616-LPS-CJB, 2020 WL 6120186, at *3 (D. Del. Oct. 16, 2020) (ordering a partially remote civil trial over defendant's objection, arguing "[s]killful trial counsel will be able to conduct effective examinations" even with both witnesses and counsel remote).

- ➢ *Gould Elecs. Inc. v. Livingston Cty. Rd. Comm'n,* 470 F. Supp. 3d 735, 742 (E.D. Mich. 2020) (allowing a remote trial despite objection of due process, reasoning that the case had a "protracted history" and "pushing off trial until possibly a year from now or later would be a far cry from proceeding to trial on an expedited basis" since the case had been pending for over a decade).

➤ *Kieffaber v. Ethicon, Inc.*, No. 20-1177-KHV, 2021 WL 425822, at *3–4 (D. Kan. Feb. 8, 2021) (rejecting defendant's objection to remote civil trial and disagreeing with the contention that "logistical difficulties [would] interfere with efficiency" of trial and would lead to juror distraction).

Criminal matters will bring even more wrinkles. Defendants challenge denial of requests for in-person proceedings as violations of their constitutional confrontation clause rights and right to a public trial. Compare these two decisions from different criminal proceedings:

➤ *Vazquez Diaz v. Commonwealth*, No. 13009, at *9–11 (May 5, 2021) (holding a virtual suppression hearing during the Covid-19 pandemic is not a per se violation of a criminal defendant's constitutional rights "so long as the videoconferencing provides adequate safeguards," including the ability of the defendant to virtually consult with the lawyer, listen to the evidence, and assess witness credibility).

➤ *State of Missouri v. Smith*, No. SC99086, at *19–20 (Jan. 11, 2022) (reversing defendant's conviction and holding live video testimony via Zoom from an expert witness about DNA evidence in a sexual assault case was not harmless error and violated the constitution's confrontation clause requirement).

No matter the type of case, large-scale change with virtual court proceedings will offer a steady stream of operational, budgetary, constitutional, administrative, and technical growing pains as court systems and processes evolve.

And evolve they will. Stay tuned for new technology in this space. During the rush of the pandemic, most courthouses were forced to use general platforms like Zoom or Skype that are not designed for a courtroom experience. Some used designated

YouTube channels for real-time audio livestreaming. "Smart courts" are popping up around the world with innovative remote platforms, tools, and even chatbots. Innovators and technologists are developing law-specific virtual conferencing platforms that better mimic the in-person decorum expected of the courtroom experience, facilitate secure testimony, support greater accessibility, and explore forward-thinking options like 3D technology, holograms, and virtual reality. What the "see" in "see you in court" means will be an exciting area for the modern lawyer to watch.

## "See" You in (Cyber) Court: Online Dispute Resolution (ODR)

We just covered court proceedings where people need help, but for decades people have also helped themselves and resolved legal matters without courts through private resolution. Alternative Dispute Resolution (ADR) captures arbitration, mediation, and negotiation. You've heard these terms; law schools offer entire courses on them. Even though law students read judicial case law, there's far more voluntary "private" resolution going on in our world. The percentage of matters litigated through court systems is minuscule compared to the number resolved in private.

ADR that moves online is called **Online Dispute Resolution** (ODR) and we'll cover two flavors of it: private ODR and quasi-public ODR. Private ODR allows parties (and third-party mediators or arbitrators) to interact remotely with one another to resolve conflicts, usually in quicker and less expensive fashion compared to court processes. A growing new type of ODR is quasi-public, whereby court systems get into the resolution-outside-of-court game and experiment with online platforms that aim to guide individuals who would otherwise be in the courthouse to resolve disputes themselves.

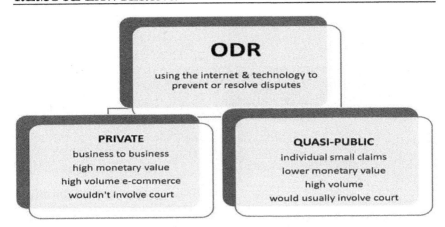

* Figure 8D: ODR overview: private and quasi-public.

## 1) Private ODR

On the one hand, private ODR is nothing new. Sometimes it involves lawyers and sometimes it doesn't. In 1999, the online marketplace company eBay used an internal system known as its Resolution Center for buyers and sellers to resolve common disputes, such as someone never receiving an item they purchased or a seller never receiving payment. eBay uses ODR software alone—no human intervention—for the vast majority of the many millions of disputes it helps users resolve each year. So do PayPal, Amazon, and other consumer companies.

On the other hand, the new reach of private ODR is expanding. Arbitrations, mediations, and negotiations that have almost always occurred in person are moving online. In part this was because of forced distancing during the Covid-19 pandemic, but it was also fueled by growing attention to cost-effective resolutions in lieu of the billions of dollars and many years spent litigating. Business-to-business, business-to-consumer, and consumer-to-consumer disputes (and not just those with low monetary values) can be resolved through mediation, arbitration, or negotiation using private online or in-person/ remote hybrid digital platforms. Instead of paying a lawyer for services in connection with litigation proceedings, parties pay to resolve a dispute privately (often still with a lawyer's service).

> ## LIT TIP
>
> "Traditional litigation is cumbersome, time-consuming, and expensive. It diverts bandwidth and resources from more beneficial and productive applications. The world has become so technologically capable. The legal industry needs to adopt and utilize those capabilities to run litigation quickly, efficiently, and virtually."
>
> Collin Williams
> Founder, New Era ADR, Inc.

One such platform, New Era ADR, aims to streamline traditional litigation by allowing parties to resolve disputes online. New Era ADR builds custom software with features such as real-time messaging, document uploading, calendaring, videoconferencing, and on-platform resolution drafting with e-signatures, while also offering a panel of handpicked neutral arbitrators and mediators. The image in Figure 8E shows a sample dashboard for an "Expedited Virtual Arbitration" in a hypothetical commercial contract dispute.

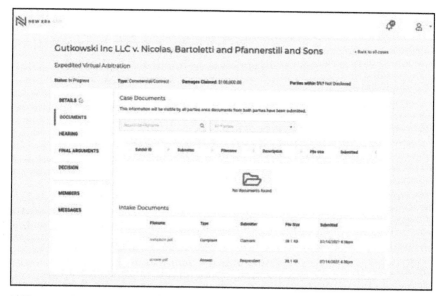

\* Figure 8E: New Era ADR virtual arbitration dashboard; reprinted with permission.[10]

## 2)  Quasi-Public ODR

Quasi-public is the second arm of ODR and it's growing fast. By quasi-public, I mean court-related, court-annexed, or court-sponsored online platforms that aim to spark voluntary resolution of conflicts that otherwise would require court involvement. This is sometimes labeled "cyber court." This form of ODR is most often directed to self-represented litigants, with no lawyers, and is viewed by many modern lawyers and technologists as a promising piece to improving the Access to Justice crisis.

Suppose you live in Connecticut and receive a traffic court citation for speeding after a small car accident. You've never received a violation before and want to challenge it to avoid a hike in your auto insurance premium. Instead of going in and out of court with a stack of papers on an assigned day(s) over many months, you might opt in to Connecticut's Online Ticket Review program by pleading not guilty to the traffic violation through checking a box on a website. From there, you might upload photos, documentation, and an explanation of your side of the story. Prosecutors review the information along with other public data such as crash reports and choose whether to prosecute the case or make a settlement offer. Three weeks later, you get an email notification of an offer for you to pay a nominal monetary fee. You pay the fee and "have your day in court" without ever setting foot inside a Connecticut courtroom or hiring a lawyer. [Virtual] justice is served!

This example isn't a hypothetical. Countries around the world and state and local counties throughout the United States like the ones listed here are experimenting with and developing court-backed, public-facing ODR, usually for low(er)-value, high-volume individual civil conflicts such as small claims disputes (under a designated monetary value), landlord/tenant, traffic, insurance, and debt collection.

> ➤ Michigan: Statewide MI Resolve launched in 2020 with a commercial vendor as a free opt-out program, helping parties negotiate matters such as financial disputes, contract cancellations, and property dissolution.

> ➤ Utah: An ODR program expanded statewide by 2021 aims to aid Utah's rural population across the geographically large state and includes volunteer "navigators" to support new users.

> ➤ New York: A small claims ODR system launched in 2021 in Manhattan for disputes up to $10,000; parties may "bid" on how much they'd settle a case for and negotiate directly or work with an ODR mediator.

> ➤ Georgia (Clayton County): An Online Traffic Resolution Program allows individuals to register with an $8 dollar fee and negotiate with prosecutors before being placed on the court's calendar for qualifying traffic citations.

Quasi-public ODR isn't one size fits all, but the goal is the same: spark voluntary resolution requiring little or no court intervention. What does ODR actually look like? Some jurisdictions contract with commercial ODR vendors such as TurboCourt; others, such as Connecticut and Utah, have built their own. Most courts working with ODR processes give basic legal information on their website to guide early processes, to help individuals diagnose their legal issue, and to set expectations. Depending on the approach, quasi-public ODR platforms might include:

✓ direct-messaging "chat" negotiation tools

✓ file upload options and directions

✓ an option to use a third-party mediator or court facilitator

✓ "FAQ" links with substantive (but simplified) legal information on the topic

✓ real-time and asynchronous (at different times) communication options

Quasi-public ODR brings advantages and disadvantages. Yes, there is hope of lower cost, lighter imposition on judicial dockets and clerk of court offices, greater efficiency, improved transparency, and personal convenience. But it's not cheap. Who pays for it? Out of what budget? For how long? Who ensures timely feedback and assessment? How do local community members learn about court-sponsored ODR tools and become comfortable with the new processes? The traditional court system has been around for centuries and transitioning any of it to quasi-public ODR is no small undertaking.

Whether private or quasi-public, ODR will look different the moment you finish reading this book. One report projects a global ODR market size of $210 million in 2028, up from $57 million in 2020.[11] I hope this overview sparks interest—or even excitement. As ODR gains traction, a modern lawyer should remain aware of how disputes get resolved both inside and outside the physical courtroom.

## Let's Make a (Virtual) Deal

Virtual courts make us think litigation. But remote lawyering impacts transactional attorneys just the same. Deals aren't only done in a high-rise boardroom with 25 lawyers reviewing documents for a corporate acquisition around a conference table. That might be how it looks in the movies, but not in real life.

Consider a simple transaction such as a real estate closing for the sale of a new home. Attorneys, real estate agents, title examiners, sellers, and purchasers used to dash around to and from different locations with stacks of paper and pens (chapter 7 touched on e-signatures).

While jurisdictional rules vary, today closings and refinances are accomplished remotely. Parties review and sign documents at their convenience, communicate using videoconferencing tools, and enjoy cost savings and greater convenience. Many practices started under temporary permissive orders during the pandemic and states wrestle with whether and how to make them permanent—or mandate a return to in-person transactions. Whether called an e-closing, online closing, or virtual closing, parties to many real estate transactions never share the same physical space.

**Virtual Data Rooms** (VDR, also called Virtual Deal Rooms) are one of the most significant aspects of transactional remote work. Considered industry standard, VDRs are centralized online repositories where electronic information is stored, organized, reviewed, and distributed, and where multiple people involved in a transaction can simultaneously access and exchange information and communicate and collaborate remotely.

Here's some background for readers unfamiliar with transactional work. Clients prepare for, negotiate, and execute transactions in all shapes and sizes, such as:

✓ partnership formations

✓ corporate acquisitions

✓ mergers

✓ preparation of an initial public offering (IPO)

✓ financial restructurings

✓ intellectual property licensing deals

✓ debt financings

When they do, they receive and review information from each other and often from more than one other entity. For example, suppose your corporate client wants to buy a smaller company that's expressed interest in finding a purchaser and closing up shop. You and your client and maybe your team review that smaller company's finances, tax receipts, contracts, and other relevant materials. If others were interested in buying that same company, they too would be provided access to the same information.

The process of reviewing information in this transactional context is known as due diligence. Decades ago, due diligence happened in "war rooms"—physical locations in a hotel, office, or law firm conference room where attorneys (often from across the globe, or from different clients "taking turns" with material) would congregate with boxes of documents and laptops. Today, physical "war rooms" are a thing of the past.

---

### LIT TIP

"As a junior associate in the early 2000s, I began my career working on merger and acquisition transactions for one of the largest law firms in the world. I spent weeks cooped up in conference "war" rooms across the United States performing due diligence on companies my clients were selling or acquiring. Reviewing the paper material was not only isolating, but even the most organized person was challenged by keeping track of the details of each contract, ensuring newly added items were not overlooked, and locating reviewed documents amidst the boxes.

After I returned to M&A work from a 10-year hiatus, I transitioned to VDRs. I can now peruse a VDR from my home office. The search features allow me to easily find a document I've reviewed. VDRs are typically organized by document type (customer agreements, employee benefit plans, etc.) and there is a roadmap that is easy to navigate. I'm able to quickly search for provisions in agreements using buzzwords such as "Change in Control." Some VDRs also let me take notes in a file associated with the documents that other teammates may view and add to. Overall, my work product and work environment today as a transactional lawyer in this context has improved dramatically."

Meghan L. Tufts, Esq.
Corporate Associate, Ruban & Rudman LLP

---

No 21st century transactional deal lawyer is relying on isolated searches through conference room boxes.

What does a VDR interface look like for a lawyer navigating today's modern "war room" landing page for collaborative transactional work? A data room such as the one in Figure 8F from SmartRoom™ offers one example, although there are many vendors in this space. Transactional lawyers could use this data for one or more clients or entities, with main-level folders, files, and subfolders to organize and track digital content.

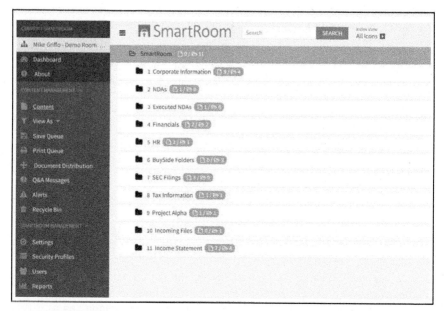

* Figure 8F: SmartRoom™ landing page; reproduced with permission by SmartRoom™.

Speaking of mounds of digital content, VDRs might remind you of chapter 5's discussion of ESI. Due diligence involves producing and reviewing ESI, although in a collaborative and strategic sense instead of an adversarial litigation, investigation, or prosecution. Transactional attorneys and those with whom they work, such as accountants, review ESI using VDRs. VDR technology has exploded in sophistication and covers not only due diligence but often an entire transaction start to finish. Just as with ESI platforms, the ins and outs of VDR options vary, but the basics for a modern transactional lawyer to be aware of are the same:

    ✓   ease of use and intuitive interface

    ✓   ability to track unauthorized viewing of select content, to "lock" access, and to disable copying, printing, or forwarding

    ✓   top security features (different levels of user access, data encryption, firewalls)

    ✓   communication tools such as messaging or "live" online discussion

    ✓    integration with separate messaging tools such as Slack

    ✓    mobile accessibility

So next time you read or see the news about a high-stakes transaction worth billions of dollars and picture a large group of lawyers and others sitting around a long conference table in fancy business suits, just imagine—that deal may have negotiated and executed from the comfort of a living room couch.

## Staying Invisible While Remote: Unauthorized Practice of Law

Remote practice means lawyers hop across all sorts of state lines. Where a lawyer lives, sits, downloads files, calls in from, and physically works is less relevant than it's ever been. Maybe I'll attend a remote arraignment in a Massachusetts criminal court session from my vacation home in New Hampshire, where I'm not a member of the bar. Or I'll videoconference clients back home in Indiana where I'm licensed while stuck at a month-long trial down in Oklahoma. It's all very convenient, but is it allowed? Is it **unauthorized remote practice** of law? When and to what extent is a modern lawyer allowed to work remotely from a physical location in a state where they are not admitted to the bar?

Remember the history here. A lawyer's actual, physical, in-the-flesh presence was (and still is) the original premise of why and when a lawyer is authorized to practice in a particular state. Ethics rules prohibiting unauthorized law practice and state bar exam passage requirements are intended to protect the public against unauthorized services by unqualified persons in *that* physical state—local rules to protect local citizens.

The wrinkle, of course, is that many lawyers don't always stay in just one geographic state. Some lawyers reside in a state where they are admitted to practice, but some don't. If you live over the border in Rhode Island but are a member of the bar in Massachusetts, Massachusetts is where you engage in legal practice and Rhode Island doesn't regulate anything you do just because you happen to have a residential address there. Think of the many lawyers in the tri-state area who practice in New York City and are members of the New York bar, but live and work remotely a train ride away in the suburbs of New Jersey or Connecticut. Even decades ago, before remote practice was feasible, if a lawyer vacationed in Florida for a few months but was not a member of the Florida bar, that lawyer could never represent clients in Florida during his vacation or attend court proceedings there. The exception to this is temporary admission to the bar of another state in connection with a specific matter, known as *pro hac vice* ("for this occasion"), which lawyers routinely seek when appearing as counsel of record for clients in out-of-state matters across the country.

---

### LIT TIP

"A lawyer shall not practice law in a jurisdiction in violation of the regulation of the legal profession in that jurisdiction, or assist another in doing so. A lawyer who is not admitted to practice in this jurisdiction shall not:

(1) except as authorized by these Rules or other law, establish an office or other systematic and continuous presence in this jurisdiction for the practice of law; or

(2) hold out to the public or otherwise represent that the lawyer is admitted to practice law in this jurisdiction."[12]

Model Rule 5.5

---

Consider the push and pull here: tension between state-specific rules regarding unauthorized practice to protect their local citizens and the reality that lawyers work remotely with and for citizens of any number of different states. Whether for vacation, work, or other reasons, it's common for lawyers to be physically present for extended periods of time in jurisdictions where they are not a member of the bar. You might think of this as the give-and-take as between a lawyer physically being a sort of guest in a "host" or "remote" jurisdiction and away from their "home" or "licensing" jurisdiction(s). Lawyers are on the move but existing state regulations still keep a tight grasp.

The answer for the modern remote lawyer is to move freely but keep law practice tied only to your home licensing jurisdiction(s). Put another way, the mere fact of being physically present in a different "host" jurisdiction is not unauthorized practice in that jurisdiction so long as a lawyer remains "invisible." This connects to the "hold out to the public" language of Model Rule 5.5. Working remotely rarely creates a "systematic and continuous presence" in a host jurisdiction because the lawyer's physical presence is incidental. Whether a lawyer logs in from a beach in California, an apartment in New York City, or a cabin in Maine, a lawyer working remotely for a Massachusetts law firm as a member of the bar in Massachusetts isn't holding themselves out for services to the citizens of California, New York, or Maine. That lawyer stays "invisible" and there is no potential for harm to the public, so the temporary "host" state has no interest in regulating the Massachusetts lawyer's practice.

---

### LIT TIP

"Lawyers may remotely practice the law of the jurisdictions in which they are licensed while physically present in a jurisdiction in which they are not admitted if the local jurisdiction has not determined that the conduct is the unlicensed or unauthorized practice of law and if they do not hold themselves out as being licensed to practice in the local jurisdiction, do not advertise or otherwise hold out as having an office in the local jurisdiction, and do not provide or offer to provide legal services in the local jurisdiction . . . [h]aving local contact information on websites, letterhead, business cards, advertising, or the like would improperly establish a local office or local presence under the ABA Model Rules."

ABA Standing Comm. on Ethics and Pro. Resp., Formal Op. 495 (2020)

---

This is general guidance; each state decides for itself what is or is not authorized within its borders. A modern lawyer working remotely in a jurisdiction where they are not a member of the bar even for a short time period should:

- ✓ Review that local jurisdiction's rules about unauthorized practice of law.

- ✓ Ensure they do nothing to establish a presence such as open a physical office location, develop signage, do public advertising, or make official appearances on record.

  ✓   Consider becoming admitted in the host state where they are physically located if they intend to stay for an extended period (don't worry—this doesn't always mean taking a bar exam; sometimes a lawyer can be admitted to the bar in a jurisdiction by a simple motion and fee payment).

## Hybrid Work Models

Past generations saw in-person lawyering as the norm and remote interaction the intermittent exception. Now, that's flipped.

For the next generation of lawyers and legal professionals (plus clients, businesses, and individuals with whom we'll work), a remote or **hybrid work model** will become the default. Years from now, we likely won't need the "virtual" modifier for firms, offices, courthouses, or deal rooms—some virtual component will be a given.

Any reader who has ever attended a videoconference wearing comfortable sweatpants or slippers knows a thing or two about the upsides to remote work. It can offer:

  ✓   flexibility

  ✓   convenience

  ✓   enhanced productivity

  ✓   less expense

  ✓   improved work-life balance/integration

  ✓   less office disruption and distraction

  ✓   additional free time to focus on well-being and mental, physical, and spiritual health (avoiding that long commute goes a long way!)

> ### LIT TIP
>
> "The hybrid model of legal work we were forced to develop quickly during the Covid-19 pandemic is the future, but we must be purposeful about work culture. Our lawyers learn so much from informal mentorship and discussion—chatting in the office kitchen about what they're working on, popping into another attorney's office to brainstorm, or grabbing coffee to take a break. Widespread remote work makes that difficult. Making frequent use of chat software such as Jabber for informal questions, actively participating in practice group or office Zoom meetings, and picking up the phone to call (instead of email) colleagues with questions are just a few examples of things we can do to stay connected to colleagues while working remotely."
>
> Kathleen C. Burns
> Former Managing Partner Boston Office, Nixon Peabody LLP

Of course, remote lawyering has a downside too (beyond just not wearing slippers all day). There will be some "culture shock" across different generations of lawyers and clients navigating the new workplace norms. Remote access from all places all the time can make it difficult to ever put down work, or separate work from our personal life and remember that they aren't the same thing. Across the legal profession, remote work practices have the potential to have a disparate negative impact on certain groups, chief among them lawyers of color, women, and others more likely to juggle significant personal, family, and childcare responsibilities while out of the office but working from home. Remote lawyering may also muddy the waters with:

- ✓ workload assignments
- ✓ mental health and well-being (pressure to always "be on")
- ✓ evaluations of junior lawyers
- ✓ increased billable-hour expectations and burnout
- ✓ feelings of isolation and loneliness
- ✓ mentorship and professional friendships
- ✓ professional development and training
- ✓ compensation and advancement

✓   workplace culture and creativity

✓   resentment between those required to be in-person and those who are not

✓   trust between lawyers and those with whom they work

---

### LIT TIP

"When it comes to maintaining focus in the midst of distractions, remote work presents challenges for anyone, not just lawyers. Because we are not robots, we can't just sit and work countless hours expecting continued focus and productivity. Whether in or out of the office, scheduling and taking breaks—for food, coffee, to check your email, or take a walk—is essential. Use a timer or an app, like the Pomodoro Focus Timer, to guide you. The technique is simple: 25-minute focused work sessions combined with five-minute breaks. True singular focus in manageable chunks of time takes discipline when working remotely; lawyers who don't take breaks will overload their on-the-go brain and are likely to see their productivity—and well-being—suffer."

Professor Shailini J. George
Author, The Law Student's Guide to Doing Well and Being Well[13]

---

There are even reports of law firms monitoring productivity of lawyers working remotely with facial recognition technology that mounts to a lawyer's computer to track how often the lawyer gets up to take a break, uses the restroom, or does several "normal" things any lawyer might do instead of being chained to a desk chair for eight hours.

\* \* \* \*

As you move forward in your career, I trust you'll share my hope that the next generation of modern lawyers steers away from privacy intrusions and "big brother" watching towards an emphasis on efficient use of remote technology, substantive productivity, and personal career satisfaction—whether that's on Main Street, on a mobile device, in the metaverse, or somewhere in between.

*Review Your Knowledge*

1) Alejandro is a criminal prosecutor in a suburban county outside of Phoenix, Arizona. He finished presenting a complicated child pornography case to a grand jury. Alejandro took a short vacation after the proceeding and planned to work with an assistant in the prosecutor's office to iron out some final details in the draft indictment. Alejandro pulled up the Microsoft® Word document on his phone at the airport and made a few important edits to one section using the Word app. He quickly emailed his assistant with the subject line, "Final—all set" but didn't realize that he needed to "tap" one more time again to actually attach the document file. The assistant received the email and assumed Alejandro meant that he had changed the document as stored in the office's cloud document system, so the assistant printed and filed that wrong version from the office. Upon return, Alejandro realized the error and was furious. Alejandro:

   a) has no responsibility for this error by an assistant with whom he works and has every right to be frustrated.

   b) has no responsibility for this error because we all know these things happen when tapping quickly on a phone, and it's a part of our 24/7 mobile society today that everyone accepts.

   c) should avoid similar future mistakes by never working remotely from his phone and saving all document work for the office.

   d) should take responsibility for the mishap and try to avoid future similar mistakes with mobile document work, including editing a cloud-based collaborative version of a document instead of a local file he creates only on his phone (or triple check when sending a locally saved mobile attachment).

2)    Rene is a legal aid lawyer at Rhode Island Legal Services, where he represents low-income individuals on matters ranging from family law to housing to public benefits. He represents a 22-year-old with cognitive disabilities at the center of a guardianship conflict after the client's parent filed papers to request legal guardianship over him. The county scheduled a remote hearing on the matter, but on a day Rene was working at home with his young twins home sick from daycare. An hour before the hearing, Rene's twin toddlers are screaming. Rene had to cut short his preparation meeting with his client, who due to his disabilities has more trouble than others navigating the court's online interface. In all the chaos, Rene forgot to have his client test his microphone, forgot to take a shower or find a fresh jacket and tie, and forgot to charge his laptop such that he must do the remote hearing from his phone propped up against the wall in his basement so the court hopefully doesn't hear his toddlers screaming. Given these circumstances, Rene:

    a)    must push forward no matter what because remote work challenges like this are a part of everyday practice, and if he makes a joke about it the judge and client will understand.

    b)    should make a careful judgment call based on this combination of challenges and consider whether he can fulfill his ethical duty to competently represent the client at the hearing.

    c)    should explain the situation to his client and let him decide whether they should move forward with the videoconference guardianship hearing or not.

    d)    must immediately file an emergency motion for a continuance.

3)    You are involved with your local state bar association and serve on its committee on public service. The state court has asked the association to look into developing an ODR system for small claims disputes with less than $8,000 at issue. After over a year of work exploring vendors and customizing the platform, two local state counties move forward with

piloting the ODR tool. Months later, you are informed that the use rate remains in the very low single digits. The committee works with the commercial vendor who built the platform to investigate and plan improvements. Which of the following would be among the most important topics the committee should consider?

a) The amount in controversy requirement of $8,000, because more people would probably use the tool if more money was at issue.

b) The type of disputes, because more people would probably use the tool if the category of allowable disputes captured complex matters.

c) Accessibility, because you discovered that the chat negotiation and settlement discussion function only worked on PC computers, not Mac operating systems, and that state email system notifications to users were going to users' "junk" email folders.

d) None of these topics, because early roadblocks are to be expected with quasi-public ODR platforms and there's no such thing as a perfect tool—state resources can't fix everything for everyone.

4) As a member of the same bar association referenced in the last question, you frequently attend networking events and transitioned to a new law firm position where significant business development is expected (bringing in new clients). The firm has developed a robust virtual hybrid practice with a client portal but in-person practices, too. During the year, you attended countless events, receptions, and conferences and received hard-copy business cards from well over 100 people. Unfortunately, the cards are stacked in a pile on your office desk or stuffed in jacket pockets and you've never found the time to enter them into the firm's portal database. The best way to revamp your approach to mobile contact management and business development as a modern lawyer would be to:

a) set aside time each day to type the business card contact information into the firm's portal or ask a more junior associate to record billable time doing so.

    b)   take pictures of the business cards when you receive them, such that even if they are mixed up with the thousands of personal photos and videos stored on your phone, at least you'll have them stored somewhere.

    c)   run the small business cards through the office photocopier and keep copies handy in a folder in your desk drawer.

    d)   download an inexpensive business card scanning app with the capability to extract printed information (name, company, address, email) with a quick snap of your camera, categorize it, and automatically get it included in the cloud-based firm portal.

5)   Ruth (pronoun they/them) works among several dozen attorneys at the City of Detroit Law Department, where they represent the city (defending actions against it, drafting city ordinances, etc.). Following the Covid-19 pandemic, as the lawyers and staff transitioned back into the office, Ruth and their colleagues used a slate of collaboration tools. They continued to use Teams and Zoom, as they did while working at home, although some of the newer lawyers preferred sending Google Hangout invitation links instead. To increase camaraderie, leadership initiated Slack as an internal messaging platform. Department lawyers also started an SMS text exchange on their personal cell phones for social events and coffee breaks and communicated throughout the day via email too. Within their litigation-focused smaller group, Ruth used Taskworld, a remote tracking tool to collaborate on projects. When it comes to remote lawyering practices, Ruth and their colleagues:

    a)   may see their collaboration and communication suffer or be siloed because of too many tools and options for remote connection, with small groups using different tools.

    b)   are nailing it—the more tools, the better availability, communication, and productivity.

    c)   are nailing it—different lawyers have different preferences as to their favorite remote technology and firms, offices, and departments should be ready to cater to them all so people are comfortable.

d) may have their collaboration and communication suffer because lawyers should use remote lawyering tools for work-related tasks and business discussion only—not social efforts like coffee breaks.

---

 *Practice Your Knowledge*

**Exercise #1: A Message About Messaging**

Suppose you are a lawyer at a law firm that is updating the communication new clients receive as part of the automatic case-opening process. Draft a Messaging Policies paragraph for inclusion in the uniform client engagement letter, thinking about the pros and cons this chapter covered and your ideal approach to setting expectations.

**Exercise #2: Quasi-Public ODR First Impressions**

Do some online research to dig deeper into the quasi-public court-involved ODR platforms this chapter mentions (or other state court initiatives that you find). Put yourself in the shoes of a person without a lawyer seeking to understand and use the different ODR platforms and take notes comparing first impressions. Consider aspects such as the user design, clarity of information, FAQs, and substantive legal guidance. What's helpful? Overwhelming? Confusing?

---

 *Expand Your Knowledge*

➤ California Standing Comm. on Pro. Resp. & Conduct Formal Op. Interim No. 20-0004, https://www.calbar.ca.gov/Portals/0/documents/publicComment/2022/20-004-Ethical-Obligation-when-Working-Remotely.pdf [https://perma.cc/4YWQ-4TKG].

➢ THE PEW CHARITABLE TRUSTS, HOW COURTS EMBRACED TECHNOLOGY, MET THE PANDEMIC CHALLENGE, AND REVOLUTIONIZED THEIR OPERATIONS (Dec. 2021), https://weblive.ibj.com/lawyer/PDFs/2021/december/Pew_court tech_report.pdf [https://perma.cc/B5JW-AM8F].

➢ Lee Rosenthal, et al., *The Zooming of Federal Civil Litigation*, JUDICATURE (2020), https://judicature.duke.edu/articles/the-zooming-of-federal-civil-litigation/#02da9d10-07b1-4450-8032-2924d08d8a7e [https://perma.cc/CN5B-FA WQ].

*Answers & Explanations*

*Knowledge Kickoff*

b)   No lawyer can avoid every mistake, and Maria's career is by no means over—but in the realm of remote lawyering, lawyers can take specific steps to prevent mishaps. Remote lawyering moves fast and with speed often comes distraction, sloppiness, and a risk of ethical violations such as Maria's work conversation at home, which could be overheard by an attendee on a videoconference from a different device. Expectations with remote practice take time to establish, and letting clients take the lead early can help (as does erring on the side of caution instead of messaging clients like we do friends). Avoiding interaction with others outside the office is probably unrealistic in our 24/7 connected society, but Maria should be more purposeful about her separation of work and personal life, such as aiming to maintain a private area at home for work.

*Review Your Knowledge*

1)   d)   Mobile document work need not be avoided but lawyers must ensure it's done competently (Need to Know #3 Ethical Duty of Technology Competency). Lawyers must supervise and try to ensure competent, ethical work by others with whom they practice. It would be unprofessional to blame the misunderstanding solely on the assistant. Alejandro could improve his processes to ensure document changes get made directly on a version others can access in the cloud. While we've all made mistakes on our phones and tablets, technologically competent modern lawyers don't make excuses or risk their reputation under the guise of "well, these things happen."

2)   b)   No one remote lawyering situation is identical to the next, and Rene's situation could play out in many ways depending on the forum, parties, personal circumstances, and the expertise and experience of the lawyer. While we all aim to prevent these types of scenarios, life gets in the way and that's not always

possible. Rene—not his client—must make a careful judgment about whether the unforeseen circumstances impair his ability to provide thorough and competent representation at the videoconference. While a wrinkled suit jacket wouldn't be the end of the world, problems with his client's audio or ability to address the court and hear Rene would be serious. "Rolling the dice" from a propped-up phone may prove foolish and risk an adverse result for Rene's client in this important substantive proceeding (as opposed to a quick procedural low-stakes court matter). An emergency request for a brief continuance may be warranted but it's a delicate decision only Rene can make.

3)   c)   Quasi-public ODR platforms are complex but the answer isn't to be content with subpar systems. Progress over perfection, and early roadblocks such as accessibility can be overcome with careful assessment, communication among stakeholders, and feedback from users. More complex disputes for more money won't improve underlying poor processes, technical glitches, or system inefficiencies.

4)   d)   The possibilities are endless for mobile apps lawyers find useful in practice. The remote lawyer is a busy lawyer, and processes with fewer steps usually offer the best result. Many people still exchange hard-copy business cards—even in our remote electronic world. Business development is part of many lawyers' practices and no client would be thrilled to see "enter business contacts" on a billable-hour timesheet. Manual input or storage sounds good in theory but takes time. Exploring a mobile scanning app that can integrate with the firm's cloud-based central portal would be the best approach at modern contacts management for business development.

5)   a)   Every workplace, in law or otherwise, finds its own balance with remote and in-person collaboration tools. In this scenario, Ruth and their department seem to be drowning in an overflow of collaboration options. With some lawyers home and some in an office, it's tempting

to overcompensate with efforts to connect. But when information comes from 12 different places at 12 different times, staying streamlined and organized is next to impossible and the effort does more harm than good. While preferences matter, modern lawyers are open to learning and using new tools when necessary and appropriate to simplify collaboration instead of complicate it.

## Endnotes

1   The Honorable Jeanne Robison, *Access to Justice and Kayak Court*, UTAH BAR JOURNAL, Nov./Dec. 2021, at 14–16.

2   MDFAMILYLAWYER.COM,   https://www.mdfamilylawyer.com/   [https://perma.cc/ WFG6-YK9V].

3   CLIO, 2021 LEGAL TRENDS REPORT (2021), https://www.clio.com/resources/legal-trends/2021-report/read-online/ [https://perma.cc/2LSX-F6PA].

4   AM. BAR ASS'N, ABA LEGAL TECHNOLOGY SURVEY REPORT, VOL. V: LIFE & PRACTICE (Sasha Goncharow 2021).

5   Hannah Levitt & Benjamin Bain, *JPMorgan Bosses Hooked on WhatsApp Fuel $200 Million Penalty*, BLOOMBERG (Dec. 17, 2021, 8:30 AM), https://www.bloomberg.com/news/articles/2021-12-17/jpmorgan-bosses-addicted-to-whatsapp-fuel-200-million-in-fines [https://perma.cc/HMU3-ECMC].

6   MODEL RULES OF PRO. CONDUCT r. 1.4 (AM. BAR ASS'N 2020).

7   LinkedIn   post   available   at   https://www.linkedin.com/posts/judgeschlegel_ utilizing-simple-off-the-shelf-technologies-activity-6664532694929596416-tKvn [https:// perma.cc/NAK5-B9TC].

8   David K. Li, *Virtual Court Hearing Takes Turn After Prosecutor Spots Assault Suspect in Victim's Home*, NBC NEWS (Mar. 11, 2021, 1:04 PM), https://www.nbcnews.com/news/us-news/virtual-court-hearing-takes-turn-after-prosecutor-spots-assault-suspect-n1260698 [https://perma.cc/6Q4D-S6L2].

9   *Arconti v. Smith*, No. CV-15-527178 (Ont. Sup. Ct. 2020) [https://perma.cc/83ST-EX66].

10   Copyright attribution New Era ADR, Inc., www.neweraadr.com [https://perma.cc/LB7L-3BYP].

11   Emerson Research, *Legal Online Dispute Resolution (ODR) Market Size & Share Prediction Research Report and Forecast to 2020–2028*, NEWSWIRES (Dec. 1, 2021, 7:13 AM)   https://www.einnews.com/pr_news/557349323/legal-online-dispute-resolution-odr-market-size-share-prediction-research-report-and-forecast-to-2020-2028 [https://perma.cc/EWZ9-TVKV].

12   MODEL RULES OF PRO. CONDUCT r. 5.5 (AM. BAR ASS'N 2020).

13   SHAILINI JANDIAL GEORGE, THE LAW STUDENT'S GUIDE TO DOING WELL AND BEING WELL (2021).

CHAPTER 9

# CONFIDENTIALITY, SECURITY & PRIVACY

*Core Concepts*

| | |
|---|---|
| *confidentiality* <br> *security* <br> *privacy* <br> *personally identifiable information (PII)* <br> *threat model* | *operations security (OPSEC)* <br> *encryption* <br> *SaaS due diligence* <br> *duty of supervision* <br> *incident response planning* |

*Knowledge Kickoff*

The Law Office of Devon A. Banta in Los Angeles offers advisory services specific to international tax law. Clients receive advice from lawyers, financial and estate planning advisors, and certified public accountants. As the founder and managing partner, Devon handles document management, client communication, billing, and all office policies. The firm regularly receives credit card information from clients at time of payment, as well as sensitive documents such as invoices, receipts, payroll records, bank statements, and W-2 year-end tax forms with names, Social Security numbers, and addresses. Devon is frustrated with separate expensive charges for office tools and wants to consolidate. A client who owns a start-up technology company tells Devon about another start-up company, BlockFlow, that uses blockchain technology to digitize paperwork and electronic files. Devon reviews BlockFlow's website, which promises "uncompromised" information security. Devon is ecstatic about the option and intends to transition as much of the firm's records and systems as possible. Before doing so, Devon must:

a) obtain consent from each of the firm's clients, because a lawyer's ethical obligation to keep clients reasonably

       informed about their matters extends to every detail
       about practice management tools and office policies.

  b)   use reasonable due diligence efforts to ensure security
       by researching the reputation and reliability of
       BlockFlow as a third-party provider beyond its general
       website representations, including reviewing its terms
       of service and privacy policy, given that Devon's practice
       involves very sensitive personal information.

  c)   do nothing, given that BlockFlow was a reliable referral
       from a trusted client and ethics rules give lawyers wide
       and absolute discretion to engage third-party services.

  d)   do nothing, but ethics rules would prohibit Devon from
       engaging BlockFlow due to the heightened sensitivity of
       the personal tax client information and fact that no
       third-party service would be as secure as the firm's own
       internal record keeping and systems.

---

Confidentiality. Security. Privacy. You've heard these terms. Have you considered them through the lens of your new role as a modern lawyer? Have you considered what they mean for your communication, document and file storage, written work product, remote work habits, personal reputation, loss of business, insurance premiums, and ethical obligations? If you've thought about these ideas, terrific. If you haven't, this chapter will get you going.

One early clarification: there is a difference between a lawyer who specializes in advising clients on substantive legal questions related to these topics and a lawyer who is concerned about the same topics for themselves. This chapter focuses on the latter. Many large law firms have established data security and privacy law practice groups. Boutique law firms grow niche specialties to help clients navigate the many legal frameworks that surround things like data and information security, breaches and breach notification, and storage and use of personally identifiable information (PII). Your law school likely has courses on these subjects. The aim of this chapter isn't to prepare you to be an expert advisor to someone else. It's to consider these topics for yourself—for *your* data; for *your* client confidences; for private information that crosses *your* desk. Not every lawyer will develop a specialty in these substantive areas of law. But every lawyer who aims to be technologically competent in any practice area must understand the basics.

If I had written this chapter in 1970, 1980, or 1990, confidentiality, security, and privacy still would have been relevant. I would have covered closing your office door to protect privileged oral communication, using "lock-and-key" and office alarm systems, keeping an eye on who might be reading over your shoulder on an airplane, and completing careful hard-copy redactions of personal information like bank account numbers before you handed documents over to a court clerk.

The legal profession isn't talking much about those things anymore. Instead, we're talking about:

> ➢ In 2022, pranksters used music and pornographic images to "Zoombomb" and interrupt a high-profile videoconference in Australia's court system in a proceeding involving tennis superstar Novak Djokovic's appeal over his visa cancellation due to non-compliance with a vaccination requirement in advance of the Australian Open tennis tournament.

> ➢ In 2021, the Department of Justice announced that hackers had accessed a large percentage of Microsoft® Office 365 emails in four United States Attorney's offices in New York, and that Russia was suspected of installing malicious code on the office systems through a false software update.

> ➢ In 2020, hackers gained access to about 756 gigabytes of client information through a cyberattack against Grubman Shire Meiselas & Sacks, a top entertainment law firm in New York City. The bad actors allegedly leaked information about celebrity clients such as Lady Gaga and Madonna and demanded millions of dollars in ransom.

We've previewed and inched toward this topic throughout the book. Security is a big idea that covers small ins and outs of modern practice. We've touched on it in past chapters—from uploading work product to a new legal research Document Analyzer tool in chapter 4, to considering client portal messaging as part of law practice management instead of SMS texts from a personal cell phone in chapter 7, to ensuring a secure internet connection before joining a virtual proceeding in chapter 8. But touching on this topic isn't enough. It's critical for a modern lawyer and deserves more attention. This chapter aims to give a big-picture framework through which you can think about confidentiality, security, and privacy as you navigate practice.

I should have titled this chapter "The Perfect Storm" because that's what a lawyer faces when technology meets confidentiality, security, and privacy. Decades ago, life was easier for lawyers when the big concerns were keeping track of a file cabinet key or not leaving handwritten notes on a table during a lunch break at a negotiation. As society moved online, so too did a lawyer's many ethical obligations. Convenience created complications. Data prompted data privacy concerns. Security became cybersecurity. Consider what today's lawyer has more of compared to past generations. We have more:

- ✓ electronic data
- ✓ devices where data is created, communicated, and stored
- ✓ ways to access data
- ✓ people who want data for financial or other gain
- ✓ physical locations from which people access data
- ✓ third-party services and providers to help us with data
- ✓ sophisticated means for others to find data
- ✓ rules, regulations, and ethical guidance about what we should and shouldn't do with data

The perfect storm. Don't signal SOS on the radio yet. A little awareness goes a long way. This chapter will cover:

1) definitions of confidentiality, security, and privacy
2) lawyers as targets and the need to create threat models

3) cybersecurity basics (common risks and risk mitigation)

4) best practices for individual everyday law practice

5) assessing third-party providers (including cloud-based software)

6) supervision, communication, and incident planning and response

I dislike the saying, "what you don't know can't hurt you." It can. On this topic, it will. In the introduction to this book, I acknowledged that not every topic in every chapter would relate to every lawyer's career path. This one does. Avoiding it is impossible, plus foolish. We can't predict the specifics you'll need for practice but we can prepare for some of them.

## Confidentiality, Security & Privacy Defined

Navigating technical topics is difficult without added confusion about underlying core terms. Confidentiality, security, and privacy are related and of equal importance to most lawyers. Many people use the words interchangeably. But they're different things.

1) Confidentiality

Keeping information confidential means keeping it secret from someone else. It's a lawyer's foundational ethical duty. **Confidentiality** protects against unauthorized use of information, such as telling another person something a client tells you. It is broader than attorney-client privilege. For example, suppose you meet via videoconference with a client and their former business partner advisor, and they both share details about a proposed corporate transaction for which you will represent that client. That conversation would not be protected by attorney-client privilege because of the presence of the business advisor. But does that mean you could post about it on a social media account or laugh about it with a friend at a party that weekend? No. Your client would have every right to consider those discussions held "in confidence." The general principle of confidentiality isn't limited to lawyer-client scenarios. Think of other people in your life such as a physician or therapist who shouldn't divulge personal information you tell them to third parties without your consent.

> **LIT TIP**
>
> "A lawyer shall not reveal information relating to the representation of a client unless the client gives informed consent, the disclosure is impliedly authorized in order to carry out the representation or the disclosure is permitted by [the exceptions in] paragraph (b) . . . [a] lawyer shall make reasonable efforts to prevent the inadvertent or unauthorized disclosure of, or unauthorized access to, information relating to the representation of a client."[1]
>
> Model Rule 1.6(a) and (c)

## 2) Security

**Security** is broader than confidentiality. Model Rule 1.15 requires lawyers to "appropriately safeguard" client documents and property.[2] Return to the hypothetical of the videoconference meeting with your client and the business advisor. After the conversation, your lips are sealed and you would never think of divulging the confidential information shared. But what if the videoconference wasn't secure? Unbeknownst to you because you accessed the videoconference via phone and couldn't view meeting participants, your client's business competitor had "Zoombombed" the session. (You never password-protected the meeting and had texted and emailed the videoconference link to your client, their assistant, their advisor, and his assistant.) Unauthorized access here would reveal a lack of security of the information and, in turn, a breach of confidentiality. The intersection between confidentiality and security could play out in many scenarios, whether high-tech, low-tech, or no tech at all:

- ✓ Typing a confidential settlement strategy on your laptop while flying to a mediation? What if someone is reading it over your shoulder from the airplane row behind you? Not so secure.

- ✓ Keeping a confidential scanned photo from a defendant client in a criminal matter as a key piece of potential evidence on a small USB thumb drive on your desk? What if it falls into the trash can? Not so secure.

    ✓   Storing confidential financial information from your client's forensic accountant on the hard drive of your office computer? What if there is a fire, hurricane, or other disaster and the computer is destroyed? Not so secure.

    ✓   Emailing confidential information about licensing agreements as part of a negotiation in a high-stakes copyright infringement matter? What if you accidentally tap the letter t from your phone in the CC field and mistakenly copy your friend Tom, a reporter at a national newspaper? Not so secure.

Good intentions to maintain confidentiality are laudable. Efforts to keep information confidential *and* secure are even better.

3)   Privacy

**Privacy** is a concept we're familiar with, from locking a diary as a child, shutting the door to an apartment bedroom during a phone call, or not saving credit card information when purchasing something online using a public computer. Think of the last time you "gave" away personal information on a website, such as your name, address, email address, or phone number. Do you know where it went? Can you be sure it was going *only* to the gym you joined? Or that it was going *only* to the store where you signed up for a promotion?

We have the right to keep sensitive, personal data called **personally identifiable information (PII)** to ourselves. It's private. It's not for disclosure. Or maybe it is, but *we* get to decide, as in the case of a new gym membership or retail promotion. We dictate how information about us is handled and shared (or not), to whom, and for what purpose. Some do a better job of this than others but either way, it's our right.

Data privacy in lawyering circles is, once again, broader than traditional ethical notions of confidentiality and privilege. Back to our same hypothetical with the videoconference with your client and the business advisor. Suppose during the meeting both individuals (not just your client) gave information that would likely qualify as "personal" under applicable privacy laws in the jurisdiction: driver's license number, passport number, checking account number, educational transcripts, and a business partnership tax ID number. You'd keep the information from both of them confidential and try to maintain security. But that may not be all that's required.

Privacy laws vary by jurisdiction. They are inconsistent and complicated. A lawyer might have no obligations, minimal obligations, or significant obligations as a "covered business" under privacy protection statutes such as California's Consumer Privacy Act (CCPA), the most well-known data privacy law in the United States. Such laws are growing in popularity, as is interest in protecting consumers in the midst of so much storage and exchange of our precious and valuable PII.

Modern lawyers will keep a close eye on applicable privacy laws to ensure compliance. This may be beyond basic steps lawyers take to ensure confidentiality and security, especially because privacy protection extends not just to clients but any PII a lawyer might have, whether it belongs to a client, witness, third party, opposing party, employee, or anyone else.

Most large law firms make public their comprehensive privacy policies, which include what information the firm collects or receives, why it is collected, how it is used, how records of it are kept, to whom it gets shared (such as third-party vendors), and what it will do if a data breach occurs. Many law firms have Chief Information Officers or similar roles to oversee issues of security; many also have roles such as Data Protection Officer to ensure fulfillment of these related but more specific obligations for PII. But many law firms and organizations, especially smaller ones, don't have the financial capacity to staff these type of positions—meaning even more responsibility falls to the lawyers.

---

**LIT TIP**

Since 2018, the European Union's General Data Protection Regulation (GDPR) law is regarded as having revolutionized data privacy regulation. It imposed huge new obligations on businesses around the world, including law firms, that have sensitive personal information of EU citizens (whether lawyers operate in the EU or not). It defines "personal data" as "any information relating to an identified or identifiable natural person . . . one who can be identified, directly or indirectly, by reference to an identifier such as a name, an identification number, location data, an online identifier or to one or more factors specific to the physical, physiological, genetic, mental, economic, cultural or social identify of that natural person."[3]

EU GDPR Directive 2016/679 of the European Parliament

---

In sum, privacy and confidentiality are concepts that set up a "right" to some later form of protection. Security is the broader principle this chapter focuses on, to get at how a modern lawyer safeguards that information and protects those rights.

## Lawyers as Prime Targets

Any discussion of security in the legal profession includes some variation of this refrain: "It's not *whether* lawyers will face a cyberattack, it's *when*." Security breaches need not always be of the cyber variety, such as an unattended laptop in a coffee shop or a phone home screen left facing up to display messages on a conference table in the middle of a deposition. And not everything cyber is criminal or outright theft. Many confidentiality and security mishaps among lawyers (both cyber and non-cyber) are accidental—the result of careless errors, sloppy practices, poor legal document proficiency (remember tips from chapter 3, such as careful redaction of a PDF document) or failed internal policies and communication. Or data gets altered, viewed, or accessed by someone not authorized to do so. But many security breaches result from intentional attacks, and many lawyers' cyberspaces might as well have a bullseye. Before we turn to what those threats are and how to protect against them, let's review why lawyers draw the attention of those up to no good.

The term cyberattack—referring to a malicious, intentional effort to breach someone else's cyberspace for nefarious purposes—makes us think of prime targets like banks, government organizations, and financial institutions. Everyone and everything with any information system infrastructure (computers, networks, devices) is at risk. Lawyers and law firms are no different. They are a treasure trove of valuable information for cybercriminals, from personal consumer information to sensitive tax return data to non-public business activities. Imagine two Fortune 500 publicly traded companies in early secret talks to merge. In the wrong hands of someone looking to make early plays on the stock market with non-public information, that nugget of data would be valuable treasure. Or confidential information about patent inventions relating to a patent lawsuit between competitors could be worth millions of dollars to someone's opponent.

Besides the fact that we possess valuable information, lawyers are targeted for cyberattacks and extortion threats because they often:

- ✓ exchange a high volume of electronic documents going "in and out" with others

- ✓ have access to substantial amounts of money, whether through client trust accounts or business accounts (to potentially pay demanded ransom)

- ✓ face strict deadlines and pressure to keep security blunders or attacks under wraps from the public and get internal systems back up and running, such that they may be more likely to negotiate or "give in"

Lawyers also make tempting bait because—let's face it—they focus on their law practice. They're in the business of legal advice. Most didn't take the bar exam to worry about the latest cybersecurity tools and defenses. On top of deadlines, substantive legal advice, business development, meetings, disclosure deadlines, court appearances, document drafting, and client communication, who has time to worry about cybersecurity?

Lawyers must make the time to worry or find someone with expertise to do so on their behalf. Some do. Many don't. You will. What's sufficient on the day you read this chapter might be insufficient months later. Whether protecting individual work product or collaborating on security decisions across a global law firm, forward-thinking planning, communication, and constant awareness will be the name of the game.

---

**LIT TIP**

According to the American Bar Association
2021 Profile of the Legal Profession[4]

- 29% of lawyers surveyed said their law firms experienced a security breach, compared to 14% several years prior

- 36% of lawyers surveyed said their law firms have cyber liability insurance, compared to 11% several years prior

---

## Cybersecurity Basics: Risks & Risk-Mitigation Measures

Forward-thinking prevention depends on practice area, habits, work environment, and nature of the information. The overarching guidepost is an ethical duty to make "reasonable" efforts at security. Just like the "reasonable person" you met in Torts class, what is reasonable is broad, vague, and context specific. This duty has always existed but is tested more today as modern lawyers work remotely and cybersecurity threats become even more widespread and troublesome.

The American Bar Association's first formal guidance for security of electronically transmitted client information came in 2017, opining that "what constitutes reasonable efforts is not susceptible to a hard and fast rule, but rather is contingent upon a set of factors."[5] When transmitting information relating to the representation of a client over the internet, a lawyer must use a "fact-based" analysis to determine what reasonable efforts they must use to prevent inadvertent or unauthorized access, depending on factors such as the:

- ✓ sensitivity of the information
- ✓ likelihood of disclosure if additional safeguards aren't employed
- ✓ cost of added safeguards
- ✓ difficulty of implementing safeguards
- ✓ extent to which safeguards impact the lawyer's ability to represent clients

Cybersecurity is a balancing act among many factors. The more sensitive the information, the more a lawyer must do. The greater the threat, the more a lawyer must do. The lesser the burden and expense of safeguards, the more a lawyer must use them. High-risk scenarios should not be treated the same as routine non-sensitive communications. In the landscape of ever-changing risks and new technologies, no one cybersecurity decision should be the same as the next.

In 2021, the ABA reconsidered cybersecurity amid the explosion of lawyers working remotely during the Covid-19 pandemic and gave lawyers additional guidance:

---

**LIT TIP**

"At all times, but especially when practicing virtually, lawyers must fully consider and implement reasonable measures to safeguard confidential information and take reasonable precautions when transmitting such information. This responsibility does not require that the lawyer use special security measures if the method of communication affords a reasonable expectation of privacy. However, depending on the circumstances, lawyers may need to take special precautions. Factors to consider to assist the lawyer in determining the reasonableness of the expectation of confidentiality include the sensitivity of the information and the extent to which the privacy of the communication is protected by law or by a confidentiality agreement."

ABA Standing Comm. on Ethics and Pro. Resp., Formal Op. 498 (2021) (internal quotations omitted)

---

A lawyer tasked with making reasonable efforts must first determine the threat(s). How can we decide what efforts to make without understanding what we are up against? Understanding the big-picture landscape relating to security decisions is called creating a **threat model** or referred to under the umbrella term of **operations security (OPSEC)**. OPSEC is a broad security concept that originated in the United States military for protecting "mission-essential" information from enemies.[6] A lawyer may not know the precise "enemy" they'll face, but they (along with technology professionals with whom they work) can use the concept of threat modeling in different forms. For our basic purposes, a lawyer should:

1) determine threats and vulnerabilities

2) identify objectives and prioritize risks

3) figure out and assess countermeasures

You do this in everyday life. Suppose you have an evening class and walk home late in a high-crime downtown area or to your car in a dark parking lot. That's your known vulnerability—walking by yourself. Then you think about your objective—to arrive safely. You brainstorm countermeasures to mitigate or prevent harm, such as carrying a whistle, walking with a friend, or hovering your finger above the keychain car alarm button just in case. You're proactive instead of reactive.

The threat for the modern lawyer won't be as obvious. Actors involved in threats, breaches, or attacks don't often knock down an office door or jump a fence. The risks are sneaky, subtle, and keep us guessing. To help prepare, here are some common risks and risk-mitigation countermeasures.

1) Common Risks

Tomorrow's risks will differ from today's and we can't predict or prepare for every new flavor of threat. But this preliminary list expands your vocabulary and lays a foundation for some early threat modeling as you begin your career.

| phishing | Fraudulent emails, such as the one shown in Figure 9A, appearing to be from trusted accounts that typically include a link or attachment that carries malware. This often leads to credential threat, where personal login information gets stolen and confidential data is accessed. |
|---|---|

| | |
|---|---|
| smishing | Fraudulent SMS texts like email phishing, in which the message asks for a text reply with personal information or asks a user to click on a link to a fake website asking for personal information (or installing malware on the mobile device). |
| vishing | Fraudulent voice calls or voicemails usually claiming to be from a bank, financial institution, credit card company, IT professional, or computer vendor asking for personal information over the phone. |
| malware | Catch-all term for types of malicious software designed to cause errors in a computer system, slow it down, or destroy or obtain unauthorized access to data. Examples include Trojan horse viruses, worms, and spyware ("spying" on a user and recording computer keystrokes). |
| ransomware | Unauthorized encryption of data on an entire computer system often via installation of malware, by someone motivated by financial gain who takes control of the information then demands a ransom to decrypt and release it back. |
| "Zoombombing" | Disruptions of videoconferences on Zoom or other platforms by unauthorized persons who infiltrate the session, usually by featuring inappropriate or lewd audio or video material. |
| malicious quick response (QR) codes | Square barcodes a smartphone camera scans to access a fraudulent website or application that embeds malware and allows access to a user's device, or directs a user to enter personal login information on a fraudulent site. |

---

**Urgent notification regarding your USPS/FedEx shipment 4544 1711
8555 91 from Sat, 05 Mar 2022 13:29:44 +0000**

**Dear USPS Customer,**

We tried to arrange the delivery for you but you were not home.

Please submit a redelivery request within 48 hours.

**NOTICE:**

Please note that if a redelivery is not shceduled within 48 hours, you can't
submit a redelivery request again. The shipping and handling feed will not be
refunded.

---

\* Figure 9A: Sample phishing email.

You may have encountered examples of phishing, smishing, and
vishing already. As part of your strategy as a modern lawyer to
address common risks, be sure to stay alert to these messages by
keeping watch for:

✓ emails designed to look like they are from a
legitimate bank, government agency, or business
organization such as Federal Express or PayPal,
asking you to click a link or open an attachment
(often to give login or personal information)

✓ abnormalities such as grammatical errors,
misspellings (note the misspelling of "scheduled" in
the bottom notice of Figure 9A), or odd use of colors
or highlighting

✓ language seeking URGENT or IMMEDIATE action
or saying YOU MUST ACT NOW

✓ an unusual URL or odd file extension such as .exe,
or phone messages from a number with only a few
numerical digits

2)   Risk-Mitigation Countermeasures

Mitigating risk to common cybersecurity threats is about
balance. A law firm probably won't ask employees to use 12

passwords and facial recognition to access a single file or keep laptops and devices under lock and key in a basement at night. Forbidding lawyers from working outside the office or in public locations would mitigate risk but at great cost to productivity and convenience. And it's unrealistic for a modern lawyer to stop using mobile devices just to eradicate mobile security threats. Just because we can't do everything to prevent breaches doesn't mean we do nothing.

| | |
|---|---|
| firewall | Akin to a home security system, software or hardware that acts like a first line of defense for a computer network to monitor and create a barrier against threats. (Firewalls come preinstalled, built into a device's operating system, part of a Wi-Fi router, or added on separately). |
| anti-virus/ anti-malware software | Software installed on information systems and devices to detect and remove malware; usually includes patches, frequent updates, and variations like a "pop-up" blocker or spam email filter. |
| **encryption** | A basic starting point process that converts data into an unrecognizable and "scrambled" form that only authorized users can "unscramble" with some encryption key (password). Can apply to data "at rest" that is stored and data being sent "in transit." |
| two factor (2FA) or multifactor authentication (MFA) | Using a secondary means as a line of defense to verify a first password, such as an additional numerical code sent to a mobile device or a biometric marker like a thumbprint or facial recognition. |
| password hygiene | Policies and tools to encourage strong and long passwords with a unique mix of symbols, letters, and mixed lower- and upper-case numbers that include no personal information and are changed regularly. |

---

**LIT TIP**

If you find it impossible to remember all of your different passwords each time you manually log in at different sites, consider a secure password manager tool that encrypts and stores passwords in one personal "vault" accessible only by you with a master password of sorts. Some popular password manager tools among lawyers include KeePass, 1Password, Keeper, Dashlane, and LastPass.

---

These risk-mitigation countermeasures are a good start. Let's dive into best practices with everyday tools lawyers use and everyday situations most lawyers will encounter.

## Security Tips for Everyday Law Practice Tools

Now we know what we're securing, what some common risks are, and what risk-mitigation options we might want to consider. Here are more specific tips to help the modern lawyer put these ideas into motion and take some early action to set up reasonable security practices.

1)   Physical Security

Despite all the high-tech chatter, no-tech physical security is as important a starting point as it has ever been, given the many locations from which remote lawyers work and the information floating far beyond office walls.

   ✓   Pay attention to your surroundings, especially in communal and public locations, including positioning a device's screen to prevent others from viewing it ("visual hacking") or using a privacy filter screen to restrict the angles from which content on a screen can be viewed.

   ✓   Aim for a "clean desk" and "clean screen" policy in a home or shared public workspace, ensuring you put away potentially confidential hard-copy materials, avoid leaving devices unattended, close out of browser windows and files, and shut down access to your computer(s).

   ✓   Ensure to the best of your ability a private space for phone calls or videoconferences, or at least step outside or away from crowds if speaking by phone in a crowded public setting.

✓ Take reasonable precautions to protect physical infrastructure at a work space or central office from disaster or criminal activity, such as making sure fire alarms and sprinkler systems work, using keys or coded locks, and considering alarmed security systems and cameras. Ensure secure backup of important paper files and local electronic data.

2) Personal Hardware

The on-the-go remote lawyering tools chapter 8 discussed cast another wide net of concerns. This is so when a firm or organization provides devices to employees, but the potential for security headaches grows with the prevalence of bring-your-own device (BYOD) policies where employees use their own tablets, laptops, and phones for work.

✓ Keep your device's operating system up to date and use anti-malware software with regular updates.

✓ Use at least basic methods to encrypt devices, as easy as setting up a PIN, passcode, or facial/ fingerprint recognition on your phone or tablet (remember password hygiene), or making a few clicks within your system preferences on a Mac (turn on FileVault) or Windows (turn on BitLocker) laptop. Do not store device passwords on the device itself.

✓ Set devices to go to an automatic lock screen after five minutes of nonuse.

✓ Help ensure you can find a device if you misplace it by enabling location-tracking features (go to Settings and turn on "Find my [device]" for both Android and Apple iOS).

✓ Avoid saving confidential information locally on a personal device and if you do, delete it as soon as possible.

---

**LIT TIP**

Be cautious about sharing personal devices. Letting a roommate or family member use your laptop, tablet, or phone is innocent enough but expands the risk of users clicking on unsafe links. Or maybe you'd just end up with a funny story, as with a lawyer from Texas who used his assistant's computer to log into a court videoconference Zoom hearing and struggled to remove a cat filter covering his face—earning himself the viral nickname LawyerCat with over three million views on YouTube and over 26 million on Twitter.[7]

---

3)  Wi-Fi

Many lawyers enjoy the convenience and accessibility of coffee shops and hotel lobbies to get some work done. So do hackers. Being connected online in a public setting or even through an unsecured connection at home poses a security problem for a modern lawyer who fails to minimize risk.

- ✓ Avoid using unsecured public or guest Wi-Fi networks and don't let a device join them automatically (unclick "automatically join this network"). Only consider joining password-protected ones when necessary.

- ✓ When necessary, use the phone data plan hotspot from your personal device instead of a public network (known as "tethering").

- ✓ Check that a home or office wireless network has an up-to-date router compatible with WPA2 or WPA3 level security. (WPA stands for Wi-Fi Protected Access.) Set a strong Wi-Fi password for your home connection or device hotspot and change the manufacturer's default name of your home Wi-Fi network.

- ✓ Use Virtual Private Networks (VPNs) (introduced in chapter 8) to encrypt your online activities when connected to a network by installing an app on your device (avoid free VPN tools from untrustworthy providers and use one approved by your firm or organization instead).

✓   Pay attention to how you connect to websites via browsers through either *http://* or *https://* protocols. *https* is more secure and most websites today use it; *http* is not and you might see a "NOT SECURE" warning. Most browsers have a small icon next to the website address with a picture of a padlock you can hover over or click on to confirm a site's security, as shown in Figure 9B.

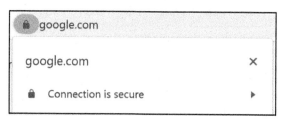

\* Figure 9B: Sample image of secure *https://* connection.

4)   <u>Printing, Scanning & Document Disposal</u>

Printing, scanning, and disposing of hard-copy documents are such routine aspects of practice that many lawyers wouldn't consider the security risks or threats of exposure of confidential information. But they're there.

✓   Only print when necessary and be cautious with common group or public printers where others could unintentionally or intentionally pick up your document.

✓   Consider secure printing software and procedures in settings with many lawyers or employees, including authentication by entering credentials such as a PIN.

✓   Require that documents scanned from office machines be sent from the machine only to email addresses within the firm or organization, to prevent inadvertent transmission.

✓   Set up and follow procedures for disposal of hard-copy documents with confidential information, including a shredding option or designated physical location.

## 5)  Document & File Sharing

We've touched on some best practices for document and file sharing in chapter 3 and chapter 7 but since it's something most lawyers do on a daily basis, a few more can't hurt.

- ✓  Use watermarks on documents, spreadsheets, and presentation slides when appropriate to help designate them as "confidential" or "internal use only."

- ✓  Protect individual files such as .pdf or .doc or .docx with passwords, especially if transmitting via unsecured means such as non-encrypted email. Communicate file passwords separately, and preferably using different means (such as a phone call instead of a subsequent email).

- ✓  Remove metadata from internal documents to prevent exposure of attorney work product or client confidences, by using a document inspector for an individual file or more sophisticated metadata "scrubbing" batch software for multiple files (chapter 3 touched on document metadata and chapter 5 explored metadata with ESI).

- ✓  Use caution with everyday file-sharing platforms such as Google Drive or Box, including checking account privacy settings, turning on two-factor authentication, and disabling (or not installing) third-party add-on extensions.

---

**LIT TIP**

Watermarks range from fancy icons or fonts embedded in graphics or a website, to simple text labels superimposed across the face of a document, shaded in the background. A watermark noting a document is CONFIDENTIAL or some custom term doesn't guarantee it won't be compromised or shared, but it can help keep such documents organized and prevent inadvertent transmission. Look for your Editor function on a PDF document to add and customize one, or the Design tab in Word.

---

---

LIT TIP

"As an enforcement attorney with the United States Securities and Exchange Commission, I must be mindful of federal laws and regulations that govern the unauthorized disclosure of nonpublic information. That includes nonpublic information about my investigations and enforcement matters. As a practical matter, this often comes up when I need to send a subpoena or some other communication by electronic means to an outside party. We have systems in place to send communications by an encrypted email system or by secure file transfer."

Michael Moran
Senior Counsel, Asset Management Unit
United States Securities and Exchange Commission

---

6)   Email

As ubiquitous as email is, it's often not the most secure option for file sharing or communication of confidential information (chapters 7 and 8 touched on secure messaging and client portal options). I've heard use of unencrypted email compared to shouting confidential information from a megaphone or sending it in the mail on a postcard (not even a sealed envelope) for the world to see. Every modern lawyer will still use email to some extent; we might as well take precautions.

    ✓   Avoid unencrypted email. Although many web email providers such as Gmail include message encryption by default, depending on your version and provider you may need to enable it manually or pay additional charges.

    ✓   Set up email to include a confidentiality disclaimer automatically with all emails, replies, and forwarded messages as an added layer of security, as shown in Figure 9C—but don't rely on it alone.

---

*This email message and any attachments are being sent by Sample Law Firm LLP, are confidential, and may be privileged. If you are not the intended recipient, please notify us immediately—by replying to this message or by sending an email to postmaster@samplelawfirm.com—and destroy all copies of this message and any attachments. Thank you.*

---

\* Figure 9C: Sample email confidentiality notice.

    ✓   Delete and do not open questionable email messages or odd attachments; check the sender's email address (not just the name) and notify any IT professionals with whom you work.

✓ Some email systems such as Microsoft® Outlook include a feature that tags incoming emails from outside an organization with a prominent label such as [EXTERNAL]. Turn this feature on to help flag suspicious messages.

✓ Review the entirety of an email thread before forwarding the most recent email in the chain, as there may be content from an earlier date that should not be shared.

✓ Be careful with address autocompletion of suggested recipients in the TO, CC, or BCC fields. Common sense gets lost when things get busy or stressful; fill in the "TO" field last and double-check recipients.

---

**LIT TIP**

"Technology multiplies the opportunities for man to do dumb things and increases the speed at which he can do them."

*Crockett Capital Corp. v. Inland Am. Winston Hotels, Inc.*, Civ. A. No. 08-CVS-000691, 2009 WL 10481837 (N.C. Super. Ct. June 29, 2009) (ordering application of a clawback provision to protect otherwise privileged documents where a lawyer included emails with attorney-client information with an email message to their spouse venting "frustration at work").

---

7)  Mobile Messaging

We know from chapter 8 that lawyers use mobile messaging all the time. How can they aim to do so in a secure way?

✓ Use secure encrypted messaging apps and portals instead of SMS cell phone texting. (Note that both sender and recipient must use the same tool, so use of such platforms should be included with client engagement.)

✓ Keep mobile messages short and on quick topics like scheduling or reminders; save substantive legal advice for more secure means of communication. ("That's not a great option. Pls call me to discuss.")

✓ Use a separate phone for personal and work communication or, if available on your device, create a work profile to keep your personal data and contacts separate and avoid embarrassing autocomplete messaging mishaps. (If your client's name starts with Michael and your best friend's name is Michelle, you don't want to text Michael a fun picture from your weekend meant for Michelle's eyes!)

✓ Enable read receipts to track whether clients or others have received and read your messages. For example, iPhone Settings > Messages > Chat Features.

✓ Disable message previews so content does not appear on your "home" lock screen immediately upon receipt, if your device is within view of someone else's eyes. (Remind clients you message with to do the same.)

8) Videoconferencing

Chapter 8 touched on videoconferencing best practices such as using quality hardware and an appropriate background. Security is just as important in videoconferencing as a professional remote presentation—if not more.

✓ Use up-to-date versions of reputable videoconferencing tools with encryption enabled (it may not be the default feature). The more sensitive the information, the more secure a level of encryption you need.

✓ Generate random meeting IDs with passwords instead of always using one continuous personal meeting ID. Require attendee registration with email address for larger meetings and do not make videoconference links public (such as by posting on social media).

✓ Take advantage of in-meeting security controls such as enabling a waiting room feature to manage attendees, restricting screensharing to "host only," and locking the meeting once in session.

✓ Close out of files not needed for the videoconference to avoid inadvertent disclosure of confidential information, such as work product from another matter, attorney-client emails in your inbox, or a client portal with billing details.

✓ If necessary to speak via phone or videoconference when others are within earshot, use a headset or AirPods so bystanders hear only you.

## 9) Internet of Things (IoT)

*Alexa, keep my work product secure.* Not quite. Billions of smart devices are everywhere in our offices and homes—from refrigerators to voice assistant devices to televisions to alarm systems. They are listening, and they swing open another access door for cybercriminals looking to infiltrate digital systems. Troubling examples of the security risks of IoT devices include strangers who have hacked into a bedroom baby monitor with a smart camera to watch and even talk to a child. Not as horrific but relevant for the modern lawyer are the privacy policies (or lack thereof) with the IoT devices we've introduced into our home and work environments. The safest bet is to turn off smart recording devices such as an Amazon Echo or Google Home when speaking about work-related matters.

---

**LIT TIP**

"Unless the technology is assisting a lawyer's law practice, the lawyer should disable the listening capacity of devices or services such as smart speakers, virtual assistants, and other listening-enabled devices while communicating about client matters. Otherwise, the lawyer is exposing the client's and other sensitive information to unnecessary and unauthorized third parties and increasing the risk of hacking."

ABA Standing Comm. on Ethics & Pro. Resp., Formal Op. 498 (2021)

---

## Turning to the Cloud: Assessing Third-Party Providers

Security is the job of every modern lawyer. That doesn't mean you go at it alone or need to become an information technology expert. You may delegate, get help, outsource, and rely on third-party services with greater expertise and technical capabilities. Doing so is often the most secure option—as long as you do your homework first. Many reputable third-party providers with whom lawyers work use far more advanced security measures than the average lawyer could afford or manage. No lawyer would turn over hard-copy documents to any random person for safekeeping; no lawyer should turn over electronic information to any random third-party service provider.

Model Rule 5.3 details a lawyer's Responsibilities Regarding Nonlawyer Assistance and applies to any third-party service, cloud-based or not.[8] A lawyer has duty to use reasonable efforts to ensure outside services upon which they rely comply with the lawyer's own ethical obligations; for example, a private investigator, electronic discovery company, phone answering service, or simple document printing vendor. Take, for example, the legal research tool CARA AI from Casetext, discussed in chapter 4, which allows a researcher to drag and drop work product into the platform to prompt return of research results. Using the tool with zero concern or effort to review it for security would be unethical—but that doesn't mean you need to spend months reviewing Casetext's proprietary algorithm or perform an expensive and technical security audit (although many large Am Law 100 law firms do).

Turning to cloud-based storage tools, Comment 3 of Model Rule 5.3 specifically addresses "using an Internet-based service to store client information." It suggests that determination of whether a lawyer has taken "reasonable efforts to ensure that the services are provided in a manner that is compatible with the lawyer's professional obligations" depends on whether the lawyer considered the third-party provider's experience and reputation, the nature of the service, and contractual terms about protection of information.

With that backdrop, we'll focus on third-party providers of cloud services because that's where modern attorneys are headed (most have already arrived). You may hear these tools referred to under the big umbrella of SaaS: software as a service. We've touched on cloud computing in prior chapters—a type of SaaS with large, centralized data centers for computing resources, whereby data gets stored, shared, and accessed from anywhere at any time over the internet.

Things may sound like they're getting technical here but bring it back to a simple level. When you use a Gmail.com email address, you are using the cloud for email data. When you store photos in an iCloud account or keep documents in a Google drive folder instead of saving them locally on your computer's hard drive, you are using cloud storage. Many lawyers take steps to avoid storing enormous amounts of data on computer hard drives or their own physical network server they have to maintain, fix, and update. Instead, they rely on cloud-storage providers and pay them to store the data on remote servers. Cloud services are often called hosted or web services.

---

### LIT TIP

The legal profession's use of cloud-based services is exploding. Lawyers use general business providers such as Dropbox (62%), Microsoft Teams (41%), Microsoft 365 (48%), iCloud (20%), Box (11%), and Evernote (11%). They also use legal-specific cloud services such as Clio and NetDocuments. But "while lawyers talk the talk about security concerns in cloud computing, to a shocking degree they do not walk the walk . . . If you take only one thing from this [ABA TechReport] to add to your . . . agenda, it should be to up your game on cloud security, for your sake and, even more so, for the sake of your clients."[9]

ABA TechReport 2021

---

How do lawyers satisfy their ethical obligations with cloud-service providers? On one hand, **SaaS due diligence** doesn't require becoming an IT expert, and a lawyer need not consult with clients on every detailed decision about information storage or security. On the other hand, blind reliance with zero diligence, monitoring, or appropriate client communication is inadequate. Thankfully, guidance from the ABA and many states sorts out a middle ground between those two extremes. Lawyers may use cloud services subject to, once again, a reasonable care analysis to ensure security as noted in this sampling of opinions:

➤ ABA Standing Comm. on Ethics & Pro. Resp., Formal Op. 482 n.12 (2018) ("Lawyers must understand that electronically stored information is subject to cyberattack, know where the information is stored, and adopt reasonable security measures. They must conduct due diligence in selecting an appropriate repository of client information 'in the cloud.' ").

➤ Pro. Ethics Comm. for Tx. Op. 680 (2018) ("Considering the present state of technology, its common usage to store confidential information, and the potential cost and time savings for clients, a lawyer may use cloud-based electronic data systems and document preparation software for client confidential information.").

➤ Wis. Formal Ethics Op. EF-15-01 (2015) ("[W]hatever decision a lawyer makes must be made with reasonable care, and the lawyer should be able to explain what factors were considered in making that decision" including a "base-level comprehension of the technology and the implications of its use" and a "cursory understanding" sufficient to explain the advantages and risks to a client).

➤ OSBA Informal Advisory Op. 2013-03 (2013) ("We do not conclude that storing client data 'in the cloud' always requires prior client consultation, because we interpret the [ethics rule language] 'reasonably consult' as indicating that the lawyer must use judgment in order to determine if the circumstances call for consultation.").

➤ Fla. Bar Ethics Informal Op. 12-3 (2013) ("[L]awyers may use cloud computing if they take reasonable precautions to ensure that confidentiality of client information is maintained, that the service provider maintains adequate security, and that the lawyer has adequate access to the information stored remotely. The lawyer should research the service provider to be used.").

➢ N.Y. Comm. on Pro. Ethics Formal Op. 842 (2010) (" 'Reasonable care' to protect a client's confidential information against unauthorized disclosure may include . . . ensuring that the online data storage provider has an enforceable obligation to preserve confidentiality and security . . . [and] investigating the online data storage provider's security measures, policies, recoverability methods, and other procedures to determine if they are adequate under the circumstances.").

Not every lawyer will be "in the weeds" using reasonable care to select and manage third-party providers. Early in your career, if you work for a government agency, court system, large corporation, or large or medium law firm, chances are these decisions will be made for you—you'll be expected to follow suit and only use approved software services. But other lawyers will find themselves entrusted with these nuanced judgment calls and need preliminary guidance for how to make them, as is provided in this "due diligence" security checklist.

---

*Cloud-Service Providers: Reasonable Care*
*"Due Diligence" Security Checklist*

☐ Need Evaluation & Sensitivity of Data:

   o Consider the scope and amount of data storage needed

   o Decide on heightened needs for particularly sensitive practice groups/materials

   o Weigh convenience, costs, and integration with existing on premises tools

☐ Reputation & Experience:

   o Ensure at least a business level account for tools like Dropbox

- o Research customer references and industry reputation, including past breaches or service interruptions

- o Consider content-specific needs, certifications, or compliance metrics relevant to privacy or financial information such as HIPAA compliance for medical records (Health Insurance Portability and Accountability Act protecting sensitive patient health information) or laws about collection of credit card information

☐ Service Agreement Terms:

- o Read the service agreement contract, even if realistically you aren't able to negotiate select material terms

- o Learn the location(s) of servers where data will be stored (often called "data centers"), including whether there is geo-redundancy (servers in different physical locations as an added safety net)

- o Confirm the provider makes no ownership claims of the data and claims no right to sell or transfer it

☐ Security Features:

- o Understand basic data-protection measures, including who has access to data and what encryption measures are used (you might hear "128-bit encryption" or "256-bit encryption" standards)

- o Dive deeper past general claims of "bank-level security" or "industry standard" security to ensure they are substantiated

- o Confirm acceptance of measures such as two-factor authentication and lengthy, complex passwords for access

☐ Data Access, Backup & Retrieval:

- o Understand any limitations on your access to data, including during routine maintenance or software updates

- o    Review business continuity and disaster recovery backup policies

- o    Review data retention and return policies if you end the service

- ☐    <u>Ongoing Diligence & Support</u>:

- o    Review notification procedures if a breach occurs or a third party requests data (such as if a storage provider is subpoenaed)

- o    Understand what audits or other vulnerability "stress" tests get performed to gauge ongoing security quality

- o    Learn what technical support and training the provider offers

Lawyers using third-party cloud storage providers must also be careful about PII that may be subject to applicable privacy laws. Solid security measures don't always guarantee compliance with the regulatory or statutory privacy obligations that a lawyer may have. The potential for inadvertent disclosures of PII is something the modern lawyer will keep a close eye on, depending on the type of information they collect in practice and jurisdiction-specific laws.

As part of any third-party due diligence, a lawyer should first confirm a provider has a privacy policy and then review it carefully. For example, comprehensive privacy policies of service providers should include information as to:

- ✓    collection of account registration information such as email or billing details

- ✓    automatic capture of website and device information such as a user's IP address, access times, pages and links visited, and mouse movements

- ✓    to whom a provider can disclose PII and under what circumstances

✓ whether a provider uses marketing or promotional partners and whether users can opt out

✓ how a provider can change its privacy policies and what notice (if any) it must provide

✓ jurisdiction-specific "opt-out" details such as requests under California's consumer privacy law

Consider the general "data protection rights" outlined in Figure 9D in connection with a law practice management tool offering cloud-based storage that a lawyer might consider.

**User Rights**

We would like to make sure you are fully aware of all of your data protection rights. Every user is entitled to the following:

The right to access – You have the right to request copies of your personal data. We may charge you a small fee for this service.

The right to rectification – You have the right to request that we correct any information you believe is inaccurate. You also have the right to request that we complete the information you believe is incomplete.

The right to erasure – You have the right to request that we erase your personal data, under certain conditions.

The right to restrict processing – You have the right to request that we restrict the processing of your personal data, under certain conditions.

The right to object to processing – You have the right to object our processing of your personal data, under certain conditions.

The right to data portability – You have the right to request that we transfer the data that we have collected to another organization, or directly to you, under certain conditions.

The right not to be discriminated against – Unless otherwise permitted, we will not deny you goods or services for having exercised your rights as outlined in this policy.

* Figure 9D: Panther Software, LLC privacy policy for PracticePanther.[10]

Checklists and suggestions don't guarantee reasonable care. If at any step you lack confidence in your capacity to decide whether and when to entrust confidential or private data to a third party, that's OK. It's an important decision; pausing and doing it with caution means you are doing it right. Find an expert, consultant, or security advisor who specializes in helping lawyers (and others) make those exact decisions. Rely on their expertise to make an informed choice.

Why is the extra time, attention, and effort worth it before you choose a third-party provider? Because doing your legwork at the outset can save you—and your clients—time, money, and headaches later.

---

**LIT TIP**

In *Harleysville Ins. Co. v. Holding Funeral Home, Inc.*, No. 15-CV-00057, 2017 WL 4368617 (W.D. Va. Oct. 2, 2017), the court considered whether attorney-client privilege and work product protection was waived after plaintiff insurance company used the online file-sharing service Box to send a video of a fire scene to a third party. The problem was that months later, the plaintiff used the same non-password-protected link to send different files that included privileged and work product material and opposing counsel eventually obtained the link through discovery and accessed and downloaded the materials. The defendant argued the privilege was waived when documents are available through public file-sharing websites with no protections, and a magistrate judge agreed, holding that using the unprotected link was akin to leaving the file in a briefcase on a public park bench and telling someone where to find it. The district court disagreed and held there was no waiver because reasonable precautions were used and the plaintiff employee believed, albeit mistakenly, that he was restricting access to just one non-privileged document (not an entire folder).

---

## Supervision

A chain is only as strong as its weakest link. Technology aside, in the quest for reasonable security people are often the weakest link who break the chain. This might be due to human errors, misunderstandings, haste, ignorance, laziness, lack of knowledge, or just plain sloppiness. Just like substantive work product is often a team effort, so too is security. A lawyer's ethical **duty of supervision** requires clear communication, teamwork, and an ongoing effort to train and monitor those with whom we work.

Model Rules 5.1 and 5.3 instruct lawyers to make reasonable efforts to ensure that others' conduct complies with ethics rules just as a lawyer's must.[11] Beyond assistance from third-party SaaS providers, this applies to supervision of everyone else with whom a lawyer works:

- ✓ paralegals
- ✓ administrative support staff
- ✓ investigators

- ✓  law clerks and interns
- ✓  litigation support and knowledge management professionals
- ✓  intellectual property specialists
- ✓  financial or accounting consultants

Anyone with access to client information, attorney work product, or personal information subject to privacy laws must receive oversight and training to understand ethical obligations extend to them—not just to lawyers.

Oversight is no easy feat. For starters, lawyers are busy enough with substantive work, and it is tempting to let administrative tasks related to security fall to the bottom of the to-do list. Every professional has their own habits and practices, and introducing rules and restrictions can be challenging. This is especially so as law firms, law offices, and law departments become decentralized as staff and others work remotely. Remote work by staff opens up additional security risks just as it does for remote lawyers, as everyone uses different means to connect to different devices from different locations.

---

### LIT TIP

"In the context of electronic communications, lawyers must establish policies and procedures, and periodically train employees, subordinates and others assisting in the delivery of legal services, in the use of reasonably secure methods of electronic communication with clients. Lawyers also must instruct and supervise on reasonable measures for access to and storage of those communications. Once processes are established, supervising lawyers must follow up to ensure these policies are being implemented and partners and lawyers with comparable managerial authority must periodically reassess and update these policies. This is no different than the other obligations for supervision of office practices and procedures to protect client information."

ABA Standing Comm. on Ethics & Pro. Resp., Formal Op. 477R (2017)

---

Developing a culture of security awareness is not something a modern lawyer masters from one book chapter. It will vary greatly as between, for example, a global law firm with thousands of employees or a small practice with two lawyers and a paralegal. Just as with evaluation of third-party service providers, we can set the stage to help you ensure everyone with whom you work understands that security is a top priority:

- ✓ Establish clear security policies in writing, accessible from a central, easy-to-find location.

- ✓ If allowing "BYOD," ensure those policies extend to all employees' devices, including strong passwords, access through VPN, antivirus updates, and notification procedures for lost devices.

- ✓ Implement training procedures, including with new hires, and specific to remote practices, mobile devices, and common risks such as phishing emails and credential theft.

- ✓ Maintain ongoing vigilance through frequent communication and "stress" tests, where IT professionals can help gauge how protected the work environment is and report areas of concern or fixes (such as an employee who constantly opens fraudulent phishing emails and attachments).

- ✓ Consider whether to use a confidentiality or non-disclosure agreement for employees or individuals accessing confidential information in certain circumstances (such as a one-time expert witness or consultant).

An ounce of prevention is worth a pound of cure, the saying goes. Cybersecurity depends on cybervigilance. Team prevention trumps any super security-conscious individual effort.

## Client Communication & Incident Response (IR) Planning

We conclude with a topic I hope you'll never need. What's required when things go wrong? There are two angles to this discussion: before and after. First, what planning and prevention efforts must you make vis-à-vis clients *before* a breach occurs? Second, what are the obligations *after* disaster strikes or problems arise?

As to the *before* question, beyond the preventive measures already discussed, a technologically competent lawyer prepares for the worst with **incident response planning**. Once again, the nature of a plan will vary and will look different for a small or solo practice compared to an in-house legal department, agency, or larger firm. But the goal is the same: to proactively detail how the lawyer or organization will address security incidents. Although a lawyer is not always obligated to inform clients of an incident response plan and broader details about storage and security, it's almost always best practice to do so, such as including the information in a routine engagement letter or otherwise offering it with client intake.

> ### LIT TIP
>
> Consider what's known as a "Tabletop Exercise"[12] to help test an incident response plan by creating a fire drill breach or security incident. Lawyers help clients do this and can and should do it for themselves. Internal employees (with or without outside security consultants) simulate a realistic situation and complete their planned response and related communications, helping to find gaps or strengthen the incident response plan if it becomes not a fire drill but a real event.

As to the *after* question, no such discretion exists: lawyers must take certain steps upon any incident (or suspected incident) that impacts security of clients' confidential or private information.

The ABA defines a "data breach" as a "data event where material client confidential information is misappropriated, destroyed or otherwise compromised, or where a lawyer's ability to perform the legal services for which the lawyer is hired is significantly impaired by the episode."[13] Beyond ethics, lawyers may have state or federal data breach obligations too, including in the event PII is unlawfully disclosed or stolen. Every state in the United States has some form of a data breach notification law.[14]

Most incident response plans include some version of these considerations:

✓ Investigate (alone, or with internal or external expert support) and gather information to ensure the problem is "over" or has stopped.

✓ Take steps to contain the incident and prevent further exposure.

✓ Notify criminal law enforcement authorities as appropriate; for example, with a hacker or ransomware demand.

✓ Evaluate what information if any was lost, compromised, inadvertently disclosed, or deleted (and for how long, to whom, etc.).

✓ Comply with data breach notification obligations under state or federal law if PII from clients, former clients, employees, or others is compromised.

✓ Notify a cyber insurance provider, whether part of general malpractice liability or cyber-specific coverage.

✓ Depending on the scope, consider external crisis management and communications to maintain professional reputation.

This book can't teach you the ins and outs of a incident response plan you might find yourself involved with someday. But no matter what, client communication will be a top incident response priority. Model Rule 1.4(a)(3) requires a lawyer to "keep the client reasonably informed about the status of the matter" and Model Rule 1.4(b) details that a "lawyer shall explain a matter to the extent reasonably necessary to permit the client to make informed decisions regarding the representation."[15] As to potential disciplinary actions, isolated security blunders are of lesser concern compared to patterns of incompetence or mistakes that get covered up. Repercussions from any breach or incident will depend on how sensitive the compromised data is (or is not).

---

### LIT TIP

"The nature and extent of the lawyer's communication will depend on the type of breach that occurs and the nature of the data compromised by the breach . . . if a post-breach obligation to notify is triggered, a lawyer must make the disclosure irrespective of what type of security efforts were implemented prior to the breach. For example, no notification is required if the lawyer's office file server was subject to a ransomware attack but no information relating to the representation of a client was inaccessible for any material amount of time, or was not accessed by or disclosed to unauthorized persons. Conversely, disclosure will be required if material client information was actually or reasonably suspected to have been accessed, disclosed or lost in a breach. The disclosure must be sufficient to provide enough information for the client to make an informed decision as to what to do next, if anything. In a data breach scenario, the minimum disclosure required to all affected clients under Rule 1.4 is that there has been unauthorized access to or disclosure of their information, or that unauthorized access or disclosure is reasonably suspected of having occurred."

ABA Standing Comm. on Ethics & Pro. Resp., Formal Op. 483 (2018)

---

\* \* \* \*

I wish this chapter supplied everything you'll need to keep confidential materials and PII secure throughout your career. It doesn't. Data and PII of all sorts will continue to be a valuable asset. Cybercriminals move just as fast as technology does and the hits will keep on coming, such as with advanced "deepfake" fraudulent techniques that mimic familiar faces or voice-cloning tools that look to gain permissions to infiltrate a network or computer system. Federal and state regulation and legislation relating to cybersecurity requirements and privacy protection will keep expanding. A modern lawyer stays prepared, not paranoid—confident that advisors and experts with whom we work will move fast to keep pace. More law firms and organizations will rely on industry security standards, frameworks, and certifications for added peace of mind. Perfection may be impossible, but a reasonable effort is not.

*Review Your Knowledge*

1) Christina is a defense attorney representing a defendant in a sexual assault prosecution. The defendant saved text messages and a voicemail from the victim and, although he was embarrassed, he shared with Christina screenshots of highly personal "snaps" and pictures the victim and defendant exchanged through Snapchat. Christina's client gave her the files on a small portable USB flash drive because they were too large to email. Christina does her best trial preparation from home where she can focus, so she slipped the USB drive into the front zippered pocket of her work bag with her trial binder. At home, Christina worked at her kitchen table and loaded the files from the drive onto her personal laptop, to crop and add them to her opening statement presentation slides. When her children arrived home from school, Christina took a break and forgot to close files or shut down her laptop. Later that evening when Christina turns back to trial prep, she's horrified to find her daughter staring at a vulgar picture of the defendant on the laptop screen. Which of the following is the most correct statement about Christina's conduct?

a) Christina's primary mishap was using a portable drive for sensitive client property because cloud-based options are always the most secure.

b) Christina's primary mishap was her decision to work remotely from home at her kitchen table because lawyers should only access confidential materials "in office," where the environment is always more secure.

c) Christina made no significant mistake, given that only one person in her family saw her client's sensitive and confidential material and some of the material would be public record anyways as digital trial evidence.

d) While not a significant security breach, Christina did not ensure reasonable security and was sloppy in her remote work practices, given that the materials were sensitive, and she could have backed up the portable drive files and made a better effort to close and secure her laptop.

2) Graciela Rocha is the managing partner at Rocha, Hernández, & Watson, LLP, a mid-size real estate firm that handles residential and commercial closings, mortgage refinances, and title examinations. It employs 9 administrative assistants, 17 paralegals, and 2 bank specialists. Several years ago when Graciela founded the firm with a handful of employees, she started a BYOD policy and instructed employees to install some anti-malware software of their choice. The firm conducts no trainings or security tests and employs a "hands-off" approach. Recently, a computer virus damaged the firm's programs, erased some employees' hard drives, and crashed the firm's entire network for days. Graciela discovered that the source was through a paralegal who accessed the firm's network from her personal laptop. The laptop was seven years old and the paralegal had never updated the anti-malware software installed when he first joined the firm. Because the paralegal clicked on a phishing email link and entered login credentials, the firm suffered interrupted business, unhappy clients, and expensive consults to try to restore lost information. As managing partner, Graciela:

a) should rethink the firm's "hands off" approach because as the firm took on more employees, Graciela had an ongoing duty to supervise and ensure others used reasonable efforts at security; she should have trained employees about phishing emails and credential theft and better monitored updated malware and antivirus protections on BYOD devices.

b) has every right to be furious because a professional paralegal should be more responsible with password protection and Graciela's top priority as the firm's leader is post-incident response.

c) fulfilled her duty to supervise others with whom she works by instructing them upon hiring to install anti-malware software as a solid countermeasure.

    d)    should end the firm's BYOD policy because it clashes with her obligation to ensure reasonable security, as there's no way she could do so perfectly with almost 30 employees and over 50 devices.

3)    Amari is Assistant Litigation and Regulatory Counsel at Spirited Airlines, an international airline company. Amari's group recently switched from Microsoft® Teams to Zoom as its preferred videoconferencing service, as did the entire company management C-suite. Amari has read about "Zoombombing" and carefully reviewed Spirited Airlines' rules and suggestions for security. When using Zoom on his company-approved MacBook, he creates a non-public unique meeting link and separately distributed password. He uses the lock meeting feature, limits screensharing capabilities, and maintains a strong password, especially with recorded discussions of sensitive topics such as recent talks to merge with another airline. Weeks into the merger discussions, Amari reads in the New York Times that Zoom announced a security vulnerability; months earlier, hackers had targeted Apple users and exploited a "bug" in an older Zoom update to gain unauthorized access to computers. Amari is nervous about whether the confidential merger videoconference discussions could have been exposed. Which of the following is the most accurate statement about Amari's conduct?

    a)    Amari should immediately notify his direct boss the General Counsel and the CEO about the security breach and advise them to inform the outside company that was the subject of merger talks.

    b)    Amari should have studied the Zoom terms of service more carefully to understand the intricacies of the software so he could have made more reasonable efforts to ensure security of the videoconferences on his MacBook.

    c)    Amari should double check that the versions of his Zoom software, antivirus, and anti-malware tools are up to date and touch base with the company's IT professionals to confirm there is no evidence his MacBook was infected.

    d)   Amari should take extra security measures now and avoid any videoconferencing using Zoom on his MacBook for any future discussions about the proposed merger.

4)   Xander is an associate at a Virginia law firm specializing in intellectual property litigation. Xander is working on a case on behalf of a well-known social media influencer and jewelry designer. After videos featuring the jewelry line went viral, the firm filed a trademark infringement lawsuit against the influencer's former partner, who started online sales of a counterfeit version. As discovery begins, Xander meets with the client at the client's office to prepare for document requests. The client has several relevant hard-copy documents she just found. Nervous about taking originals, Xander snaps a picture of each of the 17 documents with his password-protected phone and then uses his phone's picture-to-PDF converter so he has files to store in his firm's case management portal. Later, as he waits for his Uber, Xander opens his personal Instagram account on his phone and uploads pictures of his friends from a baseball game the night before—a process made simple because Xander tapped "Allow Access to Photos" years ago when he installed the Instagram app. As to his ethical duty to use reasonable measures to safeguard these client documents, Xander:

    a)   fulfilled his duty by using a secure mobile device to capture the information instead of loose hard-copy documents he could have easily destroyed by accident or left in the Uber.

    b)   fulfilled his duty because he transferred the documents to the firm's case management portal instead of having pictures of client documents in his digital photo album alongside personal ones like the baseball game.

    c)   did not fulfill his duty because he didn't reasonably consult with the client as to what measures she expected and intended him to use regarding transmission and storage of her documents.

d) may not have fulfilled his duty to the best of his ability because his phone settings for the Instagram app allowed photos on his phone (which included photos of client documents) to be shared with an outside third-party company.

5) Suppose you are a transactional lawyer in a corporate advisory practice, helping companies with matters such as partnership formation and corporate board of directors communication. You do pro bono work for CEF, a nonprofit education foundation that raises money for urban elementary schools. Early on, you helped with bylaw drafting but as the relationship grew, you consulted on tax and other matters. CEF shared electronic files with you, including its fundraising records with donor name, email, address, and spouse/child names and birthdates. Your practice is exploring a cloud-based document management tool called Flash Lawyer and a partner asks you to "take a look at its policies to make sure we're good." In doing due diligence on this SaaS company, you were pleased to see a security and privacy policy but noticed that it read, "Flash Lawyer may change the provisions of this policy at any time." The biggest problem is that:

a) the practice may be putting PII of third parties at risk by using a cloud-storage provider with a vague policy that provides little guarantees of protection, so more investigation or negotiation is required before using Flash Lawyer.

b) the partner would ask a junior and inexperienced colleague to do legwork for such an important decision.

c) the practice is collecting PII in the first place, as it should aim to avoid doing so and encourage its corporate clients to avoid sharing any electronic files with such information.

d) there is no problem, because a lawyer's obligation under the Model Rules only extends to client materials, not information from or about third parties such as CEF's individual donors.

*Practice Your Knowledge*

### Exercise #1: Device Cleanup

If security tips stay on book pages, they don't do much good. Pick five suggestions to implement with your own personal laptop, tablet, or phone, such as updating antivirus software, changing your automatic lock features or timing, or creating stronger passwords with two-factor authentication.

### Exercise #2: Statutory Data Privacy Protection

Suppose a supervisor asks you for a summary of examples of personal data to better grasp what's covered in the growing number of data privacy protection laws across the United States. Go online and review the table of contents and relevant definitions in at least three state privacy laws (California, Virginia, and Colorado would be good options). Draft a short paragraph giving your supervisor the big-picture concept but also include specific examples of categories of PII, such as credit history information or a student ID number.

 *Expand Your Knowledge*

➢ AM. BAR ASS'N, THE ABA CYBERSECURITY HANDBOOK: A RESOURCE FOR ATTORNEYS, LAW FIRMS, AND BUSINESS PROFESSIONALS (Jill D. Rhodes, et al., eds., 3d ed. 2022).

➢ Anthony G. Volini, *A Deep Dive into Technical Encryption Concepts to Better Understand Cybersecurity & Data Privacy Legal & Policy Issues*, 28 J. INTELL. PROP. L. 291 (2021).

➢ Jan L. Jacobowitz & Justin Ortiz, *Happy Birthday Siri! Dialing in Legal Ethics for Artificial Intelligence, Smartphones, and Real Time Lawyers*, 4 TEX. A&M J. PROP. L. 407 (2018).

*Answers & Explanations*

*Knowledge Kickoff*

b) Devon faces the delicate balance between keeping information secure but doing so in an efficient and cost-effective way. Lawyers engage third-party services all the time; internal systems are not necessarily more secure than relying on external expert providers (and are often less secure). There is no one right answer, but in Devon's situation engaging BlockFlow as a third-party service based on a general referral and vague website representation would clash with the ethical duty to ensure reasonable security of client information and property. Most jurisdictions don't require that lawyers inform clients about detailed practice management decisions—but Devon might consider doing so as a best practice for transparency and client comfort, given the sensitivity of the information exchanged and kept in this tax practice. The sensitivity of the information combined with the "newness" of BlockFlow as a service provider means Devon must approach this decision with extreme caution and thoroughness, including at least reviewing BlockFlow's security and privacy policies and even engaging an expert security consultant to offer advice.

*Review Your Knowledge*

1) d) Christina's duty of confidentiality for the client materials does not diminish just because she will use them in court or because they weren't subject to a massive public cyberattack. Confidentiality is confidentiality, whether one picture or thousands of documents. Never working remotely is not a realistic choice for most lawyers but when they do so, they must take measures appropriate for that remote environment, whether at a coffee shop or kitchen table. Christina should have done a better job with a "clean desk" effort to avoid inadvertent disclosure and should have also backed up the files to a secure cloud-based or other storage option instead of (or at least in addition to) keeping a USB drive in a zippered bag pocket.

2) a) Graciela took baby steps down the path to reasonable security measures but fell short. One general communication about malware upon hiring is not reasonable under the circumstances of a BYOD policy with about 30 employees. BYOD policies are not per se unreasonable and are common but they necessitate robust security guidelines for lawyers and staff, such as ongoing trainings and testing that might have prevented this paralegal from entering credentials on a fraudulent page. If Graciela does not feel qualified or comfortable leading that effort, she should consult with experts instead of making the post-incident reactive response her only concern.

3) c) Tools indispensable in modern practice such as videoconferencing are inherently unsecure. But so is any communication method short of whispering to someone in a private room. It doesn't mean modern lawyers don't use them; it means they do so with reasonable caution. Here, Amari used services from a reliable, well-known third-party provider and tried to ensure reasonable security. He need not overreact based on one report of hackers involved with similar computers and the software he used, if he confirms with IT experts and knows of no evidence of unauthorized access. There are hundreds if not thousands of communication tools modern lawyers use, and hackers, bugs, breaches, and evidence of weak security spots will be in the news more often than not. Amari takes his ethical obligation seriously and needs to maintain a healthy balance between staying abreast of news announcements related to security, but not becoming paranoid such that it interferes with his regular use of videoconferencing tools to do his job.

4) d) Xander's conduct may not jump off the page as troublesome, but it's not ideal and is an example of the blurry line between professional and personal use of mobile devices. Snapping a picture from a password-protected phone instead of stuffing documents into a bag seems harmless enough, and Xander doesn't need

client permission for every document storage decision. But Xander should think twice about how apps and digital tools he uses in his personal life impact client security, because the decision to allow a photo-sharing app such as Instagram to access *all* of his photos means every client-related photo he takes is not as secure as it could and should be. Modern lawyers must pay close attention to their digital connections, whether that's connecting a phone via Bluetooth in a rental car that could transfer the phone's contacts or allowing an online dating app to access location. The point is not that these things are never appropriate. It's that a lawyer must be aware of the privacy and information-sharing settings on devices they use for work, pay attention to "pop-ups" from apps or software that request access, and proceed with caution if using their device for work purposes in a manner like Xander did.

5)  a) Lawyers in certain practice areas can't avoid information that may be subject to the growing regulatory and statutory landscape protecting PII. Remember that while the legal profession's ethical rules run between a lawyer and client, data privacy protections are broader and could extend to anyone's information a lawyer has. Depending on the jurisdiction, this practice may have obligations with the donors' PII. Although a third-party storage service can be a secure option, they are not one size fits all and it's not unheard of that a junior lawyer would be tasked with diving into the weeds. Absent more investigation and information, the unilateral change provision with no notice in Flash Lawyer's policy offers little comfort that storing PII in this manner is the practice's most secure option.

## Endnotes

[1] MODEL RULES OF PRO. CONDUCT r. 1.6(a) and (c) (AM. BAR ASS'N 2020).

[2] MODEL RULES OF PRO. CONDUCT r. 1.15 (AM. BAR ASS'N 2020).

[3] European Parliament and of the Council of 27 April 2016 on the Protection of Natural Persons with Regard to the Processing of Personal Data and on the Free Movement of Such Data, and repealing Directive 95/46/EC, 2016 O.J. (L. 119).

[4] AM. BAR. ASS'N, PROFILE OF THE LEGAL PROFESSION 2021 90 (2021), https://www.americanbar.org/news/reporter_resources/profile-of-profession/#:~:text=Downloadä-,PDFöf%20the%202021ÄBA%20Profileöf%20the%20Legal%20Profession,-or%20view%20the [https://perma.cc/U5E6-MQ2T].

[5] ABA Standing Comm. on Ethics & Pro. Resp., Formal Op. 477 (2017).

[6] *Why OPSEC is for Everyone, Not Just For People With Something to Hide*, TRIPWIRE (Oct. 18, 2017) https://www.tripwire.com/state-of-security/security-data-protection/opsec-everyone-not-just-people-something-hide/ [https://perma.cc/F7TV-8U FM].

[7] Daniel Victor, *'I'm Not a Cat', Says Lawyer Having Zoom Difficulties*, THE NEW YORK TIMES (May 6, 2021), https://www.nytimes.com/2021/02/09/style/cat-lawyer-zoom.html [https://perma.cc/4NQ8-HJYQ].

[8] MODEL RULES OF PRO. CONDUCT r. 5.3, cmt. 3 (AM. BAR ASS'N 2020).

[9] Dennis Kennedy, *2021 Cloud Computing*, ABA (Nov. 10, 2021), https://www.americanbar.org/groups/law_practice/publications/techreport/2021/cloudcomputing/ [https://perma.cc/V24C-UK4S].

[10] User Rights (PracticePanther) available at https://www.practicepanther.com/privacy/ [https://perma.cc/A5X3-A3BD].

[11] MODEL RULES OF PRO. CONDUCT r. 5.1 (AM. BAR ASS'N 2020); MODEL RULES OF PRO. CONDUCT r. 5.3, cmt. 3 (AM. BAR ASS'N 2020).

[12] Linn F. Freedman, *Don't Wait for the Perfect Time for a Tabletop Exercise*, NATIONAL LAW REVIEW (Fed. 10, 2022), https://www.natlawreview.com/article/don-t-wait-perfect-time-tabletop-exercise [https://perma.cc/XD55-QMVD].

[13] ABA Comm. on Ethics & Pro. Resp., Formal Op. 483 (2018).

[14] SECURITY BREACH NOTIFICATION LAWS, NCLS (Jan. 17. 2022) https://www.ncsl.org/research/telecommunications-and-information-technology/security-breach-notification-laws.aspx [https://perma.cc/2CVH-LUGX].

[15] MODEL RULES OF PRO. CONDUCT r. 1.4 (AM. BAR. ASS'N 2020).

# CHAPTER 10

# CREATING & MAINTAINING ONLINE PRESENCE

*Core Concepts*

| | |
|---|---|
| *multi-channel marketing* | *email signature* |
| *pay-per-click advertising* | *drip content marketing* |
| *search engine optimization (SEO)* | *customer relationship management (CRM)* |
| *website design and naming conventions* | *thought leadership* |
| *profile page* | *social media strategy and ethics* |

*Knowledge Kickoff*

Sebastian is a lawyer at a criminal defense firm. Looking to create a splash fresh out of law school, Sebastian volunteers to take over the firm's social media efforts, which have been bare bones. Sebastian sets up Twitter and TikTok accounts with the username @CrimTrialExperts. He creates a heading on the firm's website called CrimTrialExpert Insight for blog posts, and updates each lawyer's profile page with a detailed list of past and present clients, matters, and court victories. His first blog post criticizes a recent trend of rulings excluding digital satellite evidence from automobiles, which often helps defendants. He links to the blog from the firm's social media. Sebastian later gets a visit from his furious managing partner. As it turns out, tomorrow the partner is arguing a motion *against* admission of that same satellite evidence Sebastian's blog said should be routinely allowed. Sebastian checks the @CrimTrialExperts Twitter notifications and sees several comments relating to the blog post. He responds to the thread with "chill out & simmer down folks—no chance Judge Linhart gets this one right!" Sebastian's approach to the firm's online presence:

a)     is misguided, because lawyers should focus only on individual profiles and accounts and avoid taking risks on behalf of an employer.

b)     is on point, because today's competitive market requires an aggressive social media strategy across many platforms and Sebastian's heart was in the right place trying to help.

c)     is well intentioned, but may overlook jurisdiction-specific ethical considerations such as confidentiality, professional decorum, conflicts of interest, public representations of expertise, and names that could mislead the public.

d)     is appropriate, because it's unrealistic for legal ethics rules to apply to short online posts or quick comments in today's connected social media world.

---

This book covers many angles of future lawyering skills. But what good are excellent skills if no one knows about them? This chapter is last for a reason. It introduces how modern lawyers tell the world about who they are and what they know: their success, ability, experience, and knowledge.

Like many subjects in this book, advertising, marketing, business development, solicitation of clients, and community reputation are not new to the legal profession—they're very different. Throughout the 20th century, people held firm to the notion that legal services were "above" traditional billboard-style direct advertising and communication tactics. Regulators in the United States took a strict approach to lawyer advertising and communication. For many, it was unimaginable that esteemed lawyers would feel the need to brag about their reputation, use competitive tactics, or showcase themselves "for hire" as a film company might showcase a new movie or a food company might showcase a new candy bar. Lawyers were skilled and trusted advisors in the highly insulated legal profession tasked with the monumental burden of upholding society's rule of law. It was a public calling, not an everyday service. Their reputation and work should speak for itself. They need not be "ambulance chasers." What reasons could lawyers possibly have to publicize their worth alongside run-of-the-mill consumer services or products like a movie or candy bar?

Great reasons, at least according to the Legal Clinic of Bates & O'Steen in Arizona in 1976. After state bars began to allow lawyers to do limited telephone directory advertising, Bates & O'Steen created a newspaper ad promoting its low-cost legal services. It fought the resulting state bar disciplinary action all the way to the United States Supreme Court, which held that the attorney newspaper advertising was protected commercial free speech.[1]

---

**LIT TIP**

"Advertising, the traditional mechanism in a free market economy for a supplier to inform a potential purchaser of the availability and terms of exchange, may well benefit the administration of justice."

*Bates v. State Bar of Arizona*, 433 U.S. 350 (1977)

---

The floodgates opened. Lawyers moved beyond local word of mouth to expand their client bases, bring in business, and develop and sustain their reputations. They advertised services and marketed themselves through newspapers, phone books, billboards, television, and radio. It wasn't a free-for-all. State bar ethics rules still limited what lawyers could do and say—rules that still exist in some form today, of course—but the *Bates* decision marked a crossroads and paved the way for the endless options modern lawyers enjoy.

Fast-forward to today. As a consumer yourself, you know the ways service providers reach the public—and it's a far cry from small black-and-white print newspaper ads. Online discussion forums such as Reddit have replaced in-person community gossip about the best lawyer in town. Blogs and e-newsletters replaced glossy magazine features. Instagram reels have replaced formal conference speeches. For every television commercial that still runs or billboard that still goes up, there are millions of social media posts and search engine ads for legal services. What's obvious is that the internet expands the opportunities lawyers have to publicize work, connect with others, and impress the public. What's less obvious is that it has also expanded the risks, complications, and potential drawbacks of doing so.

Creating and maintaining a robust online presence is as necessary today as it's ever been. This is because consumers of legal services have more choice than they've ever had about whom to consult and whom to hire (remember Need to Know #4 Legal Services Without (or Alongside) Lawyers and chapter 7's discussion of serving the modern consumer client). Amid such choice, online presence means finding fresh ways to shine—whether from an individual or macro-organizational standpoint.

Approach this chapter from both angles. If you pursue a small or solo practice, online presence will be on your shoulders. If you work at a large organization, company, agency, or firm, you may not be involved with big-picture decisions but you'll always be in charge of your own reputation, brand, expertise, business development, networking, credentials, and style. Differentiating yourself could be the difference between:

- ✓ business growth or business demise
- ✓ financial stability or financial stress
- ✓ successful career mobility or being stuck in positions that don't suit you
- ✓ meaningful personal networking relationships or professional isolation

How the public finds, sees, and interacts with lawyers in today's interconnected digital world is just as important as the legal advice they eventually receive. Your top-notch skills may get you in the door, but can you accomplish your professional career goals if no one ever knows about them? About you? Maybe. Maybe not. Why take the chance?

## Back to Basics: Marketing, Advertising, Solicitation & Business Development

Before you think about how to create an online presence, let's start with some basic building blocks. You've heard the concepts of marketing, advertising, solicitation, and business development before. But let's put a finer point on them, consider how they've evolved, and understand how the ethics rules have tried to keep pace and keep central the overarching goal of protecting the public from falsehoods, deceptive practices, and misleading communication. The ethical framework around "Information About Legal Services" as titled in the Model Rules of Professional Conduct is very specific to different jurisdictions and often confusing.[2] Rules and guidance from decades ago when phone book Yellow Pages were the concern have bent and stretched—or not—in many states to capture the reality that advances in technology have changed the way society communicates.

1)   Marketing

Marketing is a broad starting point. It's the behind-the-scenes effort of any business or service provider to research and identify what people want or need and how to satisfy that (and often how to do so in a profitable way). Marketing might be directed to other businesses or consumers of a product or service. Suppose you are starting a new clothing company. Your marketing strategy might include things like identifying your target demographic customer base, style, image, price point, and delivery methods. Aspects of marketing are not always within your control; for example, when a social media influencer goes viral after wearing clothing from your new company (positive) or a news reporter writes a story about poor warehouse conditions overseas where the clothing is made (negative).

2)   Advertising

Advertising is narrower. Advertising might bring a broader a marketing strategy to life with paid or unpaid promotion. If marketing sets intention and purpose, advertising is a component of that bigger picture. We see and hear advertisements all the time as consumers, whether a large print ad on the side of a bus, a podcast interruption, or an annoying pop-up over our internet browser window. Using the earlier clothing example, your company might create a new seasonal slogan with television ads to further the marketing strategy or create a social media hashtag to promote a "2 for the price of 1" sale on new sweatshirts. Figure 10A shows the 1976 newspaper advertisement the Bates & O'Steen clinic used that was (at first) held to violate Arizona's rules against lawyer advertising.

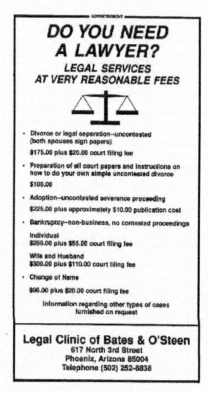

* Figure 10A: Bates & O'Steen newspaper ad, *Bates v. State Bar of Arizona*, 433 U.S. 350 app. (1977).

Advertising often conjures up a negative connotation in the legal profession for perhaps being crass or too direct but it serves an important purpose: letting the public know about available legal resources from which they may choose.

3)   Solicitation

To solicit means to entice, lure, make petition to, or approach with a request or plea. In the clothing example, solicitation might be the company's making a direct ask of a model or influencer to wear a new sweatshirt style. In the ordinary course, solicitation is often annoying but no big deal. Children fundraising at a school might solicit me for a donation. A door-to-door salesperson from a landscaping company might ring my doorbell to ask if I need gardening help. But people in need of legal services are often vulnerable, desperate, confused, and upset. That's what differentiates them from someone who might need help pruning roses.

State bars have always had the goal of protecting the public from unscrupulous efforts by lawyers to "chase" clients; the aim is to ensure professional decorum and an arm's-length process for how and why someone chooses their lawyer. But technology has changed what an arm's-length process might mean. Today, I'm more likely to get an email from a landscape company than I am a knock at the door—and solicitation by a lawyer is far more likely via text message or online chat room than it is by wandering the halls of a hospital handing out business cards to accident victims. In-person solicitation has gone electronic and online, which opens up a new era of permissible and impermissible communication.

4)   Business Development

Business development is a catch-all term capturing everything a lawyer does to give information about their services—with the goal of growing them. Business development is the longer road with many marketing, advertising, and solicitation stops along the way. Business development means building bridges with other lawyers, clients, potential clients, and experts. The goal is a sustainable framework that supports a legal practice for the long run, whether that's one lawyer or a thousand. It's the networking, referrals, references, and relationship-building tips you've heard about during law school. Back to the clothing company example, pursuing national sponsorship opportunities with athletic teams might be a business development plan to complement a broader marketing strategy.

Lawyers' business development efforts capture a wide net of activities:

    ✓   networking with existing or potential clients

    ✓   soliciting new clients

    ✓   writing about and developing expertise

    ✓   sustaining positive referral relationships

    ✓   diversifying publicity opportunities

✓    expanding to a new geographic area

✓    developing a new revenue-generating practice specialty or tool

Lawyers benefit from core ethics guidance applicable to marketing, advertising, solicitation, and business development efforts. Keep in mind Model Rules are just that—models—and given significant updates on these topics by the ABA in 2018, different states have different frameworks about what lawyers wishing to give information about their services can and cannot do.

➤    Model Rule 7.1 Communication Concerning a Lawyer's Services (prohibits lawyers from making false or misleading communications about the lawyer or their services, meaning "it contains a material misrepresentation of fact or law, or omits a fact necessary to make the statement considered as a whole not materially misleading.").

➤    Model Rule 7.2 Communications Concerning a Lawyer's Services: Specific Rules (updated rule omits the term "advertising" and focuses on rules about "communications" more generally, such as paying for recommendations and referrals, giving nominal thank you gifts, and stating or implying specialty certification).

➤    Model Rule 7.3 Solicitation of Clients (regulates "live person-to-person contact" with pecuniary gain being a significant motive for doing so, including situations where, according to comment 2, a person is subject to "a direct personal encounter without time for reflection" but not chat rooms, text messages, "or other written communications that recipients may easily disregard" where situations are less likely to be "fraught with the possibility of undue influence, intimidation, and overreaching").

We'll unravel the patchwork of this and other guidance throughout this chapter as it relates to opportunities and restrictions modern lawyers have when creating and maintaining online presence.

## Multi-Channel Presence: Where & How People Find Lawyers

Before we dive into the digital channels that combine to create online presence, think about how people find those channels in the first place.

Imagine that instead of reading this book you earned a bonus and dream of a tropical vacation to Costa Rica. You've never been. What would you do? Where would you start? How would you plan your trip? I know what you wouldn't do. You wouldn't go to a travel agent's office to peruse brochures on their coffee table. You wouldn't go to your local bookstore (assuming you live near one of the few left) or library and read about Costa Rica in a travel book.

You'd start online, probably with a general search for "top Costa Rica beach hotels." You'd skim the first page of results and stop there. Off and on you'd ask around and chat with friends who have traveled there. Maybe you'd turn to sites like Hotels.com or Expedia to check out ratings or read user-submitted reviews on Tripadvisor. If the mobile version of a hotel's website was ugly or confusing, you'd give it a second or two and then move on. You'd circle back and check the advice of strangers through Airbnb reviews, scroll through a Costa Rica travel and tourism page on Reddit, or type "What is Costa Rica like" on a Q&A site such as Quora.com. You'd follow social media accounts from hotels and check out key tourist attractions on Yelp.

---

**LIT TIP**

If you're a quick skimmer of online search results, you're not alone. Do any of the following surprise you?

- ✓  the #1 search result rank gets about 39.6% of clicks; #2 gets 18.4%; #3 gets 10.1%[3]

- ✓  only about 25% of users make it to the second page of search results[4]

- ✓  66% of all consumers—and 80% of those under age 35—perform online research every time or almost every time they buy a product or service (the most important consideration being online reviews, especially for lawyers)[5]

A search about a Costa Rica vacation is a far cry from a client seeking legal advice—but the approach to how someone finds what they want along the eternal digital highway is the same. Past generations would consider it wild to rely on the internet for big life decisions such as which lawyer to hire. Today's consumer would consider it wild not to. Yes, sometimes people book a hotel based on the personal recommendation of a neighbor, many people still find a lawyer through direct "friends and family" referrals, and clients with repeat business might use the same law firm or lawyer for decades. But in all those scenarios, they'd still check them out online. For many of the more than one million lawyers in the United States, people needing services are learning about them—and will learn about you—through some combination of these and other sources:

| | |
|---|---|
| ✓ direct website | ✓ podcasts |
| ✓ search engine results | ✓ radio |
| ✓ online discussion forums | ✓ television |
| ✓ social media | ✓ legal directories |
| ✓ blogs | ✓ direct mail |

That's a lot of traditional and not-so-traditional channels to cover—and cover in an efficient, effective, and ethical way. But if you aren't creating an attractive digital footprint accessible to millions of people through **multi-channel marketing** efforts, another lawyer you may compete with will.

### Find My Lawyer: Pay-Per-Click & Search Engine Optimization (SEO) Basics

Meet a hypothetical lawyer Nicoletta. She is a family law lawyer at a small firm in Albany, New York who tries to focus on multi-channel marketing. The firm has a terrific website featuring great work. Nicoletta is an active participant with the local bar association and churns out blog and social media content on hot topics in family law. But Nicoletta's client base has not grown. Out of curiosity, Nicoletta does a Google search for "Albany family law lawyer" and is shocked to see her firm's personal profile page doesn't appear until the fourth page of results.

Google processes more than 3.5 billion searches every day. That's more than 1 trillion searches every year.[6] Add to that more queries on other search engines, and you get the picture. It's how we access life information. Even if we already know what we're looking for, we've become accustomed to using a search engine to get us there. If I want to check out Joe's Pizza in Times Square, I don't type *www.joespizza.com* into an internet browser window or app. I type or tap "Joe's Pizza" into a search box with my location turned on from New York City (or I say "Hey Siri" and search on my Apple Watch) and enjoy the usually accurate top result that takes me to the website I'm looking for (or, better yet, gives me dining hours and walking directions).

Search result pages are crowded. They're the ultimate lawyer referral service. We wade through paid advertisements (the results at the top that seem like "results" but are marked with a bold **AD** label upon closer look), maps, one-tap phone call options, related search suggestions at the bottom such as the ones shown in Figure 10B, and—eventually—hundreds, thousands, or millions of search results. There's a lot going on. There's even more going on behind the scenes with the hidden and not-so-hidden ins and outs of complex methodologies behind why certain sources appear "higher" or more prominently than others. In our search-dependent world, the rich (those featured prominently) get richer and the poor (those featured "below the fold" or not on the first page) get poorer.

Related searches ⋮

| | |
|---|---|
| Q  pro bono family court lawyers albany, ny | Q  colwell law group reviews |
| Q  albany divorce lawyer | Q  colwell law group saratoga springs |
| Q  child custody lawyer albany, ny | Q  child support lawyer albany, ny |
| Q  colwell law group | Q  albany, ny attorneys |

\* Figure 10B: Sample Albany family law lawyer Google related searches.

This leads to two primary ways lawyers navigate search engine visibility:

| Pay-Per-Click (PPC) Advertising * Search Engine Optimization (SEO) |
| --- |

In the **pay-per-click advertising** model, lawyers pay to ensure a platform like Google Ads shows their advertisement when someone searches certain relevant keywords. Think of it as a win-win-win. For every "click" on a lawyer's ad, the client wins by finding a lawyer, the lawyer wins by bringing in new business, and the search engine wins by getting paid. If you are in a position to consider paid search engine advertising, consultants and marketing experts can help with design, keyword optimization, and analytics to track return on investment (ROI) because those details are far beyond what we cover in this introductory chapter. Online advertising isn't cheap, and a lawyer pursuing a PPC model ensures it's worthwhile to do so.

The second approach to search engine visibility, **search engine optimization (SEO)**, is often called "organic" because it happens more on its own and is not one discrete thing a lawyer pays for—unlike PPC. Think back to hypothetical Albany family law lawyer Nicoletta. She was doing great work and did not pay for online advertising, but the public had a hard time finding her on the fourth page of search results. SEO means optimizing web presence in a purposeful way to drive traffic to a website. It's like a modern-day popularity contest: a game of moving chess pieces in a strategic way to advance a website up the precious Google chain (or Bing, or any of several search engines).

The technical particulars of the algorithm of a search engine such as Google are far beyond this chapter; those algorithms use hundreds of different ranking factors and people pay a lot of money to make sense of it all. Large law firms and organizations have digital marketing experts whose only job is to navigate SEO; many other lawyers and firms hire third-party SEO expert consultants. We won't approach the topic from the perspective of spending many thousands of dollars on SEO or technical professionals. Even if you aren't involved in marketing at an organizational level, introductory SEO basics can help you understand why people see what they see when they search for your name or the name of your employer.

So if you end up creating an excellent online presence, how might you think about improving the likelihood that the public can find it?

- ✓ Focus on substantive online content such as articles, newsletters, white papers, and other ideas we'll cover. The more you publicize expertise and experience through different channels, the better.

- ✓ Be purposeful with keywords. If you have the word "divorce" all over a webpage but never mention a broader family law practice, a search algorithm may not easily push your page forward upon a search for "family law lawyer near me." Aim for breadth and specificity to cover different angles depending on your practice.

- ✓ Get other sites to drive traffic to yours. This is sometimes called "off-page" citations or backlinks. The more people click on the link to your website from other ones, and the more different websites mention yours, the more a search engine algorithm "thinks" your website is worth directing traffic to. (Remember this concept when we turn to "drip" marketing and gradual efforts using different platforms to broaden your network.)

SEO is complicated. Google has pages of webmaster guidelines advising how to improve search results, ensure a site "looks" its best on a results page, or exclude a site from being included in certain search results.[7] Those pages give more detail than most readers (and lawyers) ever want to know. If you pursue a solo or small firm career, SEO is something to which you may find yourself paying close attention (or finding an external consultant to help). On the back end, some lawyers and law firms dive into advanced analytics that measure metrics such as where web traffic comes from and what spots on a site get the most clicks. As with most topics related to online presence, a modern lawyer should favor a gradual and meaningful approach to SEO over the long term instead of a "quick fix" instantaneous mindset in the short term.

## Website Design & Naming Conventions

*www.modernlawyer.com*

Years ago, online presence meant a simple website with a simple URL. That's it. Today it means more, but you still never get a second chance to make a first impression after someone lands on your site (or your profile). Whether someone finds it through a business card or online ad, the goal once they're there is the same: to impress.

**Website design** is itself the subject of entire books. Here we'll scratch the surface. Some readers may have developed a website themselves; others wouldn't know where or how to start. Many professional templates and platforms such as WordPress are available to create a website easily; even so, lawyers often seek help from third-party consultants. Even if you aren't ultimately responsible for the ins and outs of website design along your career path, it's helpful to recognize best practices and understand necessary limitations.

Website **naming conventions** are a modern angle to an old issue for lawyers: trade names. What name or names lawyers and firms can use to present their services to the public has long been a subject of ethics guidance—whether on a large sign hanging outside a physical office or in a URL. A small number of states still have rules governing firm names and letterheads that prohibit use of any trade names; others are in line with the Model Rules, which cover the topic of naming under the more general prohibition against false or misleading misrepresentations. Despite movement toward increased flexibility when it comes to a creative or catchy name in their multi-channel marketing, lawyers still don't enjoy a completely blank slate.

A website root (modernlawyer) and top-level domain name (.com) are the unique and hopefully identifiable and easy-to-remember word or words that become part of the website address. Just like my example of *www.modernlawyer.com*, it seems simple enough to select a root and domain name and create your URL, right? Wrong. There's a reason most law firm names sound more like "O'Leary and Associates" rather than "O'Leary Gets You Out of Jail." Names associated with websites are subject to certain restrictions such as still showing the actual name of the firm on the website, not making the domain name false, deceptive, or misleading, not implying special expertise, and not suggesting a particular result. This is why a "www.olearygetsyououtofjail.expert" naming convention probably wouldn't stand a chance, whether on a shingle outside an office or as a URL.

---

### LIT TIP

"[A] lawyer who practices family law might use www.divorcelawyer.com. The mere fact that the domain name indicates a field of practice does not, in and of itself, make it false, deceptive or misleading. Although Kentucky does not recognize specialists, Rule 7.40 permits a lawyer to indicate his or her area of practice as long as the advertisement otherwise conforms to the rules. If a lawyer can state that he or she practices divorce law, there does not appear to be any reason why that same lawyer cannot use a domain name that conveys the same information. This is not to suggest that all domain names will withstand scrutiny under the rules. Just as a lawyer could not say she is the "greatest lawyer in Kentucky," because that is likely to create unjustified expectations (and compares her services with others), she could not use the domain name www.greatestlawyerinky.com for the same reason."

Kentucky Bar Ass'n. Ethics Op. E-427 (2007)

---

Before we turn to some bells and whistles that help a website stand out, beyond domain names there are many other jurisdiction-specific ethical considerations to watch for in the world of lawyer and law firm websites such as:

- ✓ client testimonials
- ✓ substantive legal information and FAQs
- ✓ security verifications (if, for example, you accept payment)
- ✓ misleading statements
- ✓ claims of specialty or expertise
- ✓ privacy notices and policies

- ✓ unauthorized practice of law
- ✓ disclaimers
- ✓ establishment of an attorney-client relationship by collection of too much information either by form, chatbot, or some other intake creating a "prospective client"
- ✓ confidentiality with past clients
- ✓ confidentiality with prospective clients

As website development exploded, there was no shortage of ethics guidance on these and other issues for a lawyer to research further as may be relevant in their own jurisdiction. For example:

> ➢ *In re Hyderally*, 32 A.3d 1117, 1122 (N.J. 2011) (criticizing lawyer for improper use of a New Jersey Board on Attorney Certification "seal" on website, warning that "attorneys are responsible for monitoring the content of all communications with the public—including their websites—to ensure that those communications conform at all times" with ethics rules).

> ➢ ABA Standing Comm. on Ethics & Pro. Resp., Formal Op. 10-457 (2010) (analyzing obligations for lawyers' websites, including offering substantive legal information instead of particular legal advice and carefully considering whether and when two-way internet communication results in someone becoming a "prospective client" under Model Rule 1.18).

> ➢ Vermont Advisory Ethics Op. 2000-04 (allowing lawyer to use a FAQ format to give accurate legal information, so long as they include a clear statement to website visitors that it does not constitute legal advice).

> ➢ Arizona State Bar Op. 02-04 (2002) (opining that lawyer website with links to invite email communication should include disclaimers that

clarify whether emails from prospective clients will be treated as confidential or not).

THE MATERIALS ON THIS WEBSITE PROVIDE GENERAL INFORMATION AND DO NOT OFFER LEGAL ADVICE. THEY ARE NOT GUARANTEED TO BE COMPLETE OR UP TO DATE AT ALL TIMES. USING THIS WEBSITE IN ANY FORM, INCLUDING SENDING OR RECEIVING INFORMATION THROUGH IT, DOES NOT ESTABLISH AN ATTORNEY-CLIENT RELATIONSHIP. YOU SHOULD NOT SEND CONFIDENTIAL INFORMATION IN RESPONSE TO THIS WEBSITE. FOLLOWING THE LAW FIRM ON SOCIAL MEDIA, INCLUDING TWITTER, LINKEDIN, AND INSTAGRAM, DOES NOT IMPLY OR CREATE A RELATIONSHIP BETWEEN ANY FOLLOWER AND THE LAW FIRM OR ANY MEMBER ATTORNEY OR STAFF. AN ATTORNEY-CLIENT RELATIONSHIP WITH YOU AND THE LAW FIRM IS CREATED ONLY BY AN EXPRESS WRITTEN AGREEMENT SIGNED BY THE LAW FIRM AND YOU.

\* Figure 10C: Sample law firm website general disclaimer.

After a lawyer ensures they've met relevant ethical obligations, some foundational design ideas can start them in the right direction toward a top-notch site.

✓ Include easy-to-navigate content pages with navigational headers such as About, Contact(s), and Media/News.

✓ Showcase expertise and experience with robust individual profiles.

✓ Consider color, images, and design to match style and intended brand.

✓ Link to social media and other channels of interest to site visitors.

✓ Focus on accessibility.

✓ Ensure the site is mobile-friendly (and be sure to test out new content or changes on different devices).

- ✓ Highlight substantive content such as blogs, webinars, newsletters, or other helpful sources of information or tools (for example, a simple child support calculator on a family law firm website).

- ✓ Consider communication options such as a secure client portal, live chat, virtual receptionist, or automated consultation scheduling tool.

A strong website is a no-brainer for a modern law firm. Put yourself in the position of a potential client and ask yourself what would be helpful—and then, once you have a draft design, ask yourself whether you like what you see.

## Individual Profiles & Email Signatures

A personal **profile page** is a critical part of any professional services website. You could work at the most prestigious law firm in the world with a million-dollar marketing budget, but if your individual profile page falls short, or if your email response to someone is unprofessional or unhelpful, folks may move on to the next stop on their digital highway. In your personal life, I hope you've given some thought to creation of your online profiles. As a modern lawyer, it's time to do that—and more—for your new professional ones.

Any individual profile page is a chance to enhance your online presence. It's also a place where ethics rules apply. Bear in mind opportunity and risk. Here are some dos and don'ts to consider for this small slice of the digital universe that's uniquely yours:

*Don't* include:

- ✓ language certifying that you are a "specialist" or "expert" unless paired with the name of a certifying organization as ethics rules may require

- ✓ mention of other jurisdictions where you aren't licensed to practice

- ✓ past or present client names without informed client consent

    ✓  confidential information about past or present matters without informed client consent, even if it is already public through other channels

Do include:

    ✓  professional, high-quality headshots

    ✓  educational background and past work experience

    ✓  organizations, certifications, accomplishments, and memberships

    ✓  hobbies, interests, talents (you never know how a connection may form!)

    ✓  presentations or publications about you

    ✓  presentations you've made or publications you've authored

    ✓  general descriptions of recent legal matters of interest without "naming names"

    ✓  a list of jurisdictions where you are licensed to practice

    ✓  disclaimers to help limit obligations to prospective clients (if not elsewhere)

    ✓  a contact form (if not elsewhere)

Your individual profile page is for the world to see, but even a single email can contribute to—or detract from—quality online presence.

Emailing without a professional **email signature** is like serving chips without salsa: it leaves you hanging. It feels OK but incomplete, like a lost opportunity. Including a modern signature block such as the one in Figure 10D at the end of email messages furthers your professional presence and informs recipients where else they can find you.

**Catherine Coleman**
Junior Associate

email: catherine.coleman@rockwellgraham.com
phone: (800) 555-0199 | mobile: (800) 555-0299

Rockwell & Graham, 260 Park Ave 18th Floor 10017 New York, NY

f 🐦 ▶ in 📷  www.rockwellgraham.com

The content of this email is confidential and intended for the recipient specified in message only. It is strictly forbidden to share any part of this message with any third party, without a written consent of the sender. If you received this message by mistake, please reply to this message and follow with its deletion, so that we can ensure such a mistake does not occur in the future.

\* Figure 10D: Sample law firm email signature.

An email signature isn't complicated; in fact, less is more: a photo (if you're comfortable with that); an attractive yet simple graphic, font, and layout; social media icons linked to your pages; a disclaimer (although, depending on the jurisdiction, a confidentiality disclaimer may not carry much weight in relation to other privilege and confidentiality disclosure rules); and clear contact details. Your employer may have its own rules and suggestions to fit a broader branding effort beyond just your page. Some lawyers include an automatic scheduling link so recipients can book a meeting with them (remember chapter 7's discussion of efficient law practice management technology and integrated calendaring tools). Just like the content, the purpose of an email signature isn't complicated either: to create opportunities, further your reputation, enhance your brand, and foster positive attention for you and your employer.

---

### LIT TIP

Many email signature generator applications and websites exist to help create this small but important aspect of a modern lawyer's online presence, no matter your email platform of choice. Check out options such as HubSpot, WiseStamp, Designhill, and Gimmio.

## Drip, Drip, Drip: Cultivating & Maintaining Relationships

*Keep in touch*! It's a casual phrase we say to friends, colleagues, and acquaintances we meet along life's path. In your role as a modern lawyer, keeping in touch is part of your online presence. Having a useful website and informative profile discoverable through search engines is a start. But don't adopt a set-it-and-forget-it mentality. No lawyer builds relationships overnight. They're built with a slow and steady "drip."

Have you ever received a "Happy Birthday!" email from a company you've never heard of? I have. At some point, I must have entered my birthday on its website or app. Unlike family and friends, that company didn't forget. Or if you've used your email to sign up for a discount or free gift, it's no surprise when that company emails you at seemingly random times in the weeks that follow until you unsubscribe. But it's not random. It's predetermined. Companies in all industries use drip marketing techniques, whether through direct mail, telephone, email, text, or social media. **Drip content marketing** is a strategy of sending small, set messages spaced out over time (hence the drip). The idea is simple: make your approach to marketing and communication with customers more automated and purposeful than sporadic and inconsistent. If a large highway billboard is like the faucet at full stream, drip marketing efforts are a more gentle and gradual nudge usually triggered by certain events (like someone clicking on your website and entering an email address, attending an in-person conference at your firm, or subscribing to your blog).

Lawyers may turn to **customer relationship management (CRM)** tools to cultivate and maintain relationships, often with the help of third-party consultants. A deep dive into CRM is beyond the bounds of this chapter. Suffice it to say CRM tools come in many shapes and sizes. The goal is to help a law firm track, manage, and learn from its interactions with clients and potential clients—to keep the old and attract the new. CRM systems can:

- ✓ sync with client intake and "follow" a client throughout matters with features such as billing and text communication

- ✓ capture data from website landing pages and website forms

- ✓ support "lead tracking" to determine the source of online attention and what follow-up seals the deal

- ✓ automate marketing and communication and improve integration across law practice management tools such as client portals

- ✓ provide visualization data to inform marketing, staffing, billing, and other decisions

Imagine a law firm spent $15,000 a month on magazine advertisements and 2 new clients reported hearing about the firm via those ads. If the firm welcomed 39 new clients that same month who reported clicking on the same PPC ad that cost the firm a total of $2,000, that data would be vital (and telling).

CRM is one technical angle but cultivating relationships need not be fancy. Don't forget what you're trying to make people remember: *you*! Companies promote products. Teams promote players. Schools promote facilities. You promote you. If you're wondering what you can "drip" out to the public to be a modern lawyer who keeps in touch, you needn't look far.

**Thought leadership** and content marketing are two important concepts for the modern lawyer looking to keep in touch. As a lawyer, you're not selling a pair of pants. You're selling your knowledge and skills. Showing authority in your field attracts attention and helps build relationships such that people want to trust you with their problems. As your legal career takes off, keep this runway in mind and make small, steady efforts to keep your drip constant. What's your niche? What expertise have you developed? What area of law fascinates you? If you're interested in cannabis compliance laws, learn about them. If you worked on design patent litigation involving fashion and clothing for years, write about it. Follow others with expertise on the topic and join the club. Keep yourself in the conversation. Before you know it, others may be looking at you to lead it.

---

### LIT TIP

"I talk to lawyers about creating a presence that positions them and their firms well within the industry. Whatever they're not doing, someone else is. It's what the world expects. The absence of quality online activity for a lawyer today is conspicuous. Starting a blog, social media account, or e-newsletter effort and then ignoring it and letting it get stale is worse than not doing anything in the first place. Lawyers should make relationship building and marketing part of their daily and weekly routines just like timekeeping and traditional legal work. Don't rely on your firm's efforts and broader network—create your own and get over the awkwardness of self-promotion. Promote others you respect and they'll promote you, but do so with a purposeful contribution. Every time you post, share, or email someone, add a sentence or two about the value of the content. 'Thought you'd like this' or a quick tap of a 'like' icon isn't all that helpful or impressive. It doesn't whet others' appetites to want more from you as a thought leader in an area in which they are interested. Even if new lawyers don't have much experience yet, they can demonstrate personality and initiative. A network doesn't magically happen. It takes time and effort to create but the payoff is worth it."

Trish Lilley
Chief Marketing & Business Development Officer
Stroock, Stroock, & Lavan LLP

---

Building a quality presence with consistent thought leadership is not easy. There are many different ways to approach it and many channels through which modern lawyers spread knowledge. Although you'll be in it for the long haul, here are some initial avenues to consider, tips to get started, and ethical cautions to remember along the way:

1)   Email Alerts, Newsletters & White Papers

Keeping in touch via email can be effective if you do so with purpose and content-rich substance. Many law firms send periodic client alert emails with news about recent case representations, positive outcomes, or new talent and recognition. This approach could be practice-specific on behalf of one group in a massive law firm or a catch-all effort on behalf of a solo practitioner or small firm. Content-based communication in e-newsletters, year-end announcements, free legal guides, or informative white papers are helpful. A firm might offer its reaction to a major United States Supreme Court decision or analysis of pending state regulation in an area of high interest to many. Every time a client, prospective client, or anyone else signs up for an e-newsletter mailing list or provides their email address to download a white paper, the reach of the online presence grows that much bigger.

2)   Blogs

We read blog posts about fashion, sports, travel, cooking, and everything else. Why not about law? Lawyers have been blogging for years. Despite new emerging platforms, law blogs remain a reliable tool in the modern lawyer's arsenal—so much so that years ago they earned the designation "blawgs."[8] Blogs are an excellent channel to show off thought leadership in a personable way. Noteworthy content delivered with a conversational writing style keeps the drip of trustworthy information flowing. Many firms have blogs embedded in their websites. Many lawyers maintain individual blogs through free or paid platforms such as the popular LexBlog[9] site, and others spread their work through larger-scale blog-distribution and hosting services and sites such as JD Supra.[10] Some pay others to create blog content in a process known as ghostwriting, although doing so requires careful consideration of jurisdiction-specific guidance about whether ghostwritten blogs in certain situations could be considered false or misleading to the public.

This chapter won't cover best practices for blog writing, but if you find yourself bit by the blogging bug (as I hope you will be), seek out additional resources and remember these core ideas:

- ✓ Set goals and intentions. Will you blog to reach clients? Establish yourself as an expert?

- ✓ Choose your lane. Do you have a niche? Will you stick to one practice area or straddle a variety of topics? Do some digging to see if existing blogs already cover your topic(s).

- ✓ Who will do all the writing, and when? Set a realistic regular schedule and stick to it. If it's a solo endeavor, it's on you. If it's a firm blog, the workload may be shared but who will take the lead? Few people are impressed by a "hot topic" post that's years—even months—old.

✓ Invite guest bloggers. They'll likely return the favor, thus increasing your visibility, driving more traffic to your blog, and helping with organic SEO efforts if that's a goal.

✓ Share blog posts on website profiles, across social media platforms, in newsletters, and anywhere and everywhere else.

✓ Be realistic and honest with yourself and others. Agreeing to do a blog post every week and then churning out subpar content when life gets busy is not ideal.

Blogs are a flexible and personal form of lawyer communication to the public but not a free-for-all. Ethics rules still apply on several fronts, from advertising restrictions to confidentiality obligations to conflicts of interest. There is no one clear rule on whether and when blog posts qualify as lawyer advertising or regulated information about a lawyer's services. The short answer is that they might. The line is hazy: on one side is commercial speech that brings blog content within the bounds of ethics rules about communications about legal services; on the other side is pure opinion, general commentary similar to an online article that is, at least on its face, not motivated by business or financial gain.

---

### LIT TIP

"Most 'traditional' blogs expressing the blogger's knowledge and opinions on various topics and issues, legal and non-legal, will be regarded as core or political speech. However, if a blog post advertises the attorney's availability for employment, according to the standards established by the Rules of Professional Conduct and statutes adopted in light of the court cases applicable to attorney advertising, the blog may be held subject to those rules and statutes. This opinion is not intended to chill or limit the protected speech of any lawyer, but rather to provide guidance to attorneys engaged in blogging activity as to the types of blogs or blog posts that may fall within the ambit of those regulations and statutes."

State Bar of California Standing Comm. on Pro. Resp.,
Formal Op. No. 2016-196 (2016)

A lawyer writing even a single blog post should take a jurisdiction-specific, post-by-post cautious approach to ethics considerations, such as with these steps:

- ✓ Check for potential conflicts of interest. What if your blog takes a legal position directly adverse to a position your colleagues just took on behalf of an important client?

- ✓ Be careful not to make false or misleading statements or representations of yourself as an "expert" without supporting certifications.

- ✓ Remember client confidentiality. Stay general or, if blogging about recent matters, obtain the client's informed consent to do so. Using hypotheticals based on a real case is risky if a reader would be reasonably likely to be able to identify the real situation or client. Write everything as if your clients, colleagues, presiding judges, etc. will be reading it.

- ✓ Carefully respond to any blog comments, clarify that your professional obligations support you not doing so, or disable the comment feature. (More on responding to negative comments or reviews later.)

- ✓ Include a disclaimer that the blog is not legal advice and creates no attorney-client relationship.

---

**LIT TIP**

"Lawyers who blog or engage in other public commentary may not reveal information relating to a representation that is protected by Rule 1.6(a), including information contained in a public record, unless disclosure is authorized under the Model Rules."

ABA Standing Comm. on Ethics & Pro. Resp., Formal Op. 480 (2018)

---

## 3)   Webinars, Vlogs & Podcasts

Many lawyers don't just want to write for existing and prospective clients—they want to speak directly to them. And many clients don't just want to read what their lawyers write—they want lawyers who speak to and with them. Webinars, vlogs, and podcasts are other tools lawyers use to put out small segments of thought content. For example, a securities enforcement and government relations law firm might put together a panel webinar about a hot topic on SEC enforcement trends that is relevant to its public company clients. Or a criminal defense lawyer might put out vlogs explaining basic concepts such as indictments and bail. Large law firms—often in the plaintiff and personal injury space—have become known for their vast referral networks and heavy advertising efforts beyond the television ads most readers have probably seen, and are now exploring podcasts, contests, and all sorts of new ways of spreading their name to the public.

I hope the phrase "drip, drip, drip" sticks in your mind throughout your career to remember to take a gradual approach to cultivating professional relationships. There's no one perfect way a modern lawyer builds a network. Like every chapter, this one offers options, ideas, and food for thought as you find your unique presence. As consumers on the receiving end, we've all seen others who overdo it. I can't decide how much is too much or how little is too little. That will be your job.

## Building Your Brand Through Social Media

You know social media. You use it, read it, skim it, ignore it, enjoy it, or detest it. It's so engrained in readers' lives that you may think it's odd to "learn" about it from a textbook. But using social media in your personal life does not make you an expert at it in your professional one. We approach this topic as one aspect of online presence and reputation. What we won't do is explore the very different topic of substantive use of social media information in the actual practice of law (for example, evidentiary admissibility of an Instagram post, lawfulness of a third-party search warrant to Snapchat, or sanctions for not producing Twitter comments in a discovery battle).[11]

Take a mindset-over-expertise approach to social media. This chapter doesn't address how best to use every feature of every platform nor does it recommend particular ones. Bring general considerations with you in practice for whatever social media option arrives next.

Like every topic in this chapter, consider **social media strategy and ethics** from both individual and organizational perspectives. You might be:

- ✓ posting on your own behalf
- ✓ posting on behalf of your law firm or organization
- ✓ commenting on a post by a colleague, client, former client, or adversary
- ✓ deciding whether a live video or still image is more appropriate
- ✓ deciding whether to "friend" or connect with a certain person
- ✓ deciding whether to make a profile public or private
- ✓ wondering whether to share someone else's post
- ✓ responding to disagreeable comments on a post by you or someone else

These and other decisions will leave an online trail. Create that trail with purpose and caution. This discussion isn't about "proper" social media use. Readers have received that lecture from parents, teachers, and career advisors. This discussion is about how to leverage social media effectively to create the online presence you want—whether that's hundreds of thousands of strangers who follow you or four practice area experts who comment on your LinkedIn posts and invite you to attend conferences. Social media for lawyers may be the ultimate double-edged sword. It offers huge advantages for the lawyer who uses it well. All publicity is good publicity, right? Not so fast.

Here are five suggestions to help your social media presence head in the right direction and stay out of trouble.

1)   Do Some Cleanup

Before we think about future online presence as a modern lawyer, we need to think about past online presence as [fill in your own blank!]. If you're transitioning from a prior professional career, or don't use social media in your personal life, you won't have much if any cleanup to do. But many new lawyers were undergraduates not too long ago and we all know how some of those college-era photos could look years later to a prospective client or colleague. Take a pass through your social media accounts as if you were a client or employer thinking about working with you (better yet, check your privacy settings while you're at it). Do an audit of sorts. Spend some time searching your name online using different search engines. Would you hire yourself?

2)   #planyoursocialmediaplan

Building a social media presence should be a careful exercise, whether alone or on an employer's behalf. Here are some early questions to consider.

- ✓   Who is your target audience and what are your goals? This will inform the best platform(s) on which to focus and other decisions, such as what #hashtags to use.

- ✓   Who will manage which platform? If someone sends a direct message to you personally or to a professional organizational page and receives no response, that won't further your online presence.

- ✓   What disclaimers might be necessary to comply with local ethics rules?

- ✓   Who will ensure consistency across platforms, such as using the same logo, picture, or image, or paying for a social media management tool like Hootsuite?

- ✓   What social media policies might you need to create for others or follow yourself?

- ✓   How will you ensure regular, quality content and attract the followers you want?

- ✓   Do you plan to "measure" the success of different platforms as part of a broader marketing picture? If so, how?

First impressions on social media are instantaneous. People viewing an account may have a shorter attention span than the average goldfish—about eight seconds before they'll lose concentration on whatever they're seeing.[12] A well-thought-out social media plan makes the most of the precious window you have to impress people before they swim away.

3)   Keep Tabs on Who Is Using What—and How

Keeping with the fish theme, fish where everyone else is fishing as the saying goes. If no one is fishing in a particular spot, it might be because there are no fish to be caught there. Using a social media platform that was popular a decade ago may not be the ideal path to online presence today.

According to the American Bar Association, three-fourths of lawyers report they use or maintain some social media presence for "professional purposes" across different platforms.[13] About half of all law firms report having a formal social media policy, as do 90% of large law firms with 500 lawyers or more. Figure 10E shows apps popular with lawyers; they won't surprise you. But this is just one snapshot in time for one book chapter. If I had written this book in 2015, no one would have known what TikTok was. A modern lawyer stays abreast of changes over their career and what platforms other lawyers—and clients—are exploring.

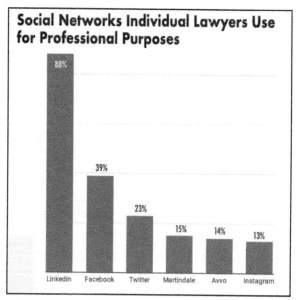

**Social Networks Individual Lawyers Use for Professional Purposes**

- LinkedIn 88%
- Facebook 39%
- Twitter 23%
- Martindale 15%
- Avvo 14%
- Instagram 13%

* Figure 10E: Social Networks for Professional Purposes, ABA Profile of the Legal Profession.[14]

Let's look at a few of the top social networks in turn.

LinkedIn is (at least as of when this book was published) *the* online networking and connection spot for lawyers—and many other professionals (it boasts 810 million worldwide users as the globe's "largest professional network").[15] It's often the first stop for someone searching your name even before your firm or other website profile. LinkedIn can transform your traditional paper résumé into a dynamic and engaging one. You want others to know what you are about today—not what you worked on or enjoyed months or years prior. LinkedIn is also a terrific research resource if, for example, you are looking to learn more about a new or prospective client about whom you know very little. LinkedIn pages are the new online business card. Make your profile specific and show off your skills and experience. It's a high-visibility, real-time source for endorsements, referral and recommendation comments, content-rich articles, and shared information and thought posts. If you are already on LinkedIn, terrific—keep up your profile, make sure you have a new professional picture, and keep exploring more ways to connect, engage in a substantive way with others, and produce content to "find" your voice as a modern lawyer. If you aren't on it or rarely engage, check out additional resources that teach you not how to use LinkedIn but how to use it well.

Modern lawyers also post short 280-character bursts on Twitter in many ways and for many reasons. Some do so from a simple research angle. As chapter 4 noted in the context of next generation research paths, daily social media feeds from other lawyers or industry professionals "in the know" can be a valuable source. Lawyers follow lawyers, judges, experts, academics, clients, and client competitors to stay current with discussion of notable trends, recent decisions, or efforts at new laws or regulations. Being "inactive" on Twitter is a lower-risk approach, although that may mean lower reward, too. Lawyers with a more active presence post content, link content from other platforms (such as directing followers to their more in-depth LinkedIn post), retweet content (hopefully with some added helpful commentary), direct message others in their network, or even create Twitter Live videos to bring more personality and interactive engagement to their Twitter community.

Speaking of videos, we all know other popular image, video, and messaging platforms such as Snapchat, TikTok, YouTube, Instagram, and Facebook. Remember the tip about planning social media efforts with an intended audience in mind. If you do estate planning or elder law, Snapchat probably shouldn't be your first stop, given that most "Snapchatters" (and TikTokers) who send Snaps, Stories, and Memories and watch billions of videos a day are of a younger generation. Modern lawyers are taking advantage of the storytelling aspect of these platforms—content is less polished and more personal, depicting quick insights in an approachable and relatable way. Whether it's a 20-second introductory Story, a 60-second YouTube Shorts video summarizing your expertise, or a TikTok video discussing a legal issue as shown in Figure 10F on the topic of whether schools can block students' cell phone signals, remember to use a professional approach to video quality—save the shaky cell phone reels for another time.

\* Figure 10F: Screenshot of @bradshear Web3Lawyer (business, technology, privacy) with more than 1.1M TikTok followers @bradshear, TIKTOK (March 10, 2022).

4)  Be Social with Social

There's a reason it's called *social* media. Don't go at it alone. A successful online presence requires a community, and those who give will receive. Remember to:

✓  engage with others in your network and join groups

✓  be purposeful about who you follow and what you share or comment upon

✓  pay it forward by mentioning others and drive attention and traffic back to your profile or page when they do the same for you

✓  bookmark feeds from thought leaders in fields that interest you or relate to your practice or clients' businesses

✓  keep goals and priorities in mind and focus on quality engagement—not just quantity

5)  Ethical Cautions

Against the upside to social media comes some caution. Remember the Model Rules that protect the public from false, deceptive, or misleading practices when it comes to distribution of information about a lawyer. At first glance, social media for advertising and marketing seems harmless. It's no or low cost, convenient, easy, and spreads your messaging far and wide. How much trouble can short and sweet posts or videos cause?

You'd be surprised. Just like with blogging, ethical concerns with social media communication tiptoe along some fine lines between protected speech and unpermitted communication about a lawyer's services. Marketing, advertising, and solicitation efforts that were once one-way now have the potential to become two-way and interactive on social media, opening up a host of potential traps.

Consider the following social media posts or comments by a lawyer. Do they give you pause?

> **"Great win 2day in district court on behalf of Craig Smithfield. Privacy rights for drivers prevail!!!"**
>
> **"Facing a traffic ticket or DUI? Call me for another victory #expertDUIlawyer"**
>
> **"Tragic warehouse accident in Providence. Alan here to help—DM me"**

They should give you pause, although whether they cross the line from an ethics point of view depends on your local jurisdiction. Just like with blogging, one safer bet is to stay general with non-targeted posted content. If you intend to contact people directly through, for example, direct messaging to solicit business, triple-check your jurisdiction's guidance to research if doing so is permitted solicitation (akin to a text message in some states) such that individuals are free to ignore the online outreach with no risk of undue pressure or potential for overreaching. Whether a post, image, or video is subject to attorney advertising rules such as needing a disclaimer or specific label is another blurry line that depends on the substance of the content, its purpose, and state-specific interpretation of ethics rules.

Confidentiality under Model Rule 1.6 is another concern. Social media is about sharing; lawyers try not to share. Lawyers should not use social media to communicate with clients or anyone else about a matter and assume anything and everything on social media is public—even if using platform privacy settings. This includes information that's already in the public domain or public record—absent client consent, it's not your role to shout any client information from the online rooftops. Innuendo about clients or current cases can also cross the line if a third party could infer the subject of the post, as was mentioned earlier with listing specifics from past matters on a lawyer profile page. Many people let their guards down on social media. Take caution to ensure you don't.

Another ethics spot to heed is Model Rule 1.18 Duties to Prospective Client. Just as with contact through a firm website, lawyers on social media must avoid inadvertent creation of an attorney-client relationship and the resulting protections and privilege that then attach. The same general-over-specific rule of thumb applies. Social media exchanges should focus on general legal information instead of applying information to the facts of any one scenario for someone. A person "DM'ing" you on social media with details relative to a legal situation can have implications even if you eventually don't agree to represent them, such as conflicting you out of other cases if you received confidential information. Although the quick and short nature of social media makes it tricky, be sure to include disclaimers that information is not legal advice, is not confidential, and does not create an attorney-client relationship.

Here's some sample guidance spanning these and other topics across different jurisdictions:

- ➤ *In re Sitton*, 618 S.W.3d 288 (Tenn. 2021) (posting of social media comments were an aggravating factor supporting sanctions and a four-year suspension for a lawyer who gave gratuitous legal advice endorsing criminal activity on a public Facebook post that "fostered a public perception that a lawyer's role is to manufacture false defenses").

- ➤ State Bar of California Standing Comm. on Pro. Resp., Formal Op. No. 2012-186 (2012) (post to 500 followers of "another great victory in court today" did not trigger ethics rules but addition of "my client is delighted" and "who wants to be next" qualified under state advertising and client testimonial rules as prohibited communication about an attorney's services absent an explicit disclaimer and label).

- ➤ *In the Matter of Office of Disciplinary Counsel v. Magee*, 137 DB 2015 (Pa. Oct. 4, 2016) (attorney admitted to the Colorado bar disciplined for unauthorized practice of law because his LinkedIn profile represented that he also practiced in California and Pennsylvania).

- ➤ *Illinois Disciplinary Board v. Peshek*, No. 23794 (Wis. May 18, 2010) (assistant public defender suspended after public blog posts revealed confidential information with client names, jail identification numbers, or criminal case details from which one could infer identities).

- ➤ *Fla. Bar v. Conway*, 996 So. 2d 213 (Fla. 2008) (public reprimand to a lawyer who called a judge an "evil, unfair witch" on a local legal blog).

## Rankings, Reviews & Testimonials

What's worse than everyone taking about you? No one talking about you. The public is talking about lawyers. We read testimonials and reviews about a pest control company if we need to hire someone to help with a mice problem. The public reads about us if they need to hire someone to help with a legal problem.

Years ago, Yelp was the sole subject on this topic but chat room apps, Q&A information sites, and ranking and review pages are everywhere today. Some professional directories are more formal and lawyers may pay to be listed or may need to take active steps to claim their listing as with the popular Google My Business (GMB) source. Others are free, local, and informal. All require another delicate balance between optimal use and ethical traps.

First, talk to your colleagues, do some research on your own, and think about whether it makes sense to get yourself into the conversation with some of these directories and sites (or whatever new and popular ones you learn about during your career):

| Lawyer-specific | General |
|---|---|
| ✓ FindLaw | ✓ Yelp |
| ✓ Avvo | ✓ Better Business Bureau |
| ✓ LawInfo | ✓ Google My Business |
| ✓ Super Lawyers | ✓ Nextdoor |
| ✓ Martindale-Hubbell | ✓ Expertise.com |
| ✓ Justia | ✓ Reddit |
| ✓ Lawyers.com | ✓ Clubhouse |

If you dive in, tread water carefully. Take a proactive approach to this reputation management both with obtaining good reviews and responding to (or ignoring) bad ones. Lawyers have always faced limits about "bragging" and publicizing their clients' statements of satisfactions, whether with billboards, radio ads, or online reviews. Check local ethics guidance (and guidance from whatever platform you're using) but start with this as a general rule: lawyers can encourage clients to post favorable reviews or give high ratings but can't script the review themselves, draft fake ones, or give anything more than a small incentive in exchange for a review—a nominal, token gift or expression of thanks.[16]

---

**LIT TIP**

"A lawyer may give clients a $50 credit on their legal bills if they rate the lawyer on an Internet website such as Avvo that allows clients to evaluate their lawyers, provided the credit against the lawyer's bill is not contingent on the content of the rating, the client is not coerced or compelled to rate the lawyer, and the ratings and reviews are done by the clients and not by the lawyer."

New York Bar Comm. on Pro. Ethics Op. 1052 (2015)

---

Some questions with reviews and client testimonials are clear cut: there's no dispute that threatening solicitation of reviews is wrong, or that posting fake ones yourself is false and misleading. But other questions are cloudier, such as what qualifies as a "nominal" expression of thanks. A $10 gift card for coffee? Probably. Professional sports playoff tickets? Probably not.

Some safer—although not surefire—approaches for sourcing authentic online reviews and ratings include:

- ✓ waiting until the end of a matter instead of bothering clients about it in the midst of a case
- ✓ keeping it authentic by making a general open-ended ask and letting your satisfied client lead the way in describing your excellent work
- ✓ making it convenient for satisfied clients by folding an ask for a review into a standard case management and wrap-up process, such as via email or secure client portal alongside final invoicing or a conclusion of engagement letter

All lawyers hope for great reviews, but what about the ones that aren't so great? There's no shortage of negative discourse online. Stay above it and be careful. Beyond a matter of professional decorum, a client's negative review of you (even if it's false or outrageous) likely does not qualify as a lawyer/client "controversy" and does not open the door to allowing you to defend yourself and respond with case or client information that breaches confidentiality.

> ### LIT TIP
>
> "Lawyers are regularly targets of online criticism and negative reviews . . . [a] negative online review, alone, does not meet the requirements of permissible disclosure in self-defense under Model Rule 1.6(b)(5) and, even if it did, an online response that discloses information relating to a client's representation or that would lead to the discovery of confidential information would exceed any disclosure permitted under the Rule. As a best practice, lawyers should consider not responding to a negative post or review, because doing so may draw more attention to it and invite further response from an already unhappy critic. Lawyers may request that the website or search engine host remove the information. Lawyers who choose to respond online must not disclose information that relates to a client matter, or that could reasonably lead to the discovery of confidential information by another, in the response. Lawyers may post an invitation to contact the lawyer privately to resolve the matter. Another permissible online response would be to indicate that professional considerations preclude a response."
>
> ABA Standing Comm. on Ethics & Pro. Resp., Formal Op. 496 (2021)

Not breaching client confidences doesn't mean you have to stay silent. Use discretion responding to negative online reviews or comments; Figure 10G shows one option that may be permissible.

> **Sample Bad Client Review**
>
> A lawyer's duty to keep client confidences has few exceptions and in an abundance of caution I do not feel at liberty to respond in a point by point fashion in this forum. Suffice it to say that I do not believe that the post presents a fair and accurate picture of the events
>
> 0   Share  ✓ Approve  ⊘ Remove  ☒ Spam   ⬭  ···                    100% Upvoted

* Figure 10G: Sample lawyer response to negative online review.[17]

* * * *

No matter the size or shape of the footprint your online presence creates, keep it authentically you. Professional presence varies just as our personal one does. The pace of online communication is fast. But the deliberateness with which a lawyer should navigate it is slow. Within the bounds of ethics rules, a modern lawyer can have it all—compelling ads, strong thought leadership, informative niche daily news feeds, and countless business development opportunities. That need not mean jumping at every new gimmick in the future legal marketplace. During your career, you might have the option to advertise on the side of downtown city Ubers, promote your expertise through digital ads on a touchscreen inside of self-driving cars, or get your law firm's name on grocery delivery robots. Digital lawyer avatars might interrupt online gaming or gambling platforms to advertise or share content while networking with colleagues in a virtual reality setting. Will your law firm brand itself in the metaverse with a virtual office or information spot like companies such as Nike and Coca-Cola have started to do? Online presence isn't all or nothing. Find what works for you today and stay abreast of new opportunities tomorrow.

---

 *Review Your Knowledge*

1)  Randall is an M&A corporate lawyer at the Palo Alto, California office of a large global law firm. One of the firm's biggest clients is Fallgreens, Inc., a major health-care company headquartered in Palo Alto. Rumors have been circulating in the national news and government regulatory circles that Fallgreens is in the works to pursue an acquisition of health-care company CHS, Inc., which is headquartered in Reno, Nevada. Randall is sitting at the Palo Alto airport waiting for a delayed flight to Reno for a meeting between some key executives and both companies' respective boards of directors. Bubbling with excitement about the potential deal closing, Randall opens his Twitter app and tweets *"boarding now! can't wait for trip to Reno— hot deal in the works 4sure let's hope not a hostile one!!"* Randall's Twitter handle with 89 followers is @RandallM&A and his profile includes the name of his firm. Under general ethics rules in most states, would Randall's tweet likely be a prohibited disclosure of confidential information?

a)    No, Randall tweeted from his personal page and not an official law firm account so the strict ethics rules don't apply.

b)    No, Randall's tweet didn't "name names" and was too vague for anyone to realistically figure out what he was referring to, especially because Randall only has 89 Twitter followers.

c)    Yes, Randall should never post anything on social media relating to his law firm or his work as an M&A corporate lawyer.

d)    Yes, Randall's tweet combined with the national news reports of a potential large corporate acquisition in health care and the fact that CHS is headquartered in Reno would probably be sufficient for a third party to infer what Randall's tweet referred to.

2)    Miguel is an appellate litigator and friend of yours from law school. You do land use zoning work for a large municipality. You run into Miguel at a 15-year law school alumni event and he mentions connecting on LinkedIn. The next week, Miguel emails a note that says "Great to see you last week. I've helped beef up your skimpy LinkedIn profile. U can thx me later, ha!" As it turns out, Miguel encouraged his friends, family members, and colleagues to endorse your skills and add recommendations to boost your LinkedIn profile. You notice a few short recommendation paragraphs with general remarks about your expertise as a trial lawyer and fierce negotiation skills. You haven't had a trial since law school clinic and never do ADR or any negotiation in your zoning land use practice—but you must admit your LinkedIn page looks more robust and impressive. Should you delete the new recommendations and endorsements?

a)    Yes, a lawyer has a duty to monitor their social media and other networking websites, verify accuracy of any information posted, and remove or correct inaccurate or potentially false and misleading endorsements like the ones from Miguel's acquaintances who you don't know and who posted things about skills you don't have and practice areas you aren't in.

b)   No, although a lawyer cannot post false or misleading information about their services, they can't be expected to police postings, comments, reviews, and endorsements of strangers and random members of the public across social media platforms.

c)   No, you are only responsible for content other people post if they qualify as your "agents" and Miguel's friends, family members, and colleagues are not your agents; you should leave the information to help beef up your LinkedIn page.

d)   No, you should keep the new recommendations and endorsements because you did have some trial experience once in law school and took a negotiation continuing legal education (CLE) seminar so the information isn't technically wrong.

3)   Catori is an attorney with Legal Aid of New Mexico, working in its Native American Program to provide services for tribal members on or near the federally recognized Mescalero Apache Tribe. Catori grew up on a tribe, so issues of poverty, religious freedom, and economic rights in the southwestern United States are near and dear to her heart. When she's not working, Catori pays for and maintains a blog called *Healthy Tribe Life*, about pursuit of a tribe lifestyle through mental, physical, and spiritual health. She has more than 250k blog subscribers and a huge social media following— she even created t-shirts to sell at a local market with *Healthy Tribe Life* on the front. A recession resulted in cuts to legal aid in New Mexico, and Catori could not resist taking to her blog to criticize the government's approach. She wrote almost 40 posts in the last year about A2J challenges, problems with tribal court processes, issues of sovereignty and land use in the face of pressure to monetize, and the need for lawyers with and without Native American heritage to enter the field. Catori's bio across platforms includes the Legal Aid of New Mexico website and other resources about tribal law. Is Catori's online presence likely permissible?

a)   Yes, only because personal blogs such as this commercial one that Catori pays for herself are protected constitutional speech and lawyers have wide discretion to use them for any business development, legal advice, financial gain, or advocacy to communicate information on a broad scale to the public.

b)   Yes, only because Catori has pursued an effective gradual approach to thought leadership and marketing for the legal aid clinic by sharing information in small pieces at different times with her 40 posts.

c)   Yes, only because Catori is not disclosing case specifics or client confidences, nor offering specific legal advice; she's using her blog as an informative outlet for general advocacy positions to bring attention to issues about which she is passionate.

d)   No, Catori should not mix personal blog topics such as healthy lifestyle with legal topics given that the content could confuse the public.

4)   Williams & Williams is a general law firm run by two lawyers (a mother and daughter team) in a rural suburb of Bismarck, North Dakota. The younger Williams lawyer has taken several CLE classes and wants to revamp the firm's outdated basic website. She works with a consultant on improved design and is excited by the suggestion of a "welcome chatbot" to automate information sharing and impress prospective clients. Months after the site goes live, Williams meets with a new prospective client Mr. Barry, who seeks representation for a contentious divorce. Williams takes his case. The next month at a court conference, Mrs. Barry files a motion to exclude Williams as counsel for Mr. Barry because she already tried to hire the Williams law firm and, in doing so, disclosed details about alleged infidelity, secret bank accounts, and her spotty criminal record to the website chatbot. Mrs. Barry says the chatbot asked questions in reply, and the back-and-forth typing went on for about eight minutes. Williams scoffs at the request, denies having confidential information about Mrs. Barry or a conflict of interest, says her mother is the one who might have reviewed that data, and suggests to the judge that there is no way a website chatbot set up by a technology vendor creates any relationship between her

firm and Mrs. Barry. Which of the following statements is most accurate about this scenario?

a) Williams is correct—there's no realistic way to monitor the quick and informal nature of social media and website interaction in our modern society such that a simple outreach by a member of the public could create any expectation of confidentiality with a stranger.

b) Williams is correct—no reasonable person would expect that a chatbot is an actual human being and it's Mrs. Barry's fault for carelessly disclosing confidential and personal details about her upcoming divorce dispute on a website.

c) Williams may be conflicted out of representing Mr. Barry because material confidential information was disclosed and website chatbots should be set up only to gather very basic contact information; Williams should have understood the tool better and had better processes for review of the incoming data, and probably can't rely on a small disclaimer somewhere else on the site.

d) The Williams law firm does not need to adjust its chatbot processes and the judge would deny the motion to exclude Williams as counsel for Mr. Barry, so long as the Williams & Williams website had a disclaimer somewhere on the site that said nothing should be construed as providing legal advice.

5) Britta is a sixth-year junior partner at a boutique employment law firm in Washington, D.C. She's spent three years working on developing legal questions about employer vaccine requirements that create a need for a reasonable accommodation when employees claim religious exemption. A lead partner at Britta's firm recently retired and the firm saw a sharp decline in new business. The managing partner asks to meet with Britta and explains that the retiring partner had a huge social media following, recorded weekly podcasts on hot topics in employment law, and was a frequent contributor on webinar panels with the government. Everyone "guesses" that his presence created a

lot of business and so his departure explains the decline. Britta is told that she needs to step up her business development and take the lead over the next month or so to bring back some positive attention—and hopefully more clients. What should Britta do?

a)  Tell the partner that the firm might want to explore customer relationship management (CRM) analytics tools because guessing at whether significant new business came from the retiring partner's online presence isn't too reliable.

b)  Tell the partner that she feels awkward about public self-promotion efforts but will do her best to build her thought leadership and presence based on her niche employment law expertise.

c)  Tell the partner that a month is a short amount of time to thoughtfully build up relationships and a quality online network likely to get Britta invited to join worthwhile webinars and panels.

d)  All of the above.

 *Practice Your Knowledge*

## Exercise #1: Online Presence Spotlight: Yay or Nay?

Go online to your social media platform(s) and search engines of choice to find two examples of lawyers with an excellent online presence and two you consider not as great (or even poor). Review as much content as you can for the same lawyer or law firm across different sites and platforms, including reading website disclaimers, lawyer profiles, ratings and recommendations, substantive legal information, etc. Rate their presence and take notes to explain the similarities and differences and why the online content left you with a positive or negative impression.

**Exercise #2: 280 Characters of Supreme Court**

Pick any United States Supreme Court decision from the past year or so on any topic that's of interest. Pretend you work with counsel of record on the case (for either side). Read the decision and any related commentary to ensure you understand the issue and the court's decision. Pretend it's the day after the decision is released and you are tasked with drafting a 280-character tweet that announces and summarizes it in an effective and concise way while also shedding favorable light on your side's representation. Draft the content of the tweet within the limit of 280 characters.

---

 *Expand Your Knowledge*

➢ Trevor Molag, *The Complete Guide to Social Media for Lawyers*, CLIO (Feb. 6, 2022), https://www.clio.com/resources/digital-marketing-lawyers/social-media-lawyers/ [https://perma.cc/677E-TEWQ].

➢ Elizabeth H. Munnell, *LinkedIn for the Reluctant Lawyer, Part I*, LINKEDIN (Feb. 14, 2019), https://www.lawpractice today.org/article/linkedin-reluctant-lawyer-part/ [https://perma.cc/2YQ5-9KZK].

➢ Cassandra Burke Robertson, *Online Reputation Management in Attorney Regulation*, 29 GEORGETOWN J. OF LEGAL ETHICS 1 (2016).

---

*Answers & Explanations*

*Knowledge Kickoff*

    c)   Sebastian's initiative with his new firm's online presence is an opportunity to make a positive contribution but he can't treat it as casually as he might have treated his personal presence in the past. Sebastian's username choice may violate a prohibition against lawyers stating or implying they are certified as experts, and his list of clients and active matters on profiles could disclose confidential information. Sebastian would be better off sticking to general descriptions or obtaining informed client consent. His blog post created an awkward potential conflict of interest on a point of law for his partner; informative legal summaries would be a more careful bet. There's no minimum when it comes to communication subject to ethics rules; short (and unprofessional) comments or tweets can get a lawyer into murky disciplinary or reputational waters just the same as long speeches or lengthy television ads.

*Review Your Knowledge*

    1)   d) Randall's duty to keep client information confidential applies to any medium, online or otherwise. Although he didn't give specific client names, a lawyer can breach the duty of confidentiality if they disclose enough information for a third person to reasonably read between the lines and infer the actual facts or parties involved. The combination of circumstances here would probably qualify, given the specific reference of Reno in the tweet, the fact that Randall's law firm is listed on his Twitter handle, the reference to the substantive topic of an acquisition, and the context of national news reports. The fact that the information was disclosed only to Randall's 89 personal Twitter followers may be relevant to an appropriate penalty but it does not excuse a prohibited disclosure on social media.

2)  a)  Lawyers may create and maintain whatever online presence they'd like within the bounds of ethics rules (and professional judgment!). Although you aren't responsible for the posts like you would be if you directed an "agent" such as an assistant or paralegal to make them, once you learn of them some duty does kick in. Allowing endorsements on a LinkedIn profile that you know are baseless and potentially misleading would likely qualify as a violation of Model Rule 7.1, depending on local rules. Ethics rules are concerned with verifying truthfulness and avoiding deception of the public, and this scenario clashes with both principles (most reasonable people would agree that limited clinical experience from law school 15 years ago does not support claiming expertise as a trial lawyer). If a lawyer's goal is to make their LinkedIn page more robust, the way to do so is by adding substantive content or soliciting endorsements and reviews from people who actually know you within the bounds of what a jurisdiction permits, such as a nominal thank you gift.

3)  c)  Subject to restrictions from her employer, this scenario is an appropriate way for Catori to create an online presence and pursue discussion of and attention to legal issues that are important to her. There is no general rule against mixing personal and professional topics, and the fact that Catori is licensed in New Mexico does not mean she can't also use her blog to sell lifestyle t-shirts having nothing to do with her work as a lawyer. The gradual content is an effective "drip" thought leadership and content-marketing approach to keeping her blog active. Whether blogs are commercial protected speech or unethical business communication is jurisdiction and content dependent, but Catori's overall approach should not raise many red flags in most states.

4)  c)  Interactive website communication can enhance online presence but ethics traps continue to arise as technology advances. Most jurisdictions wouldn't forbid a chatbot feature but intake like this should be limited

in nature to basic Q&A without substantive fact details to avoid this exact type of scenario. Williams wouldn't necessarily face discipline but it's probably unfair for the judge not to disqualify her from representing Mr. Barry, given that it's her fault that the chatbot invited the information and interacted with Mrs. Barry in a way that may have triggered a reasonable expectation of a lawyer/client relationship under whatever version of Model Rule 1.18 North Dakota imposes. Williams should go back to the consultant to ensure the chatbot itself includes a specific disclaimer and instruction not to provide any detailed facts. The firm should also improve its processes between lawyers regarding who is responsible for reviewing incoming chatbot data.

5)  d) Online presence is an individual decision but modern lawyers working on a team might need to stretch their comfort zones. The partner's request to Britta isn't an unreasonable one based on Britta's niche expertise and it could be a great opportunity for Britta to enhance her reputation and grow business as a junior partner. Self-promotion is not easy for everyone; lawyers can find their own style and voice. But that takes time, and compressing efforts into a single month is not an ideal approach likely to generate new clients. The firm may want to use CRM tools and consultants to get a broad view of lead tracking and aspects to new business growth now that the retiring partner with the significant online presence is gone.

## Endnotes

[1]  *Bates v. State Bar of Arizona*, 433 U.S. 350 (1977); Kenneth Bennett, *Lawyer Advertising: The Practical Effects of Bates*, 1 NEW ENG. L. REV. 349 (1978).

[2]  MODEL RULES OF PRO. CONDUCT r. 7.1–7.3 (AM. BAR ASS'N 2020).

[3]  Dave Chaffey, *2022 Comparison of Google Organic Clickthrough Rates (SEO CTR) by Ranking Position*, SMART INSIGHTS (Jan. 25, 2022), https://www.smartinsights.com/search-engine-optimisation-seo/seo-analytics/comparison-of-google-clickthrough-rates-by-position/ [https://perma.cc/6DNN-5DLD].

[4]  *95 SEO Statistics from this Year That'll Transform Your Strategy*, Web FX, https://www.webfx.com/seo/statistics/#:~:text=How%20many%20users%20go%20to,first%20page%20of%20search%20results [https://perma.cc/6LPX-ULSW].

**5**   Celia Colista, *How Do Clients Research and Find Their Attorneys?*, MARTINDALE-AVVO (Jan. 9, 2020), https://www.martindale-avvo.com/blog/how-do-clients-research-and-find-their-attorneys/ [https://perma.cc/WWG7-VSDB].

**6**   Dave Chaffey, *Search Engine Marketing Statistics 2022*, SMART INSIGHTS (Jan. 26, 2022), https://www.smartinsights.com/search-engine-marketing/search-engine-statistics/ [https://perma.cc/QP9S-FWPR].

**7**   *Webmaster Guidelines*, GOOGLE, https://developers.google.com/search/docs/advanced/guidelines/webmaster-guidelines [https://perma.cc/WT3L-5TU2].

**8**   *ABA Journal Blawg Directory*, https://www.abajournal.com/blawgs [https://perma.cc/CQS6-ZTTE].

**9**   LEXBLOG, https://www.lexblog.com/ [https://perma.cc/86Z7-8NZD].

**10**   JDSUPRA, https://www.jdsupra.com/ [https://perma.cc/8C35-BH4C].

**11**   For additional exploration of these and other social media topics, see Thomas Roe Frazer II, Symposium, *Social Media: From Discovery to Marketing—A Primer for Lawyers*, 36 AM. J. TRIAL ADVOC. 539 (2013).

**12**   Kevin McSpadden, *You Now Have a Shorter Attention Span Than a Goldfish*, TIME (May 14, 2015) https://time.com/3858309/attention-spans-goldfish/ [https://perma.cc/TZC5-5AXR].

**13**   AM. BAR ASS'N, PROFILE OF THE LEGAL PROFESSION 92 (2021), https://www.americanbar.org/content/dam/aba/administrative/news/2021/0721/polp.pdf [https://perma.cc/PQF4-YFPN].

**14**   AM. BAR. ASS'N, PROFILE OF THE LEGAL PROFESSION 2021 92 (2021), https://www.americanbar.org/news/reporter_resources/profile-of-profession/#:~:text=Downloadä-,PDFöf%20the%202021ÄBA%20Profileöf%20the%20Legal%20Profession,-or%20view%20the [https://perma.cc/U5E6-MQ2T].

**15**   LINKEDIN, https://about.linkedin.com/#:~:text=Welcome%20to%20LinkedIn'%20the%20world's,200%20countriesänd%20territories%20worldwide [https://perma.cc/U7UE-GCYK].

**16**   MODEL RULES OF PRO. CONDUCT r. 7.2 cmt. 4 (AM. BAR ASS'N 2020).

**17**   Pro. Ethics Comm. for the State Bar of Texas Op. 662 (2016).

# CONCLUSION

Some say a law professor's job is to teach students how to think like a lawyer. My job as the author of this book was to get readers to start acting like modern ones.

| LIT TIP |
|---|
| "Every accomplishment starts with the decision to try." |
| President John F. Kennedy |

Your job now? Try. Try to turn thought into action. Turn examples into effort. Will finishing this book be just one day in your life as a lawyer, or day one of a new approach? I hope my words, figures, images, LIT TIPs, examples, questions, quotes, and sources have inspired you to keep an open mind. Your task is not to incorporate everything in this book into your future practice. I'm overwhelmed just thinking about that. Find small pockets of inefficiency or frustration in your day-to-day lawyering and make those pockets just a little bit faster or smoother. Reflect on what you aren't great at and work to become a bit better. Be honest about your strengths and weaknesses. Focus on your attitude with new approaches as much as your aptitude with new tools. Read, listen, or watch things about innovation and technology opportunities and challenges in the legal profession. Keep your legal practice habits relevant, not stagnant. This book is a starting point, not a finish line. Your skills today—as excellent as they may be—won't be the ones expected of you tomorrow.

Anyone who stops learning is old. That's true for me, a new law student, or a veteran lawyer with decades of experience. Nothing in this book demands expertise. It demands a willingness to never stop learning not just the substance of the law, but the day-to-day practice of it. You're now familiar with some foundational technological competencies but that's not enough. Engage in your broader professional community to ensure you enhance these competencies instead of letting them deflate as life and law practice get busy. If you've ever saved some money or practiced a new hobby, you know a little investment can go a long way. Make modern technological competence your new hobby with some practice each day. You'll be amazed at where you end up.

I wrote this book with a "mindset first, technology second" approach. I included specific tools and examples in the background to help main ideas come to life. Concepts over products. Awareness over ability. Effort over expertise. Suggestions over software specifics. For every concept covered, the future holds a new vendor, update, bug fix, enhanced feature, user design, or invention. No one lawyer will keep up with every one of them. The substantive issues modern lawyers face will grow more complex; so too will the complexity of the skills necessary to tackle them.

The title of this book promises a "practical skills guide for the modern lawyer" on the topic of innovation and technology. How will you know if you've succeeded? How will you know whether you've earned the right to call yourself a modern lawyer? It won't be with numerical test score grades, victories in a courtroom, or billable hour bonuses. Measure your success with small, sometimes invisible steps as your career progresses—a few minutes of personal time saved because of automation of manual tasks, a client ecstatic with your modern communication and payment services, one quick headache instead of an everyday migraine over cybersecurity concerns, or perhaps a simple, "Wow, that's a great new approach!" appreciative note from an impressed colleague. Success with your developing legal innovation and technology skillset will be continuous and gradual. Mine is too.

So where to from here?

- ✓ Take more classes on skills and technology topics that interest you.
- ✓ Subscribe to blogs and newsletters on legal innovation and technology.
- ✓ Follow a few new sources you learned about in this book on your social media platform of choice.

✓   Read a few suggested sources listed at the end of a chapter that piqued your interest.

✓   Avoid the temptation to delete every email about technology trainings and information sessions from your school or employer.

✓   Check out a LinkedIn Learning course or instructional YouTube video relevant to something new from this book.

✓   Keep watch for relevant CLE courses or bar association workshops.

Every new lawyer will create their own unique path toward what I hope is a goal we all now share: "upskilling" throughout our careers as advances in innovation and technology move forward.

The content of this book was up to me. What you do with it now is up to you.